Vita Sackville-West

VITA SACKVILLE-WEST

SELECTED WRITINGS

EDITED BY MARY ANN CAWS

palgrave

VITA SACKVILLE-WEST
Copyright © Mary Ann Caws, 2002.

First published 2002 by
PALGRAVE™
175 Fifth Avenue, New York, N.Y. 10010.
Companies and representatives throughout the world.

PALGRAVE™ is the new global publishing imprint of St. Martin's Press LLC Scholarly
and Reference Division and Palgrave Publishers Ltd (formerly Macmillan Press Ltd).

ISBN 0–312–23760-X hardback

Library of Congress Cataloging-in-Publication Data
can be found at the Library of Congress.

Design by Letra Libre, Inc.

First Palgrave edition: July 2002
10   9   8   7   6   5   4   3   2   1

Printed in the United States of America.

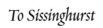

To Sissinghurst

CONTENTS

Part X: Animal Reflections

Part XI: Summary of Works Not Excerpted

ACKNOWLEDGEMENTS

A few years ago, when I first had the idea of assembling a selection of Vita Sackville-West's writings, some previously published and others not, her son Nigel Nicolson, with his customary generosity and elegance, gave me just the encouragement I needed. That encouragement has continued and I can only express my warmest gratitude. Without his gracious permissions, none of these unpublished writings would appear. My thanks to Michael Flamini and my editor Kristi Long at Palgrave, to the unfailing assistance of the librarians at the Lilly Library in Bloomington, Indiana, and at the Berg Collection at the New York Public Library, to my cousin Deborah Gage, and to my friends Carolyn Heilbrun, Rosemary Lloyd, Carolyn Gill, and Sarah Bird Wright, with whom I had the joy of writing *Bloomsbury and France: Art and Friends* (New York and Oxford: Oxford University Press, 1998), in which some of this material was first discussed.

A good part of the information here comes from the superb biography by Victoria Glendinning: *Vita: The Life of V. Sackville-West* (London: Weidenfeld & Nicolson; 1983). Other invaluable works include Nigel Nicolson's *Long Life* (London: Weidenfeld & Nicolson, 1987); Suzanne Raitt's *Vita and Virginia: The Work and Friendship of V. Sackville-West and Virginia Woolf* (London: Clarendon Press, 1993); Louise DeSalvo and Mitchell A. Leaska's edition of *The Letters of Vita Sackville-West to Virginia Woolf* (London: Virago Press, 1992); and Robert Cross and Ann Ravenscroft-Hulme's *Vita Sackville-West: A Bibliography* (Winchester: St. Paul's Bibliographies; New Castle, Delaware: Oak Knoll Press, 1999).

This work was supported by a faculty research award from the City University of New York, and a visiting fellowship at the Lilly Library at Indiana University.

FOREWORD

BY NIGEL NICOLSON

This is an anthology, but an unusual one, because it is selected from the writings of one person only, my mother, Vita Sackville-West. Most of her books have long been out of print, and some of her early poems and novels have become so rare, even in secondhand copies, that she ceased to mention them in her entry in *Who's Who*, but her name is still familiar as the author of *The Edwardians, All Passion Spent*, and "The Land," as the creator of the famous garden at Sissinghurst, and as the subject of Victoria Glendinning's remarkable biography. Here Mary Ann Caws has contrived a highly original method of reintroducing Vita to a new generation, not only as a prolific author but as a woman whose experiences and ideas are still influential today.

Vita lends herself particularly well to this treatment since her range was so wide and her life so extraordinary. She was a poet, novelist, travel writer, biographer, journalist, and historian. She kept a diary, but only intermittently, and wrote innumerable letters, never leaving one unanswered whether it be a love letter from Virginia Woolf or an enquiry—and she received dozens every week—from a reader of her garden articles.

She wrote with equal ease an intimate letter or a key passage in her latest book. Her manuscripts, apart from her poems, for which she wrote many drafts, reveal a fluency that was lacking in her conversation, for she remained shy and hesitant in company. I have at Sissinghurst a dozen unpublished plays and novels that she wrote at Knole during her childhood, and page after page is as free from correction as one of Anthony Trollope's manuscripts. Some of them are in French, others in Italian, for she had a great gift for languages, and all are suffused with a romanticism that never entirely left her.

Not many of her books are autobiographical. She wrote only one memoir, recording a torrid episode in her youth when she eloped to France with another woman, Violet Trefusis, which I published after her death in *Portrait of a Marriage*. From time to time she recorded in diary form specific journeys, like her holiday in France with Virginia Woolf in 1928 and her lecture tour of North America in 1933, and her two travel books, *Passenger to Teheran* and *Twelve*

Days, are accounts of personal experiences. Characters like Lady Slane in *All Passion Spent* and Sebastian in *The Edwardians* are vaguely reminiscent of my grandmother and brother, and Vita herself figures marginally in the final pages of *Pepita* and in the history of her family, *Knole and the Sackvilles.* But about her personal life she was reticent, never writing for publication about lesbian love or the happiness of her marriage. It is therefore an added bonus that Mary Ann Caws has included in this volume examples of her letters and diary. In total it forms the autobiography she never wrote.

Vita, for all her mixed ancestry—her maternal grandmother was a Spanish dancer—was English to the core. Intensely patriotic, romantically attached to the countryside both wild and tamed, and to the traditions of England as reflected in its literature and ancient buildings, she was nonetheless emotionally aroused by other cultures, particularly those of France, Italy, Greece, and Persia. Her only journey to the United States was less of a success because it was conducted in the least attractive circumstances—in midwinter, at the depth of a financial crisis, and in pursuance of an exhausting lecture tour that obliged her to hurry by train from city to city, constantly meeting people whom she would never see again and enduring a degree of entertainment and adulation which she felt wholly undeserved. But turning the troubled pages of her diary, one comes across sudden gleams of delight in an unusual person or a place like Niagara Falls or an Arizona ranch.

She was conservative, for instance, in her politics, but at the same time adventurous as a traveler, a writer, a gardener, and in her enduring regret that she was not born a boy who could have inherited Knole and who could have done the things that girls were not allowed or expected to do. But for all that she was a woman too, showing great tenderness toward people who were lonely or in trouble, and as a mother she revealed an understanding of schoolboy traumas well beyond her own experience.

So here you have a portrait of a remarkable person. It not only salvages an important part of her published work—from which I would specially commend her short story *Seducers in Ecuador* and her long poem "The Garden"—but reveals the private person behind the very public one, a woman of passion and determination beneath her outward gentleness and calm.

INTRODUCTION

Vita Sackville-West, an aristocrat from a long and distinguished British lineage, delighted in the colorful mingling of Spanish and gypsy blood, with which she was endowed through the unusual circumstances of her maternal ancestors. She often portrayed herself as a hot-blooded irrational being, a fantasy played out in her acting the part of Julian or Mitya for her various lovers—in particular Violet Keppel Trefusis, who represents Eve to Vita's dark, romantic, masculine gypsy side.

Raised in privilege and speaking several languages, she was herself a surprising mixture, at once imperious and bashful, a public personality but essentially reclusive. Mostly schooled at home and with governesses, she was always conscious of not having had a lengthy formal education and this contributed to her shyness in the witty society of Bloomsbury, in relation to which she felt herself to be slow. "Donkey West," as Virginia Woolf called her affectionately, was a friend of the group, and in particular of Virginia and Leonard Woolf, but not at its intellectual center as were the Woolfs.

Bisexual, with an androgynous mingling of male and female traits, Vita was the wife of Harold Nicolson, a diplomat who was similarly androgynous. Vita, with her many lovers, mostly female, was a gender rebel of the first order. Virginia Woolf modeled the title character of *Orlando* (termed "the longest love letter in history" by Nigel Nicolson) on her and greatly admired the aristocratic lineage she represented. Writing in many genres, Vita epitomized the all-around creative personality in an eccentric and distinguished mode.

Life and Loves

Vita was brought up speaking upperclass French as well as English, as was her mother. The Sackville-Wests were a long line of aristocrats, notable in their being and their actions. Their family home, Knole, which had been given to Thomas Sackville in the sixteenth century by Queen Elizabeth, remained Vita's lifelong place of choice, even when she could not inherit it. In contrast to this aristocratic bloodline, Vita took a particular interest in her grandmother Pepita

Duran, a dancer, who, despite being married already, had an affair with her grandfather, Lord Sackville-West. Pepita had inherited gypsy blood from her own mother, a Spanish ex-acrobat married to a barber, and that heritage appealed greatly to Vita's romantic fantasy, which would encourage and enhance own her various love affairs. The beautiful Pepita—about whom Vita wrote one of her most popular books, called simply *Pepita*—was known as "the Belle of Andalusia," and had many lovers in addition to her Spanish dancer husband, from whom she was never really divorced. Lionel Sackville-West named her as his wife on his deathbed in Arcachon, France. He confessed to his son Henry, however, "I never married your mother. . . ." Despite this, they produced three daughters and two sons.

One of these daughters, Vita's own extraordinarily beautiful mother, Victoria Josefa Dolores Catalina Sackville-West, was raised in the convent of St. Joseph in Paris. She was called to Washington to be her father's young and brilliant hostess at the British Legation, where Lionel was the minister, and then went with him to Knole, which he had inherited. Vita was always to call her mother "B.M.," for Bonne Maman, a title bestowed with a certain irony given their often surpassingly difficult relations. Victoria also had an array of celebrated lovers, including J. Pierpont Morgan. William Waldorf Astor and Auguste Rodin were also in love with her. She married her first cousin, also called Lionel. Their only child was Vita, born on March 9, 1892.

Victoria's companion from 1897 to 1912, Sir John Murray Scott, whom Vita and her mother called Seery, was an immense man, standing six feet four and quite round, something like five feet around his middle, and was as generous in his being as in his girth. He had two gloriously appointed Paris apartments, one on the rue Lafitte, and it was there that Vita spent much of her time when she was young, contributing to her already fluent knowledge of French. Between 1906 and 1910, she wrote eight full-length novels, one in French, and several plays, some of which are also in that language.

Vita met the young diplomat Harold Nicolson in 1910 and married him in 1913. They would have a long and happy marriage in spite of—or, as some would have it, in part because of—their each being involved with members of their own sex. They had two sons, Benedict—an art historian and editor of the *Burlington* magazine—and Nigel—a writer, publisher, and biographer, who wrote *Portrait of a Marriage* about his mother and father, and edited their selected letters (*Vita and Harold: The Letters of Vita Sackville-West and Harold Nicolson).* Nigel's own memoir, *Long Life,* honest and witty, offers a self-portrait of the kind Vita might well have written, had she chosen to do so. Some of her writings, published and unpublished, included here, give enough of her story to create her own portrait.

Vita lived an extraordinary life, both in her extensive and wide-ranging work and in her emotional attachments—those passing and those more lasting, those she envisaged as belonging to "Julian," the masculine side of herself, and the one in which she dwelled every day by presence and by correspondence as Harold's lifelong partner. Vita was as lively as her name indicates, although additionally in Harold's letters to her she is "Mar," her mother's name for her, and he is "Hadji" or pilgrim, his father's name for him. So they represent, in that fashion as in others, something handed down and symbolic, a tradition, even as their own marriage was, strictly speaking, highly nonconformist. The marriage worked, both surprisingly and well. The contradictions in their lives made them all the more interesting as persons, private and public, and as writers.

In general, it was quietly that Vita arranged and carried on a great many love affairs, a number of appearances and radio broadcasts as author and expert on gardens, and a massive amount of work, which she never discussed with her family. She lived precisely as she wanted to, traveling extensively with and occasionally without Harold, and finally spending more time in her garden and her writing tower than in society. Harold's love affairs were less public than Vita's and appeared to mean less to him. Hers, as her son Nigel put it, endured longer and were more significant: She was never without a love. As a young debutante she had been courted by an Italian, Orazio Pucci, and later, in 1914, had an affair, on her part as literary as it was passionate, with Geoffrey Scott, author of *The Architecture of Humanism*. After the affair ended, Scott's own marriage also eventually expired. This was to be the case with many of Vita's lovers, all women after this. Many of them found their marriages ruined over their passion for Vita.

Notoriously, the person Vita most loved, aside from Harold, was the woman with whom she was intimate from April 1918 to 1921, Violet Keppel, the daughter of George and Alice Keppel; Alice Keppel was King Edward VIII's mistress. Violet represented the greatest threat to the marriage of Vita and Harold. Vita and Violet had known each other at school, had exchanged an impetuous embrace, and had shared a precocious European childhood: "I had learnt Italian with her in London, and we had been together in Paris, and had acted part of a play I wrote in French in five Alexandrine acts, about the Man in the Iron Mask, and in those days we rather ostentatiously talked to one another in French in order to tutoyer one another [to use the informally intimate form of the verb] and so show what great friends we were."[1] This, I think, already indicates Vita's relating of language to life, using speech to display intimacy.

Violet Keppel Trefusis, beauteous and seductive, sketched in words the best portrait anyone has made of Vita, describing the two halves of her face with the upper half pure and grave, the lower half domineering and sensual. Vita herself continually experienced this profound division, this actual split in her personality and in her many loves. She had had a close childhood friend, Rosamund Grosvenor, with whom she became intimate and then tossed aside, as she was to do with her many other female lovers in ensuing years. Only her love for her husband remained in its inviolate state: "Harold, who is unalterable, perennial, and *best;* there has never been anything but absolute purity in my love for Harold, just as there has never been anything but absolute bright purity in his nature. And on the other hand stands my perverted nature, which loved and tyrannized over Rosamund and ended by deserting her without one heart-pang, and which now is linked irremediably with Violet."[2]

For a while, the male part of her personality, suddenly liberated in 1918 by a change in costume and her encounter with Violet, became dominant. She exhibited this in her newly donned breeches and gaiters: "I went into wild spirits; I ran, I shouted, I jumped, I climbed, I vaulted over gates, I felt like a schoolboy let out on a holiday. . . . that wild irresponsible day. It was one of the most vibrant days of my life."[3] So, for a number of years, until 1921, the tug of war between the two parts of her persona was unresolved, for "Violet had struck the secret of my duality. . . . I had been vouchsafed insight, as one sometimes is . . . all the gentleness and femininity of me was called out by Harold alone. . . . I might have been a boy of eighteen, and she a woman of thirty-five."[4]

Violet was able to state, in her purple lyric style, exactly what Vita represented for her. Vita was, she wrote, like "the wild hawk and the windswept sky . . . splendid and dauntless, a wanderer in strange lands. . . ."[5] Who, made like Vita in body and mind, could resist being the wild hawk rather than the faithful wife? Violet could write in scorn of what she despised and claim loudly what she admired: "Heaven preserve me from littleness and pleasantness and smoothness. Give me great glaring vices, and great glaring virtues, but preserve me from the neat little neutral ambiguities. Be wicked, be brave, be drunk, be reckless, be dissolute, be despotic, be an anarchist, be a suffragette, be anything you like, but for pity's sake be it to the top of your bent. Live fully, live passionately, live disastrously. Let's live, you and I, as none have ever lived before."[6]

Radclyffe Hall, the author of *The Well of Loneliness,* a celebrated lesbian novel, so determined to break all the rules, had never managed, alas, to write like this, but then Violet, like Vita, was nourished on Baudelaire and the romantic poets. On and on went the affair, with Vita dressing as a young man, in London, in Paris, in Monte Carlo. Vita would wear a khaki bandage around her head, browning her face and hands, and all were deceived. She would present Violet as her wife and wondered in delight if anyone would recognize in "the slouching boy with the bandaged head . . . the silent and rather scornful woman" they might have met at dances or dinners.[7] In many of Vita's novels, such as *The Dark Island,* the dark romantic figure is Vita herself, doomed to love a place and to figure an unusual destiny.

When Violet was about to be married to Denys Trefusis, Vita fled to Paris, terrified of what she might do—interrupting the service or worse. Just before the marriage took place on June 16, 1919, Violet wrote a one-sentence note: "You have broken my heart. Goodbye." But of course it was not goodbye, for their affair continued, and they in fact eloped to France in 1920. The husbands came after them in a small airplane: All her life, Vita remained much impressed with Harold's energy in undertaking the trip. She returned to Paris with Harold, already exhausted with Violet, who fled south through France, telephoning Vita from various places, her voice becoming faint as the distance grew between them. It all ended badly, as we read in Vita's diary entries: "My God, what a day. I am broken with misery, and if things were as bad as I at first thought I should put an end to myself . . . I had to go, I should have killed her if had stayed an instant longer. I have told her I cannot even see her for two months. She calls this banishment—it is not, it is simply the impossibility of bringing myself to see her for the present."[8]

What remains of that long-lasting affair is a florid collaborative novel by the two women: *Challenge.* It had originally been called "Rebellion," then "Enchantment," then "Vanity," and at one point "Foam," as well as a few other things. The prolonged hesitation over the title seems to me symptomatic of the fascination both of them found in the experience of this writing, and the writing of this experience. This novel is the fullest expression of the Julian/Eve relationship in its tormented excitement. When the novel was already in proof, Vita's mother objected forcefully to the publication (shame on the family, the children, etc.), so when the book finally broke into print, it sank without a trace. Doran in New York published it in 1924, and it reappeared in 1975, with a preface about the affair by Nigel Nicolson. The scandal is long gone, the book long forgotten; but the entire last part is included here as the intimate and creative witness of the famous affair.

Vita's double nature continued to get her into "muddles," as she and Harold called the messes she would make of others' lives and marriages. This was an important factor in Vita's life; to put it delicately, she did not have a green thumb with the marriages she became involved with. Vita devastated the emotional lives of many women, notwithstanding her essential modesty, benevolence, and that magnanimity that Virginia Woolf felt hovering about her. From early to late, from the longer-lasting to the briefer, Vita's loves were numerous. Vita's quite amazing number of amorous adventures and her secrecy about them mingled with her ability to keep many things going at once, and her erotic exploits, while maintaining her dignity, make her a heroine to many, in spite of the hurt her affair with Violet and her other involvements caused in others.

A partial list of her involvements, with the beginning dates simply and very roughly documenting one of the years in which the particular relationship mattered, would include many women and far fewer men. (For details, see Victoria Glendinning's thorough and engrossing 1983 biography, *Vita: The Life of V. Sackville-West*.) As a general reference point, these names may suffice with the initial dates of the affairs, which petered out over time, or more suddenly, as Vita would tire of the complications and jealousies:

>Kenneth Campbell, 1908
>Rosamund ("Roddie," "Rose") Grosvenor, 1909–1911
>Orazio Pucci, 1909
>Violet Trefusis (Eve, Mitya), 1918–1920
>Dorothy (Dottie) Wellesley, 1921
>Margaret (Pat) Dansey, 1922
>Geoffrey Scott, 1924
>Virginia Woolf, 1925
>Mary Campbell, 1927
>Margaret Goldsmith Voigt, 1928
>Hilda Matheson, 1929
>Evelyn Irons, 1931
>Olive Rinder, 1931
>Christopher (Christabel Marshall) St. John, 1932–1934
>Gwen St. Aubyn, 1934
>Violet Pym (Vi), 1947
>Edith Lamont, 1947
>Bunny Drummond, 1947–1952

Vita's multitudinous love affairs are never explicitly discussed in her diaries or her writings but only referred to in passing. However, the many traces of them and the personalities involved are as easily detected as Violet Trefusis in the florid writing of *Challenge* or Gwen St. Aubyn in the highly melodramatic novel *Dark Island*. Of course, apart from her lifelong and devoted relationship with Harold, Vita's most crucial involvements were with Violet Trefusis and then Virginia Woolf. In her affair with Virginia, she is scarcely loquacious, even to herself. Melodramatic she is not. Here are her diary entries for a few days during 1925:

>*November 7.* Long Barn. A lovely warm golden day. Sat in the sun all the morning. Went to tea with Eddy—Leonard went back to London, Virginia remained.
>   ! [in circle]
>   V. told me about re-reading the first 30 pages of "To the Lighthouse" & how she had had to rewrite them.

November 8. Virginia stayed till the evening. Such a wet day.

November 10. Spent the evening with Virginia, dinner with the Drinkwaters. Very dull.

November 24. Went up to see Virginia. . . . After to a party at Vanessa Bell's.

November 25. Went to Virginia in the evening. Went afterward to Clive's rooms, found Virginia there.

November 27. Virginia came to Mount St. to see me.

November 29. Spent the afternoon with Virginia.

December 4. Long Barn. Virginia came.

December 5. Alone all day with Virginia.

December 6. Went up with V. in the evening.

December 17. Alone.

December 20. [X at top of page] Spent the afternoon with Virginia; dinner with her at Mount St.

Virginia was eventually to see in Violet Trefusis what Vita had so cherished. When Violet went to see her about the Hogarth Press perhaps publishing her novel, called *Tandem,* Virginia wrote Vita: "I quite see now why you were so enamoured . . . what seduction! What a voice—lisping, faltering, what warmth, suppleness and in her way—it's not mine . . . how lovely, like a squirrel among buck hares—a red squirrel among brown nuts. We glanced and winked through the leaves."[9] This encomium produced in Vita an instant disquiet. For Virginia's friendship was, most likely, the deepest and most important of all those in Vita's life, except for Harold's, just as Vita's friendship was the most important one in Virginia's, except for those with Leonard and with her sister Vanessa. From the time of her first meeting with Vita, Virginia Woolf found the contrast between her aristocratic air and her modest regard for her own talents as attractive as it was disarming. She took a flirtatious tone in many of her letters, issuing a warning to them both that was not entirely without some basis: "But you don't see, donkey West, that you'll be tired of me one of these days (I'm so much older). . . ."[10] Virginia's own point of view about their affair was that Vita, in her full-breasted and mature plenteousness and maternal protectiveness, was like rich fruit: "the grapes are ripe; and not reflective. No. In brain and insight she is not as highly organised as I am. But then she is aware of this and so lavishes on me the maternal protection which, for some reason, is what I have always most wished from everyone . . ."[11] Vita's affair with Virginia was followed by a longstanding and close friendship in which each placed a high value on the other's company. After their brief trip through Burgundy in 1928, much of which was taken up with their writing to and waiting to receive mail from their husbands, they remained friends; over the years, however, the degree of closeness varied. Writing in her diary entry of September 26, 1937, about a visit just paid to Sissinghurst Castle, Virginia speaks of Vita's "silent goodness, and Harold too, a sense of the human understanding unspoken. . . ."[12] And in 1940, when bombs were exploding around Vita's house, and Virginia thought that "she might be killed any moment," she was at once more forthrightly affectionate with this great friend. "What can one say—except that I love you and I've got to live through this strange quiet evening thinking of you sitting there alone. . . . You have given me such happiness."[13] And, writing to Vita on March 4, 1941, shortly before her suicide, Virginia says feelingly: "I suppose your orchard is beginning to dapple as it did the day I came there. One of the sights I shall see on my death bed."[14] And perhaps, in her dying moments, so far from a deathbed in the conventional sense, she did: Who is to say? Vita's poem on Virginia Woolf's death is included here as her final tribute to her friend.

Vita and Harold

Vita, so close to her land and garden and work, managed to live what one might call a happy married life, despite all her other involvements—or perhaps, seen from another angle, because of them she was able to value her relationship to her husband as greatly as she did. Writing to Harold in 1953, she says it succinctly, explaining their love of living and their intense dislike of growing older: "the real deep reason for us, you and me, is that we hate the idea of leaving Life, as we must, twenty to thirty years hence, and we both love life and enjoy it."[15]

They had two kinds of lives, of course, as Harold pointed out, just as Vita had the two parts of her being. What with Vita never even knowing what the League of Nations was, her world was a different one from his. And yet, in the long run, perhaps that saved their marriage, this nonconcordance of worlds that permitted their concord in salvaging the thing that mattered: their love and their marriage. Letter after letter makes the enduring quality of the love between Vita and Harold clear and authentically vibrant. Their quite remarkable relationship, documented by well over two thousand letters exchanged, seems never to have lessened in any impact: Over and over during their very long life together they express their gratitude for it.

The Second World War affected Vita and Harold seriously; each of them carried a small vial of poison, as did Virginia Woolf, in case of catastrophe. Vita's reactions were clear-cut: she refused to attend a banquet at Buckingham Palace, not wanting to have to purchase the proper clothes; her difference from her mother's delight in her jewels could scarcely be more radical. Vita: " I am writing this letter with my jewels littered all around me—emeralds and diamonds, just taken out of the bank—and they make me feel sick; I simply can't subscribe any longer to the world which these jewels represent. I can't buy a dress costing 30 pounds or wear jewels worth 2,000 pounds when people are starving. I can't support such a farce when people are threatened that their electric light or gas may be cut off because they can't pay their arrears." Harold replied with admiration for how "sound" she was in her values.[16]

By contrast, her mother thought nothing of spending those 2,000 pounds on a diamond necklace and then, directly after, would write on the toilet paper in Harrods's Ladies Cloakroom, finding it was excellent for letters and writing to Vita (in French of course), and in how well it took the ink.[17]

In one of her last published letters, Vita writes of seeing Harold out the window, in his blue coat and black hat: "It is the sort of sudden view of a person that twists one's heart, when they don't know you are observing them . . . I often think I have never told you how much I love you—and if you die I should reproach myself, saying, 'Why did I never tell him? Why did I never tell him enough?'"[18] The truth is, as all lovers know, that enough is never enough in such a realm. And it is this that twists the heart.

Her son Nigel, who has edited their letters and Vita's autobiographical writing with discretion, courage, and love, states unabashedly his viewpoint about his mother. "I love her more, as my father did, *because* she was tempted, *because* she was weak. . . . She fought for the right to love, men and women, rejecting the conventions that marriage demands exclusive love, and that women should love only men, and men only women. For this she was prepared to give up everything."[19]

Harold knew all about Vita's duality and was always worried by the two parts of her personality: As he wrote to her, "The one tender, wise and with such a sense of responsibility. And the other rather cruel and extravagant."[20] He believed the first part was the essential one but was alarmed by the latter, always unfathomable to him. What in fact he emphasized, as Vita did, was the importance of their love and their marriage.

On their last cruise together, when Vita was aware that she was seriously ill, she hid it from Harold, knowing how much pain it would cause him. He was always her primary concern, and their marriage, her primary reassurance along with their work in their garden at Sissinghurst and her constant devotion to her writing, particularly her poetry. Vita was made a Fellow of the Royal Society of Literature and then a Companion of Honour in 1948. She died at Sissinghurst Castle at the age of seventy.

Garden and Tower

Sometimes a tragedy can lead to a triumph for a strong person and writer. So it was with Vita Sackville-West. If she had her own private tragedy, it was no less a public and indeed a cultural tragedy, symbolic of tradition and what it can do. In her time and her country, women could not inherit the royal title and attendant lands of their family. Not being a man, Vita was deprived of her ancestral home at Knole, which she loved with the kind of original devotion that inspires not just our admiration but our compassionate complicity in her loss. Her cousin Edward (Eddy) Sackville-West inherited it, and even though she was finally given a key to it, she rarely used it. The trauma remained. Her dream book, which she called just that, is reprinted here, where it is noticeable that the single dream in which she is reconciled to Knole and feels no anguish at returning is prefaced by her remarking on that rare event. Writing Knole's history and that of her family in *Knole and the Sackvilles* and creating her garden at Sissinghurst, which we might see as a substitute garden, scarcely sufficed to make up for what she should have had. She deserved it by her ancestral passion, loved it more than anyone else could have, and would have cherished it best.

Given Vita's passion for and extensive knowledge of French literature along with her acknowledged mastery of everything related to the art of gardening, it is doubly ironic to think, in relation to her life, of Voltaire's *Candide*. His all-too-often quoted ironic statement and lament about this not exactly being the best of all possible worlds leaps to mind: "*Il faut cultiver son jardin*"—you do have to cultivate your garden, whichever one you happen to have or be allotted. So Vita Sackville-West worked in and thought about, year in and year out, her garden at Sissinghurst, which was obliged to replace what she might have cultivated at Knole. Her garden still flourishes, visited by an increasing number of persons every year. Indeed, Vita's newspaper columns and her radio broadcasts about the cultivation of gardens far more fame than did her writings on other topics, fictional and factual. Yes, she cultivated her garden, but in a sense it was the wrong one. The way in which she eventually made it the right one took great force of will and managed what we might call a translated passion.

Vita Sackville-West did not mope about and shared neither her grief nor her work, which took place in her tower at Sissinghurst at a comfortable distance from the house in which everything else took place. The house, actually a castle, had no guest rooms. In Vita's tower upon her desk, there remains the photograph of Virginia Woolf, where it always was. Her still-remembered and much-celebrated affair with Woolf yielded the triumphant and unWoolfian text of *Orlando,* whose hero/heroine is based on Vita, and in which Vita's elegant and willful changeability, in personality as in costume, is rendered in different genders over the ages. And Vita's brief *Seducers in Ecuador,* with its play on varying views dependent on the color of one's glasses, is quite as Woolfian any of Woolf's stories, short or long.

Vita's life was both busy and quiet. She wrote, lectured on literature and family life as well as gardening, and made radio broadcasts, but was eventually more at ease at Sissinghurst, in her tower and with her family and dogs, than out in the public arena. There she lived a casual life in her favorite costume: long pearls and silk shirts worn with pants and high boots. That is the way she would choose to be remembered, as well as in her fashionable hats and costumes for her public performances. Here too her double nature and chosen appearance was an intimate part of her being.

Among the verbal portraits of Vita offered by those who knew her best, those by Virginia and Leonard Woolf stand out sharply. After a dinner in December 1924, which Roger Fry attended, Virginia Woolf described the difference between her friends and Vita: "She has the habit of praising & talking indiscriminately about art, which goes down in her set, but not in ours. . . . dear old obtuse, aristocratic, passionate, Grenadier-like Vita."[21] It is that very enthusiasm that attracts many of us to Vita the writer: She was passionate to the point of irritating others—how very wonderful indeed.

In a letter of the same period to Jacques Raverat in France, the very ill husband of her friend Gwen Darwin and recipient of many of her letters, Virginia Woolf gave her famous description of Vita's legs: "Oh they are exquisite—running like slender pillars up into her trunk, which is that of a breastless cuirassier (yet she has 2 children) but all about her is virginal, savage, patrician; and why she writes, which she does with complete competency and a pen of brass, is a puzzle to me. If I were she, I should merely stride, with 11 Elk hounds behind me, through my ancestral woods."[22] That "pen of brass" should be taken here in context, as it often is not, with its admixture of understandable envy and of admiration for her other qualities.

Leonard's own description is no less vivid: "To be driven by Vita on a summer's afternoon at the height of the season through the London traffic—she was a very good, but rather flamboyant driver—and to hear her put an aggressive taxi driver in his place, even when she was in the wrong, made one recognize a note in her voice that Sackvilles and Buckhursts were using to serfs in Kent 600 years ago, or even in Normandy 300 years before that. She belonged indeed to a world which was completely different from ours."[23] The very difference of her world remains part of her appeal for present day readers—not so much the envy of it, as its foreignness to many, and its naturalness to her.

A Note on Vita's Irony

Vita, in her awareness of emotions, style, and language, had—even in her moments of intensity or despair—what I would like to call the dignity of irony. This preserved for her a certain distance from her involvements and, in my view, made the quite extraordinary marriage of herself and Harold, whom she never ceased to cherish, a success. One example may suffice. In her best-known novel, *All Passion Spent,* the last part of which is included in this volume, Vita, in the voice of the elderly and nonconformist Lady Slane, reflects on happiness in this fashion: ironic, scholarly, and precise: "But what was happiness? Had she been happy? That was a strange, clicking word to have coined—meaning something definite to the whole English-speaking race—a strange clicking word with its short vowel and its spitting double p's and its pert tip-toe at the end."[24]

Writing and Reception

In a real sense, the life pictured in Vita's garden writings, in her reflections on the architecture of various country houses, in her explicit poem "Sissinghurst," and in the long poems "The Land" and "The Garden" is her true life. Against the current of what we think of as the poetry of the early to middle part of the twentieth century, she composed long poems of epic nature, taking as theme and backdrop the world of nature and its loving cultivation. Yes, she would have preferred to be remembered as a poet rather than a novelist. During her lifetime she was known and celebrated as one, and both her Georgic poems, "The Land" and "The Garden," won prestigious prizes, respectively the Hawthornden and the Heinemann. Yet something that she found hurtful in the extreme happened in March of 1946. At a meeting of the poetry committee of the Society of Authors (a committee that included Edith Sitwell, Walter de la Mare, Dylan Thomas, and Louis MacNeice), she was not asked to participate in a poetry reading to be held in Wigmore Hall in the presence of the Queen. Four years later she wrote in her diary of her despair over that: "I don't think I will ever write a poem again. They destroyed me for ever that day . . ."[25] Clearly, they did not think her poetry good enough to read. The problem was not her voice or her presence, since she was continually lecturing on the radio and in public. She always valued her critical writing and even her novels—for which she is best known—less than her poetry, a judgment with which the present day reader may argue. Her poetry has, on the whole, been far less appreciated than her other work, particularly her fiction and her essays.

As for the writing on gardening, that simply encompassed her passionate knowledge and practice. In any case, most of her novels (except *Dark Island, Grand Canyon,* and *La Grande Mademoiselle*—which she herself disliked) were immediate successes, particularly *All Passion Spent* and *Seducers in Ecuador,* which upon its appearance took top billing over Virginia Woolf's *Mrs. Dalloway.* In *Seducers,* it was often said, she had "out-Bloomsburied Bloomsbury."

Her own idiosyncratic nature is apparent in her other writings as well. One of my favorites is the delightful, if eccentric, series of reflections on dog portraits collected in her late work called simply *Faces,* many of which have autobiographical reflections about her reactions to those portraits based on her own dog family. These quieter musings make a high contrast to her travel writings, particularly those about Persia and the Bakhtiari Mountains, and the hitherto unpublished diary of her travel in the United States. The extraordinary range of her activities, her writing genres, and her knowledge, together with her own dual nature, as documented in her fiction and letters and in Virginia Woolf's *Orlando,* render her, as Nigel Nicolson so rightly terms it, a subject of growing fascination.

The enthusiasm with which she entered her various love affairs always helped her to produce quantities of work: translations (of Rilke's *Duino Elegies,* with Margaret Goldsmith Voigt and later with Eddy Sackville-West) as well as fiction and more learned material. Writing in 1931 to Evelyn Irons, with whom she traveled in Provence and to whom many of the poems in Les Baux are dedicated, Vita remarked on her own prolific output: She said she never stopped "writing stories and articles. . . . I must make the most of it while the fit is on me—but they are cheap stuff."[26]

In Vita's prose and poems, the details are resoundingly clear, especially those of food, clothes, colors, landscapes, and seascapes. Her highly visual sense of things is evident in her dream book, as in all her writing. Everywhere her wit manifests itself in her discussion of external details that seem often to give the essential clue to the characters in and the character of her fiction. What is most credible about them is not so much their personal makeup as the things they love and the roles they play in relation to them. They are, more often than not, possessed by the houses and traditions they inhabit, the worlds they live in, and the things they love. They can have, as Vita did, a passion for their land—as in *Dark Island* and in her long poems "The Land" and "The Garden"—for their inherited traditions—as in *Family History* or *The Edwardians*—or, perhaps no less believably, for their dog—as in *Easter Party.* All these passions were so strongly part of Vita that they give her, together with her acknowledged dual nature, a particular fascination for those who were close to her and for her readers then and now.

Fully conscious of this double-sidedness, she explored it in many of her writings in different guises.

Her sense of self, of land, and of work, was always a positive one. As an example, take the way in which her long poem "The Land" is a response to T. S. Eliot's "Waste Land":

> The land and not the waste land celebrate,
> The rich and hopeful land, the solvent land,
> Not some poor desert strewn with nibbled bones,
> A land of death, sterility, and stones.

As for her fictional self, she portrays herself and her impassioned love of Knole as a dark and romantic lover torn between sentiment and a sense of land. Perhaps the most vivid picture she gives of herself as a writer, picturing that self from within and without, is found in the odd story "The Poetry Reading," in which the poet (and Vita always thought of herself as that) has a special allure for the young person listening, who is enchanted by the dress and the person, the appearance and the reality of the poet as woman.

> Charlotte was also surveying Sackville-West; she saw the dark felt hat, the heavy cream lambskin coat, black dress, scarlet earrings, scarf, and shoes, yet apart from these externals the quality that held the audience and Charlotte in particular was not the beauty of the rather tired face, but its exceptional sincerity.

> Charlotte was interested in her personally, what did such a face reveal? So many things, almost everything that is save happiness; it was passionate, instantaneously receptive, sometimes childish, discontented, shy, imperious.

That story, included in this volume, reveals her willed duality as well as anything could.

Vita was a feminist of true stripe. Incensed at being addressed as Mrs. Harold Nicolson, she was "flung into a rage." "You know," she wrote Harold, "I love you more than anybody has ever loved anybody else, but I really do resent being treated as if I were your dog. The whole thing is an insult to human dignity. . . . Why not get me a collar with your name and address engraved upon it?"[27] She was no more pleased by the title Lady Nicolson. As Victoria Glendinning points out, when Harold and Vita became Sir Harold and Lady Nicolson in 1953, after the publication of his biography of George V, they considered turning down the honor, which seemed to them "dreary and middle class." Vita greatly disliked being called Lady Nicolson and remained V. Sackville-West.[28]

Finally, although her upbringing in privilege and her decidedly chilly attitude toward those of different classes might seem to disqualify Vita Sackville-West for the idealized role of female intellectual, her extraordinary production and passion in relation to creativity and the literary life go far to override that perception. She spent much of her life writing and lecturing for radio and literary audiences on society; on gardening; on England and its literature and history; on the various figures of interest to her, from saints (such as Saint Teresa)—she went through a mystic phase—to royal mistresses (La Grande Mademoiselle), from writers like Andrew Marvell to typical Edwardian figures. Her courageous old women (as in *All Passion Spent*) encourage the younger women to eschew normal values of society and take up what they really care about. Traditions can be profited from and overcome. Few things hold Vita back: She is a true representative of critical excitement, of creative passion, and of female rebelliousness against masculine-set mores. It was this that Virginia Woolf admired and loved in her, along with much else.

In a sense, Vita Sackville-West personified the best and most valorous part of what the Bloomsbury culture has come to mean to us: an unending enthusiasm for creation and for life and a nonchalance in regard to what a generally normative society believes one's behavior should be and represent. Vita did exactly as she pleased, worked double-time at her poetry and her other writing, as well as her gardening, she traveled immensely and with resourcefulness and knowledge, and excelled in multiple genres she encompassed as fearlessly in her writing as in her living. Overall, and most crucial to her reception as author and person now, I believe that her essential quality was her great and lasting courage: in the vast range of the things she did, the people she loved and was loved by, and in her intensity of living, in which she never failed.

PART I

DIARIES

The best way to approach the workings of Vita's mind and her occupations, and those of her mother, is through their personal diaries, which are therefore transcribed here at length.

Comparing Vita's diaries with those of her mother is certainly instructive about the kind of relationship they had as well as about the kind of lives they lived. Victoria's diaries, often reading like some sort of caricature of high society, are fascinating for what they reveal of another epoch. ("It was such a pretty sight, as so few people were asked and all had their best clothes and diamonds on.") We see her dresses and those of the upper-class ladies surrounding her, see their emeralds and rubies and diamonds (pale pink and pale green, in her own case), and follow their ups and downs in relation to the Palace. Of course, given Vita's attachment to Violet Keppel, Victoria's reflections on Violet's mother (the king's mistress) wearing a Cartier copy of Marie Antoinette's famous necklace is all the more riveting.

Vita's diaries, on the other hand, are concerned with her extensive travels, with her professional life, and with her numerous friends. These journals are far more down-to-earth than those of her mother. Of especial interest is the way she transcribes her encounters with Virginia Woolf, the most intimate of these simply marked as "X" or "!" in her diaries.

In Vita's memoirs, as in her daily life, her keen eye for detail is responsible for the accurate tone of presentation. It is never hard to picture what she describes, so acute is her description—one stroke, as with a painter's brush, can define a portrait or place.

In order to preserve the feeling of the diaries, such things as exclamation marks, capitalizations, and ampersands are left intact.

SELECTIONS FROM
VICTORIA SACKVILLE-WEST'S DIARIES,
1902–1905 AND 1922

In the diaries of Vita's mother, Victoria Sackville-West, the main topics of interest are, as one might expect of an Edwardian aristocrat, her clothing: the dresses from Lucile and Paquin, the jewels worn with them, and the occasions on which she wore them. Her social sphere is of primary importance, of course: this dinner, that visit, the frequent encounters with royalty. She notes her own sensitivity and various nervous states: she weeps at Lady Windermere's Fan and is unable to sleep with the noise above her flat. As for her commentary on the perhaps unusual, but in fact, highly successful relationship between Vita and Harold, it, too, is more or less what might be expected.

Regarding Vita's writing, her mother might have wished her to choose another subject matter, but her reflection on her daughter's carrying over her personal style of calm poise to her writing is perceptive. This poise gives us a clue as to the workability of Vita's wide range of subjects: her general calm, a sort of detachment, permits this imaginative stretch.

1902

18th June. Opera to hear Caruso and Pancini in "Lucia." Have been invited to the abbey by the King; have ordered white dress at Lucile's. Gave Lionel a Cartier pin today.

29th June. London. The poor king had to be suddenly operated on the 24th, just 2 days before the coronation. Every one was stunned! Lucile had made me a beautiful cream salon dress for the "Loose Box!"—

No time for diary writing.

I have got a lovely pendant with a pale pink and a pale green diamond from Cartier, also a pair of tiny diamond and ruby aiguillettes from Cartier too. He is mounting, according to my design and suggestion, my fine alexandrite as a ring.

1903

10th March. London. Small dance at Buckingham Palace. Wore lovely new gauze dress—trimmed lace and pink chiffon from "Berthe." Emerald and diamonds. I hoped to escape having to shake hands with the king, but I had to come in, *quite* at the end of the line, & shook hands with King, Queen, Prince of Wales & Princess, they were standing in the middle of a big room and no one was announced; they knew everybody by name at once.

I had a long talk with the Prince of Wales. It was such a pretty sight, as so few people were asked and all had their best clothes and diamonds on; Mrs. G. [George] Keppel has had Marie Antoinette's famous necklace copied by Cartier! The Queen looked so lovely & not a day over 30. I saw her so well, under a blaze of electric light; she has no wrinkles and is not painted up; her hair only is too young to be natural; her neck, shoulders, figure are truly *wonderful.*

18th December. We also went to *Lady Windermere's Fan;* where I cried stupidly— I can't go to the play without crying, as my nerves are in such a weak state. [. . . went] to see Sir Anderson Critchett for my weak eye; he said the same as Dr. Ferrier as to my nervous system. Have new palpitations all the week. Have ordered spectacles!!!

1904

Christmas Day. I had 45 presents & Vita had 50 (Reference for details to my red Book) The local band played on the 24th. We are very short of servants, our 2 footmen have influenza. Stubbs is dying of Delirium Tremens and poor Papa never knew that Stubbs drank! A "nipper." My best presents have been the lovely pink enamel frame from Fabergé from Lio & the Fabergé Clock from Seery and Vita had such a nice book-cover designed by her for me.

1905

January. I am not going to write any more my journal very regularly, but only now and again. . . . My sittings with [the American painter John Singer] Sargent are quite pleasant, as he is very sympathique and talks well and all the time. I am done in a simple black dress and a lovely lace scarf and I wear some of my fine emeralds. I go 4 times a week—and sit over three hours. He wants to do it with my mouth slightly open, but I don't like that.

24th January. Bought some table-linen at the sale yesterday, as Lionel did not think our tablecloths were good enough!!! [. . .] Awful riots in Petersburg. The Czar will not listen to the strikers and has fled from the Winter Palace. He is very much blamed in England for having the mob fired at, women & kids.

12th February. London & St. Albans. We motored over to lunch with George & Jenny Cornwallis West at Salisbury Hall near St. Albans; a charming small old place—very well done up. We took Hans von Pless in the motor. The others were: Lady Lester-Kay & W. de Cuadra, Mr. Jack Churchill, Lady C. Hatch. Lionel had a game of golf there; he often goes out of London with Connie Hatch to play golf.

17th February. London. We have decided to go to Monte Carlo, so I am ordering a dress at Paquin's: light fawn voile, with *big high* sleeves again! We dined at Mrs. Hope Vere's on the 15th. I saw again that nice Marquis de Villavieja, whose death was reported from Ostend (playing polo) last July. I took Lucienne Grosvenor to Derby House where there are some delightful lectures on the 18th century.

18th February. I have been 4 times this week to Sargent. Lady Lester-Kaye called to see the flat. We are thinking of leaving the dear little flat on account of the terrible noise the new tenants (Mrs. Willie Portal) make upstairs. It drives me crazy as I can't have a minute sleep after 6 o'clock in the morning. And I feel so tired, to go to Sargent at 10:30, when I have not slept. Vita has been laid up this week with a very bad cold, caught at Knole when she went for L. I keep her in bed.

20th February. Lots of hunting talk here. Poor Lio came back with a chill, as he had to drive on the box of the brougham this morning when it was bitterly cold. I made Lio stay at home & nursed him.

21st February. Sargent did a charming drawing of me, which I will give Vita for her Birthday. It took him an hour to do it, and played the piano beautifully for me, while resting.

24th February. London. I have met the great Rodin twice at dinner, yesterday and today. Burne-Jones's model (so ugly now) also a daughter of Mrs. Hunter's,

Lady Cynthia Graham who was not en beauté, & the lovely *lovely* Lady Helen Vincent, who was radiantly beautiful that night.

Old Mrs. Cornwallis West was there too; she said it was a pity her face was wrinkled and that she could not show the best part of herself that was not wrinkled as she was sitting on it! She was most gushing to me. We all adjourned to Mrs. Hunter's house and very good music. We dined with the Becketts also to meet Rodin. I sat on his right and found him so much less shy than last year when I met him at Seery's *for the first time.* I suggested that he should go & see Sophie Arnould at Seery's who has invited Rodin & Sargent at once. My other partner was Mr. Ernest Beckett, doing up his new house in the Renaissance style, the mania that everybody has got in Paris now! Lady Londonderry was there, très aimable et en beauté.

I wore yesterday my Lucile Coronation dress & rubies. Tonight, Hayward's dress & emeralds. Lio said I looked very well.

25th February. London. I could not go to my sitting as it was so foggy yesterday. It would have amused me to hear Sargent's impressions on the ladies at the big dinner of Mrs. Hunter. I called on Mrs. Hunter where I met Lady Colin Campbell! Seery took me to see the Whistlers at the New Gallery. I think his "famous portraits" except his Mother from the Luxembourg & his Carlyle, are *abominable.* I like some of his watercolours and most of his etchings.

MALADE. We gave up going to the Beauforts, as I felt getting bad.

26th February. London. Lio has been looking at many houses, but none seems to suit us, or they are too expensive. Sargent has sent me the drawing, *framed,* and has written on it: to my friend, Mrs. S. West. for Vita's Birthday 1905. & signed it. Lio likes it *very* much and so does Vita.

1st March. London. I went to Sargent's again this morning. I went down to the studio, thinking Sargent would be away & took Lio, Vita, & Seery. But Sargent was waiting for me and begged me to take off my hat—redid my face; he made me look away & I much preferred when he made me look straight at one. Lio said I was not very vain not to mind taking off my hat & sitting in a dishevelled manner! I was much surprised to receive a white dress from Lucile, which I had tried on only once & did not fit me at all, such a failure. Miss Wolff writes in the most laudatory way about Vita & her classes.

4th March. I have told Mrs. Brown that I should like her to become housekeeper in the flat & Nellie would take her place at Knole. She has accepted. The poor woman has been such a worry to me! Let us hope Nellie will be a treasure, as she has been in the flat.

8th March. London. I have been with Lio to look at a nice little house in Grosvenor Street, no. 61, which we might get for £9000. Seery likes the idea as he knows how badly I sleep in the flat with Mrs. Portal on the top floor. Oh! That maddening noise in the early morning!!

Went to Sargent's again & Lio liked it again, although he redid my fan for a ninth time. Dress is not finished.

9th March. London & Paris. We celebrated Vita's thirteenth birthday last night. We all had a great discussion after dinner over the Lucile dress which does not fit & which is sent back, backwards & forwards. Vita got a lot of books & we gave her some petit-gris furs. Seery dined at Buckingham Palace on Tuesday & felt very tired last night at dinner, after having been 3 hours with the King & Prince of Bulgaria. He has been so kind & nice & not at all cross lately, the dear old friend. We crossed to Paris today.

10th March. Paris. We slept last night at Rue Lafitte. [Seery's apartment]. Did some hat-shopping (some chocolates for M.) and started for Monte Carlo at 8:00 A.M. in a lit salon.

11th to 30th March. Monte Carlo. We could not get our usual rooms at the Victoria & got a fairly nice little suite at the Prince de Galles: Double bedroom & sitting room with balcony. Single room & bathroom & elec. light. All 1st floor. The Arthur Wilsons are building a fine villa at St. Jean. We lunched with them to meet the Duke & Duchess of Schleswig-Holstein; she was a Coburg & seems half-witted. We went over to see the Ralph Curtis[es] in their lovely villa Sylvia; they are great friends of Sargent's & cannot understand why he has written that he cannot let me have the picture, as he is so dissatisfied with it & it is so bad, that he has destroyed it & feels he never can do me well. It is a *great* disappointment, after all this trouble.

1922

"Book of Reminiscences" [inscribed on the flyleaf: "The book of Happy Reminiscences for My Old Age. Started on my 61st Birthday."] This diary included a list of her suitors.

23rd September 1922. Brighton. I am 60 today. I feel as if I was 30 and even younger.

But . . . I am entering old age for all that . . . and I want to have a golden old age. . . .

[. . . .] She [Vita] *hated* rice pudding.

She is a very difficult person to know . . . She is or *seems* absolutely devoted to Harold, but there is nothing whatever sexual between them which is strange in such a young and good-looking couple. She is not in the least jealous of H. and willingly allows him to relieve himself with anyone, if such is his wont or his fancy. They both openly said so one evening when I was staying at L. [Long Barn, Vita's and Harold's home from 1915–1932]. . . . It shocked me extremely. People may do what they like, but it ought to be either sacred or absolutely private. . . . I am glad they [Vita and Harold] will be interested when Granmama is not there any more and it will show them how lovingly she thought of them. . . .

Her calm descriptions fill me with admiration. She carries into her writings the quiet and tranquility of manner which is so characteristic of her. I only wish she did not choose the kind of subject she seems to be partial to.

SELECTIONS FROM VITA SACKVILLE-WEST
DIARIES, 1907–1929

Vita's diary entries between 1907 and 1933, from which this selection has been made, offer the fullest picture of her interior and exterior landscapes. The identifications in brackets are of people and places important in Vita's personal life.

Vita's diaries compose a startling contrast to those of her mother: They are terse, rapid, and concern themselves more with other people and the outside world than with formal society, its procedures, and her place in it. Quite the opposite of her mother, Vita never comments on what she is wearing and is far more interested in the monuments she sees on her travels, the people with whom she travels, and—at times—in their relations with others and herself. As for her relationship with her mother, it had much secrecy in it: Suspecting that her mother would read her diary, the young Vita kept it in Italian for four years, partly for privacy, but mostly for enjoyment of the language. (Vita was fluent in both Italian and French.)

What she notices and notes defines her point of view: Her acute perception is trained above all on the necessity of feeling alive to her experiences and to those events that matter to her and her companions, rather than to a preordained social set. The role of diary-writing was crucial in sustaining her personal intensity, whether she was traveling or simply writing, gardening, reading, and lecturing. In contradistinction to the way in which she felt herself so inarticulate and so slow with the members of the Bloomsbury group in their witty and rapid exchanges, ("I am distinctly not clever," she says in her memoir)[1], her diaries show her as determined, acute, sensitive, and perceptive to a fault.

This is the compensation for the way she had so often perceived herself: "I see myself . . . plain, lean, dark, unsociable, unattractive — horribly unattractive! — rough, and secret. Secrecy was my passion; I dare say that was why I hated companions."² Her diary was, from the beginning, her companion, but a companion to whom she never talked excessively. Vita, for all her passionate living, was almost a classicist in her words.

The first diary entries here record her third trip to Italy, where she had two years before been sightseeing with Violet Keppel; they had had private Italian lessons together, and Violet had already announced her affection for Vita — whose own affection for Rosamund Grosvenor had been her own first lesbian attachment. The intense and long-lasting affair with Violet, which nearly destroyed both their marriages, was to take on its full flavor later.

Vita, always an enthusiastic traveler, comments succinctly on the details that most impress her: people, landscapes, monuments. Like a Jamesian heroine, she could be counted as one on whom nothing is lost. Nor does anything take up too much space.

July 1907-July 1910

May 8, 1910. Hotel Royal Daniele, Venice. We [Vita and Rosamund Grosvenor] went to San Marco and through the Doge's palace: both are fine in their way, but nothing seems to stand out here above anything else; all the buildings are so crowded one on the top of the other. But I like some of the old palaces, especially in the small canals. . . .

May 9. We went to the Belle Arti; fascinating Carpaccios! And right down the Canal Grande in the afternoon, after which we wandered into a few churches where there was nothing very remarkable. Orazio Pucci [her suitor] turned up in the evening! We packed him off to another hotel, as he proposed to stay here.

May 14. Chiasso, over Swiss frontier . . . Weather ascribed to Halley's comet, through the tail of which I believe we are passing now.

May 15. I suppose the scenery is magnificent, but it is rather like a colour picture-postcard, or a scene from a pantomime.

May 17. All day by the St. Gotthard route, which I have gotten to know well. I remember how enthusiastic I was over it two years ago. It is horrible to feel oneself getting blasé.

May 29. Heavenly crossing delayed by king's [Edward VII's] funeral. It was very magnificent but not at all like a funeral except when the guards reversed arms and everyone cried when they saw the King's little dog following the coffin. The German Emperor talked all the time to the King [George V], which everyone thought very bad taste.

July 2. Ellen Terry, who is quite charming. Lady Tree is appalling. The Party stayed here: Miss Campbell, Rosamund [Grosvenor], Felicia, Mrs. Godfrey Baring, Harold Nicolson ["Harold Nicolson" underlined in red].

1913

July 25. Friday. Knole. [The court case, brought by the family of Sir John Murray Scott (Seery) contesting his will, in which he left Vita's mother £50,000, had taken up much of Vita's time, but Victoria triumphed, to Vita's admiring eyes.] Poor Harold, let's hope he isn't forced to return here this morning. I have been very involved . . . but thanks be to God, everything is all right.

October 1. Wednesday. Coker. WEDDING DAY! Today Harold and I got married. Mother didn't get up in the morning, just carried on with her regular schedule, then toward midday, I got dressed all in gold, which was a great success. Olive sang in the chapel. [Olive Rubens was a close friend of Lionel Sackville-West, whom he had, at one point, wanted to move into Knole with her tubercular husband.]

October 2. Thursday. We didn't do anything but write and sleep in the garden. . . . I never would have dreamt of such happiness.

1915

August 3. Alone, lunching with Harold, and I feel newly married. 182 Ebury Street. Get up late, lunch and dine alone with Harold. [The initial sentence is written in Italian, the following in English—this is Vita's first entry in English since 1911!]

1916

May 1. Long Barn. A long day all alone with Harold, lovely weather. We do forestry. Paddle with Ben . . . Ben says "boat," "ball," and "my good tea, Amen."

November 29. Violet [Keppel] lunches and we go to Chu Chu Chow & to tea with Osbert [Sitwell]. Ezra Pound brings his little Jap to try on Buddha clothes.

1918

April 29. On. Polperro. . . . drive out to Polperro [Cornwall] by wagonette. Staying in a fisherman's cottage, very primitive—rice pudding & no drains!

Harold plants nuts. Ben goes up to a little girl in the village and says "Buckle my shoe" to her by way of opening a conversation.

April 30. Nigel goes into short frocks. Go to Hugh Walpole's cottage. He isn't here but lets us use his room and his books.

May 2. Polperro. Go to Fowey [nearby town to Polperro] in the local butcher's pony cart. The harness comes all to pieces. Have tea, or rather cider, in a little restaurant at Fowey, V. [Violet] meets a man like Mallory. V. steals wisteria & lilac from a deserted garden by the wayside.

May 3. Polperro. Spend the day at Hugh Walpole's cottage again, reading his books

May 4. Leave Polperro.

[Vita and Violet Keppel initiated their affair with various trips to Paris in November 1918, then to Monte Carlo from December 1918 until March 1919, returning to England only after Vita's mother and husband prevailed on her to do so. In March 1919 Violet Keppel announced her engagement to Denys Trefusis and, despite her passion for Vita, married him in June of that year, having extracted from him an agreement that she could continue her affair with Vita. In October 1919, Vita and Violet again traveled to Monte Carlo, and the intensity of their affair grew: They agreed to leave their husbands to live together. Vita intended to inform Harold of their decision when she went to see him in Paris. Finding him ill, she postponed her announcement of the intended "elopement" until mid-January 1920, after she and Harold had reunited in England and Violet and Denys Trefusis had returned from France.]

1920

January 1. Hotel Matignon, Paris. H. [Harold] has his knee finally stitched up.

January 2. Hill Street [Victoria's house, acquired in 1907]. Come over from Paris. A jolly crossing by moonlight. Sit up on deck almost alone; cold, but love it. Read life of Rimbaud which thrills me; also Claudel.

London beastly, fog.

January 3. Knole. Spend the morning in London looking for a governess—object of value and rarity. Lunch with Rose, & come down here afterwards, where I am alone with Dada [her father, Lionel Sackville-West]. Ben and Nigel are here, very well; and the former immensely grown. Bitterly cold.

January 4. Take Ben & Nigel out for a walk in the morning, and go to see B.M. [Bonne Maman, Victoria] who is very seedy.

January 6. Spend the day in bed, very cold and bored and stupid; read Hippolytus and try quite vainly to write.

January 8. Hill Street. Go with Dada to see movies of Allenby's campaign and pictures of Pepita [her Spanish grandmother, about whom Vita wrote a biography] which simply enchant me.

January 9. Knole. Spend the day in London with L. [Lushka, Vita's name for Violet Trefusis] Take "Rebellion" to Collins who think they can get it out by May next [one of the early titles of the novel *Challenge,* written in collaboration with Violet. It was not published in the United Kingdom until 1974 because of Vita's mother's strong objection.] Go to see the pictures of Petra again, with L.

January 10. It pours. Go over to Long Barn to get a few things. The place is just one large puddle.

January 11. It pours and blows a gale. Resume the soap book. Kenneth renews his usual ludicrous proposals to me. [Her godfather, Kenneth (Kenito) Hallyburton Campbell, a friend of Seery's, the age of her mother, who tried to rape her when she was 16.]

January 12. Go to London for the day & see L., also D. T. [Denys Trefusis]—an unpleasant interview. [Violet remained in love with Vita, who reciprocated her affection: Violet's husband, Denys, was understandably upset.]

January 13. Walk Ben, Nigel, and two dogs to Sevenoaks, a strenuous undertaking. Walk over to Long Barn in the afternoon & get things there, & retrieve the beginning of the soap book which I thought was lost.

January 14. 34 Hill Street. Spend the day with L. Dine with Kenneth and Dada at Jules and go to "Home and Beauty." Kenneth comes back with me afterwards here.

See Ozzie [Oswald Dickinson, Harold's friend], a gossip, as befits his post of Secretary to the Home Office Board of Control in Lunacy! In the evening, about B.M. & Knole, etc. Kenneth rather a dear; tell him I am in trouble, to stop him making love to me, and he instantly becomes the most concerned of friends, & puts himself wholly at my disposal. Poor thing: if he only knew! . . .

January 16. Basil Hotel. Clear out of Hill St. under the impression that H. and B.M. have had row & come to this hotel with L. Harold arrives in evening and we both dine at Cadogan Gardens [Harold's mother's house in London]; his father is very old and can barely lift his right arm. Go to H.'s room afterwards and tell him about things [her planned elopement to France with Violet and the unpleasant interview with Denys].

B.M. arrives from Paris.

Spend half the night writing letters.

Met H.'s mother on the stairs as I was leaving C. Gardens, and told her everything.

January 17. Knole. A perfectly awful day. Come round early to C. Gardens & stay until midday talking to H. who refuses to agree to my going today. Go round to see L. Lunch with Harold and take him to Grosvenor Street afterwards. L. agrees to wait a fortnight [before eloping with Vita to France], then when H. has gone she says she won't come back to Knole in a state of collapse.

January 19. Nigel's birthday.

January 22. 34 Hill Street. Come up with H. Lunch with L. Don't see B.M. until the evening, when we have a strained and impersonal conversation. Dine at the Ritz with H. and go with him to Home and Beauty. On my return I again talk to B.M., who tries to get me to agree with all she says about Dada [Lionel, whom she is about to leave]; when she finds I won't she goes off very angry. An *impossible* situation.

January 23. Knole. I see B.M. for a moment this morning before leaving Hill St. but she is frigid to me and writes H. a letter refusing to see him at all—though what he has done as he wasn't even in the room during her conversation with me Heaven only knows!

January 26. Knole. H. and I take Ben to the pantomime—his first. He is less impressed than I expected, but at his best all day. See L. for a brief moment just before lunch.

February 1. Still at Knole. Harold goes back to Paris. I go up to London with him. To the station, then straight back to Knole.

Walk over to Long Barn with Dada in the afternoon. The suspense is almost unbearable. The whole fortnight has been sufficiently odd, esp. as H. has never mentioned the subject [her predicted elopement with Violet] until I simply forced it on him in the train today.

When shall I see him again? What is going to happen?

February 2. Come up to London early with my things & go to the dentist. See L. at 11:30 and lunch with her. It is, at any rate not for today. . . . Spend the afternoon with her, and come back to Knole in the evening, leaving my things at Charing Cross. At the last moment she wants to come with me, but, having promised D.T. not to give him the slip, she goes back to Grosvenor St. Also she was rather insufficiently equipped with her wax Bacchante & and box of brandy cherries!

February 3. Saracen's Head, Lincoln. Come here with L.

February 4. Lincoln. Walk up to the cathedral; Lincoln is rather jolly, but o Lord! the cold!

February 5. Lincoln. Meant to go to the Fens today, but spend the day in bed instead.

February 6. Lincoln. Spend the day in bed.

February 7. Go to the Fens today. Meant to spend the night here, but having forgotten the Bacchante at Lincoln we come back to fetch it.

February 8. Liverpool Street Hotel. We come back from Lincoln this afternoon, arriving at dinnertime. L. telephoned for D.T. who comes at once & remains a comparatively short time. L. very silent & unhappy.

February 9. King's Head Hotel, Dover. D.T. comes for a second to our hotel early this morning, and L. & I leave for Dover by the boat train. She goes alone, very frightened, leaving me at Dover. After lunch Denys appears, having followed us by motor. Spend a grim afternoon with him in my hotel, send telegrams, write letters, etc. A fierce storm gets up & rages all night.

February 10. Hotel Meurice, Calais. Cross to Calais with Denys, the roughest crossing I have ever known. L. comes unexpectedly to meet me, and we meet in the buffet; she looks terribly ill & collapsed. D. and I take her to a hotel, & put her to bed & get a doctor. Impossible to discuss anything tonight. This ludicrous situation resolves itself into our all three dining most amicably in L.'s bedroom, & even into D. suggesting that we should all live together in Jamaica growing sugar!

February 11. Hotel du Rhin, Amiens. We take a motor in Calais and motor to Boulogne in piercing cold across desolate country. In the train between Boulogne & Amiens, D. suddenly says he will go on to Paris when we get out at Amiens. This he does, after an interminable 2 hours in a train that stops at every station. L. and I here alone.

February 12. Amiens. We go out in the morning & look at the remains of the bombardment, and at the very lovely cathedral. L. spends the rest of the day in bed, but comes down to dinner, and after dinner "Papa" [Violet's father George Keppel] suddenly arrives in L.'s room and we have a ridiculous & abusive scene with him.

Learn meanwhile by telephone that H. has left Paris for London this morning, & I wire for him.

February 13. Amiens. Papa mercifully keeps out of the way. L. spends the day in bed, only dining downstairs. She has another scene with Papa after dinner, at which I do not assist.

February 14. Hotel Alexandre III, Paris. Denys & Harold arrive together by aeroplane from London, landing at Amiens. Return to Paris with H. In the middle of dinner L. comes in & I feel restored to life to a certain extent. My god, what a day! I am broken with misery; if things were as bad as I had at first thought, I should put an end to myself. I *had* to go, I should have killed her if I had stayed an instant longer. I have told her I cannot even see her for two months. She calls it banishment—it is *not*. It is simply the impossibility of bringing myself to see her for the present.

February 15. Paris. L. leaves Paris by motor this morning. Lunch at Laurent's with H.

February 17. Go with H. to "Le Bonheur de ma femme."

February 18. Paris. Ash Wednesday. Bright, warm sunshine. L. telephones to me every day from various provincial towns in France, on her way south, and every day her voice is a little fainter . . .

February 20. Paris. Get the proofs of "Rebellion"; about the only thing which has stirred me to any interest since Amiens.

February 21. Paris. Have a chill and spend the day in bed, feeling rather wretched. Reading "Anna Karenina" again. Write a new last chapter to "Rebellion," and decide to call it "Endeavour" since Rebellion has been already used. Sorry about this, but Endeavour seems perhaps more applicable.

February 22. Paris. Still feel rather seedy, & don't go out, as it has turned cold. Jean de Gaigneron [one of Harold's lovers] comes and Herman Norman.

February 23. Paris. Send off corrected proofs of "Rebellion."

February 24. Paris. Lunch with Jim Barnes and H. at La Perouse and go to Leon Vannier to see if H. can pick up any information about Verlaine, particularly as he has taken up against idea of his biography of Verlaine. Wander around Paris, the most lovely sunny day, quite warm. Buy two little birds.

February 25. Paris. Harold is telephoned up mysteriously, and goes off to London in the afternoon.

February 26. Paris. Alone here. Lunch with Jim Barnes at Voisin & go to various shops & Musee Rodin with him; he comes back to tea. Dine with Uncle Charlie [(Baron) Charles Sackville-West] & go to "Mademoiselle ma mère"— funny. Get a wire from H. asking me to come over.

February 27. Paris. Wretched day. . . . Desperate telephoning between me and L. who is at Bordighera with Pat [Margaret "Pat" Dansey, one of Violet's lovers, who later became one of Vita's].

February 28. Come across with Dido and Miss Williams. H is going to Russia with the L. of N. [League of Nations] commission. B.M. Brighton. An awful blow meets me here: B.M. has read my proofs, and thinking that the book will give rise to gossip wants me not to publish it.

March 2. Long Barn. Change my title to "Challenge." I can't give it up; B.M. asks too much.

March 9. Long Barn. My birthday. Harold gives me a cocker spaniel puppy (Judy). Spend the day in London with B.M. and go with her to a matinee.

March 12. Hill St., Richmond. Mrs. Belloc Lowndes rings me up out of the blue and says she wants to know me. [Marie Adelaide Belloc Lowndes, to whom Victoria will write about the awfulness of *Orlando.*] Will I go and see her? I go. She is much au courant with my circumstances, and with the question of publishing "Challenge" or not. I am to send her the proofs.

March 15. Hill St., Richmond. Go to see Mrs. Lowndes, and have a long discussion with her about "Challenge," which she has now read in proof. She wants me to cancel it—says if L. were dead, would I publish it, etc.? This hits me— gossip I don't care a damn about. Mrs. Lowndes is kindness itself. So I give it up. I hope B.M. is pleased. She has beaten me.

March 19. In the train. I leave London early this morning, and catch the train to Avignon in Paris at 8. Sit up all night, but what do I care?

March 20. Hotel de l'Europe, Avignon. Arrive at 8 in the morning, and find L. at the hotel. We go out to look at the Palais des Papes, which we liked so much when we were here before. Quarreling already, because she apparently thought she could persuade me to stay with her after these allotted ten days were over, and it angers her to find she can't.

March 21. Cap d'Antibes. We hire a motor and come thus far, about 200 kilometres—right through Provence and over the Esterel, which is lovely but alarming. Find this rather jolly hotel, & dine over the sea in a pavilion.

March 22. Bordighera. Alas, my Monte Carlo! I get whirled past in a motor with drawn blinds . . . Reach Bordighera in the evening & dine with Pat who has a villa here.

March 23. San Remo. Motor to San Remo, a beastly place. L. horrible to me all day, and makes me very miserable and exasperated. After dinner I lose my head & say I will stay with her—Paradise restored.

March 24. Nervi. We leave S. Remo in the morning, joining Pat & Joan in the train, and travel all day getting to Genoa in the evening. There is no room in the hotels at Genoa, so we have to motor out to this perfectly beastly place. L. is however so sweet, having got the promise she wanted, that it makes up for everything.

March 25. Milan. Get to Milan latish and have a job to find room. I've got an awful cold.

March 26. Danieli Hotel, Venice. Spend the morning in Milan (with a streaming nose!) come here by Orient Express. It is very late as usual, & we don't reach Venice till nearly midnight. L. falls in love with the Orient Express, and it's all I can do to make her get out at Venice, as she wants to go on.

March 27. Venice. Spent part of the day trying to find Louis Mallet's palace & part of the day in shops & sightseeing. Had forgotten the beauty of San Marco.

Reading nothing but Shakespeare—an undiscovered country to me, which I swear I won't leave till I've explored every corner. What a wealth, what *afflatus,* what wind-filled sails! I feel that at last I've found the real thing; think I must have been mad not to embark on it before.

March 28. Venice. Everything is black again. I have had to tell L. I should only be followed and brought back. It is horrible. She is in the depths. So am I. I feel the Grand Canal, in spite of the floating onions, would be preferable.

March 30. Venice. L. not at all well.

March 31. Venice. L. still very seedy, and the doctor says she has a touch of jaundice. She stays in bed all day. It pours. Anything better than Venice in the rain is hard to conceive.

April 1. Verona. L. a little better, so we leave Venice and come here, arriving late.

April 2. Verona. Verona is very attractive, or would be if it wasn't raining. We go to see the Scaliger tombs, and in the afternoon drive round the town seeing the amphitheatre, the Scaliger Bridge & castle, the Duomo, and San Zeno.

April 3. Verona. We try to catch the Orient Express, in which we have reserved places, but miss it & have to return to the hotel. Take a carriage & drive out into the country in the middle of a thunderstorm.

April 4. Verona. Today the Orient Express is 13 hours late, so we renounce all hope of catching it. Unfortunately it continues to pour.

April 5. Albergo Sempione, Domodossola. We actually succeed in leaving Verona this afternoon, a grand regret, and think we shall really get to Paris at last, but no, the fates think otherwise; we get turned out of the train at the frontier for not having an Italian police permit. Nearly get locked up as a spy, and nearly get sent back to Venice as an alternative, but avoid both these things, and come to this hotel. Can't help feeling this is a reprieve.

April 6. Domodossola. Still here. Spend all day in bed. Get up at one A.M. in the morning to try & catch the train, then hear it won't arrive till 5, and give up the attempt, especially as we have heard nothing about places being available.

April 7. Orient Express. Get up and go for a delicious drive into the hills with L.; lie on a warm sunny bank and talk. Catch the blessed old train at midnight (only four hours late today!). Dreadfully sorry to leave.

April 8. Hotel Powers, Paris. Arrive in Paris about two o'clock, and much to my surprise are met by Harold who has come over on L. of N. business. B.M. is alone at Long Barn. Go out for a walk with H. in the afternoon. He comes round to our hotel after dinner, and remains talking to L. and me about the future until nearly one in the morning. Simply dead with tiredness.

April 18. Grand Hotel, Dover. Leave Paris this morning, meaning to reach London tonight, but change our minds & stay at Dover. Beastly grey country!

April 19. Long Barn. Leave Dover early & travel with L. as far as Ashford where we part. Come on here, and find B.M. rather sceptical as to the genuineness of all my delays. I don't blame her. She's had a lot to put up with from me, poor darling.

April 21. Hill St., Richmond. Spend the morning with L. & lunch with her & take her to a play after. A beastly unsatisfactory day. (Raquel Meller at Hippodrome, marvelous Spanish singer)

April 22. Come up to London with H. . . . . Meet L. after lunch & come down here with her alone. Hate seeing her in her own house—hate the hypocrisy of it all.

April 27. Long Barn. Bicycle home & get drenched, but rather enjoy flying down the hill with the rain lashing my face.

April 28. See L. in morning. Tired, absentminded, and dispirited.

April 29. Long Barn. Seedy, which annoys me. I suppose I get spoilt by being always well, and feel injured when my usual health fails me—like a millionaire who can't put his hand on £10,000 cash at a given moment!

April 30. Long Barn. Oh my good Lord! I *can't* write nowadays. It drives me wild to remember my fluency of once upon a time—ten or twelve sheets a day! And as for poetry, it's gone, gone, gone from me.

May 1. Long Barn. Lose the ring I always wear [The missing ring was one Violet had given her.] & am miserable & superstitious about it.

May 2. Long Barn. Walk to Hildeborough station after lunch to see if by any chance I have dropped my ring there, but fail to find it.

May 3. L. very unhappy & haunted. I *wish* I knew what to do.

May 5. Long Barn. I don't know what's the matter with me. I think I've got softening of the brain. I've been sitting all day in front of a barely begun review of some book, reading over & over again the few sentences I had written, not taking them in in the very least—oh wind, come & blow away the clouds! I smoke endless cigarettes, which help to addle my brain. I long for vigour and clear thought, but only meet with chaos. How I envy H. his clear-cut intellect!

I *must* shake myself out of this inertia. I wish I was poor, dirt poor, miserably poor, and obliged to work for my daily bread or go without. I need a spur. I am a rotten creature.

. . . Later, made myself finish the review.

May 7. Long Barn. Spend all today in bed. Write two poems, one of them slick off so perhaps I haven't got softening of the brain after all? Distinctly more cheerful in consequence.

May 11. Write another poem—bad, but better than nothing.

May 14. Long Barn. Pat comes down for the day. H.'s mother comes to stay in the evening. Very restless and unhappy.

May 17. Lower Grosvenor Place. Come up in the morning, lunch with L. We go to a matinee at the Hippodrome. We are both staying with Pat. Dinner all three at a little hotel opposite; happy.

May 18. Long Barn. Spend a rather miserable day with L. in London, after a row with Pat in the morning. Come down here with H. See B.M. in the morning & get slandered by her too. It blows a gale. Am I a good sailor? A burning question.

May 19. Long Barn. L. comes down for the night.

May 20. Sumurun [Lord Sackville-West's yacht], Calshott. Sail very slowly down to Calshott. Lovely weather.

May 21. Swanage. Sail from Calshott to Swanage. I *am* a good sailor! Harold immersed in his life of Verlaine.

May 23. Dartmouth. It has turned warm, and we had a perfect day though very little breeze. Lay on deck in the sun. Even Harold was weaned for a little from Paul Verlaine.

May 25. At sea off Start Point. Start well, but get suddenly becalmed and befogged and hurried heave to in a swell and a thick mist, with foghorns hooting all around.

May 26. At sea off Fowey. A perfect day again, but very little breeze till dinnertime, when we get about 4 hours moonlight sailing; then the wind drops and we are left rocking about in an awful swell all the rest of the night.

May 27. Falmouth. Wake up not knowing where we are, and believing ourselves to be off Fowey (o my Polperro!) but suddenly round a headland upon Falmouth. Find a telegram from H. saying that the Bolsheviks have invaded Persia, so he can't rejoin us yet. Go for a walk with Dada.

May 28. Falmouth. Go with Dada by steamer to Tregothman, a place belonging to Lord Falmouth. Such marvelous wood! Run a mile & a half to catch the return boat. Perfect weather.

May 31. Meet L. Hindshead.

June 4. Long Barn An alarming "literary" party! Clemence Dane [Winifred Ashton], Hugh Walpole, Marcus Hewlett, Virgilia [Enid Bagnold] & Sir Roderick [Jones] and Rebecca West—an attractive ugly young savage.

June 6. Long Barn. Write a lot, so does H. who kills off P.V. [Paul Verlaine]

June 7. Long Barn. Spend most of the day in bed, trying to write poetry, and enviously reading Shakespeare.

June 15. Gloucester. We go over the cathedral in the morning, very fine tombs (especially of Robert of Normandy) and a fine early 14th century window. We motor out to Berkeley after lunch, quite overwhelmed by its charm, magic, & mystery. We have to break our way in over hedges & through soaking hayfields, but it's impossible to get inside. A jolly day. Go to the local music hall in the evening.

June 26. Long Barn. L. makes me go up to London to see her; so I go up with Mrs. Lowndes.

July 2. Hill St., Richmond. A ghastly day. Get a note from L. in the morning saying she is going away, etc. Incapable of doing anything but slouching round Ebury St. after B.M. L. telephones to me in the evening; there ensures a scene between H., B.M., and me, which is interrupted only by the necessity of dining with Sybil Colefax. Pull myself together. . . . Go afterward to a dance at Mrs. Gordon's where I see L. and the whole of her family, whom I've conscientiously met.

July 3. Long Barn. Spend a disturbed morning with L. in Pat's house. . . . Lovely evening, walk up and down the terrace talking to Hugh till nearly midnight.

July 4. Long Barn. Hugh reads "Challenge," and is very complimentary about it, he prefers it to "Heritage." (I don't.)

July 5. H. staying up for dinner so I come here, and argue with Clemence Dane over the abstract and the concrete in literature and their rival merits. Afterwards L. and I tell Clemence Dane all about ourselves.

July 6. Long Barn. Stay till the evening, after an awful morning with Clemence Dane trying to make L. and me give each other up.

July [8?]. Sonning. Come down here & find L. very seedy, with her heart gone wrong.

July 9. Sonning. Not well, so I chuck going to the opera with L. I'll stay down here—not reluctantly. A perfectly happy day.

July 12. Sonning. H. to Paris, I come here, alone with L.

July [13, 14, or 15]. Long Barn. Sale at Ebury St. See L. first at Pat's; attend the sale, rather fun.

July 16. 34 Half Moon St. L. comes this afternoon. As she has not told D. where she is, he telephones to her after dinner, and he forces her to go up to London. She misses the last train, so I motor her in, without luggage or anything; I get a room here, while she goes to the Curzon Hotel.

July 17. Beacon Hotel, Hindhead. L. comes round to me before 8 this morning and says she has had a scene with D.T. [Denys Trefusis], and has left him, so after seeing Pat, lunching at our little Rubens hotel, we motor down here. O Christ, how I long for peace at Long Barn! but she is in such distress of mind & so seedy into the bargain that I must give way to her. It is lovely here, but I had been so looking forward to being at home. However . . . She writes D. a note asking him to see her for a final discussion on Monday.

July 18. Moorlands Hotel, Hindhead. We transfer to this hotel, as it is nicer. We go for a lovely walk across the moors. Very happy.

July 19. Long Barn. Go for another walk this morning, lovely day. No answer from D., so we motor up to London after tea, and L. gets him on the telephone; he is very rude to her, so she motors down here with me.

July 20. Long Barn. L. very seedy this morning, so I take her up to London.
 It seems that I am *never* to have any peace!
 B.M. comes to dinner on her way to London from Brighton

July 22. Sumurun, Deal. Race this morning in a heavy wind. Brittania wins. Anchor off Deal; horribly rough.

July 23. Sail round from Deal to Dover this morning in a very rough sea after a beastly night of rocking about in a swell. On the way to Dover our dinghy gets washed adrift by a specially heavy sea. One of the crew gets his head cut open by a block. Altogether an adventurous trip.

July 24. Long Barn. Alone here. Writing an autobiography, started today.

July 27. Long Barn. Go up to London and lunch with L. and see Pat for a short time. B.M. stops here to dinner, she is *specially* charming tonight.
 (Jean de Gaigneron, he paints and I write.)

August 5. Hill Street. Long Barn. A horrible day. Tell L. on the telephone that I am going to Albania [trip with Harold], which brings her here by the next train.

She arrives ill & goes straight to bed. H. comes back in the evening & she persuades him not to go. Everything too hellish.

August 6. Long Barn. Ben's birthday. Give him Meccano. L. leaves in the morning & goes back to Sonning. Perfectly miserable. . . . There seems to be nothing but misery of one sort and another for everyone.

August 7. Long Barn. We were to have started today at 2 for Albania!

[Between *August 8 and 12.*] Moorlands Hotel, Hindhead. Spend all day in bed at Long Barn, and motor across here to join L. in the evening—a lovely drive & perfect weather.

August 13. Hindhead. Lovely day. Go for a picnic with L. Happy.

August 16. Moorlands Hotel, Hindhead. Come across here by train, and retrieve the motor on the way. Have got 5 days with her.

August 17. Marden's Head, Uckfield. Motor as far as this, where the car breaks down. Don't mind much.

[Probably *August 18.*] Mermaid Inn, Rye. Leave Uckfield after lunch, and motor here, which we stop and look at. the moat is dry for the moment, which detracts from its beauty L. likes it, but doesn't like Rye—how instinctively right she always is about things!

August 28. Sherfield, Basingstoke. Spend the day pottering about. Harold comes down in the evening. I like Dottie but can't stick smug Gerry. [Dorothy Wellesley, née Ashton, with whom she would later travel to Teheran; Gerry Wellesley, her husband; Sherfield, their home.]

August 30. Brighton. Spend the day in London with L. who is a little better, and who leaves in the evening for Holland. Come down here & find Ben & Nigel very happy.

September 4. Sumurun. H. writing a novel, with his usual indefatigable energy.

September 10. At sea I sleep on deck, in the gig, a glorious night, quite calm, studded with stars—never liked anything better, except that the swell is rather a bore as the boom and sail and blocks make such a row banging about.

September 15. Brighton. Ben and Nigel well, & still here. Most successful week on *Sumurun.* Have simply loved it.

   B.M. is having financial rows . . . O god, this bloody money means so much to her.

September 17. Long Barn. It pours, gardening, perfect weather.

   B.M. "of an angelic sweetness."

September 24. Stratford. Out shooting all day, a very jolly day. In the evening 12 farmers come to dinner, and Dada makes a speech and so do I!

October 9. Sonning. Go for a walk with M. Harwood in the morning over the Downs. Come up and go straight across London to meet L. at Padding-ton, she having just arrived from Holland. Come down here together. So happy.

October 11. Sonning. L. a little better. *So* happy.

October 12. Sonning. Spend the day in bed.

October 13. Hill Street. Come up after lunch, after four really perfect days with-out one jarring moment. Dine with L. and Harold.

1921

April 16. Snow! "The snow!"

July 21. Sherfield. A lovely day; D's monkey is too attractive.

July 23. Sailing *Sumurun.* Have a roughish sail up from Ryde.

July 24. A lovely day; we sail about.

August 2. Long Barn. John Drinkwater and I read each other's poems aloud after dinner.

August 3. Sumurun broke her mizzen boom yesterday racing for the King's Cup; Harold loved it; there was a big wind.

August 5. Long Barn. D. [Dorothy Wellesley] comes to stay.

August 6. Ben's birthday. He is too sweet. . . . Ben comes down to dinner for the first time in his life, has champagne, and falls into a drunken slumber.

August 7. Long Barn. The house catches fire in the morning & we have great fun putting it out. Play lots of tennis.

August 11. Finish a story called "The Bell Buoy," for the New Statesman. Have got the proofs of my poems & have been working on these. Are they good? Are they futile? I don't know.

August 12. Long Barn. Begin writing a new book.

August 25. Long Barn. Alone; work hard.

December 18. Long Barn. H. began to work at his book on Tennyson; I read "Reddin" from the beginning, and was infinitely *depressed by it.* [Reddin was a topic she worked on as a book, as a play—both unfinished—and as a poem: Reddin, an old, wise architect-sculptor, "gentle, mild and sure," understanding the "unimportance of life," surrounded by disciples, building a cathedral on a cliff as a monument to his ideals.]

December 19. L. comes over from Paris tomorrow.

1922

[Mostly Vita used this diary as an engagement calendar for this year, listing tennis, lunches, and parties.]

August 6. Ben's birthday. He dines downstairs. Gets *le vin gai.* VERY sweet. Give him a pony.

August 7. Play tennis most of the day & discuss poetry with Eddy. Find him devitalising.

August 8. Got seven new dogs—(one born since above entry). Watch the whole process; much impressed by manifestation of instinct—platitudinous but cosmic.

August 10. Sail to Portland. Sulky and homesick (*not* seasick).

August 11. Sail to Dartmouth. Home tomorrow! and my puppies.

August 13. H. depressed because it is the end of his leave. Play tennis. Give the four children rides on the pony. Corrected proofs of Knole [*Knole and the Sackvilles*].

1924

January 24. Quarrel with Pat in full swing; letters exchanged, she threatening lawsuits, & I being rather pompous. [Pat Dansey, Violet Trefusis's lover, a mythomaniac and madly jealous over Vita, to whom she gave a car, threatened suicide over her other lovers, and persisted in such fabrications as offering Vita nonexistent shares in the *Morning Post* and declaring she was leaving everything to Vita at her death.]

January 3. Went home with April, and dined home alone with H; talked to him about Pat, & finally wrote her a conciliatory letter. So *bored* with this row, and have moments of wishing most people at the bottom of the sea.

January 4. 34 Hill Street. Lunched at Portland Place, and in the afternoon took Ben, Nigel, Valerian, and Michael Montague to the Drury Lane Melodrama, shipwreck, motor accidents, fire, & a horse race. All very thrilling. Came home to find B.M., Gerald Berners, & Desmond McCarthy dinner; told murder stories till 12:30. He asks me to review for the *Statesman & Empire Review,* whose literary side he has just taken on.

January 6. Knole. Walked over to the cottage and back in the morning. I lay down in the afternoon, and between sleeping and waking started writing a poem about woods.

January 8. Ben came to me in tears because he had been copying out the Golden Journey & Nigel had torn it up. He has a real passion for it, and copies it out, learns it by heart. I shan't force this taste, but let it take its own course. He loves that and the "Midsummer Night's Dream" so he has begun well; also the Bible.

I spent the morning in bed, going on in the poem about woods . . . Ben had a *crise de nerfs,* so I sent him to bed for the afternoon—not as a punishment, but to rest and recover!

January 10. 34 Hill St. Geoffrey rang me up . . . at 7 he came for me, we dined at the Berkeley, & came back here afterwards; a bewildering and not very real evening. Rainy London; taxis; champagne, confusion. [Geoffrey Scott, who continued to hope Vita would go off with him; later, his marriage broke up over his affair with Vita.]

January 31. 34 Hill St. An awful agitated day. Lunched with B.M. to meet Mrs. Spears, whom I liked particularly. B.M. came back to Hill St. with me & flew into a rage about the plate-warmer, she left the house in a fury. I descended to the basement & cried for two hours, on the kitchen table. Advent of Geoffrey; consolation from him and Lily. Advent of Ozzie; laughter restored to life.

Had seven to dinner . . . Felt like death, or rather, like flu.

February 1. Lunched with B.M. who was apparently unconscious of anything having happened: Talked to Sybil [Geoffrey Scott's wife] & tried to enlist her help in diminishing talk about me and G. [Geoffrey Scott]

February 2. Long Barn. Nice here, but draughty. Dined alone, & the puppies ate my little cold joint while I was answering the telephone.

February 3. 34 Hill St. A real spring day at the cottage; we sat out on the step in the sun, read Yeats, and were quite warm, surrounded by Canute, Wolf, Swend, & Enid [her dogs]. Tulips, hyacinths, & Spiraea coming up, aubrietia just beginning, lilacs in full bud.

February 7. Dined with Clive Bell. Ethel Sands there and Desmond McCarthy. Went to Hammersmith to hear "The Way of the World"; a queer wedge of people in the dress circle: Berners next to me, Goosens, Geog of Russia, Lytton Strachey, the Jowetts, and a lot of others. Then to Mrs. Hutchinson's at Chiswick, where poor Desmond fell downstairs and broke his kneecap. This cast a certain gloom over the party. Came home, giving Duff Cooper a lift . . . to my astonishment he made love to me—I don't suppose I see him more than once in two years. Altogether a queer evening.

February 13. Knole. Spent the day alone again, but rather better, and not sorry to be shut away from a biting east wind; with Swend and Canute and books. Dover's "The Patrician," which seemed to me the worst of all—and incidents dragged in by the scruff of the neck just to give the author an opportunity to show off his fine writing or to bring in a moral point—and of course the morality *maddened* me— it all seemed so queerly out of date. Read "Les caves du Vatican" [André Gide's novel] which bored me surprisingly; and Aristophanes, which makes me laugh always. For the rest, lay very happy watching a fitful sun play along the walls of the green court. Got up for dinner and beat Dada at chess. Harold had to stay up.

February 22. Went down to Richmond by underground to dine with the Woolfs; in the kitchen as usual; Raymond Mortimer there. Virginia delicious as ever; how right she is when she says love makes everyone a bore, but that the excitement of life lies in the *béguins* [initial infatuations] and the "little moves" nearer to people—but perhaps she feels this because she's an experimentalist in humanity and has no *grande passion* in her life . . .

March 16. Went to the cottage with H. and Nigel. . . . Niggs so nice and intelligent, with a pronounced taste for the practical and the topical. Anything to do with organization or government interests him.

April 2. Long Barn. In raptures at being home.

April 21. Easter Monday. A lovely, hot day, 70 in the shade. The hedges are rushing out, but the trees are still black—a queer effect of winter trees on a really summer's day. Down to get the bee orchids, and afterwards to Nigel's woods. A very happy day—marred only by a post-prandial argument about one's duty to one's relations—only Harold maintaining that one has one to relations *as such.*

April 22. B.M. very sweet, & brought red daisies, as (I suspect) an olive branch. Pat arrived just before she left. Pat in a maddening mood, and I was thankful when Ronnie [Ronald Balfour] came back. Harold was kept up in London. Went for a walk with Ronnie across the fields, having quarreled with Pat. Dinner was strained, but R. played up magnificently. Pat collapsed after dinner and was so pathetic—poor little thing.

April 23. Spent quite a happy day with Pat, gardening—but it is cold again . . . H. came down.

April 26. B.M. saying I neglected her. Such balls.

1925

March 23. Dined with Mario Lanza.

April 9. Sherfield. Tennis talk. Read Tchekov.

November 7. Long Barn. A lovely warm golden day. Sat in the sun all the morning. Went to tea with Eddy—Leonard [Woolf] went back to London, Virginia remained.

  ! [in circle.]

V. told me about re-reading the first 30 pages of "To the Lighthouse" & how she had had to rewrite them.

November 10. Spent the evening with Virginia, dinner with the Drinkwaters. Very dull.

November 24. Monday Went up to see Virginia. . . . After to a party at Vanessa Bell's.

November 25. Went to Virginia in the evening. Went afterward to Clive's rooms, found Virginia there.

November 27. Virginia came to Mount St. to see me.

November 29. Spent the afternoon with Virginia.

December 4. Long Barn. Virginia came.

December 5. Alone all day with Virginia.

December 6. Went up with V. in the evening.

December 17. Alone.

December 20. [X at top of page] Spent the afternoon with Virginia; dinner with her at Mount St.

1928

October 1. The 15th anniversary of our wedding day!

October 2. Went up [to London] after breakfast and broadcasted (Modern Poetry) at 6 [lecture included in this volume]. Went to see Margaret and Frederick [Margaret and Frederick Voigt, later divorced]. Dined with Clive who gave me the mss of his book on "Proust." Raymond [Mortimer] there, and Frances Marshall [later Frances Partridge]. Staying with Raymond and Paul Hyslop.

October 4. Long Barn. A perfectly lovely day, & quite warm. Walked across the fields with the dogs. Virginia & Leonard came to lunch, bringing Pinker and her puppies. April came to dinner & after dinner I lectured on the Bakhtiari Road to the 7 Oaks Literary Society. [Her book *Twelve Days* was published in 1928.]

October 5. Alone.

October 30. London. Lunched with Hugh Walpole. Virginia there. Conversation all about the "Well of Loneliness" [Radclyffe Hall's lesbian novel, banned in 1928]. Went to see Pat. Broadcasted at 6 and then went to see Virginia. Dinner with Clive: Vanessa, Duncan, Virginia, Leonard, Beatrice Meyer, Frankie [Birrell, owner of bookstore].

December 2. Long Barn. Collected Nigel & John St. Aubyn in the morning & we went to Christ Church where Nigel was sick. Lunched with John Sparrow.

December 31. Delighted to see the last of 1928.

1929

March [?]. A peaceful day. Took Ben to skate on the lake. Cold but fine. Nothing out in the garden at all, not even a bit of aubrieta & scarcely any bulbs showing.

March 20. Hilda came for the night. [Hilda Matheson, Director of Talks at the BBC, "Stoker" to Vita. They would travel together in the French Savoy in July 1929.] I tidy up the house.

March 21. H. painted the front gate & cut down some things in the wood & made a bonfire. Alone all day. I fear that poor Niggs has got whooping cough.

March 22. Long Barn. Alone. Worried about Harold's cold so rang him up but he was out. Started to write my Marvell essay [*Andrew Marvell,* in Faber's "Poets on Poets" series, published 1929].

March 23. April came to stay, after lunch. Went down in the wood, and my bonfire set fire to the grass all over the Hawthornden. [Vita's "The Land" won the Hawthornden prize in 1927; "The Garden" would win the Heinemann prize in 1946.] Hadji rang me up in the morning.

April 24. April here. Sat in the sun & read poetry.
Motored Ben, Boski [the children's governess], and Nigel to Newhaven, from where they go to Dieppe. Stopped at Rodmell on the way back & lunched with Virginia and Leonard; saw their new motor & their new plot of land.

April 28. Virginia came down to dine and sleep. Heard the nightingales for the first time this year.

April 29. Virginia left before lunch. Told me about going to Greenwich in a rage. Hilda came to dine & sleep. Nightingales again, but a great wind sprang up & it turned cold at night, after one really warm & lovely day.

April 29. Virginia left before lunch.

May 8. Long Barn. Alone.

May 9. Saw Hilda for a minute at the BBC. Went to Virginia and we went to Hampstead to see Keats' house. She told me how she had discussed modern poetry last night with Blunden and how they had decided that poets today were too thin—not pouring out a flood of nonsense & poetry all in the same muddle. She also told me about Laura Riding throwing herself out of the window.

May 16. Lunched with Miss Compton-Burnett [Ivy Compton-Burnett, the novelist] & Miss Jourdain, Leigh there. Went out with Virginia. We went to see the old Roman Baths near the Strand. Broadcast at 7 [her regular broadcasts on gardening].

May 18. Long Barn. Hilda left. Went over the Penns to see the wild lilies of the valley and stayed to dine there. [Dorothy Wellesley had purchased Penns-in-the-Rocks, at Withyham, Sussex, in 1928; Yeats and Pound visited her there.]

May 27. April came over and brought me some little black pansies. Nigel goes to Eton for his scholarship exams.

July 17. Hotel des Glaciers, Pralognon, Savoie. Arrived at Moustiers at 9 A.M. Came up to Pralognon by autobus.

June 7. Alone. Finished Marvell [Her small book on Alexander Marvell].

July 18. Refuge Felix Fauré, Col de la Vanoise. Left Pralognon at 9:30. Dawdled up to the Alpine Club hut, lunching on the way. Very hot indeed. Lovely flowers: mauve & white violas in sheets.

Heavenly air, 8,000 feet up. One ought to do the walk in 3 to 4 hours, but we did not arrive till 4. More thunder in the evening & some rain. Wrote letters lying out on the grass.

July 19. Hotel Parisien, Val d'Isère. Left the hut at 8 and reached Val d'Isère at 7, a perfect day, hot & sunny. The first hour takes one across the col—grassy upland, with little lakes, and then a long stormy descent of half an hour to the valley of the Liesse, passing the chalets of Entre deux Eaux; Byronic gorge, some snow. Long but gradual climb up the valley, fewer flowers in Wilmington (because it is a north bank?), cross the river at the head of the valley, then a steep short climb, and then down to a lake, were we lunched at 12:45. Poor track to the Col de Fressa. Down across meadows (vanilla orchis) and very steep descent to Val d'Isère. Thunder threatening. Very fine view of La Grande Motte from Col de la Liesse, & of Mont Blanc from Col de Liesse.

July 20. La Curé, Val d'Isère. Last night. Slept in hotel annex, "as there were two priests staying with the curé" . . . Went for a very small walk. Reading the life of Lady Byron, which thrills me.

July 21. Val d'Isère. We took our luncheon up onto the hill & lunched on a ledge there under a little pine which smelt good. Hilda bathed in a waterfall. It became so thunderous that we had to come home after lunch.

July 22. [first three lines scratched out] A lazy day, we took our lunch out to some trees by the Isère. I read Lady Byron and finished a poem about storm in the mountains. Lots of crickets, & peasants gathering hay.

July 23. [first three lines scratched out] X. We walked up here in the morning and spent the afternoon lying on the hillside in the very hot sun. 9,300 feet. Excellent chalet.

July 24. Col d'Isère. Spent a lazy day, the morning in bed, the afternoon lying on the hillside until it became stormy. Then they lit the stove for us & I wrote my novel in the dining room.

July 26. Worked at my novel.

July 31. Nigel comes home. Bourg St. Maurice, a steep road *a lacets,* through Tignes. Took the train at Bourg, changed at Chambéry & again at Culoz, to Geneva at 4. Had an ice. Found a bookstore in the Rue de Genève with "The Heir" in it [her short story of 1922, published by Heinemann that year, later reprinted with *Seducers in Ecuador*]. Left at 6 & got to Basel at 10:15. Lovely view of the mountains from the train. Left Hilda at Geneva, to catch the Paris train at 9:30.

August 3. Hotel zur Post. Huge French tricolor was still floating over the Rhine. . . . We worked on the balcony all afternoon, Hadji at his father's book, I at my broadcasting for next Thursday.

August 5 [?]. Train to Ostende. I sat at the Cologne-Ostende station and wrote my novel.

August 11. Penns. Went for a nice walk with April over the high fields. Vanessa [Bell] and Roger Fry came to lunch.

PART II

MEMOIRS AND DREAMS

Vita's Dream Book is a remarkable document of her obsessions with Knole and with her mother in particular. I have transcribed each dream exactly as it is found therein, sparing none. The vivid quality of her imagination leaps out at the reader, whatever the source of the dream material.

The contrast between Vita's early memories of her grandmother's house and her observations about her retention of the work of these early years, with its description of the ledgers in which she kept her manuscripts and her notebook of dreams over a period of time, is startling. In each she pays attention to the smallest elements as well as to the large, so that the reader has the distinct feeling of her fidelity to both sides of the record. In both the conscious remembering and the unconscious dream state, places and figures are given in their specific and haunting detail: each contour is clear, each color and shape is definite.

BEGINNINGS

This essay by Vita, published only in a collection of essays entitled Beginnings, edited by a friend of hers, is of interest as it describes quite exactly the state in which Vita's manuscripts have been left and her own view of her beginnings as a writer. It is reprinted here in its entirety.

This essay owes its existence to two facts. First, to the suggestion of my friend L. A. G. Strong, and second, to my instinct. By my own hoarding instinct I mean my reluctance to throw certain things away. In most people this instinct proceeds from the vague idea that the object in question "may come in useful some day" (which it never does); in my case it proceeds from a disinclination to destroy the written page. Thus it comes about that I have quite unnecessarily and rather sentimentally preserved an alarming number of foolscap ledgers representing the literary activities of my early years.

They stand in a row at the bottom of my bookshelves, getting dusty and more dusty as time goes on. I never look into them. A mere glance at their backs is enough to make me blush with shame. Whenever I catch sight of them, I know that I ought to take them out into the garden and make a bonfire. But, as Mr. Max Beerbohm has pointed out, it is extremely difficult to burn a book. And here are many books. They are all in fat ledgers, stiffly bound in cardboard—the sort of ledgers which one sees piled in such alluring stacks in stationers' shops— solid ledgers such as would defeat even the holocaust of a modern Savonarola. I could not face the practical difficulty of setting them on fire. Besides, there is that hoarding instinct which makes me shrink from the final destruction of all that early energy. So they remain in their harmless, unexamined row at the bottom of my shelves. I was content to preserve them and never to look into them, until Mr. Strong's letter arrived, forcing me to the embarrassing task of exploring my literary past.

Then I blushed indeed. I blushed, but at the same time I couldn't help being slightly impressed by my own industry and neatness. I had quite forgotten the neat, industrious, and priggish child I once had been. All those conscientious historical notes; all those insertions in red ink, done with a mapping pen. . . . Looking into my first big ledger, I realized that I had worked out my first plays and my first poems much as I drew maps of the river system of France for the classes I attended in London. The mapping pen and the red ink had come into use for both my official lessons and my private poetry. The only difference was that my lessons were merely lessons, and that my plays, my poetry, and my novels really mattered to me; they constituted the whole of my secret life. Still, the neatness, the priggishness, and the red ink which permeated my lessons were present also in the writings of my private life.

I must have been an insufferable child: an impression which has subsequently been richly confirmed by my then contemporaries.

My parents treated me with creditable intelligence. In fact, my only grievance against them is that they taught me neither Latin nor Greek, and never thought of sending me either to school or to a university. Apart from this sad omission, they behaved with exemplary good sense towards the odd duckling they had hatched out. They neither injudiciously encouraged nor unkindly snubbed. Thus, I remember that my earliest ambition was to appear at a dinner party of thirty people in the banqueting hall at home, dressed in a sheet representing a ghost, in order to recite an epic poem composed by myself on the various exploits of my ancestors. This proposal, which must have proved very embarrassing to my parents, was wisely but amiably suppressed. A ghost aged twelve, complete with epic poem, was scarcely a guest to be welcomed at a dinner party of thirty grownups.

My second venture met with a more sympathetic response. By that time I was fourteen (for these statistics I am indebted to one of the ledgers I found myself so reluctant to destroy). Having, at that age, fallen strongly under the influence of *Cyrano de Bergerac* and also of *The Three Musketeers,* I had composed a tragedy which aspired to combine both the poetical romanticism of Rostand and the historical romanticism of Dumas. The result—strange bastard as it was—took the form of a five-act play on the "Man in the Iron Mask," in French Alexandrines. Of French Alexandrines I had but little experience, and still less technical knowledge. I knew only that an Alexandrine consisted of twelve syllables to the line, but knew nothing of the necessary caesura, and even less of the mute e. The twelve syllables, however, which I did know about, became an obsession. Every sentence which I uttered in ordinary speech, whether in English or in French, must be shaped into twelve syllables or their multiple. At first I counted on my fingers under the table, or behind my back; or, when I couldn't conceal my fingers, I wriggled my toes inside their shoes. It was very difficult to wriggle one's toes separately, so I thought of them one after the other instead. But soon my ear grew so well accustomed to the scansion that there was no longer any need for my fingers or toes to come into play. This trick was, I suppose, analogous to the superstitious trick some children have of stepping on the cracks in pavement stones. "If you miss a crack you will meet a bear," or "your sums will not come right." Eleven syllables, or twenty-three, or forty-seven, were to me a portent of disaster. I still catch myself playing this game sometimes.

My five-act tragedy, I fear, was a ludicrous though ambitious attempt. My parents nevertheless, not having been allowed to read it, consented to let me act part of it, supported by a friend to whom was allotted the secondary role. I myself played the part of the Man in the Iron Mask, dressed in cheap black sateen and a Vandyke collar of imitation lace. The audience consisted of my parents and the French servants. My parents listened patiently; the French cook, to my extreme gratification, burst into tears. I felt that I had at last scored a triumph.

My third venture was equally ambitious, but, luckily for my family, was conducted in greater privacy. This was a play in blank verse on the life and death of Thomas Chatterton. I had the play printed by the local stationer at my own expense; it cost me £5 for a hundred copies—£5 which I saved out of my tips and pocket money for the year.

The sentiments expressed in this play were excessively noble. So noble were they, that I felt impelled to keep them to myself, and therefore made no attempt to inflict them upon my family as an audience, but performed them secretly, and for my single benefit, in an attic at the top of the house. The attic was a strangely suitable setting: I realize now that with its bare boards and latticed window it must closely have resembled the attic in which poor Chatterton spent his last tragic days. Of course I did not realize this at the time. I realized only that as there was no cook to weep, I must weep myself, and consequently was moved to tears every time by my own performance. Each time I burnt Chatterton's manuscripts in the candle I felt I was burning my own; each time I died most uncomfortably on the oak settle, it was not only Chatterton but I myself who died. It was a case of "mighty poets in their misery dead." I especially fancied myself in the costume I had devised for this role: black breeches, white stockings, buckled shoes, and a white shirt. Luckily, nobody ever caught me at the game, otherwise I should certainly have been sent straight to bed for having run the risk of setting the whole house on fire.

What next? I remember a whole succession of historical novels, running into at least three hundred pages of foolscap each, all very neat, with dates in the margin, and sometimes the marginal comment V.E.—my private sign, meaning Very Easy; in other words, " It has gone well today." These historical novels covered quite a wide range. There was one about Alcibiades; one about the French Revolution; one about Louis XIII (this one, very Dumas-esque, was written in French, for between the ages of two and eighteen I was what, thank God, I no longer am, bilingual); one about Florence in the fifteenth century, inspired by George Eliot's *Romola;* and at least three others about my own home and my own ancestors. All these I wrote at great speed and with extreme gusto. I kept them very private; and no sooner had I finished one than I started another; sometimes, as their dates inform me, on the very same day.

A little later came a history of the Italian city-states from 1300 to 1500, full of murderous and probably inaccurate detail. I enjoyed this enormously, partly owing to the amount of research it involved, for I had not yet shed the priggishness and pedantry of my schooldays. Visconti and Sforza, Scaligeri and Baglione, Sismondi and John Addington Symonds, became my constant companions for two happy years.

Then, tiring of history, whether romantic or factual, I tried my hand at writing a modern novel. I was then twenty-five, and old enough to know better, but prose was still only a contemptible stopgap for the days on which I couldn't write poetry, and of the construction of a novel I knew no more than I had known of the construction of a French Alexandrine. I had, for instance, no idea of the number of words necessary in fiction from a publisher's point of view; ten thousand words meant no more to me than a hundred thousand. Thus it came about that my first novel, when finished, was only about forty thousand words long. Still, unconscious of the deficiency, it seemed to me very much like a novel; very much like the novels which other people wrote and which actually got printed. I was rather pleased with it; so well pleased, that in the first flush of excitement I submitted it to the only publisher I knew—the only "literary" person, in fact, with whom I then had any acquaintance at all. To my delight he consented to read it, only to return it after a week's interval with a kindly worded letter to say that although it showed "considerable promise," it was much too short for publication. So I put it away, disheartened, for a year.

During that year I went to live in Ebury Street. I lived at No. 182, but at No. 121 lived a more distinguished and more experienced neighbour, who had been practising the art of fiction, both in conversation and on paper, for many years, and who fell into the habit of arriving at my house unannounced, after dinner, whenever he had nothing better to do. Conversations in Ebury Street ensued.

They were not so much conversations as monologues; George Moore enjoyed talking about himself; but, luckily for me, his monologues in my house usually took the form of literary rather than amorous experiences. He would relate at great length the story of the book he next intended to write: thus I remember listening patiently to the whole proposed scheme of *Héloise and Abélard,* and *A Story-Teller's Holiday;* or he would rush into the sitting room in a state of great excitement, saying "Give me your copy of *The Brook Kerith* at once; I sought for a phrase of Christ for years, and now at last I have found it—let me write it into your copy, before I forget it." (Incidentally, although he called it a *trouvaille,* it wasn't a particularly illuminating *trouvaille* at all. It was a rather trite, commonplace little phrase.)

Humbly, I was content to listen to George Moore's monologues by the hour, since anybody who had not only written but had actually published many books, was then almost a god to me, or, at any rate, a superior and successful being. Then there came one magical moment when he switched off from himself and condescended to remember my own existence. "Have you," he said, "ever attempted to write yourself? A great mistake if you have; but I expect you have been guilty of that usual indiscretion of the young." He fixed me with a threatening and critical eye. "Come, now," he said, "confess."

I confessed.

Under persuasion, I told him the whole story of my unfortunate novel. He was charming about it. Not only did he listen with flattering attention, but he even suggested a means by which I might extend it to the necessary length. The means he suggested was due to what he described as "a real-life story" he had read in some American newspaper. Practically every reviewer who subsequently condescended to notice my book observed that nothing of the sort could ever have happened in real life. Thus I am wholly indebted to George Moore for the eventual publication of my first novel.

THIRTY CLOCKS STRIKE THE HOUR

The title story of Thirty Clocks Strike the Hour published by Doubleday, Doran & Company (Garden City, New York) in 1932, is really an autobiographical recollection and expresses "a wish to give shape to a fading impression" before it is too late to retrieve it. Like Vita's diary and letters, these pages exude an atmosphere at once personal and impersonal. They are impregnated with an almost claustrophobic nostalgia and sense of mystery.

Vita's memories of her great-grandmother are painfully sharp. The small figure, alone, all in black, leaning on her stick, walking down the corridor, aware of her possessions and her great dignity, makes a vivid contrast with her great-granddaughter irreverently taking out the wheelchair and propelling herself down the parquet floors, standing with frizzed hair while the visitors ooh-and-ah over the Louis Quinze and Louis Seize furnishings, hiding behind the curtain at the end of the long hall. Vita's own reactions: Her pity at the old lady's frailty and realization of her despotic, unfeeling, materialistic character are clearly drawn against the background of the bustle of the Boulevard des Italiens.

The height of the piece is the intensely portrayed scene of the strange ecstasy of her great-grandmother when the clocks chime at once. The gallant figure of the grandmother shrinks into someone much more fragile, tired, and bent, who is at the same time amused and enraptured by the sound, amidst the flame of the candles flickering like her life.

I remember being taken to visit my great-grandmother.

This is no story. It is a recollection—a reconstruction. A wish to give shape to a fading impression at the back of my mind before that impression should become irrecoverable. It is not only a personal impression, it is an impression in a wider sense, of an age that I saw in the act of passing.

She lived in Paris, in an unfashionable quarter. Hers was a vast corner house on the Boulevard des Italiens; I remember I used to count the row of windows, and there were twenty each way, twenty looking on the boulevard, and twenty on the narrow side street. There was a vast porte-cochère in the side street; one rang the bell, the concierge pulled a string, the door clicked on its latch, and one pushed one's way through, into the central courtyard, where a great business of washing carriages always seemed to be going on; a business of mops and immense quantities of water and grooms clacking round in wooden clogs; patches of sunlight, birdcages hanging in the windows, and girls arriving with parcels. All round the courtyard dwelt an indeterminate population, for portions of the upper floors were let out in flats, but these tenants were kept severely in their place, nor did I ever hear any save one, Mme Jacquemin, referred to by name. Consequently they existed for me in a cloud of alluring and tantalizing mystery, so that I spent hours inventing the inner drama of their families, and wondering what they did when they wanted to play the piano, and how they managed their exits and their entrances. I was sure that none of them would dare risk an encounter with my great-grandmother, their landlady, who occupied the whole of the first floor.

The staircase was very dark and grand. One arrived on the first-floor landing, already awed into a suitable frame of mind. Of course the bell was not electric; one pulled a cord, which produced a jangle within. The door was opened, with a miraculous promptitude, before the jangle had ceased, by either Jacques or Baptiste in white cotton gloves, white-whiskered and respectfully benevolent; at least, Baptiste was quite definitely benevolent, and often dandled me in secret on his knee, giving me meanwhile brandy cherries rolled in pink sugar, and murmuring confidences about his daughter, who had been guilty of some misdemeanour forever and perhaps fortunately enigmatic to me; but the benevolence of Jacques I had to take on trust, on the general principle that all the retainers in that house were benevolent. For Jacques was outwardly *grincheux*. In appearance he was like an old whiskered chimpanzee, and his hands, which I once saw denuded of their cotton gloves, were hairy. I never heard him make but one statement about his private life, but that statement he made with great frequency: "*Moi, j'ai mes cent sous par jour, et je me fiche du Pape.*" Whence Jacques got his *cent sous*, and what the Pope had to do with it, I never discovered. But I linger too long in the antechamber, where Jacques or Baptiste closed the door behind one and relieved one of one's parcels or one's umbrella.

Great-grandmother's apartment was on what in an Italian palace would be called the *piano nobile*. This meant that, standing in the last doorway, one could see right down the vista of rooms; that is to say, down the rooms represented by the twenty windows on the side street, until the flat turned the corner and took on a new lease of life represented by the twenty windows on the boulevard.

It was an impressive vista. Parquet floors, ivory woodwork, tarnished gilding—it seemed they must be reflected in a halfway mirror, so endlessly did they continue. I was irreverent, of course. Whenever I thought great-grandmother safe in her bedroom, I used to slide along the parquet, or, more irreverent still, get her wheeled chair out of the dining room and trundle myself down the vista. I shiver now to think of the bruised paint and dented ormolu that must have marked my progress—for, unlike great-grandmother's stately advance in the wheeled chair, my one idea was to go as fast as I could. But what did I know then of the privilege that was mine in being admitted to that beautiful house? Small and clean, with painfully frizzed hair, I would stand by, very bored, while visitors marvelled at the furniture under the direction of great-grandmother's stick. Louis Quatorze, Louis Quinze, Louis Seize, Directoire, Empire—all these were names, half meaningless, which I absorbed till they became as familiar as bread, milk, water, butter. Empire came last on the list, for the life of the house seemed to have stopped there. As the door of the antechamber closed behind you, the gulf of a century opened, and you stood on the further side.

True, there was the noise of Paris without motors, and motor horns, and clanging bells; when you opened the window, the roar of the boulevard came in like a great sea; but within the flat, when the windows were shut, there were silence and silken walls, and a faint musty smell, and the shining golden floors, and the dimness of mirrors, and the curve of furniture, and the arabesques of the dull gilding on the ivory boiserie. There was an old stately peace never broken by the ring of a telephone; shadows never startled by the leap of electric light. It seemed that the flat itself, rather than its occupant, had refused to accept the modifications of a new century. It had enshrined itself in the gravity and beauty of a courtly age, until the day when its very masonry should go down in ruin before the mattocks of the house-breakers.

Given up to its dream, in a sumptuous melancholy ennobled by the inexorable menace of its eventual end, few were aware of the existence of this fragment intact in the heart of Paris. A little museum, said the connoisseurs; but they were wrong. It was no museum, for it had preserved its life; its appointments had never been deposed from their proper use to the humiliation of a display for the curious; chairs that should, said the connoisseurs, have stood ranged behind the safety of red ropes, carried the weight of the living as well as the ghosts of the dead; the sconces and the chandeliers still came to life each evening under the flame of innumerable candles. It was then that I liked the flat best. It was then that its gilding and its shadows leapt and flickered most suggestively as the little pointed flames swayed in the draught, and that the golden floors lay like pools reflecting the daggers of the lights. It was then that I used to creep on stockinged feet to the end of the long vista, a scared adventurer in the hushed palace of Sleeping Beauty, and it was on such an evening that I saw my great-grandmother, as I most vividly remember her, coming towards me, from the length of that immeasurable distance, tiny, bent, and alone.

She was a rude, despotic old materialist, without an ounce of romance or fantasy in her body, but to me that night she was every malevolent fairy incarnate, more especially that disgruntled one who had so disastrously attended Sleeping Beauty's christening. I had often been frightened of her tongue; that night I was frightened of her magic. I stood transfixed, incapable of the retreat for which I still had ample time. I remember being wildly thankful that I had on, at least, a clean pinafore. Very slowly she advanced, propped upon her stick, all in black beneath the candles, pausing now and then to look about her, as though she welcomed this escape from the aged servants who usually attended her, or from the guests, deferential but inquisitive, who came, as she shrewdly knew, to boast afterwards of their admission into this almost legendary fastness. I realized that she had not yet caught sight of me, white blot though I must have been at the end of that shadowy aisle of rooms.

Very leisurely she was, savouring the wealth of her possessions, stealing out of her room when no one knew that she was abroad; as clandestine, really, as I myself—and suddenly I knew that on no account must she learn the presence of an eavesdropper. It was no longer fear that prompted me to slip behind the curtain looped across the last door; it was a desperate pity; pity of her age, I suppose, pity of her frailty, pity of her as the spirit of that house, stubborn in the preservation of what was already a thing of the past, whose life would go out with hers; it was her will alone that kept the house together, as it was her will alone that kept the breath fluttering in her body.

What thoughts were hers as she lingered in her progress I cannot pretend to tell; I only know that to me she was a phantom, an evocation, a symbol, although, naturally, being but a child, I gave her no such name. To me, at the moment, she was simply a being so old and so fragile that I half expected her to crumble into dust at my feet.

She crossed the dining room and passed me, flattened against the wall and trying to cover the white of my pinafore with a fold of the curtain; so close she passed to me, that I observed the quiver of her fine hands on the knob of her stick and the transparency of the features beneath the shrouding mantilla of black lace. I wondered what her errand might be, as she stood, so bent and shrunken, beneath the immense height of the ballroom. But it was evident that errand she had none. She stood there quietly surveying, almost as though she took a protracted and contemplative farewell, all unaware of the eyes of youth that spied upon her. Her glance roamed round, with satisfaction, I thought, but whether with satisfaction at the beauty of the room, or at having kept off for so long the tides that threatened to invade it, I could not tell.

Then, as she stood there, the clocks in the room began to strike the hour. There were thirty clocks in the room—I had often counted them—big clocks, little clocks, wall clocks, table clocks, grandfather clocks, and even a clock with a musical box in its intestines; and it was a point of honour with Baptiste that they should all strike at the same moment. So now they began; first the deep note of the buhl clock in the corner, then the clear ring of a little Cupid hitting a hammer on a bell, then a rumble and a note like a mastiff baying, then a gay trill, then the first bars of a chime, then innumerable others all joining in, till the room was filled with the music of the passing hour, and my great-grand-mother standing in the middle, listening, listening. . . . I could see her face, for her head was lifted, and her expression was a thing I shall never forget, so sud-denly lighted up was it; so pleased; so gallant; so, even, amused. She had, I think, her private joke and understanding with the clocks. The little flames of the candles quivered in the vibration of the air, but as the last notes died away they steadied again, like a life which has wavered for an instant, only to resume with a strengthened purpose. And as the silence fluttered down once more, my great-grandmother drooped from her strange, humorous ecstasy, and it was as a little figure bent and tired that I saw her retrace her steps down the long vista of the lighted rooms.

VITA'S DREAM BOOK

Of Vita Sackville-West's unpublished material, it is probably her Dream Book that is the most startling and the most humanly interesting. It is here that her distress over losing Knole comes through most clearly, as does the kind of resolution she finally achieves, when she is able to visit it with no trace of bitterness.

Her tender feelings for her husband are balanced by the alarming picture of her mother in the most violent dream transcribed here, in which her dog Rollo plays his own awful part. It has seemed to me unprofitable to choose among the dreams, and so I have simply transcribed them all for the readers to make their own interpretations.

"Vita's Book of a Thousand Pities" was originally attached to the dream notebook. It is a remarkable mental game concentrated around what is a "pity" and seems worth transcribing for its range of creative lamentation and its experimental form.

An undated dream

This was a dream I shall never forget: it was a voyage over landscapes of unearthly beauty; more beautiful than any hills of Italian painting—rose-red hills, grey cliffs, up-and-down roads, perilous landscapes, yet no terror in them, no fear of falling over edges, no fear of hairpin bends but just sheer delight in the beauty—all more beautiful than anything seen or painted. I woke so entranced that it took me more than the day to recover from my dream.

My dreams are so often about landscapes of this style—so seldom about people—especially people I know—always landscapes, houses, or things—

All the things I shall put in this notebook will be utterly true with no exaggeration or embellishment—because it would be no fun to keep a record otherwise.

September 21, 1941

I was in a flat in some foreign city; it might be Rome. It was a "grand" flat—the piano nobile sort—dark, overloaded, overornamented. There were two women—elderly, rather Jewish—hung with bangles, lockets, black lace. They were benevolent, not sinister. They surrounded me with kindness and *prévoyance* [foresight].

I found a lot of things which belonged to me in the flat—jewels, watches, bracelets, all very heavy work—I packed them into an attaché case. The thing which pleased me most was a box or casket of crystal and bands of white enamel (more like Limoges enamel than the Fabergé sort) with views of scenery on the enamel. The box had rounded corners. It was very beautiful as an object and gave me great pleasure to find. It was not like anything I had ever seen before.

I went away with the two women in their car. It was an ordinary car, but a grand one—a limousine. We went towards another city and on the road we picked up two other women who sat on the strap-on tins to give them a lift. I cannot see what they looked like—but they amazed me because they kept on switching on the central heating (the car had central heating, a little radiator inside it) and I kept switching it off because I saw my two hostesses wincing. The car went very fast roundabout corners and I was frightened. The swing of the car kept throwing me against one or the other of my hostesses and they were kind and consoling.

All the time I was aware that I was asleep and kept hoping that I would not wake up.

This was a thick, deep, happy dream; I felt lapped round with happiness; the flat was extraordinarily real and the objects I found were solidly real. I could see the details of each one.

Another dream

I dreamt that the whole population of the earth was floating away. They hovered just above the surface of the earth, with their feet dangling a few inches above. They were at different levels.

I wondered why this should be so, and was told (I don't know by whom) that the "better" ones floated higher and that the more earth-bound ones stayed nearer to the earth.

Every now and then a pair of feet would drop lower and I was told that it was because the person had had a mean thought or done a mean action—and was pulled back to earth for a bit. They never quite touched ground.

Eventually they all floated away—and the earth was left to itself, without any people on it at all. Then it seemed extraordinarily beautiful and unpolluted. It seemed to have returned to what it was meant to be.

I saw it in great vividness and particularity.

I cannot account for this dream in any way—it did not relate to anything I had read, seen, or heard about—or thought about—that I am aware of, except that I do always think about this sort of thing.

My "discovery" dream

This is a dream I have had for as long as I can remember.

It is very vivid (*actualité*) and upsets me a lot.

It is about finding two hidden rooms.

It is always very precise.

It starts behind the panelling on the left of the fireplace in the Great Hall—on the left as I stand facing the fireplace. It takes me up a staircase and lands me in a room no one else knows about. It is a bare room (I mean unfurnished). Panelled.

The odd thing about this dream is that the first room might easily be my bedroom—and that the second room might easily be my sitting room (because they communicate by steps) but I used to have this dream long before I ever had my bedroom or my sitting room (at Knole, I mean).

The whole point of the dream is that they are *secret* rooms, unknown to anyone, and that *I* find them—which is why I call it my "discovery" dream.

Every time I dream it, the process is exactly the same: I go through the panelling in the Great Hall and come up into those two rooms which no one else knows about—and I see them in every detail.

The dominant feature of this dream is that I am utterly happy when I arrive there—and am happy for all the next day after it.

It gets upset sometimes by another dream which is of Knole catching fire. I never dream about any other house catching fire.

This is a recurrent dream also—which I have always had, but this is of the nightmare sort—not the happier sort. I have never dreamt about Sissinghurst catching fire; only Knole.

I cannot explain either of these dreams.

Another recurrent dream which I have always had

I dream that I am a little boy at a private school. It is always the moment when we are sent out to play football, and I go down with the clatter of boots along the cemented passage. The boots make a great noise which I hate and shrink from. We come to the school notice-board where I see my name "Sackville-West" written up.

I never get beyond that. I mean I have never got out into the football field as yet—but I always have the impression that I am in disgrace for something—and being jeered at—and my name on the board is a disgrace.

In this dream I often dream that I have lost my cap and shall get into a row if I cannot find it in time.

I dreamt I was given a lioness as a present & a pet—but though her head was normal her body had no hide—and was just raw red meat, sloppy when I petted it—and she kept rubbing herself affectionately against my legs like a cat, which disgusted me although I was ashamed of being disgusted because I felt I ought to have been fond of her.

I dreamt I came up over a slope of hill and saw before me a landscape stretching away into the sea into points of headlands, *three* points—rounded points, not sharp. It was misty, rather like a Cotman [John Sell Cotman, 19th century

English landscape painter]. If I could draw I could make a plan, it was so definite. Nothing like anywhere I have ever seen.

It was opalescent, milky, there was no one there, no boats even.

I dreamt of a house, it lay at the bottom of a steep street, one went in by the lower door and came into a bricked hall—a sort of double room with a hooded fireplace in the centre of the inner half of the room. There was furniture round the walls, walnut settees with cushions of white brocade—very lovely and unusual. I was happy there until people began to arrive and hold a party—then I was angry—they spoilt it.

I can see the village street outside, it was very steep and sloping and "stepped" in wide shallow brick steps. It was not like any place I have seen in life. The houses had Gothic gables. There did not appear to be any population—only the people who came into the bricked hall. I cannot see those people in any distinctness—but they were noisy. They were none of them people I knew. I seldom dream about people I know.

I dreamt I could write poetry. I dreamt that I wrote and wrote till I nearly died. I was so unhappy when I woke up that I cried (not dream-tears, real tears). If only I could remember the poetry I wrote during this dream I daresay it would be real poetry, but it has all gone.

This dream was not accompanied by any landscape, it was just a dream in the void.

It was one of the happiest dreams while it lasted but quite the most miserable on waking.

February 4, 1944

This is not a dream but a waking experience. There was an air raid at 5 A.M., I was alone in the South Cottage, the siren woke me. I was not frightened at first, then I became so frightened I could not control my limbs from trembling. The droning procession of planes began overhead, they went on and on, I thought there must be hundreds passing over. I lay in bed waiting for the crash. I heard the London guns start. I thought it was silly to stay where I should be most frightened so I went downstairs. This was the first time I had ever given in to the wish to go downstairs. I sat on the Coronation chair because the walls seem most solid there and I could have the light on in without showing, and also there was no glass. I had Martha with me. I had forgotten to bring a book with me and dared not go upstairs again to fetch one. The planes were continually overhead and the doors rattled in the gunfire and I think some bombs. I had nothing to do except think and I tried to think how I could think myself into not being frightened. I thought, "That is one of our fighters, there are young men in it who are so excited that they are actually enjoying this, they hope they will meet a German plane and shoot it down," but none of this seemed to console me. I did not feel excited in the least or enjoying it, and could not persuade myself to feel so. So I thought I would try thinking about something else and I thought about God. I tried to *think* phrases like "I am in God's keeping," but that didn't work because I didn't know how God intended his keeping to work out. So then I tried to *see* God—staring at a knot in the wood of the door—and of course I saw nothing at all—but in about two minutes in the midst of my staring a complete peace came to me—my limbs ceased from trembling and an indifference to my fate took the place of terror. This is all quite true and so striking that I must record it.

March 17, 1944

I was in a cowshed. There were lots of cows, and wash swilling about on the concrete floor. I got shoved about by the huge forms of cows. I tried to single out my own cow, but evidently got hold of the wrong one by mistake. This wrong cow was intractable so I gave her a leather glove to chew to keep her in a good temper. Another cow then pushed me aside, and in a rage I hit her on the nose. She then looked at me with an expression of (unbearable) reproach; sat down on her haunches; and exposed her udder which was bleeding with dark blood. I then realised that she was showing me, as a sign of identification, a small misformed spleen—and that she made me understand that I had often had trouble in milking this spleen.

The dominant impression left by this dream was that the other cow was trying to take advantage over my own cow—and the bleeding udder of my own cow was unendurably pathetic.

God in the void

This is the most extraordinary dream I ever had, and through it all I was aware that I must make a poem of it. It was a dream in outer space. God was so angry with the entire universe that he decided to annihilate everything down to the smallest particle of the lightest atom. So then there was nothing left—no matter, no force, no energy, *nothing*—nothing but the mind of God left alone in something emptier than our conception of the emptiest space.

I was worried by not knowing whether God would start creating afresh.

I don't remember the date of this dream, but it was *after* the atom bomb—some time after—a year or so.

I dreamt another landscape—very northern—sort of rolling downs with grey-green turf stretching away indefinitely. There was a lot of water about—pools—and a sense of the sea somewhere—and a milestone which said *ONE DIRECTION: 500 kilometers.* All very melancholy, but somehow I was happy there.

January 16, 1950

I dreamt I was travelling along a road and I fell in with a crowd of gypsies They seemed to be all one family—there was the grandmother, and the middle-aged people, and lots of small children. The point about them all was their extreme cleanliness and their incredible beauty, and their happiness. They were not only beautiful, all of them, but their physical stature was on heroic proportions: the young men were superb, like Michelangelos, and they seemed to be about seven-feet tall. The grandmother had pure white hair, brushed back from her temples—the children were like Italian peasant children (Roman *ciociari,* perhaps) and they swarmed round me, tumbling about like puppies—and they were all clean and gay—no squalor. There seemed to be no young women—only the old woman & the young men & the children—and a medium-aged couple—of whom I saw only the man clearly, immensely tall and magnificently proportioned, in a sort of tight jerkin with a polo collar—the woman with him was dim. I couldn't see her—but knew *vaguely* that she was there. They asked me to come with them and I went—we went into a sort of wooden inn and they cooked in a big pot over the fire—and I was so happy.

October 20, 1950

I dreamt I was at the Moulin des Rats with Anna. We shared a bedroom, a very plain respectable little room, with two beds on opposite sides, and she kept me awake by making loud speeches addressed to the prime minister. This annoyed me so much that I got up & wandered down the passage and went through a door which admitted me to a completely different part of the house. Here the rooms were large and lofty, luxuriously furnished with sofas and large pieces of furniture and filled with great urns full of beautiful flowers; great rosy lilies in particular, set on pianos, blazing lights. These rooms were full of people, men and women: the men were the spiv type, the women were immensely tall, some of them, about seven-feet high and very slender and marvellously dressed; I noted one or two specially—one wore a flowery frock with a sort of bolero jacket and a tiny hat perched right on top of her head—and another one had a dress of black stiff taffeta, with the skirt slit open in front right up to the waist and nothing underneath it; this shocked me dreadfully and what shocked me most was that when she moved one saw her white thighs with brown suspenders down them, holding up her long stockings.

I met a housemaid and asked where was the lavatory and was shown into a huge room, all marble I think, also full of great pink lilies in white urns. I looked round and saw a woman watching me from a corner. This made me furious, and I said, "Who are you? What is your name? Are you a lady?" She laughed and said "I knew what you were going to do, so I watched, so I am not a lady." But she was nice, I felt, and I thought she was the only benevolent person in that awful house. She was quietly dressed in black, rather chic, and it worried me that her frock was smeared with powder.

We went out together into the sumptuous rooms, where we were immediately surrounded by all the other women and their spivs. There were more women than men. The women all had immensely long nails, like Chinese mandarins' nails; I don't think they were coloured, but they were sharp and claw-like. I felt surrounded and jostled by them all. Such a crowd. The only one who kept close to me and I felt protected me was the woman in black with that messy powder all over her frock.

Then Anna appeared; I can't see what she wore, but I know her arms were bare, and one of the spiv men came forward and threw his arms round her. I knew she ought not to be there, and I tried to get her away from him; I struggled with him and then I saw he had got an open clasp-knife in his hand and was trying to slash the upper part of her arm. I knew that if I couldn't get her away, a long thin cut of blood would appear down the whiteness of her arm.

I did get her away, and the next thing I knew was that we were all sitting at a sort of concert party in rows on chairs.

Then I woke up, but as I woke up, I heard Anna saying "Darling! Where are your pearls?"

General

I dream quite often about Knole. I dream about the deer galloping down the stable passage, their hooves rattling on the wood boards. This is a dream mixed with the vision of tangled legs of deer and arms of fighting men—rather like a Paolo Uccello. I like this dream. I like any dream that takes me back to Knole. I wish I dreamt oftener about Knole. I don't often, now. I think about Knole all the time, every day, but I don't often dream about it now. I wish I did. It used to be a sort of substitute for not going there. It makes me dreadfully unhappy sometimes, never going to Knole. Perhaps I will go there again one day, but it will never be the same—never, never the same—never, never, never.

Christmas 1950

Uncle Charlie sent me a master key to the garden gates. I had asked him for it. It was nice of him to let me have it, and he wrote a nice letter saying he hoped I would use it (which I never would) but he just spoilt the whole thing by adding "I have had the word Knole erased."

I suppose he thinks I might lose my key again.

It was not my fault that I lost it. The green leather box in which I kept it disappeared after the sale of Long Barn—but I have still got the key.

I shall get Copper to put back the word Knole on my key.

February 14, 1951

V. to H.

I dreamt I was condemned to be beheaded, & said to you "I am afraid you will mind." "Oh, don't worry about me," you replied, "I shan't mind, I've got George the Fifth." Not a very kind remark, I thought.

September 8, 1951

It is a long time since I have put down any dreams. I think it may be rather boring, meaning nothing except to oneself. I did however have a dream out of which I think I might make a poem—a real deep poem of experience.

Anyhow I don't want to put that down now—I wanted only to record a recurrent dream I have:

It is a recurrent dream about a party where I am very popular. Very much in demand. Everybody likes me—and clusters round me, and makes a fuss of me. I can very easily interpret this dream: it goes right back to when I came out and nobody liked me—and I suppose I minded.

This dream was very vivid. It took place at Sissinghurst. I went down towards the moat, and found a sort of arch like a bridge through which I went, and there I found a sort of community of young people making pots. Young potters in fact. They were all very gay and they were dressed in brightly coloured clothes, and they all seemed to accept me as one of themselves which pleased me. I forget what happened then—except that I woke up wishing I could find that arch and still feeling surprised that I had never noticed it or found my way through it—or up a sort of paved way towards the place where the young potters were working.

A dream I had in France (October 1955)

I dreamt I saw a mouse, obviously ill, so in order to give it a quick death I picked it up and threw it into a puddle of water. Somebody said "Don't you see the water is not deep enough, it won't drown, it will just go on swimming about." So I picked it out again, and as I did so it bit my finger. Somebody said "That mouse has got a disease and you will get it." I was terribly distressed by this, because I said "Harold wants me, Harold needs me, and if I get a disease I can't look after him."

September 23, 1957

It is a long time since I have written anything about my dreams.

Last night I dreamt about Long Barn. This was a very deep-sleep dream. I went to Long Barn with Bunny. I had let Long Barn and so didn't think I ought to wander about—but I did. There were lots of young people staying there, about 15 of them, all in slacks and polo-jumpers, all very gay and coloured and charming. I met my tenants; they were called Kramer. They had put a new staircase into Long Barn, and had furnished it lavishly with tapestries—they have made it all look very nice. I approved. I knew I could still find my way about, and said to Bunny, "Come this way—I know my way about my own house," but I got a bit confused owing to the new staircase, and the long room having turned into something like the hall at Penshurst or the old kitchen at Knole.

This was a happy dream. I wasn't cross or resentful about Long Barn.

1959

This was a truly horrible dream I had on the *Cambodge* [ship they took to the Far East in January 1959]. I dreamt B.M. was dead, and her body lay on one bed and her head on a pillow of another bed. I was looking at her body (covered by sheets, all decent) when I suddenly realised that Rollo had got her head off the other bed's pillow, onto the floor, and was gnawing the raw red stump of the neck.

Her face was still beautiful—just like her face in life. It horrified me to see Rollo chewing at the raw stump.

VITA'S BOOK OF A THOUSAND PITIES

My dear

This is my book of a thousand Pities.

You will not want to write in the book, but you must be gracious, and you will.
What do you think is a pity?
You may think several things are a pity.

If you cannot remember for the moment, what you think a pity, then play a game like this, and you are sure to find a suggestion.

Art
Architecture
Bores
Beauty
Bolsheviks
Committees
Clothes
Civilization
Dullness
Death
Dust
England
France
Food
Fascism
Gold
Girls
Health
Hell
India
Journalism
Kindness
Literature
Letters
Life
Meals
Mussolini
The Nation
Prisoners
Politics
Psychoanalysis
Places
Religion

Relations
Rest
Socialists
Society
Tea
Voices
Vandals
Work
Youth
and so on!

Part III

Letters (1920–1927)

Most of the family letters included here come from the years 1920–1927 and present a glimpse of life in Vita's family in that emotionally turbulent period. So Vita's letters exchanged with Harold, a few selected from a flood of affectionate and detailed communications—and a very few from their children to them—as delightful as they are amusing—provide an authentic sense of family warmth, completely unforced. Nothing gives a stronger feeling of place, person, and relations than this kind of correspondence.

The letters to Virginia Woolf are from the same period, during which Vita's affair with Virginia was in full flower.

Vita was, in my view, a wonderful letter writer, assuming entirely different tones for each correspondent. The correspondence featured here shows how, to Harold, her letters are continually affectionate, witty, and detailed, and how, to Virginia Woolf, they are both loving and literary. Vita could present herself as warm and cold, in other circumstances. I have included only letters of the first kind.

FAMILY LETTERS:
FROM THEIR SONS

These letters from Vita's and Harold's sons give an intimate look at the family and proof of the warmth of their household. While their sons' personalities were as different from one another as the letters indicate, their affection for their parents was equally clear. The original spellings have been retained.

Commenting to Harold on their contrasting letters to her, Vita compares their two sons: "Isn't it funny how much more opti [optimistic] Nigel is than Ben? So charac-teristic!" In her opinion, Nigel was the sunny, cheerful one, sharing Harold's character, and Ben, the discontented one, gloomier, more like herself. "If Nigel stays as he is, he will be happy and everybody will love him, but there is a distinct Dostoeffsky [sic] touch about Ben!" And, writing to Harold on December 26, 1926, about Nigel, she calls him "a born comic. . . . He is infinitely serviable, unselfish, and affectionate. Also sturdy, practical, resourceful, independent, humorous. I see no flaw in him, as a char-acter; everybody loves him. . . . My darling, we are very, very lucky in those two boys. They will, respectively, satisfy all that we could wish for: Ben our highbrowness, Niggs our human needs."[1]

September 12, 1922
Dear Mummy—

I eat a pin yesterday which I think is a very stuped think to do. I was suck-ing it and it suddenly it fell out of my hand and into my throat.

Melle [their French governess, also called Goggie or Gogy] was very upset is'ent she kind she does like it when we do things like that.

Mummy you ned not worry, for I had not pain at all.

Melle has look after me very well, and if it had not been for her I dont know what I would do.

Melle has stoped up all night for me.

She put Nigel in her bedroom and now we are waiting for me to sit down and Melle put's it through muslin.

Nigel send his love to you

Your loving Ben

September 15–16, 1922
Dear Mummy—

Nigel can read very well, I let him read the rainbow which is very difecoled for him. I knoly had to tell him a few words and afterwards I gave him a panny for reading so well ans when Miss Evans came I asked her if she would put him on to another more diffeculed book.

Now days I call Melle gogy for annie name, do you think that it is a good name. Thank you very much for the Post you sent me I show it to Miss Evans as you said and she said that it was the same kind of history as the History book that she is going to bring down, because we have finished the History book that we have been reading all the turm and last turm.

Joan went back yesterday she did not want to go because she liked school, she loves the handcerchefs that you gave her I notest that she had one of them in her pocket, when she came to do lessons yesterday.

Daddy gave me two french books last year that Melle found in the big cup-boaerd in Nigel's bed room and I have picted up a lot of French wored's out of it. Tell Swend that if shen evere he is naughty he will have to come back here in your bag, he wont like that I am shure.

Give my love to Daddy.

Melle is still wainting for my pin to come out, and I am quite all right.

Nigel send his love, and thank for his post card.

Your loveing Ben

November 8, 1922
My Dear Mummy,

It is so cold to day.

We are going in the litle train today because Gogy has to do some business for Grannyma, I love it. I had such a lovely letter from Miss Evans today.

I am looking forwould for Xmas.

Give my love to daddy

your loveing Nigel

November 16, 1922
Dear Daddy,

What a pity that you must go a way for your birthday. I keep my present till you come back.

Many happy returns Dear Daddy and lots of lov from Nigel

Brighton, December 24, 1922
Dear Editor [of the *Rainbow,* a comic that Nigel reads],

I am come-ing to see you on January, and the Bruin Boys too. I shald like to come on my Birth-day so look out for me.

Nigel Nicolson

December 1922
Dear Mummy,

I am sorry that I have not ritten be fore to you, because I am to busy. Last night we sow Mr. Pickwick and we all loved it, we have lots of treats we are lucky ant we.

Good-bye mummy

Give my love to Poor Daddy

Your loving Nigel

VITA AND HAROLD

These letters from Vita and Harold are from the period between the closing days of 1919 and the spring of 1923. Previously unpublished, they are in the collection of the Lilly Library at Indiana University in Bloomington, Indiana. They reflect both the emotional upheaval of Vita's affair with Violet Trefusis and the steadfastness of Harold's and Vita's love for one another.

Vita to Harold:

December 30, 1919. 23 rue Nitot, Paris
Mr. Hadji, who lives at 23 rue Nitot,

I live in room No. 37, Hotel Matignon, 6 av. Matignon, Paris.

I don't, anyhow, but it will do to write to you on. Darling, I've just come up from putting you to bed. . . . Anyhow you are out of the wood. But you will be lonely for a little *more*—but it will get better and you will be busy, and will for- get your horrid Mar [Vita's mother; later Harold used this name for Vita].

[. . .]

Darling, I must go to bed & not write any more nonsense. But you must have this tiny scribble to bring you all my love.

Mar

Harold to Vita:

January 2, 1920
My own darling,

I got up to look out of the window & wave at you—but you didn't look up, which was lucky, as my pyjamas came down at the crucial moment. . . . Oh my darling you have been such an angel to me while I have been ill. I shall never forget it—my sweet loving Mar.

Vita to Harold:

January 4, 1920
Darling,

I miss you so in the evenings—& B.M. is rather a bore with her boasting. I had to ask her last night not to talk about you—as she goes on & on, till I could scream. She has got no decency, about those sorts of things, & then every remark she manages to drag out of one she misinterprets.

Vita to Harold:

January 5, 1920
Darling, you *must* write the life of Verlaine. You would do it so excellently well, I can't image anybody who would do it better. You would produce a book which was at the same time picturesque, critical, and humourous. Why don't you start on it when you come home this time? As for me, I can't write a word and don't feel as though I never should again, whether prose or poetry.

J'ai perdu ma force et ma vie . . . [I have lost my strength and my life . . .]

Please, please don't stay in Paris longer than the 13th. I cannot bear to think of you hobbling. *Et mon coeur déchiré est, hélas, tout plein de tendresse pour toi. Reviens B.M.* [And my despairing heart is, alas, full of tenderness for you. I return to B.M.]

Vita to Harold:

January 12, 1920. Knole
[. . .] Darling, I had a dreadful interview today with D.T. [Denys Trefusis], it was very painful and I can't possibly write about it. Besides, you may never get this. Anyway I will tell you *viva voce.*

The wind is howling round Knole. It sounds terribly melancholy. Don't cross on Thursday if it is rough, but wait at Boulogne, because I am so afraid of your leg getting knocked.

No more, as I expect this letter will be a dud.

But come back Thursday.

Mar

Harold to Vita:

February 2, 1920
My darling Mar (oh my darling—it is getting dark & I do miss you so. What do you *mean* by saying I don't miss you? Why it's a great gap.)

Well I have done nothing much since I wrote this morning. It was a simply gorgeous spring day & the first thing I did was to go out & buy masses of mimosa for my sitting room. . . . I have a lovely big room with a huge writing table like a piano which rather frightens me and a room for Miss Williams next door.

Anyhow I dictated to her & then I went out to lunch with Allen Leeper at Laurents—& then I went to Edward's Shop where there was an exhibition of spring models—some really lovely ones. The D[uche]ss of Sutherland was there and asked about "Rebellion." She is a darling. . . .

And then I came here & did more work & here I am writing to you my darling darling Mar.

I do hope the tooth is better. My poor sweet.

Look here write to the [Hotel] Alexander III always.

Your loving loving Hadji

[Ed. Note: I include the following letter in this section, though it is from Vita to her mother, for the purpose of giving the reader further perspective on Vita's relationship with Violet Trefusis.]

Vita to Her Mother:

February 9, 1920 Dover.
My darling Mama,

I daren't picture to myself what you must think by now, after my telegrams today. Briefly, I got back from Lincoln late last night, & V. [Violet] saw Denys & told him she wanted to leave him. I wasn't there, so I don't know what he said, but anyway he went away after being there a very short time, and she left London this morning. I travelled with her as far as Dover, and *honestly* did my utmost to prevail upon her to go back to him, but she would not listen to a word of it. I honestly, honestly tried, though it was torture to me to do so, as you will appreciate better than anyone, knowing as you do all the true facts. I have never tried anything so hard. Well, anyway, she left Dover by today's boat & promised to wire to me. This afternoon Denys arrived, and he and I are going over to France tomorrow, (what a ridiculous journey! I can't help seeing that, even at this moment) and he will ask her to return to him and I alas! shall again do all I can to make her, but whether I succeed I very much doubt. If she *does* go with him, I think I will go on to Paris to Harold for a few days, as I shall be half way there already. But if she refuses, God alone knows what is going to happen; he says he will never have anything to do with her again.

I have never been in such an extraordinary situation in my life, and the décor is all so much in keeping,—a howling gale, and my awful little lodging-house room with a single gas jet,—it seems very unreal, and the only real thing is the anguish he & I both endure.

I put in my telegram that all this must be kept quiet, to avoid a scandal. You will be the first to agree. I have written fully to Harold.

You were very, very, very sweet over your interview with Denys, and your telegram to me & your letter,—which by the way I did not have time to answer in Lincoln, as I went to the Fens the last day & only found it on my return. I was ill nearly all the time I was in Lincoln.

I have spent the most absurd afternoon with Denys, I only hope he sees the ridiculous side of it as keenly as I do. But underneath all this I feel very near the life of an active volcano. As he said rather grimly, we can't complain that life is dull.

O Mama, don't think I'm not taking it seriously; I know only too well that somebody's heart will be broken by tomorrow night, probably mine, I *hope* mine—and I think of you.

Mar

I have also written to Dada.

[Vita had also written to Harold that same day that if Violet decided to go with Denys, as she tried to persuade her to do, "I shall come to you."]

Vita to Harold:

[Undated but possibly in late March 1920 after Vita and Violet had again gone traveling together.]

Oh Harold, my darling, I am so absolutely miserable now. I have had your letter. I visualised the whole scene, and exactly how it must have looked. But you forget I didn't know when you were coming to Paris, you had never told me by letter, and as a matter of fact the last thing you had said to me in London was that you would probably be crossing on Wednesday. You see, we thought we would get wagons-lits for Thursday (hence the telegram I sent you & which your mummy must have forwarded to you by now), but later in the day we heard they weren't certain, so we determined to set out for the station and hope for the best. Oh dear, I have told you all this already in another letter but never mind. My poor poor sweet, it must have been an awful disappointment. I do realise it so well. But look here, those telegrams which they told you V. [Violet] had sent were 1) to Roncompagni in Rome telling him not to get rooms there and 2) to Pat about a commission in London. I know, because I saw them both. They were *not* telegrams to say we were leaving Paris—so it is all not as awful & deliberate as you thought. Those beastly concierges, how dared they grin—anyway it was a foul hotel & they made up the bill all wrong, and those two telegrams *are* on the bill (I've looked) so I hope you didn't pay for them. That would be the last straw.

And look here, there's something I want to tell you, you know I always keep your letters? Well, I tore that one up, so as it shouldn't remain forever; I hated doing it, because I hate tearing anything you've written me, and never do, but I *had* to tear that letter,—*elle me brûlait les doigts* [it was burning my fingers]—so now I've told you I feel less badly about it.

I mind dreadfully your having been disappointed.

I've got a bad cold & feel ill and o so wretched to think of you.

And I *do* love you, whatever *les apparences*.

Look here, a proof: if you want me back now at once, send me a telegram saying you are ill & I will come straightaway. I'm not just saying this *pour la forme. I mean it.*

O Hadji. *Je t'embrasse.*

Your Mar

Harold to Vita:

May 19, 1920
My own darling Mar,
   A. This is just to say, don't forget:
      1. Piccy box
      2. My passport (I have got copies)
      3. Le lys rouge
      4. De Profundis (Oscar Wilde)
      5. My luggage
   B. Tell William Cooper to cut off *all* the lilac stems—you know what I mean, you'll see what I mean.

Also what about the packets of Virginia Stock?

Oh dear! Oh dear!

C. I met Enid Bagnold. Also Roderick Jones. The latter is a nice, clever, gentle, self confident, in love little man. I liked him. So does Enid Bagnold in spite of your theories. *Damn* those Amazonian theories of yours! Surely it is less ridiculous to marry & have babies, heaps of babies, than to live on through a truculent virginity. Anyway she was evidently sensitive about it all. She flamed indignation. And I thought of that foolish hard little letter which I had that morning dropped into the box. After all what on earth? . . . But I won't argue. Anyway I was tactful—according to my 1886 lights—& said I hoped she wouldn't be cross when she got your letter. She promised she wouldn't. She is a nice boy. I like her very much. I like her more than I like lots of people but less than I like you. My dear dear black gypsy (gypsy? gypsophylla? Oh dear. I'm not as good as Ben).

D. (dentist didn't hurt thank you.)

E. Less windy tonight.

F. I love you.

G. Goodnight

Hadji

Meet you at 12:30 P.M. tomorrow—take tickets for Southhampton West (Not Sackville West) & oh please PLEASE don't miss [it].

Harold to Vita:

May 21, 1920 Marlborough Club.
Darling,

That's done it!

The secretary of this club—otherwise an intelligent and quite polite man—has just said "By the way are you any relation to the Nicolson whose wife wrote *Heritage?*"

Now look here; I don't mind being Hadji or your being Vita.

Or being your husband.

I might even put up, from foolish people, with being called "Vita's husband" or "V. Sackville West's husband"

H.N. === V.S.W.

I *might* put up with being "that fellow Nicolson whose wife wrote *Heritage.*"

H.N. . . . . .V.S.W.

NOT

     BUT I WILL *NOT* BE ASKED

"if I am, by any chance (by *any* chance—mark you)

a RELATION of THE (just think, *the*)

NICHOLSON whose wife etc. . . ."

VSW

    HN

Vita to Harold:

November 24, 1922. Cottage.
My little Hadji,

I got your dear funny letter about your packing, which made me laugh, do you want an extra suitcase sent out to you empty some time before you come home? I'm glad you didn't give the fluffy suit to the waiter. I should have felt that that was indeed a link with the past gone. Oh darling, how terribly we loved each other at Cosmopoli when the fluffy suit was young and we were young too. Have you forgotten? Sorry to sentimentalise.

Yes, I will have 3 Knole books sent to you, and you can give one to the Marquis, and one to the Roumanian (how on earth had he heard of it?) and one for yourself.

I am keeping all your Lausanne letters (as indeed I always do keep your letters, silly one, so you can make a diary of them if you like, and not bother to keep a separate diary).

Darling, I hope you will be impressed by all that you will find done in the garden when you come back. The gentleman (?) who came about the new hedge says Hugh Dickson always grows in that food-of-the-giants way, and that they [a hybrid perennial rose, medium-red, introduced in 1905] should be bent over & pegged down, when they will break all along the bend, and flower.

Dots & G. [Dorothy and Gerald Wellesley] have gone off to Sheffield together. She sounded quite cold and frozen on the telephone—sort of numb. She has got claustrophobia badly. I hope it won't end by making her really hate G. More than ever do I think he was a fool not to go to India with McNeel.

Go on writing here, till I tell you to write to Ebury St., as B.M. may again put off going back to Brighton. I hope so, as Brighton is good for the babies, & I love being here. It is quite warm, rather delicious. But I *wish* you were here, nothing really nice without you.

Goodbye, my own darling, *amor de mi vida.*

I have got Ethel Mayne's *Life of Byron* for you, do you want it sent out or kept?

Vita to Harold:

[part of letter, probably from late December] 1922

[. . .] Pat informed me casual-like the other day that she had left me everything she possessed. It is rather difficult to know what to reply to such remarks. "Thanks awfully" seems inadequate; lack of interest seems ungrateful and excess of interest in poor taste. I lost my head and said I wished she would see another specialist. I really think she is the queerest fish I ever came across.

Vita to Harold:

December 31, 1922
My beloved Hadji,

It is close on midnight & my last scribble this year must be for my darling to say Happy New Year, although he won't get it till the New Year is quite two or three days old.

I enclose a letter of Nigg's. It is written to the editor of that much-to-be-deprecated publication, the *Rainbow.* Of course I can't send it, but how sweet it is, with its slight hint of menace. [See "From Their Sons," Nigel's letter dated December 24, 1922 in this book.]

Today I told Ben I was tired and was going to rest. I came into my room five minutes later to find him standing beside my bed with tears pouring silently down his face. I said Good gracious Ben what's the matter? There was an outburst. He hid a wet face in my neck and sobbed out that he couldn't bear to think I was tired (and it was only t.m. [time of the month], poor lamb, had he known), and he had come to see if he could get me a hot water bottle. I hugged him, and he turned rough and cross, and said he must go to his tea.

And when I got into bed I found a very tepid hot water bottle pushed well down to the foot.

Goodnight, my sweet, it will be 12 in a minute. I suppose I shall see you again some time next year? But it seems a long way off

Mar

I knew this letter was from Gwen [Gwen St. Aubyn, Harold's siser, to whom *Dark Island* is dedicated] so slipped this in.

Harold to Vita:

March 2, 1923
My dearest,

I send you herewith a design for the wrapper of "Reddin." [long poem about an independent spirit] It will do well enough.

I went to the luncheon for Prince Nicolas: there was
1. Caviar
2. Sole
3. Salmon
4. Lamb
5. Quails
6. Ice

And there was
1. Sherry
2. White wine
3. Red wine
4. Port
5. Champagne
6. Liqueurs

I HAD:
1. a little bit of lamb
2. coffee

Wasn't that good? But I don't think I could hold out another time.

God bless you my sweet & enjoy yourself. How I *long* to get down to our little cottage. I loathe London.

Hadji

Harold to Vita

[April or May] 27, 1923
My darling,

I won't come down tonight as I am going to the Piccoli with Reggie. I shall come down by the 5:25 to Hindenberg tomorrow. I love you.

I dined last night at Maudes; I came in looking very pleased with myself in my little flag & so tidy with my hair brushed all flat—& then found that no one else had a little flag & I had to take it off in front of the looking glass & get all untidy. There were lots of people & I sat between Maggie Greville and Lady Horner and we talked about Tennyson & why he was like that & it was rather pleasant. Lord Farquenhar was there & was either mad or drunk or both. We then went on to the dance. I was given back my little flag & had a large blue rosette on my lapel which looked very well & means "This large pink gentleman is a *Steward* and must be obeyed." So I was pleased with myself again. But not for long. There was a "royal table" at the supper party, & Lady Curzon was to sweep in on the arm of our Prince, followed by a procession of ambassadors & duchesses & other who make England what she is. But both the Princes said they didn't want supper at all & then the French ambassador went away.

Meanwhile Lady Curzon was waiting upstairs to head the procession, & we had to tell her that the procession had gone, & she had to sneak in on the arm of Pollaniani, & Marita had to go with me, the Marquis (who was trying to get away) fell down stairs, & his stick went tockle tockle tockle from step to step in front of him; and then [in tiny writing] I crept away and hid like a little mouse in a room with palms where very sadly I took off the blue rosette & put it in my pocket.

But it wasn't bad fun after all, & I saw lots of people.

The income tax people have docked my pay. That's why I was overdrawn. Damn them.

Your own Hadji.

VITA AND VIRGINIA

The choice of these few letters from Vita's 19-year correspondence with Virginia Woolf is based on their relation to the other materials in this volume. Thus the letters presented here are about Seducers in Ecuador, about Vita's travels, and about her poems; they continue the time period begun by the family letters. These letters are reprinted from The Letters of Vita Sackville-West to Virginia Woolf, *edited by Louise DeSalvo and Mitchell A. Leaska, and incorporate their notes in brackets.*

Tre Croci, Cadore [Italy]
16 July [1924]
My dear Virginia,

I hope that no one has ever yet, or ever will, throw down a glove I was not ready to pick up. You asked me to write a story for you. On the peaks of mountains, and beside green lakes, I am writing it for you. I shut my eyes to the blue of gentians, to the coral of androsace; I shut my ears to the brawling of rivers; I shut my nose to the scent of pines; I concentrate on my story [*Seducers in Ecuador,* published in this volume]. Perhaps you will be the Polite Publisher, and I shall get my story back—"The Hogarth Press regrets that the accompanying manuscript, etc."—or whatever our formula may be. Still, I shall remain without resentment. The peaks and the green lakes and the challenge will have made it worth while, and to you alone shall it be dedicated. But of course the real challenge wasn't the story, (which was after all merely a "commercial proposition") but the letter. You said I wrote letters of impersonal frigidity. Well, it is difficulty perhaps, to do otherwise, in a country where two rocky peaks of uncompromising majesty soar into the sky immediately outside one's window, and where an amphitheatre of mountains encloses one's horizons and one's footsteps. Today I climbed up to the eternal snows, and there found bright yellow poppies braving alike the glacier and the storm; and was ashamed before their courage. Besides, it is said that insects made these peaks, deposit on deposit; though if you could see the peaks in question you would find it hard to believe that any insect, however industrious, had found time to climb so far towards the sky. Consequently, you see, one is made to feel extremely impersonal and extremely insignificant. I can't tell you how many Dolomitic miles and altitudes I have by now in my legs. I feel as though all intellect had been swallowed up into sheer physical energy and well-being. This is how one ought to feel, I am convinced. I contemplate young mountaineers hung with ropes and ice-axes, and think that they alone have understood how to live life—Will you ever play truant to Bloomsbury and culture, I wonder, and come travelling with me? No, of course you won't. I told you once I would rather go to Spain with you than with anyone, and you looked confused, and I felt I had made a gaffe,—been too personal, in fact,—but still the statement remains a true one, and I shan't be really satisfied till I have enticed you away. Will you come next year to the place where the gipsies of all nations make an annual pilgrimage to some Madonna or other? I forget its name. [Santiago de Compostela] But it is a place somewhere near the Basque provinces, that I have always wanted to go to, and next year I AM GOING. I think you had much better come too. Look on it, if you like, as copy,—as I believe you look upon everything, human relationships included. Oh yes, you like people through the brain better than through the heart,—forgive me if I am wrong. Of course there must be exceptions; there always are. But generally speaking. . . .

And then, I don't believe one ever knows people in their own surroundings; one only knows them away, divorced from all the little strings and cobwebs of habit. Long Barn, Knole, Richmond, and Bloomsbury. All too familiar and entrapping. Either *I* am at home, and you are strange; or *you* are at home, so neither is the real essential person, and confusion results.

But in the Basque provinces, among a horde of *zingaros* [gypsies], we should both be equally strange and equally real.

On the whole, I think you had much better make up your mind to take a holiday and come.

Vita

Virginia Woolf comments on this letter:

"I enjoyed your intimate letter from the Dolomites. It gave me a great deal of pain—which is I've no doubt the first stage of intimacy—no friends, no heart, only an indifferent head. Never mind: I enjoyed your abuse very much. . . .

But I will not go on else I should write you a really intimate letter, and then you would dislike me, more, even more, than you do."

SS Rajputana, in the Indian Ocean
8 February [1926]

Such an absurd day at Aden yesterday: tearing across salt-marshes in a small open motor, in a hot gale; cyclones of dust; hundreds of tiny windmills madly spinning; salt-heaps in rows like the tents of a regiment; tunnels under hills; empty tanks of a hundred-million-gallon capacity (there are no springs, and it hasn't rained there for 10 years); small black boys at the bottom of the tanks, like bears at the Zoo at the bottom of the Mappin Terraces, beating their stomachs and crying reverberatingly "No father, no mother, thank you"; Scotch soldiers in kilts; then Aden again, and lions suddenly in the middle of a Ford lorry garage [the lions were in fact caged]; and tea with an old Parsee in cool rooms over an apothecary's shop. Pure Conrad, this: the merchant-prince of Aden in a shiny black cap, and shrewd eyes twinkling behind owlish glasses. A photograph of the King on a table. Bunches of herbs strung up to keep illness and misfortune from the house. Photograph groups of Parsee generations. Ledgers; a globe; models of ships. A dark young secretary in a suit of white ducks. Sweet biscuits. Talk of cargoes for Somaliland. And Aden lying outside, swept by its hot wind, the most god-forsaken spot on earth. And then a motor-launch, and the ship again, with gulls and hawks wheeling together above the refuse, and sellers of shells bobbing round in tiny canoes, and the Resident coming on board. [Aden was a British

Protectorate, under the control of the Viceroy of India.] And then the steaming out into the night, and no more land ahead for two thousand miles, and the self-contained life of the ship closing round one once more.

The Indian ocean is grey, not blue; a thick, opaque grey. Cigarettes are almost too damp to light. At night the deck is lit by arc-lights, and people dance; it must look very strange seen from another ship out at sea—all these people twirling in an unreal glare, and the music inaudible. One's bath, of sea-water, is full of phosphorus: blue sparks that one can catch in one's hand. The water pours from the tap in a sheet of blue flame. The parties of Proust gain in fantasy from being read in such circumstances (I don't mean in the bath, but on deck); they recede, achieve a perspective; they become historical almost, like Veronese banquets through which flit a few masked Longhi figures, and ruffled by the uneasy impish breeze of French Freud. I re-enter their company after struggling with the Persian irregular verbs. My own poem ["The Land'] on the other hand has ceased to have any existence for me at all: it seems just silly. I thought I should be able to stand back and look at it; but no: it is crammed right-up against my nose, and I can't see it at all. Mme de Guermantes and Khwastan-rasi alone have reality.

But by the time I come home I shall have written a book, which I hope will purge me of my travel-congestion, even if it serves no other purpose. [*Passenger to Teheran,* selections in this volume]The moment it is released, it will pour from me as the ocean from the bath-tap—but will the blue sparks come with it, or only the blanket-grey of the daytime sea? (By the way, I have discovered since beginning this letter that one can draw pictures on oneself with the phosphorus; it's like having a bath in glow-worms; one draws pictures with one's fingers in trails of blue fire, slowly fading.)

For the rest, it is a perpetual evading of one's fellow-beings. Really what odd things grown-up, civilised human beings are, with their dancing and their fancy-dress (Charles I stalking the deck with his head under his arm like an umbrella), and their sports, and their blind man's buff, and an indignant Wellesley being forced to give away prizes. [Dorothy Wellesley, married to Lord Gerald Wellesley, later the seventh Duke of Wellington, from whom she separated in the 1920s] ("Really I do think it's a little hard that because I happened to marry Gerry I should have to make a fool of myself, on a P. & O.") But I come up on deck at dawn when there is no one about but a stray Lascar cleaning brasses, and watch the sun rising straight ahead, out of the east, and the sky and sea are like the first morning of Genesis. This is all before the hearty clergymen are awake, or the people who approach and say they think they know one's aunt. (Why have aunts so many friends?)

I expect you think this is a dumb letter. It is rather. But of such things life is made at present. Everything else has been stripped away, and one remains a sponge, just drinking things up. What will happen when it's all over, do you think? What would happen to *you*, I wonder chiefly, if you could be so thoroughly disturbed out of Bloomsbury? my greatest desire at present is to try that experiment. Also I want nine lives at least—another desire. And nine planets to explore. You have no idea how silly the tiny refinements of introspection can become.

If all this happens on a mere passage to India, what oh what is going to happen to poor Vita when she reaches the heart of Asia?

Perhaps some sense of selection will blessedly return, to order the traffic, like an archangel, or a policeman.

We have crept onward a few hundred miles since I began this letter, and the sun has come tropically out, and the clergymen have put on their sun-helmets. Tomorrow I shall be bouncing across India in a dusty train.

Have you quite forgotten this poor pilgrim? I haven't forgotten that I am to tell you I think of you, but I think that will be a nice occupation for the Persian Gulf. In the meantime I think of you a terrible great deal. You make a wonderful cynical kindly smiling background to the turbulence of my brain. Shall I find a letter from you at Bombay I wonder?

I don't mind if you do laugh at me—

Your V.

Teheran
8 April [1926]

Persia has turned magenta and purple: avenues of judas-trees, groves of lilac, torrents of wisteria, acres of peach-blossom. The plane-trees and the poplars have burst into green. I know you had a lovely Easter in England—Reuter chronicled it. (Reuter is a great joy to us, because it always arrives all wrong, e.g., "Lady Fisher has just completed her 27 days' fast, undertaken to cure her of an illness caused by General de Bility.") But I suppose you are in France now, tearing about—well, I, too, am about to tear, for we are going down to Isfahan. And, dear me, I can write you only one more letter after this, for the next fortnightly bag [diplomatic mail pouch] will bring me to the eve of my starting for home. I have been studying Mme Dieulafoy, a ravishing character, in fact I wrote an article about her, which you may see in Vogue. (Vogue is illustrated, and Mme Dieulafoy is incomplete without a portrait, or I would have sent it to Leonard.) [Vogue, June 1926. Extracts from Vita's article about Jane Dieulafoy's travel journal of her voyage to Persia in the 1890s and her husband's excavation of the palace of Darius are included in *Passenger to Teheran*.] Raymond [Mortimer] and I have agreed to divide the world; rather like the Versailles peace conference we are: he is to have Palestine, Syria and the desert, and I am to have Persia, for journalistic purposes. (We are both rather resentful of Aldous

Huxley.) [Whose *Jesting Pilot* described his world travels.] Raymond has arrived, you see; he fell over a precipice and was fired on, but survived. It seems odd to see him here. He is very happy, and as good as gold: scribbles away, and gives no trouble. But we both find it difficult to write about travel. My drawer is full of loose sheets that refuse to connect up. I daresay you are right about rhythm; all I can say is that rhythm and I are out of gear. I have finished my poem though, and it goes off by this bag. There are large patches of Asia in it now. Will you approve, I wonder?

But indeed my bringing-up wasn't so very different from yours: I mooned about too, at Knole mostly, and hadn't even a brother or a sister to knock the corners off me. And I never went to school. [An invention; she did.] If I am jolly and vulgar, you can cry quits on another count, for you have that interest in humanity which I can never manage—at least, I have the interest, but not the diabolical skill in its practice which is yours. And as I get older (I had a birthday only the other day) I find I get more and more disagreeably solitary, in fact I foresee the day when I shall have gone so far into myself that there will no longer be anything to be seen of me at all. Will you, please, remember to pull away the coverings from time to time? or I shall get quite lost. It is, I think, a pity to allow oneself to come to that stage when one only wants to be with people with whom one is intimate or perhaps in love. One ought to have a larger repertoire. But there, you see, am I saying "one ought to,"—and that gives away the whole trouble: that I live by theories, or rather they revolve and jostle in my head, and then I neglect to put them into practice, or perhaps am incapable of so doing. And that perhaps is one of the reasons why I like women better than men (even platonically), that they take more trouble and are more skilled in the art of making friendship into a shape; it is their business; men are too spoilt and lazy.

There now is a long egoistic passage; but from time to time I get seriously worried, and have a longing to be gregarious, and pour it out on poor Virginia.

I met a young American poet called MacLeish [Archibald] who has a passionate admiration for you. He is a serious young man, who has come here on an opium commission. You and Eliot are the only two writers in England today, etc. etc. By the way I would like to read Middleton Murry's invectives, but you didn't say what they were in. [Attacks on Woolf's *Jacob's Room* and Eliot's "The Waste Land," in the *Adelphi*, February 1926] Will you keep them for me?

Darling Virginia, you mustn't write me any more, because I shall be coming home. On the 25th is the coronation; then we are going to climb a mountain, then I am going to start. I can't find anything about my journey; tourist agencies are unknown here, and the continental time-tables ignore Russia altogether. So I shall just launch off into the blue and trust to luck, and ought to reach England on the fourteenth, laden with rugs for old Bridges. [Robert Bridges] If you aren't very careful I shall really bring you a tortoise, as the place is alive with them. (Have you read Lawrence, D. H., on tortoises?)

Have you read "Comment debuta Marcel Proust"? I cried over it. (By the way, that might be a good book to publish in translation; it's quite short.)

How pleased I shall be to sit on your floor again.

I have got to go and see the Crown jewels, which is unexpectedly cutting my letter short, and I daren't risk the bag not being closed when I get back—I'm also going to see that they've painted the room the right colour for the coronation, and am to be rewarded for my trouble by being allowed to pour bowls of emeralds through my fingers! So, at least, says the high functionary who is gracious enough to accord me this favour. I am taking Raymond. I must fly—

Your V.

Postscript. just back from the palace, with 1/2 an hour before the bag shuts.

I am blind. Blinded by diamonds.

I have been in Aladdin's cave.

Sacks of emeralds were emptied out before our eyes. Sacks of pearls. *Literally.*

We came away shaking the pearls out of our shoes. Ropes of uncut emeralds. Scabbards encrusted with precious stones. Great hieratic crowns.

All this in a squalid room, with grubby Persians drinking little cups of tea.

I can't write about it now. It was simply the Arabian Nights, with décor by the Sitwells. Pure fantasy. Oh, *why* weren't you there?

Teheran
11 March [1927]

The posts are all awry and amok; a stray *Daily Mail* trickles in, then a detective story for Harold, then a letter for me posted on Jan. 30th, but no nice big lumps of post come as they ought to do. As for our missing Foreign Office bag, it hasn't turned up yet. And I haven't heard from my mother for four weeks! So Heaven knows when this letter will reach you.

But at least, among the trickles of the Russian post, is a letter from you, of February 16th. I gather from internal evidence that one is missing—it'll come in the bag next week, I expect. But are you really shingled? Is it true? Oh darling, do I like that? I think I preferred the dropping hairpins, that cheerful little cascade that used to tinkle onto your plate. But Mary [Mary Hutchinson, Clive Bell's lover] says you look nice shingled, does she? And Mary ought to know. It makes you go all wrong in my mind, and the photograph of you at Knole no longer tells the truth, which upsets me.

Otherwise, yes, you are a very bright bead. What amuses me most is the speculation on what you would be like here. And in Greece: Where shall we go in

October? Avignon? Italy? Or are you going to let me down over that? Tired of going abroad, after Spain with Dadie [George Rylands]!

Meanwhile our plans are ever so slightly changed: we cannot reach Athens on April 28th as I told you before, but on May 5th—a week later. Is there any hope that you will still be there? We shall be on the *Lloyd Triestino* (*Carinthia, Carniola* or *Trento,* according to which boat is running—we can't discover exactly which) which will reach the Piraeus from Cyprus and go on to Trieste. I dare not hope that you will be able to join it—or dare I? In any case, we get to London on May 9th, late at night. But oh, if you could join the boat. . . .

Do you know that my time in Teheran is drawing to an end? Every night as I walk across the compound and look up at the stars through the planes, I wonder if I shall ever see Teheran again. Everybody asks me if we are coming back. I say "So far as I know." But that is just official discretion: I cannot believe that the swords and silk stockings will exercise their charm much longer. In the meantime I remain wisely silent, observing a struggle going on in Harold, and knowing that an ill-placed word often makes people turn contrary.

What else? Yes, I have read Cowper [William Cowper, "The Task," 1785]:

> The stable yields a stercoraceous heap. . . .

It bears an unpleasant resemblance to *The Land,* doesn't it? But it has its good moments.

> While fancy, like the finger of a clock,
> Runs the great circuit, and is still at home.

I read *Les faux-monnayeurs* too [by André Gide]. I remember you said you didn't like it. Yet I wonder you weren't interested by the method of springing decisive events on the reader, without the usual psychological preparation. I thought it gave a strange effect of real life. I liked it better than *Si le grain ne meurt,* in which I liked only the beginning of the 3rd volume, about the French littérateurs; I was bored by the African part; I don't think lust is interesting *as such,* and it doesn't inspire me at all to know that Gide had an Arab boy five times in one night . . . but the Wilde part was good although revolting. How beautifully unsubtle Gide makes Fielding appear, with all his knock about fun in Gloucestershire inns, when you read them as I did in conjunction, dove-tailed, Gide in the daytime and Fielding at night.

I have come to the conclusion that solitude is the last refuge of civilised people. It is much more civilised than social intercourse, really, although at first sight the reverse might appear to be the case. Social relations are just the descendants of the primitive tribal need to get together for purposes of defence; a gathering of bushmen or pygmies is the real ancestor of a Teheran dinner party; then the wheel comes full cycle, and your truly civilised person wants to get away back to loneliness. If all my life went smash, and I lost everybody, I should come and live in Persia, miles away from everywhere, and see nobody except the natives to whom I should dispense quinine. It is only affection and love which keep one. But I think Lady Hester Stanhope must have had a good life. [Stanhope went to live in a convent in Syria in 1810 until her death in 1839.]

I've been buying, in large quantities, the most lovely Persian pottery: bowls and fragments, dim greens and lustrous blues, on which patterns, figures, camels, cypresses, script, disport themselves elusive and fragmentary. [See her poems in this volume.] How I am going to get them all home God knows. For the moment they stand round my room, creating a rubbed, romantic life of forgotten centuries. It's like looking into a pool, and seeing, very far down, a dim reflection. I make all sorts of stories about them.

Where will you get this letter? in London? in Greece? I wish I had your address. I told Leigh [Ashton] he might run into you there, he's going to the British School at Athens. Oh God I wish I were going to be in Greece with you, lucky lucky Leonard. Please wish that I might be there. Please miss me. You say you do. It makes me infinitely happy to think that you should, though I can't think why you should, with the exciting life that you have—Clive's rooms, and talk about books and love, and then the press, and the bookshop, and wild-eyed poets rushing in with manuscripts, and all the rest of it.

But I *am* going to Shiraz, it's true. This would be heaven if I didn't so much want Virginia. However, next time I go abroad it will, it shall, it must, be with you.

Your V.

P.S. I think it is really admirable, the way I keep my appointments. I said I would be back on the 10th of May, and here I am, rolling up in London at 11:50 P.M. on the ninth, with ten minutes to spare. It's like the Jules Verne man who went round the world in eighty days, and who had forgotten to turn off the gas in his flat.

Persepolis
30 March [1927]

The hawks wheel between the broken columns, the lizards dart through the doorways of the palace of Darius; Persepolis towers on its great terrace. I've driven a motor over nearly a thousand miles of Persia within the last week. I am dirty, sunburnt, well. We have got up at dawn every morning and gone to bed (on the floor) at 8:30. We have slept in ruined huts; made fires of pomegranate-wood and dried camel-dung; boiled eggs; lost all sense of civilisation; returned to the primitive state in which one thinks only of food, water, and sleep. But don't imagine that we have nothing but water to drink; no, indeed; we carry a demi-john filled with Shiraz wine, and though we may discard our beds (which we did on the first day, when our Ford luggage-car broke down and we strewed the street of a Persian village with chemises and tea-pots,) the demi-john we do *not* discard. We get up at dawn, we motor all day across plains and up gorges, tearing along, and at nightfall we arrive somewhere or other, and shake out our little diminished camp, and fall asleep. A very good life, Virginia. And now (for I have moved on since beginning this letter at Persepolis) I have seen Shiraz, an absurdly romantical place, and passed again by Sivand, and slept there, a valley full of peach blossom and black kids, and came again to Isfahan, where the post was waiting for us, and a letter from you. (But before I answer it, don't imagine, please, that this life of flying free and unencumbered across Persia is in any sense a romantic life; it isn't; the notion that one escapes from materialism is a mistaken notion; on the contrary, one's preoccupation from morning to night is: Have we cooked the eggs long enough? have we enough Bromo left? who washed the plates this morning, because *I* didn't? who put away the tin-opener, because if nobody did, it's lost? Far from finding a liberation of the spirit, one becomes the slave of the practical—

But anyway, my darling, I found a letter from you. There it was (I've now unpacked the ink and refilled my pen). We topped the pass, and came down upon Isfahan with its blue domes, and there in the Consulate was our mail-bag full of letters. You were no longer going to Greece but to Rome. [After a holiday in Cassis, the Woolfs and Vanessa and Clive Bell were going to Sicily, then to Rome.] You won't like Rome, with its squaling tramlines, but you will like the Campagna. Please go out into the Campagna as much as possible, and let your phrases match the clouds there, and think of me. I've just been to dinner with a young Persian—he's in love with me—such a nice creature—I knew him last year—he chants Persian poetry so beautifully—This letter gets interrupted all the time, but I love you, Virginia—so there—and your letters make it worse— Are you pleased? I want to get home to you—Please, when you are in the south, think of me, and of the fun we should have, *shall* have, if you stick to your plan of going abroad with me in October—sun and cafés all day, and ? all night. My darling. . . . please let this plan come off.

I live for it.

Do you really get the Femina prize? [Woolf did in 1928, for *To the Lighthouse*.] And the Hawthornden. ["The Land" had won the Hawthornden prize, presented to her after her return.] D'you remember our bet? what fun. [Presumably, that they would both win prizes that year. They did.] Yes, let's write about solitude. Oddly enough, by the same post as your letter, I got sheets from

Ethel Smyth, largely about that same subject, solitude. She likes it too.

Such a scrawl. By candlelight. The motor leaves at 4 tomorrow morning for Teheran. I'm in a queer excited state—largely owing to your letter—I always get devastated when I hear from you. God, I do love you. You say I use no endearments. That strikes me as funny. When I wake in the Persian dawn, and say to myself "Virginia . . . Virginia. . . ."

The Common Reader was in my room at Shiraz—it gave me a shock.

Look here . . . you'll come to Long Barn, won't you? Quite soon after I get back? If I promise to get back undamaged? I'll be sweeter to you than ever in my life before—

Your Vita

PART IV

TRAVEL WRITING

Vita generally kept, with some persistence, a journal of her travels. The entries, of irregular lengths, are generally of interest to the contemporary reader, sometimes for the singularity of outlook and always for the exact transmission of what she saw and her reflections upon it. To compare these passages with her published and more polished works such as Passenger to Teheran and the nearly unobtainable Twelve Days in the Bakhtiari Mountains is to glimpse her artistic judgment. Several long selections from both published books on her Persian travels are presented here, as well as selections from her various travel journals.

Italian Journey with
Dorothy Wellesley (1921)

This early travel diary about Vita's trip to Italy that started in Paris with Gerald and Dorothy Wellesley in the fall of 1921 is full of the intensity Vita always experienced when voyaging. She notes her reactions to places, weather, skies, reading, companions — in high color. A superb traveler, she will later transcribe her reactions in her travels to Persia, the mountains of Russia, and through the United States with the same sort of enthusiasm evident here.

September 14. D., G., [Dorothy and Gerald Wellesley] and I left Victoria at 11 for Paris. I was miserable because H. [Harold] had got out of our taxi halfway to the station, and had walked away looking white and unhappy. I wrote to him in the train, to try to console him a little. We had dinner in Paris at the Gare de Lyon [in Le Train Bleu, a famous restaurant up a stately staircase, with immense murals depicting French cities, an historical monument]. We left Paris at 9 and got to Lausanne the next morning, where we changed into an ordinary carriage.

September 15. We spent the whole day in the train, reaching Verona late at night. I did not much like coming back to Verona . . .

September 16. G. went out by himself in the morning to see Verona—and D. & I wandered out later and I showed her the things I liked, i.e., the Arche and the Gothic staircase. After lunch we took G. to see the staircase, and he destroyed its beauty in a few deft phrases, which made me angry. After that we went to see churches, and he admired baroque chapels, which seemed to me of an unparalleled hideousness, but I listened to his remarks on the baroque with interest, and, I hope, an open mind. We trailed about the streets getting hotter and more thirsty every minute. There were barrows of fruit at every street corner, and barrels of fresh wine standing along the river. In the evening we went to a cinema in the arena—a moonlit anachronism which was great fun. D. was thrilled. Afterwards, we walked about the streets.

September 17. G. & D. took me in a beastly open motor to Mantua, where we wandered through a dull palace of which D. and I contrived to miss the only interesting part. After lunch we went on to the Palazzo del Té, which I liked inordinately, and then to Sabbioneta in pursuit of the baroque; very dull. Then on to Parma. I did not like the motor, but I liked the grape-hung vines all along the road and the heaps of red-gold maize which men with wooden shovels were turning over & over in front of every farmhouse. I had forgotten how lovely Italy was in the autumn. At Parma we saw nothing which amused us in the least except a motor-bicycle race passing through on its way from Milan to Naples—faces caked with white dust flashing down the main street in the glare of acetylene lamps and to the scream of sirens. We wandered about the streets after dinner rather aimlessly, as nobody would say what they wanted to do, and then went back to the hotel, where I left D. to talk to G., and sat myself in my bedroom talking to the hotel housemaid for an hour.

September 18. D. & I left G. at Parma looking rather forlorn. We changed at Bologna, meaning to go to Rimini, but as we found a train that went to Ravenna we thought we would go there instead. We tore through the night as far as Castel Bolognese in the fastest and shakiest train I had ever been in. At Castel Bolognese we got out. They seemed a little doubtful there as to the train for Ravenna. One official said it went at eight, another at eight-thirty, and yet a third said it went at nine, and added, "*Qualche volta arriva*" [Sometimes it comes] which I thought cryptic, and, under the circumstances, a little casual. We filled in the time by having dinner in the station buffet: tagliatelle, vitello, and too much Chianti. We became hilarious, and nearly missed the train, but not quite. It deposited us at Ravenna at nine. We asked for the Hotel Byron, where we had our letters sent, and were told "*Non esiste piu*" [It isn't there any more]. We found, however, another one, where at first they said they couldn't take us in, as even the bathrooms had people sleeping in them, but finally they produced one room. There were quantities of mosquitoes, no mosquito curtains on either bed, and we were cross at having to share; but the general irresponsibility of the country had infected us, and we did not much care, and hunted mosquitoes more or less cheerfully for the better part of the night.

September 19. We went out rather vaguely to see the town. We thought how horrified G. would be by our vagueness, but we did not do so badly. We saw San Vitale, the tomb of Galla Placidia, San Apollinare Nuovo, and the tomb of Dante. At the latter we saw a bottle that contained bits of Dante, very nasty and rather macabre, but no doubt he himself would have appreciated the latter element as much as anybody. In the evening we went to a cinema, which at one moment gave promise of developing into a row, but this came to nothing. We got another room and mosquito curtains out of the reluctant management, and so slept undisturbed.

September 20. In the morning we took a motor and went to San Apollinare in Classe, a large, derelict, and mildewed basilica which we liked. Then to the Pineta, where we were extremely arty: left the motor and went into the wood, and lay under the pines, and read snatches of the more obscure poets to one another. We said "Here Dante, Boccaccio, Shelley, and Byron walked," and again "Oh my God how the canal does stink!" There were a great many lizards, and even more picnic papers littering the ground. Then we went back to Ravenna, and at four got into a lackadaisical train for Trieste. On the way we ate cheese and figs, and drank the Chianti. After Mestre we got into the Corso country, which was very impressive under the moonlight. The train climbed slowly up hill between mostly limestone boulders and for the first time since we had been in Italy we were cold. We got to Trieste at one in the morning, and drove to the quays where the *Sarajevo* was lying alongside, small, black, and dirty. A gale was blowing. We could not get on board, as the steward was on shore and everything was locked up. The Italian customs house officials were very suspicious, and searched everything for arms and ammunition, but finally let us through. We drove to a hotel, but could not get a room, nor was Ozzie [Dickinson, a friend of Harold's and of Vita's mother] there. By this time we were rather dispirited, and extremely cold, and began to think that we should have to spend the rest of the night in the dark. Things brightened suddenly when we discovered another hotel where they were able to give us a room, and not only that, but Ozzie was there; so we rushed to his room and woke him up (it then being about half past two in the morning)— and he hugged us both, because he thought we were never going to turn up.

September 21. After about three hours sleep we got up and went on board the *Sarajevo.* It was still blowing a gale, but this miraculously dropped as we left Trieste, and there was no sea. It was a most lovely day, blue and gold. The coast was rather dull as far as Pola [Pula]. At Pola we got off the boat, and went to see the arena, which was all overgrown inside with sage, thyme, and snapdragons. Then we walked about the town, had drinks at a café, and bought Havelock Ellis in Italian. After dark we got to Lussin-piccolo [Losinj], where we landed, and had more drinks in another café, under oleanders, and were extremely self-conscious and said "How romantic to drink golden wine on an island," and more to the same effect. During the night we got to Zara [Zadar], where we stayed for several hours in an intolerable din of coaling, and of shipping cargo. I saw Zara in the dawn, it looked rather nice.

September 22. Sailed all day past a sort of fairyland coast, between islands, on the bluest of seas. An Albanian on board entered into conversation with me and asked me to go and live with him in the mountains of Albania. I was rather tempted by this suggestion, especially as he was young, tall, dark, and good-looking. In the evening we came to Spalato [Split], which thrilled us, as being the first properly Serbian thing we had seen, and also as being built inside the outer walls of Diocletian's palace, so that mixed up with narrow slums one came suddenly upon great Roman gateways, or a Roman colonnade. We got Serbian money, and dined on the terrace of a café. A good day. The Serbian officials were very suspicious and prodded us all over before we were allowed to land.

September 23. I got up very early and slipped up on deck to watch the sunrise behind the mountains. It was impressive—blood-red, gold, and purple. The coast and the islands had been steadily getting lovelier and grander, but quite barren and uninhabited. I spent most of the morning with the Albanian, who became hourly more poetic and more ardent. By about mid-day the coast began to soften a little, cypresses and stone pines appeared, and presently Gravosa came in sight. Here we were given a sort of royal reception by the commissary of police and a posse of gendarmes, but I never made out why. We drove up to Ragusa [Dubrovnik], where we had lunch, and afterwards went out and looked at the town. I got a violent attack of liver, which made me feel so ill that I forgot to mind the ignominy of it. I had no dinner, and went to bed and sulked there while D. and G. walked about the quays.

September 24. I was better, but not quite mended. Yet we all three sat on the quays, and watched young men like bronze statues bathing. This thrilled me inordinately, as I had never before seen the human body burnt to such a colour. It was very hot and blue. After lunch D. and O. insisted on bathing; they bathed in a dark, rough cove amongst crowds of hairy men, most of whose very inadequate drawers had split in the most ill-chosen places. I sat on the beach, and sulked. After this D. and O. wanted to go for a walk, so we walked to Gravosa and I recovered my temper. On the way there we went through a rough archway and were suddenly confronted with the sunset behind the islands, a staggering sight. We dined at Gravosa at a small café, and walked back afterwards in the dark.

September 25. We spent an unfortunate morning trying to find a better bathing-place, but all the coves seemed to be populated as thick as Manchester. We didn't succeed in bathing, but all got extremely cross, tired, and so unspeakably hot that on our return to the hotel we all got into cold baths. We went into Gravosa to see Ozzie off; his boat left at six; we hugged him and said we loved him, and got *abscheidstimmung* badly. We watched his boat out of sight, and then turned back, feeling very far away from everybody and everything; we went and had dinner at the same little café, drank wine which D. said was like drinking purple pansies, and talked wildly on every subject under the sun. We walked home in the dark. On the way back a timid little man approached us, politely removing his fez, and inquired our terms. He was so meek and diffident that I did not like to snub him, and said as regretfully as I could that we were already booked. We parted with expressions of mutual esteem.

September 26. I tried to take up my book ["Reddin," an unfinished novel about a wise man building a cathedral on a cliff as a monument to his ideals] again, but with signal insuccess. We went for a walk and found a small grey hotel built on terraces by the sea, dined there, and decided to go there to live.

September 27. We continued to say vaguely that we would change our hotel, but there was an awful sirocco and we were both too limp to do anything about it. Tried to write, and couldn't. Damn.

September 28. The wind shrieked and raised clouds of dust, and in the middle of it we packed our luggage on to a cab and drove to the other hotel, thinking all the time that the cab would be blown over. It wasn't; and we were glad we had moved, as we had the sea right under the windows and a lovely view of Ragusa.

September 29. In the morning we bathed; it was extremely cold and rough, and D. was nearly drowned twice, which seemed to annoy her. After lunch we made an effort and went for a walk along the coast. I thought it was a nice walk, but D. was less enthusiastic. We saw wild irises which we could not reach, otherwise the flowers were dull—little dusty yellow things. There were, however, figs, vines, and pomegranates, and in the gardens the oleanders, bougainvillaea, and wisteria were rampant. At the other hotel we used to breakfast off muscat grapes and figs under a roof of wisteria, the only thing I regret [about not being] there.

September 30. The weather continued grey, northern, and unbecoming. I struggled with my book.

October 1. The day was hot and blue again. We went down to the harbour with two little hats and after the usual fuss with the Serbian officials who seemed to be convinced that everyone is a smuggler, we got on board the boat to Cattaro [Kotor]. We stopped at a dear little place called Ragusavecchia, and again at

Castelnuovo [Herceg-Novi], just inside the Bocche di Cattaro [Boka Kotorska]. From having been fast sleep we woke up and began to take interest in the Bocche. Castelnuovo is a railway terminus, and we saw the Belgrade train starting off, a rickety-looking affair like a toy, with two engines, three ordinary carriages crammed to overflowing, and half a dozen goods trucks on and in which clustered the superfluity of passengers. We decided *not* to come back to Ragusa by rail, as we had intended. The Bocche narrowed, becoming gradually less like the west coast of Scotland, and presently we went through the narrowest part, which opens out into a bay entirely surrounded by enormous mountains of grey stone. The sun was just about to set; some of the mountains were golden at the top, others were amethyst; we did not know which way to look as every way was so lovely. We passed two tiny islands with a church and a cypress grove on each, nothing else. We also stopped at a little village called Risano [Risan], once the refuge of Illyrian pirates; and we passed quite close to another little palace called Perasto [Perast] (which D. rechristened), right down on the water's edge, a lovely and desolate little town, with two dim Venetian campanile and several most beautiful little Venetian palaces, with gardens, which seemed to be totally deserted. I longed to stop and explore. We came now in sight of Cattaro, at the end of a long narrow bay, under the shadow of the tallest and most barren mountain of all. One of the ship's officers told me about it, and showed the road climbing in serpentines up the sheer face of the rock; and told me how during the war the Montenegrins had held the summit and the Austrians the lower reaches of the road, until by the treachery of the king of Montenegro the Austrians broke through the Montenegrins, who had receive the order not to fire. It is a terrible place, and one dared not imagine fighting under such conditions; indeed there must be something terrible about living under the perpetual threat of such a mountain. It was dark by the time we were able to go ashore. We dined at a filthy little inn, where they had delicious Turkish coffee and rather good food of unexplained nature. Afterwards we sat on deck and watched the stars above the mountain; I was excited because it was so exactly like the mountain in my book, and I thought how magnificent the cathedral would truly look, crowning it. We became quite exalteés about it, but were taken down a considerable number of pegs quite quickly by the swarms of mosquitoes that were already in occupation of our cabin. I spent the entire night killing them with a shoe against the walls of the cabin, to the light of a small piece of candle stuck onto a saucer. D. slept unmoved throughout, which infuriated me. However I scored over her, because I saw the dawn, and she did not. It broke, pale green over that sinister peak and as we slipped slowly out of Cattaro, a huge star hung in the transparent sky on the extreme tip of the cliff. I remained with my head stuck out of the porthole till Cattaro was out of sight.

SELECTIONS FROM *PASSENGER*
TO TEHERAN (1926)

Passenger to Teheran *and* Twelve Days *are both the colorful renderings, full of humor and lively anecdote, of some of Vita's more exotic travels in Persia and Russia. From the wise suggestions about what to take along, to the accounts of what a traveler in relatively harsh conditions must endure, to the tales of Gertrude Bell's insisting on her choosing a Saluki dog to the vagaries of mail deliveries, to the marvels of mountainscapes and teeming cities, she never loses her sense of amusement.*

Vita traveled widely and often most glamorously, amid and over the mountains of Samarkand and of Persia, rode on many a mule and walked in much mud, writing of her extraordinary experiences whenever she had a moment. She had chosen Salukis with kings, traveled with the famous, endured what travelers endure, and written it all up as a proud and often lonely venture. Her poems about Persia grasp something of her feeling for the country.

In November of 1925, Harold Nicolson was posted to the British Legation in Teheran as His Majesty's counselor. Vita, preferring to stay in their Sussex home at Long Barn, visited him twice, in 1926 from January to the middle of May, and then in 1927, to walk with him over the Bakhtiari Mountains. During this period, Harold was writing his most successful book, Some People.

For the first trip, Dorothy Wellesley went with her as far as India — they went up the Nile to Luxor and in India went to Agra and New Delhi, after which Vita went up the Persian Gulf by boat, then by rail to Baghdad, staying a few days with Gertrude Bell (Vita omits from Passenger to Teheran *any mention of Dorothy Wellesley being on the trip and gives scarcely any notice to India, which she disliked.) She then continued the journey in a caravan of cars over the mountains of Persia and to Teheran, meeting Harold at Kermanshah, to his excitement and her utter composure.*

She greatly liked Persia, and, as Nigel Nicolson tells us in his introduction to the 1990 edition of Passenger to Teheran, *"Persia had not welcomed since Curzon a more observant and appreciative British visitor than Vita."[1] She, Harold, and Raymond Mortimer — another Bloomsbury figure and Harold's intimate friend — went together to Isfahan. Eventually she and Harold parted and she wended her way home through Russia and Poland, in the most difficult of circumstances, all of which she took as an adventure.*

Vita was a courageous and not in any way the shrinking violet feminine traveler. She was forerunner, mulerider, and wanderer: Over deserts and wide spaces, into mountains and adventures of all sorts, in cities and royal receptions, she remained as intrepid as any of the more celebrated explorers. One of her more useful talents along these lines was flexibility, what we might call the art of making-do. She retains, fortunately, a sense of humor about the expected and unexpected details of traveling, of the British Legation, and of a diplomat's life. If every fortnight the bag of correspondence left Teheran for Bagdad, the delays were similarly noticeable: It took a letter from Vita to Virginia Woolf about six weeks to arrive. And in the other direction, there were delays no less noticeable: Having sent themselves three cases of wine from London in October, still in May—though they had once been glimpsed—they had not arrived, and there was silence on the topic. "Beyond looking with interest at every camel I meet lurching along the street, and trying to read the address upside down on the crate he bears, I accept this silence with philosophy and drink the amber-coloured wine of Shiraz instead," Vita wrote.²

When Virginia Woolf received the letters Vita sent her from Persia, she was not altogether complimentary, writing in her diary of 1926: "She is not clever: but abundant and fruitful, truthful too. She taps so many sources of life: repose and variety." But then upon receiving the typescript of Passenger to Teheran, *which the Hogarth Press was to publish in 1926, she exclaimed to Vita how good it was and admitted: "I didn't know the extent of your subtleties . . . not the sly, brooding, thinking, evading Vita. The whole book is full of nooks and crannies."³*

PASSENGER TO TEHERAN

CHAPTER 11

TO EGYPT

I

. . .

One January morning, then, I set out; not on a very adventurous journey, perhaps, but on one that should take me to an unexploited country whose very name, printed on my luggage labels, seemed to distil a faint, far aroma in the chill air of Victoria Station: P E R S I A. It was quite unnecessary for me to have had those labels printed. They did not help the railway authorities or the porters in the least. But I enjoyed seeing my fellow-passengers squint at the address, fellow-passengers whose destination was Mürren or Cannes, and if I put my bag in the rack myself I always managed to let the label dangle, a little orange flag of ostentation. How subtle is the relationship between the traveller and his luggage! He knows, as no one else knows, its idiosyncrasies, its contents; he may have for it a feeling of tenderness or a great loathing; but, for better or worse, he is bound to it; its loss is his despair; to recover it he will forego railway tickets and steamship berths; it is still with him even when he has locked himself away in the drab bed-room of a strange hotel. There is the friendly box, which contains his immediate requisites, and which is opened and shut a dozen times a day; there are the boxes which will not shut, and which therefore he takes care never to open, however badly he may need an object lurking in their depths; to unpack them altogether is unthinkable, as bad as trying to put the djinn back into the bottle. There are the miscellaneous bits—a hold-all with rugs and coats; and always some small nuisance which he wishes he had not brought; had, known, indeed, before start-ing that he would regret it, but brought it all the same. With what a distinction, too, are invested those of his possessions which have been chosen to accompany him; he knows that he has left behind him an untidy room, with open drawers and ransacked cupboards, the floor strewn with bits of tissue paper and string; a room abandoned for somebody else to tidy up, while *he* sits smug in his carriage, having got away and escaped; and with him go, stowed away in the dark rectan-gular jumble of pigskin, fibre, or alligator, those patient, faithful, indispensables which will see the light again in bewilderingly changed surroundings, but which for him will emerge always with the association of his own dressing-table, his own washstand, and all the close familiarity of home. They have shared his ordinary life; now they are sharing his truancy; when he and they get home again, they will look at one another with the glance of complicity.

There is a great art in knowing what to take. The box which is to be opened and shut a dozen times a day *must* be an expanding box, and to start with it must be packed at its minimum, not its maximum, capacity. This is the first rule, and all temptations to break it by last-minute cramming must be resisted. A cushion or a pillow is a bulky bother, but well worth it for comfort; an air-cushion is less of a bother, but also less of a comfort. A Jaeger sleeping-bag (which goes in the hold-all) makes the whole difference to life on a long and varied journey; but it ought to be lined with a second bag made out of a sheet, or else it tickles. I had neglected this precaution. Thermos bottles are overrated; they either break or leak or both; and there are few places where you cannot get tea. Other essentials are a knife and a corkscrew, and a hat which will not blow off. An implement for picking stones out of horses' hooves is not necessary. Quinine for hot coun-tries, iodine, aspirin, chlorodyne, sticking-plaster. I would say: avoid all regis-tered luggage, but there are few who will follow this sound advice. I did not follow it myself. I had a green cabin trunk, which I grew to hate, and left be-hind in Persia. I had, however, the excuse that I must provide against a variety of climates; I expected to be now boiled, now frozen; must have a fur cap and a sun-helmet, a fur coat and silk garments. My belongings had looked very in-congruous when they lay scattered about my room.

Equipped, then, and as self-contained as the snail, the English traveller makes the most of the two hours between London and Dover. He looks out over the fields which, on the other side of the Channel, will widen out into the hedgeless sweeps of Northern France. For my part I know that line all too well; it takes me through my own fields, past my own station, and a curious mixture stirs in me; there is a dragging at the heart, and then to correct it I think deliberately how often I have seen this very train hurtle through the station, and have had a different dragging at the heart as "Continental Boat Express" whisked past me— a wish to be off, an envy of those people sitting at the Pullman windows; but no, that was not a dragging at the heart, but at the spirit; it is home which drags the heart; it is the spirit which is beckoned by the unknown. The heart wants to stay in the familiar safety; the spirit, pricking, wants to explore, to leap off the cliffs. All the landmarks flash past me: there are the two factory pistons which go up and down, near Orpington, plunging up and down alternately, but never quite together; that is to say, one of them is not quite risen before the other has begun to fall; ever since I was a child those pistons have distressed me, because I could not get them to work in unison, side by side as they are. I know that I shall remember them, travelling across Asia; and that on my return I shall see them again, still going up and down, and still a little wrong. Then comes my own station, and Yew Tree Cottage, and the path across the fields. But would I, if I could, get out of the train and run home by that path across the fields? There is the orange label dangling: P E R S I A. In half an hour I should be home; and my spaniel, sitting on my glove, would run out astonished; but meanwhile the train has rushed me into less poignant country; I am carried beyond that little patch of acres, beyond the woods where the orchis grows. I wonder whether the things in my luggage have felt a similar pull? responded, as the needle of the compass to the north?

Everything begins to recede: home, friends; a pleasant feeling of superiority mops up, like a sponge, the trailing melancholy of departure. An effort of will; and in a twinkling I have thought myself over into the other mood, the dangerous mood, the mood of going-out. How exhilarating it is, to be thus self-contained; to depend for happiness on no material comfort; to be rid of such sentimentality as attaches to the dear familiar; to be open, vulnerable, receptive!

. . .

II

Earlier memories of Cairo were scarcely agreeable; very young, very shy, and very awkward, I had been made to stay with Kitchener. I had not wanted to stay with him; I had protested loudly; my relations, who thought they knew better, said that some day I should be glad to have gone. I was not then, and am not yet, glad; for the recollection survives with horror, a sort of scar on the mind. I had arrived at the Residency suffering from a sunstroke and complete loss of voice— not an ideal condition in which to confront that formidable soldier. Craving only for bed and a dark room, I had gone down to dinner. Six or eight speech-less, intimidated officers sat round the table; Kitchener's bleary eye roamed over them; my own hoarse whisper alone punctuated the silence. Egyptian art came up as a topic. "I can't," growled Kitchener, "think much of a people who drew cats the same for four thousand years." I could think of nothing more to say, even had I been physically capable of saying it. Worse followed; for as we sat on the terrace after dinner, looking across the garden towards the Nile, a quick, happy patter came across the bare floor and in trotted an alert yellow mongrel. "Good gracious, what's that? a *dog?*" cried Kitchener, glaring at his A.D.C. The sanctity of the Residency was outraged; a dozen swords were ready to leap from their scabbards. I could not sit by and see murder done; I had to own that the dog was mine.

Next day, however, my host took me to the Zoo, as pleased as a child with the baby elephant which had been taught to salute him with its trunk. The ice was broken.

This time, after the lapse of years, I was irresponsibly in Egypt again; no dog to conceal, no servants, no Kitchener, no sunstroke. I went to Luxor. I had nine days' grace between ship and ship. Blankets of magenta bougainvillaea hung over the white walls of Luxor; four creamy Nubian camels knelt beside the Nile. I remembered how on that previous occasion in Luxor I had lain in a cool dark room, sick with headache, but thankful to have escaped and to have my sun-stroke at last to myself. Instead of going to the Valley of the Kings I had lain watching the bars of sunlight between the slats of the Venetian blinds, and hear-ing, with the peculiar vividness that only the concentrated egoism of illness brings, the drops of water falling on the tiled floor outside, as the servant splashed it from a bucket; a pleasant way of spending the days—and even the pain seemed to add something, to mark off that week from ordinary life—I was not resentful, only a little wistful at having to come as far as Luxor in order to do it. Now all was changed, and full of energy I took the dazzling, naked road that leads to the Valley of the Kings. How far away now appeared the English fields—yet the two pistons were still going unevenly up and down; small and very brightly green they appeared, as though seen down the wrong end of a tele-scope, when I thought suddenly of them in the midst of the Theban hills. But above all they presented themselves to me as extremely populous, full of small busy life, rabbits at evening coming out from the spinneys, hares sitting on their haunches among the clods of ploughed lands, field-mice, stoats, slinking through the leaves, and birds innumerable hopping in branches; a multitudinous population of tiny things, with plenty of rich corn and undergrowth to shelter them; very soft, green, and cushioned Kent appeared to me, as I paused in the white dust of that lifeless landscape. A hoopoe? a lizard? a snake? no, there was nothing; only the tumbled boulders and the glare of the sun. This silence and lifelessness frightened me. The rocks closed in on the road, threatening. There is a keen excitement in not knowing what one is going to see next; the mind, strung up, reaches forward for an image to expect, and finds nothing; it is like picking up a jug of water which you believe to be full, and finding it empty. I had formed no image of the burial-ground of the Pharaohs. Indeed, it seemed incredible that within a few moments I should behold it with my eyes, and know for the rest of my life thereafter exactly what it looked like. Then it would seem equally incredible that I should not always have known. These small but stinging reflections kept me lingering; I was loth to part with my ignorance; I reproached myself with having wasted so many years in not speculating on this royal sepulchre. Never again would that delight be within my reach; for the pleasures of the imagination I was about to exchange the dreary fact of knowledge. Already I had seen the road, and, even were I magically to be whisked back to Luxor, or, like Habakkuk, picked up by the hair of the head and through the vehemency of an angelic spirit set down to give my luncheon to some one a thousand leagues distant, still I should have seen the road and might form some idea, on a solid basis, of what was likely to be revealed round the corner. It was no good turning round and going back, out of this wilderness to the narrow green reaches of the Nile: I went forward.

. . .

IV

The moon happened to be at the full while I was at Luxor, so I went out to Karnak one night after dinner, to the quick trot of two little horses. This was a thing that many people had done many times before; but to me it was egotistically invested with a special excitement; for among the ambitions that smouldered vaguely at the back of my mind, one was to see Karnak by moonlight, another was to row about Karnak in a boat; and now the first ambition was to be fulfilled. At first the horses trotted softly along the sandy track, between the trees, the clicking of their hooves forming a busy, brisk little rhythm; then the landscape began to resolve itself into its characteristic properties: an obelisk appeared, then the square portico of a lesser temple on the left, then a broken avenue of squat shapes, toad-like among the shadows, then finally the mass of Karnak itself in an open space suddenly spreading out beyond the narrow road and the trees. A strange plain country, Egypt! so true to type, so expected, plat-itudinous—yet so grandly transcending all these things, making sophistication appear so trivial, putting to shame all pedantry with that perennial simplicity recognised by sophisticated and primitive minds alike. There is no escape. Fastidiousness must split the hair down to its narrowest filament; but, tired, returns again to the simplest forms for an ultimate satisfaction. We come back, always, to those odd, false, true relationships, which stir our emotions in response to our finer, not our more educated, judgement: such relationships as that of a pagan temple under the moon—though why the moon should have any bearing on the temple we do not know, except that both are old, so old that both have become unreal to us; unreal, and charged with a significance we are quite at a loss reasonably to interpret, only we know obscurely that it is there; obscurely, un-scientifically, and in ignorance; perhaps mistakenly, but anyway with an inward, intuitive certainty; the conjunction stirs us as an aesthetic harmony stirs us: and who shall explain such mysteries as conjunction and rhythm, intuitively felt, but not by our present crude terminology to be defined? Who shall explain, either, the bearing of visual experience upon physical experience? That which we ap-prehend through the eyes can surely have no bearing on that which we experi-ence through the spirit? But all these words are so vague: "spiritually," "emotionally," "intellectually," what does all that really mean? We fumble, knowing that somewhere round the corner lies the last, satisfying co-ordination. Meanwhile, certain queer comings together, such as are made by rhythm, or by pattern, or by lights and shadows, do produce a natural harmony: a harmony suggesting that the part does probably fit, somewhere, into the whole.

Leaning against Karnak, I thought: what was a work of art if not the deliber-ate attempt to produce, artificially, such a harmony, which in nature emerges only by accident, and with the help of such adventitious advantages as Karnak itself now enjoyed, as, the moon casting shadows, and familiar constellations wryly tilted overhead. So, architecture was not and could never be a pure art, de-pending as it must on natural, accidental things. But there was no denying that architecture and nature made an astounding pair of allies. I had often puzzled over the architect's platitude, that the aesthetic value of a building was indepen-dent of its site, as a picture was independent of its frame, and now understood it less than ever. This Karnak, that rose out of rock and sand, with its columns like gigantic palm-trees and its capitals like spreading lotus, gave the violent lie to such a theory. It sprawled like a magnificent monster on Egypt, enhanced by all that Egypt could give. An obelisk, rising out of the desert, gained something surely by its spiky contrast with the broad rolling waste; I floundered ignorantly, arrogantly but still apologetically, among problems I did not understand. It seemed to me that, since I had embarked on this journey, I had shed everything but the primitive pleasures of sensation. I knew myself, theoretically, to be a reasonably educated person, ready to produce theories on several subjects; yet when I called on theory now, it behaved like an ill-trained dog that will not come to the whistle, snuffing rather at new, delicious scents in the hedgerow, flushing a bird, jumping after it into the air, and landing on all fours again with a mouthful of tail-feathers. Like Kinglake's traveller, I was fit only to report of objects, not as I knew them to be, but as they seemed to me—and to read into them, I might add, a great many attributes they could not really possess.

Walking into Karnak was like walking into one of Piranesi's Prisons, solidified suddenly into stone, and grown to natural, nay, to heroic size. Piled on fantastic ruin, obelisks pricked the sky; the colossal aisle soared, its base plunged in the deepest shadow, its head lifted to the moon; shafts of light struck the columns, lay in silver druggets across the floor. The black, enormous temple was shot through and through by those broad beams of light. Beyond the aisle, a vast space littered with fallen masonry lay open to the sky. Cavernous openings, porticos, colonnades, blocks of masonry; obelisks, statues of Pharaohs, some upright, some prone; and beyond them, beyond this magnificent desolation, shrilled the thin piping of the frogs. At every point of the compass, turn which way one might, this temple, this etching by a mad genius, offered some new aspect, now beautiful, now terrible; some massing of shadow, some lofty soaring into light. It crushed the mind, since it was not the human mind that had conceived it as it now appeared, but such inhuman factors as time upon earth; and, in the sky, the mechanism of astronomy which brought the moon once more to that path overhead. But, out of the awful shadows, came suddenly a human voice, insistent, clamant for recognition. "I am a twin," it said.

I turned, and beheld a figure in noble draperies standing beside me in a patch of light. It was my dragoman, a young Bedouin of proud and handsome appearance. He was in a state of extraordinary excitement, as though he could not contain his news, but must, under compulsion, communicate it to somebody. "I am two months older than my brother," he said, his eyes burning with pride. "My mother kept my brother two months longer than she kept me. My father gave me *two* nurses," he said, expressively, rounding his hands over his breast, "two nurses, for pleasure that I came so soon. My father never looks at my brother, he looks only at me. When my father dies, I shall be the headman of our village. I get three crops a year." He broke off, and bounded nimbly up a sort of Giant's Causeway of fallen stone; paused there, tall in his flowing robes against the sky. "Listen!" he cried, and rapped on a prostrate monolith. It gave out a note like twanged steel. He laughed with delight, as though this performance on the part of the quarried granite were one with his own excitement and his simple vanity.

CHAPTER III

TO IRAQ

I

Our return from Luxor to Cairo must have looked like a triumphal progress through the night, seen from the desert by any stray Bedouin, for the dining-car caught fire and trailed after us like the tall of a comet down the line. The train was stopped once, certainly, and some half-hearted efforts were made to put the fire out, but these being unavailing, we started off again and hoped for the best. My handsome dragoman was terribly frightened; he forgot about being a twin, he forgot about his prowess as a hunter, and insisted that the carriage would soon "be lying down on her side." Besides, he added, robbers were in the habit of putting boulders across the line, to stop the train and plunder such passengers as might survive the accident. Our particular engine-driver was a devil, it appeared, and would charge any obstacle rather than run the risk of being thought in league with the robbers. I had seen the engine-driver, a little black man with a red handkerchief knotted round his head; he had come along from his engine to watch while the railway men tried to extinguish the dining-car, most contemptuous, with a cigarette dangling from his lips; the flames lit up his dark greasy face, and he had replied scornfully to any anxious enquiries. Finally I persuaded Nasr to go back to his own compartment, which he did, remarking that he would rather break in a rogue camel than go in a train again. As nothing happened, however, and as we arrived safely in Cairo next morning, he forgot his fears and implored me to take him on to Persia. He had seen France, England, Spain, and Italy; he had told his father he would not marry until he had seen all the world; would I not, therefore, take him to Asia that he might the more speedily settle down with a wife? He looked crestfallen when I said it was impossible, but soon brightened again. If I would not do that, would I at least send him a packet of post cards (coloured) of Shakespeare's house at Stratford? This I was able to promise, and he ran along beside the train as it moved out of Cairo station, explaining that he had left eighteen pence with the postcard shop at Stratford, but that they had never sent the post cards . . . but here we reached the end of the platform, and the last I saw of him was the flutter of his white robe as he stood waving and looking after the train which might have carried him on the way to the coveted places.

He was a great dandy, and I missed him. His luggage had been a mystery to me, for he apparently carried a roll of blanket only, yet every day in Luxor he had produced new, voluminous clothes, green, purple, and white, and scarves embroidered with gold thread, and leather shoes in purple and yellow. I wished I had his receipt. My own baggage by now had increased considerably, and my supply of orange labels was giving out; I had acquired a gramophone, an ice-box, and a large canvas bag which took the overflow of my books. The gramophone and the ice-box I had accepted in Cairo to save them from being thrown into the Nile; as they had already travelled with forty-seven other pieces of luggage over Tibet on the backs of yaks, I thought it a pity they should not continue their career.

With this paraphernalia I arrived at Port Said; learnt that the ship was late; slept in an hotel on the quay-side; and woke in the morning to find the liner moored under my windows.

. . .

VI

Fever sharpens the wits and improves the perceptions; loneliness performs the same good office. I had no one to talk to, except the captain, a jovial Scotchman who accepted his fate with the usual philosophy of such men. Yes, he said, it could be quite warm enough in the Gulf, certainly; and yes, the monsoons did give you a bit of a dusting. "But it's surprising," he added, "what a hammering a ship will take from the sea and come up smiling." A seafaring life begets, not a lyrical, but a matter-of-fact point of view; there is, mentally, a family likeness among sailors, and this captain reminded me of another one who, on returning a borrowed copy of *Typhoon,* remarked only, "Seems to have been a bit of dirty weather knocking about." The captain, however, had to go back to his bridge and I was left to my own devices. There was not much to look at: Baluchistan was very faint, more like a long, low, pink cloud than solid land, nor had we any prospect of future sights, for the captain told me that we should pass through the narrow Gulf of Oman during the night. Ships seem to take a pleasure in passing during the dark hours any object which might be of interest to their passengers. So my hand flew over the paper, covering sheet after sheet, and a school of porpoises followed the ship, turning over and over because they are still looking for Solomon's ring, which he dropped off his finger in the Persian Gulf. Presently back came the captain, and pointed to the coast. "Persia," he said laconically.

VII

The next two days were rough and cold; no land was in sight; we might have been in the North Sea instead of the Persian Gulf. The fever returned with fury. But I was so elated that I did not care: I had begun a book, and I had seen Persia. Since I might not behold the pearls of Bahrain, I took refuge in the pearls of Proust, heavy on the white throat of the duchesse de Guermantes; I dived into my canvas bag and brought out those shabby volumes which had won me such black looks when they lay scattered round me on the deck of the P. & O.; for although parson and colonel's lady had enough French and enough Biblical knowledge to understand the titles, I doubt whether they had ever heard of Proust; anyway, I fished them out again now, and lost myself in that brilliant world, so real in its unreality. To read of Proust's parties in the Persian Gulf is an experience I can recommend, as a paradox which may please the most fastidious taste. Indeed, I came to believe that every book should be read in the most incongruous surroundings possible, for then it imposes its own unity in a way that startles the reader when he has to emerge again into his own world; thus, when I passed from a ball at the Hotel de Guermantes into the little dining-saloon of S.S. *Varela*, Proust's world was still truer than the ship and I was puzzled to know, really, where I was.

Then we came to Mohammerah, and, with other ships, waited outside the bar till we could begin to go up the Shat-el-Arab. It was then twilight; the ships' lights came out one by one over a wide expanse of water; the smooth sky was streaked with red and orange behind the groves of palms; again it seemed miraculous that the ship should have made her landfall, but less miraculous this time, at the head of a narrow sea, than after the opal wastes of the Indian Ocean. So we waited for a little at the gateway to Iraq, with the engines stilled, in a peace like the peace of a lagoon. Slowly we moved up the river; it was dark by now, and the waterway was narrow: a low coast, thick with groves of date palms, through which we glided all night; from time to time I got up and looked through the porthole, but saw nothing beyond the thick, tall trees, that made an opaque wall along the banks, but whose fronded tops waved gently against a clear sky.

VIII

From Basrah to Bagdad the train runs straight over the desert; yellow, hideous, and as flat as the sea, the desert comes right up to the railway line, and stretches away to the circular horizon, unbroken save by a little scrub, a few leprous patches of salt, or the skeleton of a camel. Once, the monotony is interrupted by a mound: this is Ur of the Chaldees. Otherwise there is nothing. At one station a notice-board says: Change for Babylon. But one does not see Babylon from the train. So I was glad enough to reach Bagdad at seven in the morning, to hear the shouts with which all movement is conducted in the East, and to see the goats picking their way with pastoral simplicity between the railway trucks.

I had had quite enough by then of fending for myself, and wished only to forget about the Persian Gulf and Basrah as quickly as possible; Bagdad to me meant no Arabian Nights, but the much greater and more comforting romance of friends.

This was lucky, for any one who goes to Bagdad in search of romance will be disappointed. The Tigris rushes its yellow flood through the city, and the houses which line its banks share the inevitable picturesqueness of all houses lining a waterway; the round coracles, which cross the river laden with bales and donkeys, swirling in the flood, looking impossibly unseaworthy, have a peculiar character of their own; but for the rest Bagdad is a dusty jumble of mean buildings connected by atrocious streets, quagmires of mud in rainy weather, and in dry weather a series of pits and holes over which an English farmer might well hesitate to drive a waggon. In Bagdad, however, drivers are not so particular. Ford cars, battered, bent, with broken wind-screens and no trace of paint, bump hooting down the street, while camels, donkeys, and Arabs get out of the way, as best they can: any road, in the East, is a road for a motor. I confess that I was startled by the roads of Bagdad, especially after we had turned out of the main street and drove between high, blank walls along a track still studded with the stumps of palm trees recently felled; the mud was not dry here and we skidded and slithered, hitting a tree-stump and getting straightened on our course again, racketing along, tilting occasionally at an angle which defied all the laws of balance, and which in England would certainly have overturned the more conventionally minded motor.

Then: a door in the blank wall, a jerky stop, a creaking of hinges, a broadly smiling servant, a rush of dogs, a vista of garden path edged with carnations in pots, a little verandah and a little low house at the end of the path, an English voice—Gertrude Bell.

I had known her first in Constantinople, where she had arrived straight out of the desert, with all the evening dresses and cutlery and napery that she insisted on taking with her on her wanderings; and then in England; but here she was in her right place, in Iraq, in her own house, with her office in the city, and her white pony in a corner of the garden, and her Arab servants, and her English books, and her Babylonian shards on the mantelpiece, and her long thin nose, and her irrepressible vitality. I felt all my loneliness and despair lifted from me in a second. Had it been very hot in the Gulf? got fever, had I? but quinine would put that right; and a sprained ankle—too bad!—and would I like breakfast first, or a bath? and I would like to see her museum, wouldn't I? did I know she was Director of Antiquities in Iraq? wasn't that a joke? and would I like to come to tea with the King? and yes, there were lots of letters for me. I limped after her as she led me down the path, talking all the time, now in English to me, now in Arabic to the eager servants. She had the gift of making every one feel suddenly eager; of making you feel that life was full and rich and exciting. I found myself laughing for the first time in ten days. The garden was small, but cool and friendly; her spaniel wagged not only his tail but his whole little body; the pony looked over the loose-box door and whinnied gently; a tame partridge hopped about the verandah; some native babies who were playing in a corner stopped playing to stare and grin. A tall, grey saluki came out of the house, beating his tall against the posts of the verandah; "I want one like that," I said, "to take up into Persia." I did want one, but I had reckoned without Gertrude's promptness. She rushed to the telephone, and as I poured cream over my porridge I heard her explaining—a friend of hers had arrived—must have a saluki at once—was leaving for Persia next day—a selection of salukis must be sent round that morning. Then she was back in her chair, pouring out information: the state of Iraq, the excavations at Ur, the need for a decent museum, what new books had come out? what was happening in England? The doctors had told her she ought not to go through another summer in Bagdad, but what should she do in England, eating out her heart for Iraq? Next year, perhaps . . . but I couldn't say she looked ill, could I? I could, and did. She laughed and brushed that aside. Then, jumping up—for all her movements were quick and impatient—if I had finished my breakfast wouldn't I like my bath? and she must go to her office, but would be back for luncheon. Oh yes, and there were people to luncheon; and so, still talking, still laughing, she pinned on a hat without looking in the glass, and took her departure.

I had my bath—her house was extremely simple, and the bath just a tin saucer on the floor—and then the salukis began to arrive. They slouched in, led on strings by Arabs in white woolen robes, sheepishly smiling. Left in command, I was somewhat taken aback, so I had them all tied up to the posts of the verandah till Gertrude should return, an army of desert dogs, yellow, white, grey, elegant, but black with fleas and lumpy with ticks. I dared not go near them, but they curled up contentedly and went to sleep in the shade, and the partridge prinked round them on her dainty pink legs, investigating. At one o'clock Gertrude returned, just as my spirits were beginning to flag again, laughed heartily at this collection of dogs which her telephone message (miraculously, as it seemed to me) had called into being, shouted to the servants, ordered a bath to be prepared for the dog I should choose, unpinned her hat, set down some pansies on her luncheon table, closed the shutters, and gave me a rapid biography of her guests.

She was a wonderful hostess, and I felt that her personality held together and made a centre for all those exiled Englishmen whose other common bond was their service for Iraq. They all seemed to be informed by the same spirit of constructive enthusiasm; but I could not help feeling that their mission there would

have been more in the nature of drudgery than of zeal, but for the radiant ardour of Gertrude Bell. Whatever subject she touched, she lit up; such vitality
was irresistible. We laid plans, alas, for when I should return to Bagdad in the
autumn: we would go to Babylon, we would go to Ctesiphon, she would have
got her new museum by then. When she went back to England, if, indeed, she
was compelled to go, she would write another book. . . . So we sat talking, as
friends talk who have not seen one another for a long time, until the shadows
lengthened and she said it was time to go and see the King.

The King's house lay just outside the town; a wretched building in a sad state
of disrepair, the paving-stones of the terrace forced up by weeds, the plaster flak-
ing off the walls and discoloured by large patches of damp. The King himself
was a tall, dark, slim, handsome man, looking as though he were the prey to a
romantic, an almost Byronic, melancholy; he spoke rather bad French, address-
ing himself in Arabic to Gertrude when his vocabulary failed him. They discussed what linoleum he should have in the kitchen of his new country house.
Then tea was brought in, and a sort of pyramid of fanciful cakes, which delighted Feisal, and they discussed at great length the merits of his new cook.
Gertrude seemed to be conversant with every detail of his housekeeping as well
as with every detail of the government of his kingdom, and to bring as much interest to bear upon the one as upon the other.

His melancholy vanished as she twitted and chaffed him, and I watched them
both—the Arab prince and the Englishwoman who were trying to build up a
new Mesopotamia between them. "You see," she had said to me, "we feel here
that we are trying to do something worth while, something creative and constructive"; and in spite of her deference to his royalty, in spite of the "Sidi" that
now and then she slipped into her conversation, there could be very little doubt
as to which of the two was the real genius of Iraq. As we drove back into Bagdad she spoke of his loneliness; "He likes me to ring up and ask to go to tea,"
she said. I could readily believe it.

Her house had the peculiar property of making one feel that one was a familiar inhabitant; at the end of a day I felt already that I was part of it, like the
spaniel, the pony, and the partridge (the partridge, indeed, slept in my bedroom
that night, on the top of the cupboard); I suppose her life was so vivid, so vital,
in every detail, that its unity could not fail to make an immediate, finished impression on the mind. But I was only a bird of passage. Next evening I left for
Persia, the moon hanging full over Bagdad, and my heart warmed with the anticipation of a return to that friendly little house which now I shall never see
again. The finally selected saluki sat beside me; she must be called Zurcha, said
Gertrude, meaning "yellow one"; in every street café a gramophone brayed,
through the fog of smoke rising from the hubble-bubbles of the Arabs. These

smoky, lighted interiors slid past me as my cab bumped towards the station; but I, clinging on to my bouncing luggage, had no leisure for their tinsel or their discord. What were Arabs to me or I to them, as we thus briefly crossed one another? they in their robes, noble and squalid, of impenetrable life; and I a traveller, making for the station? They had all the desert behind them, and I all Asia before me, Bagdad just a point of focus, a last shout of civilisation, lit by that keen spirit, that active life; and lying for me now—as though I looked down upon it from a height—between Arabia and Asia, midway between a silence and a silence.

CHAPTER V

ROUND TEHERAN

I

This country through which I have been hurled for four days has become stationary at last; instead of rushing past me, it has slowed down and finally stopped; the hills stand still, they allow me to observe them; I no longer catch but a passing glimpse of them in a certain light, but may watch their changes during any hour of the day; I may walk over them and see their stones lying quiet, may become acquainted with the small life of their insects and lichens; I am no longer a traveller, but an inhabitant. I have my own house, dogs, and servants; my luggage has at last been unpacked. The ice-box is in the kitchen, the gramophone on the table, and my books are on the shelves. It is spring; long avenues of judas trees have come into flower along the roads, the valleys are full of peach-blossom, the snow is beginning to melt on the Elburz. The air, at this altitude of nearly four thousand feet, is as pure as the note of a violin. There is everywhere a sense of openness and of being at a great height; that sense of grime and overpopulation, never wholly absent in European countries, is wholly absent here; it is like being lifted up and set above the world on a great, wide roof—the plateau of Iran.

Teheran itself, except for the bazaars, lacks charm; it is a squalid city of bad roads, rubbish-heaps, and pariah dogs; crazy little victorias with wretched horses; a few pretentious buildings, and mean houses on the verge of collapse. But the moment you get outside the city everywhere changes. For one thing, the city remains definitely contained within its mud rampart, there are no straggling suburbs, the town is the town and the country is the country, sharply divided. For another thing, the city is so low that at a little distance it is scarcely visible; it appears as a large patch of greenery, threaded with blue smoke. I call it a city, but it is more like an enormous village. The legend here is, that a certain speculator went to the Shah and said, "King of Kings, if I build you a rampart round your city, will you give me all the land within the rampart that is not yet built over?" and the Shah, thinking the man a fool, agreed. But the man was not a fool, and he built the rampart in so wide a circle that the city has not yet grown out to its walls.

. . .

. . . Such strange things happen in these forgotten regions of the world. As a consequence, all questions of transport furnish an endless topic of conversation. Whether so-and-so will arrive, or some one else be able to leave; whether he is to be expected on the Wednesday or the Thursday; whether the post will come tonight or not until tomorrow morning, or, indeed, be delayed for a week—all these speculations form an integral part of life. Are the floods over the Kasvin road? Has the bridge been swept away again between here and Kum? Then some one comes into the town with news of the road, and the information is passed round by word of mouth to all whom it may concern; and, more or less, and for one reason or another, it concerns everybody. So you get the curious spectacle of silk-hatted gentlemen and upholstered ladies engaged in the discussion of these truly mediaeval difficulties. "He is stuck in the mud in the desert," you hear; "they sent out an aeroplane for him, but that has stuck too." The modern and the mediaeval jostle in the same phrase. It is all taken quite as a matter of course.

So we are at the mercy of snow and flood, and also at the mercy of limp Oriental methods; three cases of wine, despatched from England in October, have not reached Teheran in May. True, they were heard of two months ago, about two hundred miles up the road, but where are they now? Nobody knows. No doubt the camels came on a patch of green, and have been turned out to graze. All that we know for certain is that they were once "seen passing through Hamadan"; the rest is silence. Beyond looking with interest at every camel I meet lurching along the street, and trying to read the address upside down on the crate he bears, I accept this silence with philosophy and drink the amber-coloured wine of Shiraz instead. The post at least arrives with fortnightly regularity, corded on to the splashboards of a muddy motor, an Indian soldier on the box; the headlights stream suddenly down the road, lighting the white trunks of the plane trees, and then there is a scramble to sort the letters as some one empties the bags out on to the table, and every one carries off his budget greedily and jealously, much as a squirrel carries off a nut to his drey. It is almost as hard, in Persia, to believe in the existence of England, as it is, in England, to believe in the existence of Persia; and to piece together, from various letters, what has really been happening to our friends, is like playing a game, or fitting a puzzle:

very neat and fascinating, but hard to conceive of as related to any real life. And yet it has its value, for it cuts a new facet on the gem of friendship; to keep in touch with our friends by means of letters only, shows them to us under a new aspect; they are detached, divorced from the apparatus of personality; appearance, voice, gestures are no longer there to mislead and confuse; what we get is an essence, incomplete certainly, and fragmentary, but pure so far as it goes. Then letters become really an enchanting game; we are compelled to contribute all the resources of our imagination; then we find little scraps put away in our memory, little puzzling scraps, that now fall into place, and we enjoy a triumph that at so remote a distance we should yet have made so illuminating a discovery. We shall go back to our friends treading on firmer ground; not, as might be expected, with a gulf between their life and ours.

But this is the exile's pleasure, and it is not to be hoped that those friends in England, with their full life, should have the time to idle over us as we do over them. Yet this, too, may be turned into a satisfaction, for it puts us into the superior position of having found out a number of things while remaining ourselves undiscovered. Sitting on a rock, with the yellow tulips blowing all about me, and a little herd of gazelle moving down in the plain, I dwell with a new intensity on my friends. I know quite well that they are not thinking of me. But they have become my prey, and they are not there to correct or to contradict. It might well be a little alarming for them, this solitary dissection; much more alarming than gregarious gossip, which is bad enough, and makes most people nervous; but fortunately they know nothing about it, so I have the laugh over them. I hold them here, quite tiny, but bright and sharp, in the merciless space of Persia. All old habits of mind have left me, so that it is possible to approach the old ideas with a new eye. The heart is renewed, and winds have blown away the cobwebs.

I had, however, strolled as far as the gate, with no intention of speaking of any of these things, but the amplitude and leisure of the place lead me into discursiveness; there is no hurry, and very little to do except sit and stare. I do not think it a waste of time to absorb in idleness the austere splendour of this place; also I am aware that its colour stains me through and through. Crudely speaking, the plain is brown, the mountains blue or white, the foothills tawny or purple; but what are those words? Plain and hills are capable of a hundred shades that with the changing light slip over the face of the land and melt into a subtlety no words can reproduce. The light here is a living thing, as varied as the human temperament and as hard to capture; now lowering, now gay, now sensuous, now tender; but whatever the mood may be, it is superimposed on a basis always grand, always austere, never sentimental. The bones and architecture of the country are there, whatever light and colour may sweep across them; a soft thing passing over a hard thing, which is as it should be. The quality of the light suits this country of great distances. Hills a hundred miles away are clearly scored with the clefts of their valleys, so that their remoteness is unbelievable; Demavend himself, seventy miles distant, looks as though he overhung the town, and might at any moment revive, to annihilate it, his dead volcanic fires. The shapes and promontories of the hills grow familiar: the spur which juts out into the plain near Karedj, the claret-coloured spine of Rhey, the great white backbone at the Elburz, beyond which lie the sub-tropical provinces of the Caspian. They stand with the hardness of an old country; one does not feel that here once swayed the sea, not so very long ago, geologically speaking; on the contrary, this plateau is among the ancient places of the earth, and something of that extreme antiquity has passed into its features, into the jagged profile of its rocks, worn by the weather for untold centuries until it could wear them no more—until it had reduced them to the first shape, and whittled them down to a primal design beneath which it was powerless to delve. Age has left only the bones.

Some complain that it is bleak; surely the rich and changing light removes such a reproach. The light, and the space, and the colour that sweeps in waves, like a blush over a proud and sensitive face. Besides, those who say that it is bleak have not looked, or, looking, have not seen. It is, rather, full of life; but that life is tiny, delicate, and shy, escaping the broader glance. Close and constant observation is necessary, for the population changes from week to week, almost from day to day; a shower of rain will bring out a crop of miniature anemones, a day of hot sun will shrivel them; the tortoises will wake with the warmth; the wasteland stirs. It is necessary to look towards the distance, and then into the few square yards immediately beneath the foot; to be at one and the same time long-sighted and near-sighted.

. . .

CHAPTER IX

RUSSIA

I

The countryside had also decked itself for the coronation; all along the roads, where the judas trees had now shed their magenta and clothed themselves in leaf instead, the jasmine and wild roses were in full flower. In the gardens, poor stunted tea-roses that in England would have been torn up by a derisive hand and flung on the bonfire, had for some weeks past been putting forth their blooms; but it is for the exuberance of the native wildling that one must wait before one understands the reputation of Persian roses. Huge bushes, compact, not straggling like the English dog-rose, spattered with flame-coloured blossom; the ground carpeted with fallen petals—this is the first impression, then a closer scrutiny reveals the lovely shape of the separate flower, the pure, early shape of the briar-rose, of a pristine simplicity which our whorled hybrids, superlative though they be, can never excel; and, allied to that early, naked design, a colour such as all our cross-fertilisation fails to produce: the interior of the petal red, but lined with gold, the two together giving a glow of orange, a burning bush. Side by side with these grew the yellow rose, which to me was always the rose of Kum, and the low, shrubby jasmine, and plumes of acacia that scented the air; the brief spring was once more making the most of its allotted season. I could not believe but that the earth was ready to break into other sudden, concealed riches, for I had learnt by now to take nothing on trust, and to ignore the disparagements of other people, for very quickly I had discovered that those who found "nothing to see" were those who did not know how to look; but although equipped with this pharisaical humour, I might no longer indulge it, for the time had come for me to return to England.

Already the promise of summer hung over Persia; the planes were heavy in leaf, and the trickle of water became more persistent, as the gardeners (with one trouser leg rolled up to the thigh, a fashion I could never wholly explain) released the pent-up streams and allowed them to pour over the thirsty beds, or padded bare-footed about the garden, splashing water to lay the dust in the early morning. We no longer courted the sun, but darkened the house all day with reed blinds, raising them only in the evening when the snows of Demavend turned red, and the dusk came quickly, and the little owls began to hoot, and the frogs hopped on the garden path, and the breeze rose and sighed in the planes. The imminence of departure oppressed me; I was beginning to say, "This time next week . . ." and to suffer when I heard people making plans for a date, not very far distant, when I should no longer be there; heartlessly they made their plans, the people for whom life flowed continuous, while I sat by and listened, under sentence of death; then the days began to rush, and the day came which was still an ordinary day for other people, but for me was a day so different. An early start, so like, so unlike, the start for Isfahan; the motor at the door; luggage being carried out; the curtained windows of other houses, whose inhabitants still slept, would sleep for three hours longer, by which time I should be sixty miles away; the early morning life just stirring, the white pony going his rounds with the water-casks; a freshness over everything; the dogs wanting to come; being refused; the servants wishing me a good journey, and bringing me little presents; the fat cook coming out in his white shoes with a basket of little cakes. My room empty upstairs, but my books still on the shelves; my handwriting, reversed, still on the blotting-paper; good-bye, good-bye; for Heaven's sake let us get this over. The guard at the gate saluting, then the streets, the Kasvin gate, the Kasvin road; what a difference, between arrival and departure! *then,* everything had been new, I had looked with curiosity, Demavend himself had had to be pointed out to me and named, I had not known what to expect next round the turn of the road; *now,* everything was a landmark to be left behind, every place had a meaning and an association; there was the shop where we had bought the pots, there was the place of meeting for the paper-chase, there was the track that led up to Var-dar-Var, where we had first found the wild almond in flower, and had marked off an unknown shrub with a ring of stones. Still the donkeys trailed along the road, though camels were few, for they had gone up to Gilan for the spring grazing; and every one I met going towards Teheran I envied; and every one I overtook going towards Kasvin I pitied for being in the same plight as I.

After Kasvin the road was unfamiliar, and the character of the landscape changed with surprising abruptness. We were no longer on the roof; the high, arid plateaus were gone; the vegetation became lush and green, the climate changed from the clear air of four thousand feet to the mild, steamy atmosphere of sub-tropical sea-level. We had dropped from over four thousand feet in a few hours, down a precipitous road into the valley of the White River. The scenery was fine, in its way; groves of trees descended the steep slopes to the banks of the river, and between the trees could be seen green meadows, as green as Devonshire, with cows peacefully grazing or—an odd effect—camels grazing in this Devonshire landscape, as who should come upon a herd of camels in the meadows above the Dart; the valley of the White River had its beauty, but it was not Persia as I understood it, and I resolved that I would never bring any one into Persia for the first time by that road, but would subject them to the rigours of the plains and passes of Kermanshah and Hamadan. Evening fell; we seemed to have been travelling interminably; the continual hairpin corners made driving very tiring; we met strings of hooded waggons, whose miserable teams could scarcely drag them up the hill; men were shouting, and tugging at the bridles, and thrashing the stumbling horses; we got past them all somehow, and drew up in a village by the river where a notice-board proclaimed the Hotel Fantasia.

It was well named, for a crazier building I never saw; an outside staircase, with two steps missing, led up to a wooden balcony, and here we pitched our camp-beds and slept as well as the fleas would allow us. There had been no fleas at Dililjan or at Kum; the rooms there had been bare and clean; it was typical of the difference between that happy and this miserable journey. There, we had gone to sleep conscious of the free space all around us; here, we were in a narrow valley with the river roaring in a brown flood fifty yards away, and no sense of Asia. . . .

SELECTIONS FROM *TWELVE DAYS* (1928)

Long out of print, the highly colorful chapters of Vita's Twelve Days, subtitled in the American edition "An Account of a Journey Across the Bakhtiari Mountains in South-western Persia," figure among her best travel writing. She may not have seen a "pleas-ing curve" in them, or any particular shape, but this most adventuresome of her adventures was clearly worth recording, with its vast spaces and arduous mountains.

TWELVE DAYS

I

For a long time I believed that it would be impossible to make a book out of these experiences; I could see no shape in them, no pleasing curve; nothing but a series of anti-climaxes, and too much repetition of what I had done, and writ-ten down, before. Yet I was loath to let the whole thing go unrecorded. Was it for this that I had gone footsore, cold, hot, wet, hungry? climbed up, and scram-bled down? covered all those miles? looked at all those goats? Surely not. There must be a possible book in it somewhere. The book was always in my mind, teasing at me, and little by little, as time receded, it began to take shape, a mean-ing began to rise up out of the welter, a few definite conclusions which really had some bearing on half-formulated ideas; besides, the fingers which have once grown accustomed to a pen soon itch to hold one again: it is necessary to write, if the days are not to slip emptily by. How else, indeed, to clap the net over the butterfly of the moment? for the moment passes, it is forgotten; the mood is gone; life itself is gone. That is where the writer scores over his fellows: he catches the changes of his mind on the hop. Growth is exciting; growth is dy-namic and alarming. Growth of the soul, growth of the mind; how the obser-vation of last year seems childish, superficial; how this year—even this week—even with this new phrase—it seems to us that we have grown to a new maturity. It may be a fallacious persuasion, but at least it is stimulating, and so long as it persists, one does not stagnate.

I look back as through a telescope, and see, in the little bright circle of the glass, moving flocks and ruined cities.

II

There they are, a long way off, and looking at the map of Asia, a kind of awe comes over me that I should be able to visualise the place represented by a name in cold black print. I know how vast are the spaces which on the map cover one inch. I know how high and arduous are the mountains which on the map deepen only into a stronger shade of brown. I think of life going on there, the same today as when I, so briefly, brushed past it. The nomads are on the move; their black tents dot the plain; the fierce dogs rush out barking, as a wild figure on horseback gallops up and flings himself from the saddle. At night the black tents cower between red fires. It is exactly the same for them this year as last, and the days which stand out so vividly for me were for them merely the uncalendared days of ordinary existence. Malamir today scorches in the sun. Do-Pulan sleeps in the shadow of the hill by the banks of the Karoun. In the dripping gorge below Gandom Kar the crown imperials rear their brilliant orange among the rocks.

The Bakhtiari country. "Bakhtiari," says the *Encyclopaedia Britannica,* "are one of the great nomad tribes of Persia." It goes on to mention the Haft-lang and the Chahar-lang as the two main divisions of the tribe; it records a stormy and blood-stained history. "Here," says Lord Curzon, "in a *mise en scène* which unites all the elements of natural grandeur—snowy crags, rugged hills, mountain ravines—are the *yelaks* or summer quarters of the tribes." Alas, how bleak and brief is the written word.

One of the great nomad tribes of Persia, the Bakhtiari are Lurs, but who the Lurs are and whence they came, as Lord Curzon says, is one of the unsolved riddles of history. "A people without a history, a literature, or even a tradition," he says, "presents a phenomenon in face of which science stands abashed. Are they Turks? Are they Persians? Are they Semites? All three hypotheses have been urged. They appear to belong to the same ethnical group as the Kurds, their neighbours on the north; nor does their language, which is a dialect of Persian, differ materially from the Kurdish tongue. On the other hand, they consider it an insult to be confounded with the Kurds, whom they call Leks; and the majority of writers have agreed in regarding them as the veritable relics of the old Aryan or Iranian stock, who preceded Arabs, Turks, and Tartars in the land. Whilst, however, we may accept this as the most probable hypothesis, and may even be led thereby to regard with heightened interest these last survivals of an illustrious stock, we are not compelled to endorse the conjectural connection of Bakhtiari with Bactria, which has been propounded by some writers, or to localise their ancestral home. (Some have gone so far as to base on this resemblance the assertion that the Bakhtiari are the relics of one of the Greek colonies left by Alexander in Asia, an hypothesis for which the further support is claimed of a similarity in the Greek and Bakhtiari national dances.) It is sufficient to believe that they are Aryans by descent, and to know that they have lived for centuries in their present mountains." Rawlinson, who travelled among the Bakhtiari, characterised them as "the most wild and barbarous of all the inhabitants of Persia"; but we, making plans for our expedition, were less interested in the history and nature of the tribe than in the road which we should have to travel.

We had spent many an evening in Teheran, poring over maps and discussing our journey across the Bakhtiari country. It had not been easy to get information; the maps were most inadequate; there seemed to be no books in Teheran available on the subject of more recent date than Sir Henry Layard's, which related an expedition undertaken in 1840, nor were there any Europeans in Teheran who had travelled over the Bakhtiari Road. We had to rely on a few letters, none of which were very reassuring. A young officer in the Indian Army wrote that he had never been so exhausted in his life, and other accounts spoke of precipices and crazy bridges, and swirling rivers to ford—all of which, save for the wail about exhaustion, proved to be completely misleading. Travellers like to exaggerate the perils they have run; so, not to fall into the common error, I say at the outset that never at any moment were our brittle limbs in the slightest danger. The Bakhtiari Road, certainly, is not for those who like a country stroll; but it may be undertaken by the most cowardly if they are but sufficiently active. Indeed, the only intrepidity which we displayed was our determination to go despite the romantic discouragement which we received.

The Bakhtiari Khans living in Teheran gave a different account of their own country. Either they were loath to acknowledge that their famous Road was not made of asphalt, or else in the amiable mendacious way of the East they wished to flatter our ears with pleasant hearing; I remember that on asking one of them if it was possible to ride over the Road, or if one must go on foot, I obtained the startling reply, "Ride? but you can go in a motor!" Now this was not true. It was indeed magnificently untrue: it was a lie on the grand scale. By courtesy it is known as the Bakhtiari Road, but actually it is a trail, a track, which leads, now up, now down, over wild and mountainous country; and as for wheeled traffic, no one could push even a wheelbarrow over it. My neighbour at dinner must have known how soon and how thoroughly his words would be disproved; but after the manner of his race he no doubt thought it more agreeable to produce a comfortable impression at the moment, leaving the future to take care of itself. Familiar with the Persian habit, I forbore from argument. Sitting there at dinner in the sumptuous house of the rich Khans, the Road seemed remote enough; a large façade of civilisation seemed to have been erected, a façade built up out of the French language, poker and poker chips, and the innovation by which the Persians laid aside their *kolahs* after dinner; but behind it rose the mountains which turned all this sophistication to a sham. The Salon pictures of 1880, the candelabra, the ormolu, even the acetylene lamps on the table—giving a glaring white light and known frequently to explode—could not wholly eliminate the sense of a certain primitive, feudal organisation in the background—the source of wealth, the domain and territory where our suave hosts abandoned their pretences, and went back to the brutalities they had known as little boys. Those carpets hanging on the walls, those amorini, that representation of Omar accepting a draught of wine from the cup-bearer—those had been woven by women of the tribes, rocking a cradle with one hand while with the other they threaded the swift shuttle. Soft and polite, our hosts had, elsewhere, a complete, separate existence. They had no intention of talking about it. Of course not. The Road? The Bakhtiari Road? Why, you can go by motor. Who among us betrays his family secrets to a stranger? All is for the best; and we talk least about what we know most intimately. In fact, the more glibly a man talks, the more you may mistrust his knowledge. Complete, detailed intimacy begets reticence. The mountains rise in the background, willy-nilly; but they are blocked out by the poker-chips; it is the façade which we all put up.

Little by little, our expedition began to take shape. The dates were settled and a letter despatched to Isfahan ordering tents and mules. Our Bakhtiari friends in Teheran promised us an escort. (An escort? Here was a hint, surely, that the Road was not quite the Route Nationale they would have us believe?) We dragged out our camp equipment, and sorted it on the landing at the top of the stairs: two beds, two sleeping-bags, a Rawkee chair, a folding table, a green canvas bucket, two felt-covered water bottles, a blue tin basin. My camera. My films, in tin cylinders. An amphora full of apricot jam. So much, and no more, would Harold Nicolson and I provide. Our dogs nosed round uneasily, scenting departure. Meanwhile, the caravan increased: to Harold Nicolson, Gladwyn Jebb, and myself, the original three, were added Copley Amory from the American Legation in Teheran, and Lionel Smith, who by letter announced his intention of coming up from Baghdad to join us; so that altogether we were five Europeans setting out on the Bakhtiari Road.

. . .

XI

Down at the foot of the hill, in the gorge where the bright-green river crept between the rocks, we halted and looked up at the hill we had to climb. The whole hillside was noisy with bleatings. It seemed, as we gazed upwards at the trail, that the hillside was in fact coming down upon us; as though the stones and boulders had been loosened, and leapt down the hill, now singly, now in a moving flood, pouring down steadily from the very summit, with incessant cries among the stunted oaks. Far overhead, in the blue, planed a couple of eagles. The morning sun blazed still in the east, throwing long blue shadows on the distant snow-mountains. And the air was filled with the distressful cries of the flock as they poured down the precipitous slopes, driven onward by the voice of the shepherds.

Twice a year, in spring and autumn, the tribes move. In spring they go up from the scorched plains towards which we ourselves were travelling, to the higher plains of Chahar Mahal; in the autumn they come down again, driving all their possessions before them, over the two hundred miles of the road. And here were we in the midst of them—very literally in the midst, for the flocks surged round our mules, making progress impossible, and we had to sit patient in the saddle, looking down upon the sea of backs, till the way was cleared and the mules were able to scramble a few yards further, up the steep rocky tract, with a sudden straining of the muscles, a sudden putting forth of strength; and when we stopped again, the green river below us seemed a little further away, the beat of the sun a little more powerful. We were going against all that moving life . . . we ourselves felt pleasantly exalted by the flattery of travelling in the opposite direction.

So many thousand faces. The long, silly faces of sheep, the satyric faces of goats with their little black horns; the patient faces of tiny donkeys, picking their way under their heavy loads; . . . a litter of puppies slithering about on a mule's pack, a baby in a cradle slung across its mother's shoulders. The hens travelled too, perched on the back of a donkey. Behind each separate herd—for each herd, in its way, represented a self-contained little family—came the men, beating the stragglers up with sticks and uttering strange cries which the beasts recognise and obey; then came the women, also beating up the stragglers, young women in bright red and yellow shawls, old women who must have crossed the mountains a hundred times. They were all too weary or too apathetic to stare much at us. Some, indeed, stopped us to make a practical enquiry: was the snow deep on the passes? were the rivers in flood? was the mud bad? for we had come down the way they must go up, and in those hills news circulates only by word of mouth. We reassured them; they nodded dully, and passed on.

We had come down the way that they must go up, and knew the exhaustion that lay before them, the passes to be climbed, the steep descents that would lead them down on the other side, the changes of weather, the long stretches up the ravines where the greasy mud checks every footstep. But for us, each difficulty conquered was conquered for ever and left behind; we should not pass that way again. For them it was different. It was only one journey among many journeys, renewed twice a year from the cradle to the grave.

. . .

The men who drive the flocks are tired. The women who follow the men are tired too; often they have just become, or are on the point of becoming, mothers. The children who drag along after their parents limp and whimper. To us,

who come from Europe, there is something poetic in a Persian shepherd calling
to his goats and sheep; but the Persian shepherd himself sees nothing except the
everyday business of getting a lot of tiresome animals along. Since romance is
the reality of somewhere else or of some other period, here, on the Bakhtiari
Road, this truth is doubly applicable. Persia is certainly somewhere else, and a
long way, too, in relation to England, and this Biblical form of existence certainly belongs to a period other than the twentieth century—it is an anachronism in our eyes, and therefore romantic; the double elements of space and
time, geographical and chronological, necessary to romance, are thus amply satisfied. We are on the Bakhtiari Road, in one of the wildest parts of Persia; let us
accept it at its face value, and see what is to be got out of it in terms of the picturesque. Let us be quite cynical about it; let us, by all means, be romantic while
we may.

The hillside, then, is alive with flocks. "Baa-a-a!" go the sheep, and "Meh-h-
h!" go the goats. They bleat, they bleat; even today, in England, when a flock of
sheep is turned loose into the meadow at the bottom of my garden, and their
bleatings reach me, I whirl back to the Murvarid Pass, and feel the sun hot on
my hands; a queer sensation, analogous to that sensation with which one wakes
at night convinced that one's bed has turned itself round the other way. There
are thousands of them, jostling, leaping, hustling each other among the boulders. Some of them are very lame, but what of that? That is reality, not romance;
lame or not lame, they must go forward. There are two hundred miles to cover
before the sun gets too hot and the already scant pasture shrivels up. So the shepherds come after them with sticks. "Oh," say the shepherds—a flat, English
"Oh" that sounds curiously out of place on the Persian hills. Oh. A real Cock-
ney vowel. But the beasts respond. They leap forward as if in terror. We, on our
mules, sit motionless while they huddle by. The men take very little notice of us,
unless they stop to ask a question; they do not seem to notice that we are Europeans, and, as such, figures of romance to them, surely, coming as we do from
another place? No, to them we are simply a caravan travelling in the opposite direction, an obstacle, albeit a patient and long-suffering obstacle, to be passed.
Oh. And the sea of backs surges round the legs of our mules. The smell of fleeces
comes up to us, acrid. The men follow, in their blue linen coats and high black
felt hats, and their sticks fall with a thud on the woolly backs. Oh. The sun is
hot and high. The jade-green river flickers in the sun down in the ravine. The
snow-mountains stretch out like a spine in the distance. An old woman passes
us on foot, carrying across her shoulders a limp baby donkey. Some squawking,
flapping hens pass, perched on a load of pots and pans on a pony's back. A litter of puppies, that presently will be savage, camp-guarding dogs, but now are
round, woolly, and frightened, pass clinging and sliding on another pack. They

try to growl as they go by, but without much conviction. A child passes, beating up his flock of lambs and kids—youth put in charge of youth. Oh. And then a fresh shower of sheep and goats, animated boulders. How stony the road is! How slow our progression! Come along, come, along. Oh.

This, then, was life shorn of all mechanical ingenuity. One forgets too readily that there are still places in the world which civilisation has been utterly unable to touch. Even the wheel, most elementary of mechanical devices, here did not, could not, exist. Dawn, the hour at which one started; dusk, the hour at which one stopped; springs, at which one drank; beasts of burden, to which one bound one's moving home; a beast from the flock, which one slaughtered and ate fresh; fire; a story; sleep. There was nothing else.

In the evenings we saw the nomads under a different aspect, when we had pitched our own camp, squatting by their black tents, the smoke of their pipes rising upwards with the smoke of their fires, while the women cooked and the animals strayed browsing. It was then, when they were at rest, and the sense of their weary progress was suspended, that the charm of a pastoral existence reasserted itself. Along the road, one was conscious only of harshness, violence, and fatigue. The limping horse, the dying ram, the woman near to her delivery, the man with his foot bound up in bloody rags—all these were painful sights, made more painful by the knowledge that there could be no respite and no relief. But in the evenings, in some quiet valley, with a spring gushing from a rock near by, and the moon newly risen from behind the hill, then the world did indeed seem to have returned to an early, limpid simplicity. Theocritus and the Bible took on a fresh and more vivid significance. The pastoral and the patriarchal, ceasing to be decorative merely as a convention of literature, became desirable also as a part of life.

Meanwhile we climbed for most of that day, conquering step by step the Murvarid Pass, only to drop down again, having reached the top; and as evening fell we came down on the lovely valley of Deh Diz, with its single sentinel poplar and a ruined castle in the distance, and the long ridge of the snowy Kuh-i-Mangasht beyond. Our camping-place this time was in an orchard of pomegranates, beside a clear mountain stream, on a grassy terrace strewn with rocks and boulders. The ropes had already been untied; the packs had fallen to the ground; the men were bending over them sorting out our possessions; the little brown lamb which the Khans had given us, and which had trotted meekly all day beside our caravan, was hanging dead and skinned from a bough with a drop of blood at the end of its nose; a thread of blue smoke was already rising from our kitchen. The evening was very soft and serene, the surrounding hills enormous and shadowy. A sense of peace crept over our weary limbs, and a sense of sudden intimacy with this quiet spot, which none of us, almost certainly, would ever see again. Already its contours were familiar, and someone had picked a handful of the little wild pink gladiolus, and put it in a glass on our rickety camp table. It is curious how quickly, in this kind of life, any resting place becomes home. It is as though the mind, instinctively rejecting the implication of transitoriness, sought, by an excessive adaptability, for compensation. Yet we knew that when we left at daybreak on the following morning, no trace would remain of our passage but the blackened ring of our dead camp fire and four squares of trodden grass, that were the floor of our tents. The golden oriole will return to the myrtle bough, and the spring will bubble without any memory of those who stooped to fill their cups.

XII

But we were not destined to leave Deh Diz on the following morning. As we were sitting round the fire after dinner, we heard a distant clap of thunder, and the muleteers came running up to say that a storm was upon us. From the minutes between a flash of lightning and the next clap, we reckoned that we had twenty minutes in which to prepare. Everybody ran in different directions—some to knock the picket-pegs of the mules firmer into the ground, others to perform the same office for the tent-ropes, others to dig little trenches round the tents, others to carry our dinner table into shelter. Scarcely were we ready for the storm when it burst upon us. We five had all gathered together into the biggest tent, and as the storm crashed above us we hung on to the tent-pole with our united strength, expecting every moment to be carried away, tent and all, in the sudden gale of wind that tore screaming up the valley. The hail came down in torrents, battering on the canvas, and we thought thankfully of our little hastily dug trenches. Peeping through the flap, we could see the valley wholly illuminated by the magnificent flashes, with which the thunder was now continuous; the snow on the distant ranges gleamed white, and the valley showed an unearthly green, as the sky was torn asunder as with a swift and golden sword. The storm swept on; we heard it cracking over the hills; it was as though the wheels of a great chariot had driven over us, in the heavens, and were now rolling onwards, above the oak forests and the black tents of the crouching nomads, describing great circles, and returning now and then to visit our camp at intervals through the night.

XIII

When we looked out in the morning, we saw to our astonishment that the ground was white with snow. There was no chance of continuing our journey that day: the mules could never have carried the weight of the soaking tents. We were condemned to a day of inactivity at Deh Diz. By ten o'clock, however, a warm sun had melted all the snow and the tents were steaming like the flanks of a horse. We hung all the wet things we could find on the tent-ropes to dry, and stretched ourselves on rugs in the sun, to the delight of a circle of inquisitive villagers. It was a change to spend such a lazy day. We read the Apocrypha, I remember, and wandered a little, but not very far afield, not much further than the spring where we refilled our water bottles; we admired the village giant, a grand figure at least seven foot high; we talked with a wandering dervish, who strayed up to our camp carrying a sort of sceptre, surmounted by the extended hand of Ali in shining brass; we listened to a blind man chanting an interminable poem about hazrat-i-ísá (his Majesty Jesus); we watched the procession of women going to the spring. They crept past, with their empty goat-skins, stealing furtive glances at us out of their long dark eyes; then scurried on, in a burst of mischievous giggling, like a lot of children caught in a conspiracy. Presently they returned in a more sober mood, weighted down by the heavy, black, dripping goat-skins that lay shining across their shoulders and drenched their blue rags. We watched them, as one watches shy animals creeping out of a wood—the wood of their secret, unrevealed lives, spent in the mud-houses of Deh Diz, among bickerings and jealousies and hardships, crouched over a pot on a smoking fire, to the upraised voice of the mother-in-law, and the cry of the child, till the figure of a man darkened the entrance, and a babble arose, and a clutching for the partridges he carried in his hand. Very secretive they looked, as cunning as slaves and as silly as children, but pretty under their snoods of blue, with the characteristic surreptitious walk of those who go barefooted under heavy burdens. So we idled, becoming acquainted with the habits of village life in Deh Diz, while our mules wandered loose among the pomegranates, cropping at the grass, and the eagles circled high over the hills where the gladiolus and the gentian grew.

XIV

The stage between Deh Diz and Qaleh Madresseh lay through the most beautiful country we had as yet seen. We were now in the very heart of the ranges. The road after first leaving Deh Diz is rather dull; it follows the valley, in a switchback of small descents and small ascents, wearisome and monotonous. We had to find our interest where best we could—in immediate anticipation of the future, and distant memorials of the past—that is, in a man ploughing with two bullocks amongst a scatter of boulders, yelling and groaning at his beasts, as his primitive plough jerked up and down the slope, turning the sod which perhaps would grow him a handful of corn in autumn, perhaps, and perhaps not—in a wayside cemetery, where among blood-red poppies stone lions of archaic design commemorated the valour of bygone Bakhtiari. Poignant little cemeteries, these, lost in the hills. Lions used to abound in these mountains, and the Bakhtiari, when they did not want to fight the lion, had a special code for dealing with him. Lions were of two kinds, they said: Moslems and infidels. They might be known by their colour, the Moslem having a bright yellow coat, the infidel a darker coat, with a black mane. On meeting the Moslem it was sufficient to say, "O cat of Ali, I am the servant of Ali," when the lion would retire into the mountains. On meeting the infidel, however, the wisest course was to take to your heels.

Lions are reported even today in the Pusht-i-Kuh, the range stretching to the northwest of the Bakhtiari range, and bears are known to exist still in the Bakhtiari country; and leopards, notably the snow-leopard, but we never saw so much as the spoor of any such animal. Wolves, lynxes, and hyenas were also common in Layard's [18th-century English archaeologist] day, adding to the dangers which that indubitably brave man had to face whenever he set out, sometimes alone, sometimes with a guide whom he justifiably mistrusted, to look for tombs or inscriptions among the unmapped hills and valleys. I thought of Layard often as I rode along. It is easy enough to confront dangers when one is in perfect health, but Layard himself never knew when an attack of ague would not compel him to dismount, and, lying on the ground with his horse's bridle fastened to his wrist, spend two or three hours in delirium and unconsciousness. An unpleasant predicament, in a country infested by murderers, marauders, and wild animals. A brave man, I thought, as I looked at the stone lions among the poppies.

By midday, we had rejoined the Karoun, and were riding along a rocky path sheer above the river, which presently brought us to the splendid gorge of Pul-i-Godar. Here the Karoun winds between pointed hills, to lose itself again in the intricacy of the ranges. We left it far below us, for after Pul-i-Godar the track rose steeply, bringing us to the top of a pass, with truly splendid views over the tumbled country. Strange geological convulsions had heaved up the hills; the strata, which were as definitely marked as though they had been gigantic slates laid flat one against the other, stood up on end instead of lying horizontally superimposed; in some of the hills the lines of strata were actually vertical, in others they were aslant, so that one could imagine one saw the huge processes still at work. In the course of ages, those masses of rock would shift under the weight of some unseen pressure; that which was now oblique would become perpendicular, and that which was now perpendicular would gradually heel over until it slanted to the opposite side. These mountains were being slowly turned upside down. It was not so much the grandeur of the landscape which impressed one—though that was sublime enough—as the awful evidence of nature labouring on a cosmic scale. The wild loneliness of the place, the ramifications of the valleys leading up into unknown fastnesses, the track made by generations of men crossing the mountains—all this produced a sense of some elemental strength which excited and yet sobered the imagination.

And now came the tribes, the slow-moving, inevitable tribes, winding up through the hills in a long and constant stream. Dwarfed though they were by their native scenery, dwarfed into crawling battalions along the narrow ledges, they still seemed an integral part of the country. It seemed right that these mountains should witness their pilgrimage in the two temperate seasons, and right also that the mountains should be left to their own loneliness during the violence of summer and the desolation of winter. On the Murvarid Pass we had met the tribes coming down upon us; now, as we made our way down into the valley towards Qaleh Madrasseh, we met them coming up towards us, their up-turned glances swiftly reckoning the best way to pass, their animals struggling up from rock to rock. Down, down, round the hairpin bends, seeing the path far below, still covered with that moving life; down, right down, into the valley where the black tents were plentifully sprinkled about. Then—rest, on an open grassy space hemmed in by hills; another day was over.

But Rahim, the well-meaning and unfortunate, tripped over a tent-rope and upset our soup.

XV

What would happen to oneself, I wonder, if one were to spend a long time in such a place as Qaleh Madrasseh? A week, a month, a year, thirty years? Thirty years. If one were to go there at the age of thirty, and remain fixed till one was sixty—the most important years of life drifting by at Qaleh Madrasseh? One would explore the paths running up into the mountains, mere goat-tracks; one would come to some unmapped village; one would meet and talk with a number of fresh, ignorant, and unsophisticated people. One would come to know every wild flower in its season, and every change of light. But what would happen inside oneself? That is really the important thing. The only goat-tracks one wants to explore are the goat-tracks of the mind, running up into the mountains; the only sophistication one really wants to escape from is one's own. To start afresh; unprejudiced; untaught. Changes of light, coming from the internal illumination, not from the play of limelight over a ready-set scene. Away from papers, away from talk (though not, I stipulate, wholly away from books); cast back on personal resources, personal and private enjoyments.

Thirty years at Qaleh Madrasseh.

Of what is civilised life composed? Of movement, news, emotions, conflict, and doubt. I think these headings may be expanded to fit every individual requirement? Now at Qaleh Madrasseh most of them would be deleted: movement certainly, except such slow and contemplative movement as could be performed on one's own legs; news certainly, except such local and practical news as would brush one in passing by word of mouth. But what of the growth of the mind? The mind would have only its own rich pasture to browse upon. It would rise superior even to these tribes flowing backwards and forwards—and in the space of thirty years it would witness the flowing of the tide sixty times—it would be filled with the sense of its own inexhaustible riches, dependent upon no season, dependent upon no change of pasture from Malamir to Chahar Mahal, no exchanging of the south for the north. The mind would browse and brood; sow and reap. Few of us have known such leisure. Those who achieve it are called eccentrics for their pains: it seems to me that they are among the wise ones of the earth. The world is too much with us, late and soon; we are too stringily entangled in our network of obligations and relationships.

. . .

But I, when I say Qaleh Madrasseh, mean Qaleh Madrasseh. I mean that exact spot, whose contours I have learnt, whose clefts I have contemplated, enviously, running up into the mountains and had no leisure to explore. So far, at least, I am on solid ground. But of the effect of solitude in such a place I know no more than did Marlowe or Milton. That is a speculation which, no doubt, would never have occurred to either of those great poets or to their humbler contemporaries; they had not acquired the habit of playing with hypothetical complications as we have acquired it. The very mention of the name sufficed, Persepolis and Parthia, Ternate and Tidore, to hang an agreeably rosy veil between themselves and reality; it brushed an Orient glow across their pages; they felt no need to follow up the implications to their logical conclusion. Had anyone suggested their visiting Parthia or Persepolis, Tidore or Ternate, they would no doubt have recoiled in dismay. For one thing, they probably had but a very vague idea of where these places were situated. But I protest that, did occasion offer, I would eagerly embrace those thirty years at Qaleh Madrasseh, though with an equally vague idea of what the consequences might be. What, for instance, would become of one's capacity for emotion? Would it become stultified through disuse, or sharpened through denial? What would become of one's power for thought? Would that become blunted, in the absence of any whetstone whereon to grind itself? Or would a new, high wisdom arise, out of an inhuman sense of proportion, accomplishing nothing and desirous of no achievement, but attaining through contemplation a serene and perfectly tolerant estimate of the frailties of mankind? For one would arrive at Qaleh Madrasseh, at the beginning of the thirty years' seclusion, not as an Oriental mystic, having no experience of the world of intellect, vanity, and science, but as a fully mapped exile from a European state in the agonies of its striving after civilisation. Glutted and weary with information, confused with creeds, the old words knocking against one another in the brain and producing no more than a tinny clatter, one would settle down either to a stagnant repose or else to a concentrated readjustment of values.

The very idea of stagnant repose being execrable, one repudiates it without further consideration. Thus one is left exiled at Qaleh Madrasseh with an army of facts waiting to be drilled into order. Facts—that incongruous assortment which accumulates—snippets of knowledge, fragments of observation, fleeting theories no sooner formed than discarded, ideas as self-contradictory as proverbs—at last one would have time to marshal all this into some sort of formation. An army indeed; and every unit as complicated as the soldier himself, as intricate and capable of as many interpretations. Personal conceit, however, suggests that one would deal successfully with the matter; so successfully that at the end of the thirty years one would emerge upon the world crying with a voice as the voice of a prophet.

. . .

XVI

I observe, however, in some dismay, looking back over these pages, that I have given an entirely wrong impression of the Bakhtiari mountains. I have, unintentionally, represented them as over-built and populous; I have mentioned villages; I have mentioned a merchant on his horse, a man ploughing, the son of the Il-Khani, the keepers of a *chai-khaneh*. All this, in the aggregate, must I fear have given the impression of a walking-tour through some part of Europe, with never more than a few niggardly miles intervening between one reminder of civilisation and the next. Nothing could be further from the truth. By the very use of the word village, with its associations in an English mind, I have probably evoked a picture of something much larger, more orderly, and more definite than is justified by the few poor hovels of Naghan or Do-Pulan. For the rest, our path lay along miles of country where not so much as a mud hut was visible. The merchant, the man ploughing, were figures so isolated and so exceptional that I have recorded them as it were greedily, for the sake of having something human to record. They were—let me emphasise it—isolated instances; and, as such, they made an impression on us which in the swarming countries to which we Europeans are accustomed they would not have made. No, the dominant impression was one of isolation. True, we were on the Road; we met an occasional traveller; we met the migrating tribes; but we knew that to the left hand or the right lay utter solitude; the solitude of nature, which draws us and holds us with a primitive, an indefensible attraction, all of us, however sophisticated we may be. And it was a double impression: of isolation and anachronism. Not only had we gone far away in distance; we had also gone far back in time. We had returned, in fact, to antiquity. We were travelling as our ancestors had travelled; not those immediate ancestors who rolled in their coaches between London and Bath, or between Genoa and Rome; but as Marco Polo had travelled, or Ovid going into exile, or the Ten Thousand hoping for the sea. We learnt what the past had been like; and what the world had been like when it was still empty. Time was held up and values altered; a luxury which may be indulged today by anyone who travels into the requisite parts of Asia. More: we knew that had we not elected to travel the Bakhtiari Road at that particular time of the year, we should not have met even the tribes, but should have had the mountains all to ourselves, eccentric invaders of majestic desolation. No merchant would have overtaken us beneath the oaks, no peasant groaned behind his plough. We should have topped the pass above Deh Diz and seen not only the lonely range of the Kuh-i-Mangasht, but known that in the whole of that valley no human being drew breath. Those whom we did meet were as transient as ourselves; the only permanence was in the hills and in the rivers that coiled about their base.

. . .

XVIII

A disagreement arose next morning between us and our muleteers. From notes which we had accumulated from other travellers we had decided to make for a place called Murdafil. The muleteers, however, denied the existence of any such place, and declared, moreover, that we should find no water except at the place they wished to go to, called Agha Mihrab. Gladwyn Jebb, who managed all that part of the expedition with a calm and haughty efficiency, would have nothing to do with their arguments. To Murdafil we intended to go, and to Murdafil consequently we were going. We set off from Malamir on a hot morning, through rolling country where the vegetation was far richer and more interesting than it had been in the hills. Orchises, iris, anemones, borage, convolvulus, Star of Bethlehem, gladiolus, eremurus grew everywhere in great profusion; and on a slope I found to my joy the little scarlet tulip for which I had looked in vain in other parts of Persia. The white, starry tulip, and the yellow tulip had been common, but so far the scarlet one had eluded me. There it was, blood-red in the sun, and I took the bulbs, and stuck the flowers into the harness of the patient Mouse.

As we drew near to the end of our day's march, wondering whether we should indeed find Murdafil or whether we should be compelled to camp in some waterless place, and own ourselves defeated, we came to a sloping valley down which rushed a stream overhung by oleanders and pampas grass. The whole character of the country had altered, and by nothing was it so well indicated as by this complete change in the vegetation, so rich and green that we might almost imagine ourselves in the tropics after the severe aridity we had hitherto associated with Persia. Just above the stream we presently descried the ruins of some small building, where we decided to camp for the night; yes, said the muleteers with smug satisfaction, this was Agha Mihrab, the site they had recommended. We gave up Murdafil with as good a grace as possible, though we were sure they had deliberately and obstinately misled us. There was certainly nothing to complain of in the site: the ruins were raised up on a little natural terrace, in the midst of what had once been a garden, for some old, unpruned rose bushes grew rampant, and down in a dip grew a grove of dark myrtle. Wandering off while the monotonous process of unpacking began, we came on a waterfall that splashed down over a high wall of rock, and here we found a goatherd piping to his goats. What was the name of the ruined caravanserai we had passed some way down the road? we asked him, and received the reply, Murdafil. We were amused rather than irritated by this characteristic example of the working of the Persian mind; for the muleteers must have known perfectly well that we should find them out in their lie, and that we should establish not only the existence of a place called Murdafil, but also the fact that it lay by a stream of clear mountain water. But when we taxed them with the lie, they only put on a blank expression and shrugged their shoulders.

It was very warm and peaceful at Agha Mihrab. I remember the place with affection and gratitude, as one of those memories which nothing can take away. The note of the goatherd's reedy flute rose above the sound of the waterfall, and mingled with the other sounds of night: the snap of a burnt stick, the tinkle of a mule's bell, the croaking of a thousand frogs down by the stream. We had been sitting in silence round the fire, smoking, while Venus travelled slowly across the sky and now was about to dip behind the hill. I knew that by climbing the hill opposite I could still see Venus for a little longer, in all the splendour of the clear, black night. But I was too tired. Better to let the day go out quietly, when Venus was thus silently extinguished; better to let it go out on the note of the flute, as the red fires burnt low in the valley, and the nomads wrapped themselves in their cloaks and slept.

. . .

XXIII

I see now that although I started this book with little hope of making it into anything more than the mere record of an expedition, it has almost of its own accord assumed a certain shape, and piled itself up into two main blocks, or-dained by the force of contrast. Two different communities have crossed the stage; the one weary, ignorant, and poor; the other energetic, scientific, and prosperous; but both equally enslaved by the habit of their different modes of thought. I wish I could say that my impartiality had been such that the reader is unable to tell which way my sympathies lie. It seems fitting that it should con-clude with yet a third image—the representation neither of an anachronistic ex-istence nor of a modern civilisation. The pastoral tribes have streamed by, simple survivals from a lost world; the steam-hammers have thudded round the site of what was once the Temple of Fire; now it is time to see what becomes of em-pires as arrogant as the British and, on so oracular a note, to end.

Persepolis is particularly suitable for such a purpose—to stand midway be-tween the Bakhtiari country and the outposts of England as typified by the Anglo-Persian Oil Company. It is suitable because, although it was once the cap-ital of the Persian Empire, its ruins now lie among surroundings as primitive as the plain of Malamir. The gaunt columns remain, thrusting up at the sky, but of the site of the city of Istakhr there is nothing but the nibbled grass. Persepo-lis gains in splendour from its isolation. Not another building stands anywhere near it; not a hut, not a guard-house, not a shepherd's shelter; only the vast green plain, encircled by mountains and the open sky and the hawks that wheel and hover between the columns. As a ship launching out on an expanse of sea, the great terrace drives forward on to the plain, breasting it, the columns rising like naked spars into the clear blue of the sky. At first sight it may seem smaller than one had expected to find it, but that is due to the immensity of the plain and to the mass of the hill against which it is pushed up. The terrace, in fact, juts squarely out, backing against the hill as though for defence; but the effect is less of a seeking for defence than of an imperial launching of defiance, a looking-out across the plain, a raised domination above the level ground: the throne of kings overhanging the dwellings of the people. But the dwellings of the people which once spread over the plain have disappeared, and nothing of the royal capital re-mains but the ruins that were once the citadel of Xerxes and Darius; the dwellings of the people, no doubt, were made of wattle and sun-dried bricks, ephemeral material, whereas the kings glorified themselves in stone. A thousand years, I suppose, will level the disparity between them. The propylaea of Xerxes, the palace of Darius, will have enjoyed a few thousand more years of survival than sun-baked bazaars which sheltered the potter and the barber.

So stands Persepolis, looking out over the deserted plain. The space, the sky, the hawks, the raised-up eminence of the terrace, the quality of the Persian light, all give to the great terrace a sort of springing airiness, a sort of treble, to which the massive structure of bastion and archways plays a corrective bass. It is only when you draw near that you realise how massive that structure really is. It has all the weight of the Egyptian temples; square, monolithic. The terrace itself is supported on enormous blocks, its angles casting square shadows; a double stairway climbs it, a stairway that at its landing-place is superbly dominated by huge winged bulls. Now you are in the midst of the ruins: the columns soar, supporting no roof; square doorways open, leading into no halls. (But see, within the jamb of one doorway is carved a king wrestling with a lion, and within another a king stepping forward under the shade of a parasol; these were the kings that ruled, but here, following the easy rise of steps, comes a procession of captive kings.) A little further, and you are in the Hall of the Hundred Columns, a wilderness of tumbled ruins, but ruins which in their broken detail testify to the richness of order that once was here: fallen capitals; fragments of carving small enough to go into a pocket, but whorled with the curls of an Assyrian beard; wars and dynasties roll their forgotten drums, as the fragment is balanced for a moment in the palm of the hand. Over this roofless desolation hangs the sun, cutting black square shadows, striking a carving into sharper relief; and silence reigns, but for the dry-leaf scurry of a lizard over the stones. This hall was roofed with cedar, says Quintus Curtius; and now the discovered ashes of carbonised cedar corroborate the account of the historians: this hall of Darius flamed indeed beneath the vengeance of Alexander. Little did it avail Darius that he should have caused the *Avesta* to be written in letters of gold and silver on twelve thousand tanned ox-hides.

The hand of man has never desecrated these ruins, no excavator's pick has ever rung upon these stones; tumbled and desolate they lie today, as they lay after the might of Alexander had pushed them over. The heat of the Persian summers has passed over them and bleached them; they have flushed in the light of many sunrises and bared themselves to the silver of many moons; the wild flowers have sown themselves in the crevices and the lizards scurry over the pavements; but it is a dead world, as befits the sepulchre of an imperial race.

Ruined cities. Ranging away from Persepolis, I remember other wrecks of pride, splendour, and majesty: the ziggurat of Ur against the sunset, the undulating mounds that were Babylon, the gay broken colonnades of Palmyra. Golden, graceful, airy, debased, Palmyra rises like a flower from the desert in an oasis of palms and apricots. At the apex of a flattened and irregular triangle between Damascus and Baghdad, Palmyra lies on the old caravan route and the strings of camels still slouch beneath the triumphal arches of Zenobia and Odenathus. But the Street of the Hundred Columns is now nothing but a transparent screen of pillars, framing the desert, and in the precincts of the Temple of Baal clusters an Arab village, the squalid houses incongruously put together with the stones of the once magnificent centre of a pagan faith. What is Palmyra now? Where is the glory of Solomon who built Tadmor in the wilderness? A few tourists motor out from Beirut, and the desert traffic of camel caravans passes through on its leisurely way. The Arab children squabble in the gutters. There is a French *poste de police*. There is a derelict building, originally designed as an hotel. But now that even Trans-Desert Mail no longer takes Palmyra in its rush—as it did when the Druses terrorised the southern route—it seems likely that Palmyra will return to the isolation to which it is geographically destined, and that the flush of its prosperity under the Roman Empire will resemble the flush of flowers over the desert in spring—with this difference, that spring for Palmyra is not recurrent. It happened once, and will not happen again; a miracle the more exquisite for its singleness and fugacity.

You come upon Palmyra unexpectedly, if you approach it from the Damascus side, going through a gorge crowned by Turkish forts, and coming out on to a full view of the desert with these surprising ruins standing in the white, pale sand. Lovely in colour, as golden as honey, the vistas of columns and arches give Palmyra a lacy quality: it is a series of frames, and nothing so much enhances the beauty of landscape as to be framed in a fragment of architecture. But on looking closer this architecture presents a puzzle: it is Roman, surely? but there is something not quite Roman about it; there are mistakes that the Roman builders would not have made. Indeed, the Romans did not build it, no; Arabs built it, dazzled by what they had seen or heard of the Roman models. Most people criticise Palmyra on this account. Certainly it is neither as pure nor as majestic as Baalbec. It lacks the grand solidity of Roman building, and the Roman sense of proportion is notably absent. But I like Palmyra. It is very feminine; it is gay, whimsical, and a little meretricious. It seems to have drunk the desert sun, and to have granted free passage to all the desert winds with a wanton insouciance. Palmyra is a Bedouin girl laughing because she is dressed up as a Roman lady.

And there, lastly, under the snows of Lebanon lie the mighty ruins of Heliopolis. The Temple of Bacchus retains its shape, but of the Temple of Jupiter only six columns survive out of the original fifty-four. Baalbec had its worthy enemies: Genghiz, Timur, and Saladin; besides the earthquakes which have crashed pediment and capital to the ground. There lie the blocks of masonry, here gapes a vault; here is a column, propping itself against the wall of the Temple. It is a wilderness of masonry; havoc such as might have been wrought in a sudden onslaught by the anger of the very god to whom the greatest temple was dedicated, that Jupiter who at Baalbec was called Baal—not the hirsute Jove of the Romans, but a beardless god, covered with scales, and holding in one hand a scourge, and in the other, lightning and ears of corn. Baalbec has gone the way of those cities of antiquity on whose ruin no later city has arisen. True, a little town has grown up beside it, so that it enjoys neither the superb isolation of Persepolis nor the native sprinkling of Palmyra, but the little town is insignificant, and it is really the wreck of Heliopolis which dominates the lovely valley between Lebanon and Anti-Lebanon.

There is another difference between Baalbec and those two other cities. The plain of Persepolis is green indeed with the short grass, and at Palmyra the fruit trees of the oasis foam with blossom in the spring, but there is no sign of cultivation anywhere. Round Baalbec the fertile land is carefully tilled; the permanence of agriculture, that detailed, laborious, and persistent craft, is nowhere more strongly emphasised than here, where it pursues its quiet way undisturbed by the presence of a crumbled civilisation. It seems not irrelevant to wonder whether in the course of centuries the Anglo-Persian oil-fields may not revert to the solitudes of the Bakhtiari hills, while London, Paris, and New York lie with the wild flowers blowing over their stones, and fields of corn bend to the breeze for the bread of the population in some distant capital whose name we do not yet know.

JOURNAL OF TRAVEL TO FRANCE
WITH VIRGINIA WOOLF (1928)

Vita's travels in France were many, and made quite frequently with her women lovers and companions—notably, of course, with Violet Trefusis, but also with Evelyn Irons, with Gwen St. Aubyn, and, most famously, with Virginia Woolf. On the latter trip, in September of 1928, the companions left Paris for Saulieu in Burgundy, where they visited a local fair, going the next day to Avallon and to Vézelay, where the old abbey was the drawing point. Vita's voracious reading stood her, as usual, in good stead: she had read Walter Pater on Vézelay in his Studies in the History of the Renaissance *(1873). She wrote Harold about traveling with Virginia: "The combination of that brilliant brain and fragile body is very loveable. She has a sweet and childlike nature, from which her intellect is completely separate. I have never known anyone who was so profoundly sensitive, and who makes less of a business of that sensitiveness."4 Vita's journal of that travel is quoted here in full from the Holograph, unsigned, dated Sept. 24–30, 1928, in the Berg Collection of the New York Public Library.*

DIARY OF A JOURNEY TO FRANCE
WITH VIRGINIA WOOLF IN 1928

September 24. I went by train to Lewes where Virginia and Leonard met me. We drove to Rodmell where I saw Pinker's puppies. Leonard then motored us to Newhaven where we caught the 11:30 boat. We took our lunch with us and ate it on board. It was very calm. We arrived at Dieppe at 3, and took the train to Paris. In Paris we went to the Hotel de Londres, rue Bonaparte. We left our luggage & walked out to have dinner in a small restaurant in Bd. Raspail. Walking out we got into a bookshop where V. [Virginia] bought *J'Adore* by Jean Desbordes, & I bought *L'Immoraliste.* There was an old man sitting in the bookshop, & he & the proprietor (a woman) fired off a rhapsody about Proust. We observed how this could never happen in England—it was about 8 o'clock. Yet there was the old customer sitting & discussing Proust, also Desbordes of whose literary success he said Cocteau would soon be jealous, "even if he had no other cause for jealousy."

Walking home from the restaurant we missed our way, so sat down to drink coffee at the Brasserie Lutetia in rue de Sèvres & V. & I wrote to Leonard and Harold respectively on the torn-out fly-leaves of our books. She told me how she & Leonard had had a small & sudden row that morning about her going abroad with me.

A rather disturbed night, as fire-engines tore down the street beneath my window.

September 25. Called at 6 & drove to the Gare de Lyons [*sic*] through a deserted Paris. Caught the 7 o'clock train to Saulieu where we arrived at 12.40. I read *L'Immoraliste.* V. read *J'adore,* & remarked that there was a tendency in our Frenchmen of today towards religion and simplicity. Hotel de la Poste at Saulieu, with excellent cooking. After lunch we went out; a fair in progress; Virginia bought a green corduroy coat for Leonard. We then went & sat in a field till it got too cold, & wrote letters. After dinner we went to the fair. There was a zoo with lion-cubs, a merry-go-round, & a Bal Tabarin which we watched for some time. A very lovely gipsy woman there. Virginia very much delighted with all these sights. People threw confetti over us.

September 26. We had breakfast in my room, and entered on a heated argument about men & women. V. is curiously feminist. She dislikes the possessiveness and love of domination in men. In fact she dislikes the quality of masculinity; says that women stimulate her imagination, by their grace & their art of life. We then went out & I bought myself a corduroy coat. After lunch we went for quite a long walk, past the station & drove down the lanes between the woods. Nice, but not warm enough. After dinner V. read me her memoir of "Old Blooms-bury," and talked a lot about her brother.

September 27. We left Saulieu at 8 and got to Avallon at 9:30. Here we walked about looking at the town; church of St. Lazare, old houses, ramparts etc.—with a fine view over a valley. I got letters from H. at the *poste restante.* V. was very much upset because she heard nothing from Leonard. We lunched at Hotel de la Poste where we fell in with Valerie motoring to Avignon with the John Balder-stions. We went again to the post; still nothing from Leonard; so I made V. send a telegram. We hired a motor & drove to Vézelay which enchanted us. Went out to look at the cathedral, and view from the terrace; then lay in a field not talk-ing much, but just listening to the crickets. V. seemed tired, & I made her go to bed at quarter to 10. In the middle of the night I was woken up by a thunder-storm. Went along to V.'s room thinking she might be frightened. We talked about science & religion for an hour—and the ultimate principle—and then as the storm had gone over I left her to go to sleep again.

September 28. A rainy morning. We sat in my room & wrote letters. At 11 it cleared up & we went out, to the antiquaire where we bought nothing. Fitful sunshine, & I took some photographs. After lunch we walked down to Asquins, & sat for some time in a vineyard & again on the banks of the Cure—where we watched the old village women doing the washing. Then up the hill, with lovely views down over the valley of the Cure. I made V. go in and rest, and walked right round the ramparts myself looking at the sunset.

Saturday, September 29. Left Vézelay with great regret at 10. A lovely warm morning. I watched the builders on their ladder handing up the stones. Motored to Sermizelles, & there caught a train at 10: 49 which got us to Auxerre for lunch. Hotel Houring. A thunderstorm burst, so we waited; then went out & found lovely stained glass in St. Etienne. Went to St. Gervain where there is an old crypt—not very interesting. Nice bridges over the river. Had chocolate in a tea-shop & found a good antiquaire where V. bought a looking-glass. Discussed Edith Sitwell. V. told me the history of her early loves—Madge Symons, who is Sally in *Mrs. Dalloway.*

September 30. Got up at 6 & left for Paris at 7. Drove from Gare de Lyons [*sic*] to St. Lazare, where we lunched & then went on to Rouen.

LECTURE TRAVEL DIARY
(JANUARY TO MARCH 1933)

One of the most valuable unpublished documents included in this anthology is Vita's travel diary from her lecture tour in the United States and a brief time in Canada. She was progressively more at ease, even "glib" as she puts it, with the lectures she was invited to give on literature, English life, and the changes in English society over the years.

The titles for her lecture of 22 cities, during which she was treated as a well-known scholar and writer, are indicative of the range of literary topics she could handle with ease. She spoke on "Novels and Novelists," "Changes in English Social Life," "The Modern Spirit in Literature," "Travels through Persia," and "D. H. Lawrence and Virginia Woolf." Most of the lectures seem to have been a great success, according to all accounts.

Her diary tour, from middle of January through March 1933, also gives a representative picture of the kind of reception visiting Britons must have found in Canada and the United States at that time. If she is highly derogatory about certain of her hosts, we can be all the more certain that those who incur her praise in any way are all the more remarkable. It is, to say the least, more than unfortunate that she seems particularly sensitive to the looks, the background, the lack of conversational ability, and the mental and aesthetic shortcomings of certain new acquaintances. Her relief at encountering fellow English-speakers with the correct accent and views is palpable.

Some of the anecdotes are especially fascinating. The person who cannot believe the redness of her cheeks is real, so she suggests he try to rub it off on his handkerchief. The high amusement of her hosts when, at a country club, they must dine in the gun room; Americans are easily and unexpectedly amused, she says. The exchange with Miss Ely at Bryn Mawr about their mutual admiration of each other's clothing. The fall of the screen in the middle of a lecture that no one appears to notice. The way Vita, who had no love for reporters—and seems to have spent a good deal of time trying to get rid of them—gets her revenge by leaving the window open for an icy blast to chill them.

The reaction of an English person to the American accent is unavoidable—we are familiar with it from Roger Fry, Virginia Woolf, and others. In the midst of a crowd—generally heard as noisy—Vita expresses her great relief at hearing an English pronunciation: someone from Sevenoaks! Her wit and scorn are visible in all their full array here, particularly directed at Midwesterners, many of them seen as large and not very bright. But everywhere, there is something to mock, heavily or slightly, in the "Amurricans," with their admiration for the "vury vury" beautiful countryside, the pseudo-Tudor style manors of the magnates, the suburban sprawl, the factories of Pitts-

burgh, the highways with the heaps of scrapped cars. It is with astonishment that she finds, repeatedly, some grassy slope with trees, a lovely situation for a building, the clapboard houses in New England, where her experiences are clearly more agreeable. Her repeated irritation with vapid conversation, with the noise level of dining rooms, with the way she is expected to respond to everything when her constant desire is to escape and to go to bed, as well as her often negative judgments, render her far more clearly than the one-dimensional aristocrat we may have formally perceived.

The college scenes are unforgettable: the lovely young ladies with too much makeup and their eternal discussion of their dates and their beaus, the bibliophiles and professors with their culture, such as William Lyon Phelps and Chauncey Tinker of Yale and Mrs. Helen Taft Manning of Bryn Mawr. No less so, the scenes of her encounters with poets such as Robert Frost and Robinson Jeffers in California, and with philosophers such as R. B. Braithwaite, as well as painters such as Dorothy Brett and cultural icon Mabel Dodge Luhan. Her lectures, on subjects from D. H. Lawrence and Virginia Woolf, to social changes in England, and novels and novelists, we might like to have heard. (The lecture on poetry, prepared for the BBC and included elsewhere in this volume, is an indication of the kind of talk for which Vita was known.)

Vita's profile comes out sharply here, in her perceptions of character as of landscape and culture, and in the details. All the telling repetitions — "I couldn't escape," "more dead than alive," "I could not get rid of them" — speak loudly of her exasperation at the trip. Frazzled, carrying too much luggage, always having to change for dinner or traveling, waiting at small stations for five hours, this visitor to the shores of America left a vivid picture of herself. It is that picture I have wanted to convey in as much color as possible. She is particularly sensitive to appearances — to this one's girth and that one's intelligent face — and to the quality of conversation. Repeatedly, she suffers from the noise of the gathering, in the clubs, at dinners, or from the lack of any provision for her dinner, or from exhaustion. Her relief at meeting Harold and her sadness at their separation for their individual lecture appearances is palpable. Vita was never to return to America.

I have transcribed this travel diary in full, with a very few omissions of brief sentences with undecipherable names. Nevertheless, some of the names included are nearly illegible in the original and I hope the reader will pardon any misspellings in what I have had to approximate.

January 28. Left Washington at 12:25 A.M. last night and arrived at New York 5:50 this morning, but was allowed to sleep till 7, when a buzzer woke me up. Very comfortable compartment, like a European wagon-lit but better: e.g., the chair was really a *chaise percée,* and one has a washing basin ingeniously fitted in, so that one need never go out of one's compartment at all.

Went straight to Hotel New Weston where I was put into the room Hadji is to have tomorrow. Washed & had some breakfast & read my letters; all American post. Walked down Madison Avenue and bought a suitcase on the way. Went to the bank to get traveller's cheque book, and then to Colston Leigh to collect my own tickets and settle about western journey. Enraged by a newspaper article saying we had been rude about America.

Return to hotel at 11, and re-pack my things in new suitcase which has now arrived. Write Hadji a note, and sign a book for some stranger who waylays me in the passage. Leave New York 12:30 for Albany, which I reach at 3:22. The train runs beside the Hudson as far as Albany. Looking out of the window I could not believe it was a river, but thought at first that it must be an immensely long lake.

There must be floods out, as I saw a sham medieval castle standing in the water, with the walls of its forecourt entirely submerged but for the battlements and the tops of two pepper-port turrets—a very odd effect. There are fine cliffs on the opposite side of the river, rising vertically to a couple of hundred feet—I should think, and a number of little houses perched on the top.

I had 40 minutes to wait at Albany, so I had some coffee in the restaurant. Left at 4:20 for Colliers. Pretty, hilly, wooded country, very like England, but it soon got dark. I was rather tired but I couldn't go to sleep because of an American young man who talked for two hours without stopping in an incessant and insistent voice about American railways. It is awful how these people talk in trains. I glared at him, but it did no good. Read the *Epic of America,* which I enjoyed.

Met at Colliers by Miss Kidd and another woman—Case? Chase? [*sic*]—and motor 16 miles in a large noisy car. Find that I have tumbled into another girls' school, which has its quarters in Hotel Otsego which becomes a hotel again during the summer holidays. The principal is a stout lady in pink chiffon called Mrs. Russell Houghton. I am put into a bedroom where I am mercifully allowed my dinner on a tray. Have a bath and dress. Get numerous small electric shocks every time I touch silk, metal, or water. Miss Kidd who fetches me at 8, explains that this place is mysteriously full of electricity, also that it is the hometown of Fenimore Cooper, whose granddaughter I subsequently meet. Lecture on "Novels and Novelists" to about 100 girls and a number of local grown-ups, including "the faculty" and Mrs. Hoyt, who is Elizabeth Lindsay's sister-in-law and who asks me to luncheon next day. A tall, sympatique [*sic*], grey-haired, slender woman with a sad face. Reason for sadness is explained later by Mrs. Houghton, who says Mr. and Mrs. Hoyt were blissfully happy in their marriage, until they went to a Swami fortune-teller, who told them (separately) that Mr. Hoyt was about to meet his fate. He met her soon afterwards at a dinner party and they fell in love at first sight across the dinner table. Mrs. Hoyt watched it happening. Result: divorce and Mrs. Hoyt's sad eyes.

The usual supper-party after my lecture, and the usual eager girls. The girls are nice, but the general atmosphere is not as pleasant as Dana Hall or Wellesley. There seems to be greater severity and discipline. My lecture went well though, and I met a lot of budding novelists afterwards, but they kept a cautious eye open to see if any of the faculty were about.

All the ceilings are fitted with a grid of water-pipes—sprinklers in case of fire. This reduces the fire insurance but entails insurance against floods.

To bed rather exhausted at 11.30.

January 29. Woke to find Cooperstown under snow and snow still falling. Mrs. Hoyt, Elizabeth Lindsay's sister-in-law, fetched me at the Knox School at 11:30 and we walked to her house, about 1/2 a mile away. Cooperstown is a regular backwater; it has a railway station, but nobody uses it as there are practically no trains. A pretty village, with green and white New England houses, hilly, on the edge of Lake Otsego, which is 10 miles long and the source of the Susquehanna. The whole place is run and financed by four brothers called Clark, who have built a hospital, a library, and a club, all in nice grey stone with green shutters. Wooded hills all round the lake. Mrs. Hoyt has a house paneled in pine; she also has twin daughters aged fourteen. After lunch Mrs. Houghton fetched me and we motored 20 miles in a blizzard to Herkimer. Very pretty rolling country, with few houses, mostly farms. Left Herkimer at 2:30 and got to Buffalo at 7:50 where I was met by Miss O'Reilly and a friend. Arrived at the house, I found two more Misses O'Reilly, also a dog called Reilly. Had expected dinner, so hadn't had it in the train, but there wasn't any and when they asked as an afterthought if I had had it on the train I said yes. So I was rather hungry. Had to dress, as there was a party—the intelligentsia of Buffalo. This produced biscuits, for which I was thankful.

January 30. Reporters arrived en masse at 10 to ask questions and take photographs. (The papers subsequently came out with accounts of my view on divorce, a subject which had never been mentioned at all, and which my hostess had specially cautioned me to avoid, since D'Youville College is run by nuns.) Then I write some letters, and am taken out to lunch "quietly" with a Mrs. Pomeroy; the "quietness" is provided by about 30 women all talking at the tops of their voices in a small room. A regular parrot-house. Then I am photographed by one Otto Gaul, who asks me to take off my rouge and refuses to believe that that is my natural complexion until I offer to let him rub my cheek with a handkerchief. Then I go to see a Mrs. Stoppes, not Marie, who is bedridden with arthritis and who likes seeing "distinguished strangers" who come to Buffalo. She is a pitiable sight, propped up on a mechanical bed worked by pulleys in a half-darkened room. She cannot move her legs or arms at all; cannot even hold anything in her hands. She has had two children, a boy who died at the age of nine and a girl who died at the age of twenty. Her husband to whom she is devoted and who is devoted to her, has got angina pectoris and is liable to die suddenly at any moment. They were rich once, but have recently lost all their money. In spite of these calamities she does not seem in the least embittered, but talks with zest about books and the people who have come to see her, especially Hugh Walpole. My hostess then brings me home—I have become "darling" to her by now—and we find the D'Youville College committee awaiting us. At 6 I am allowed to vanish, which I do gratefully.

Mr. and Mrs. Swift, Mrs. Carpenter's friends, come to dinner; Mrs. Swift a nice, good-looking woman with white hair and bright blue eyes, Mr. Swift a dryly humourous man. The lecture is at D'Youville College at 8:30—on writing a novel. A particularly nice auditorium, like a tiny theatre. It is crowded. A mixed audience with a scattering of the college girls and the grey nuns who run the college. Nan O'Reilly introduces me in a little speech. After the lecture there is a party at Mrs. Swift's house; particularly nice and intelligent people. Dr. Lappin seems a definite personality.

People in Buffalo are very extravagant about their electric light, because Niagara does it all for them!

February 1. A rainy day. Wrote letters in the morning and left Niagara Falls at 1:15 for Toronto. A dreary landscape; as untidy as America. Arrived at Toronto at 3:30 only to find that I had been expected by another train and that journalists had traveled down to Hamilton to meet me. Met at Toronto by Miss Doyle, the Governor's aide de camp Colonel Hilatine [?] and several photographers. More reporters waiting at Government House. The Governor, Mr. Bruce, is a nice old man with white hair; Mrs. Bruce is much younger, English (he met her in France where she was a V.A.D.) and a vice-regal manner. Was interviewed by several papers and then dined alone with the Bruces. Not very thrilling. Masefield & Clemence Dane have preceded me here, leaving good impressions. Allowed to go to bed early. Sumptuously lodged, with bathroom & sitting room to myself.

Write letters in the morning and talk to Maxwell Bruce aged 13, who is in bed with a bilious attack. Taken out to luncheon by Mrs. Bruce and Lady Clark (wife of Sir William Clark, British Commissioner to Canada). Luncheon with Mrs. H. D. Warren; crowds of women as usual. After lunch I go to the museum where there are really lovely Chinese pottery things. To tea with Mrs. Clarence Bogert, where I rejoin the Clarks and the Bruces. Large dinner party at Government House. Lecture to Pleiades Club afterwards: English social life. Very smart audience! Supper-party at Mrs. A. H. C. Proctor's, and to bed at 1:30.

Feel I have earned my keep today!

February 3. I leave Toronto at 8. Colonel Hilatine [?] comes to the station with me, which distresses me. A very dreary journey to Chicago which I reach at 8:30, with a view of Detroit on the way. I stay at the Drake Hotel, & reporters come and bother me.

February 4. More reporters. I revenge myself on them by leaving the window wide open. There is an icy wind blowing straight off Lake Michigan. At 11 A.M. I lecture on "Changes in English Social Life." In the middle of my lecture a screen falls down on the heads of the audience but they do not appear to mind. I am then taken to lunch with Mrs. Robert McCormick wife of the editor (or owner?) of the *Chicago Tribune,* a large party, and lovely French pictures, modern. After lunch, Mickey Kellogg & I go out by train to Lake Forest. Very cold, and lots of snow.

February 7. Wake to find Chicago under snow and a blizzard. Hate leaving Hadji in it, but have to catch the 11:30 to St. Louis. Dreary journey across snow-bound plains interrupted only by grim towns and occasional dumps of broken motors, more squalid than ever, sticking up out of the snow. My train one and a half hours late, so we get in at 7:30 instead of 6. (They light gas-flares to keep the points free of snow and ice. All the trains standing in stations are roofed with snow, and have great icicles dripping down their sides; the engines have flares lit underneath them, so that they appear to be on fire; rather a fine effect in the dusk.) Two women from Lindenwood College meet me with a motor at St. Louis. I escape from the reporters by saying I am late. I am indeed, for my lecture is timed for 8, and we do not reach St. Charles till quarter to 9. I wash but do not change, and give lecture at once; "Modern Spirit of Literature"; audience mostly the college girls, with some outside people as well. I am introduced to all of them afterwards and made to sign books. Observe that the copies of *All Passion Spent* have changed from 9th edition to 10th. Am given some dinner, which I had not yet had. Get a telegram from Hadji & ring him up. Long to go to bed, but am kept up talking; with all their kindness, these people have very little imagination.

Get to bed finally by 12. Staying at the college.

February 8. A lovely, white, frosty morning. I walk across the campus & have breakfast at a sort of tuck-shop. They then motor me in to St. Louis, to the house of Miss Helen Morgan with whom I am to stay. A nice kindly woman with an aged mother. I go to lunch with Mr. Clemens of the Mark Twain Society. A heavy and boring young man, but there is another man who enlarges on the American character with some intelligence. On the way out from lunch I am caught by reporters and remorselessly photographed. They want to take me to see the Lindbergh monument where Lindbergh keeps all the presents his admirers give him, but I evade this. Lindberg & T. S. Eliot are both natives of St. Louis, and so is Mr. Alfred Prufrock. They all loathe St. Louis & say it is the dirtiest & most stagnant place in the United States. It doesn't seem to me worse than most. A bright young thing called Roberts comes to see me; she is trying to edit a literary review here, & admires Virginia, Eliot, & E. M. Forster. She is very young & eager.

Miss Morgan has a party, with a man who sings "Ol' Man River." I meet one Mr. Clunden whose ancestors came from Cranbrook. Then we go to dine at the Chase Hotel. About 400 people all shouting, & I sit between two deaf men.

I am very tired, and fear that my voice will go. It doesn't and I lecture afterwards, "Modern Spirit in Literature." Escorted home after by a lot of bloody people I can't get rid of. Heaped with flowers, really lovely ones.

February 9. I leave St. Louis for Chicago at 8:35 & get to Chicago at 3:25 where Hadji meets me.

February 13. Leave Lake Forest at 8:48 and travel as far as Chicago with Hadji. Catch my train at 10 o'clock at Chicago, for Minneapolis, while Hadji goes to Washington. A nasty parting, for 10 days. Snowy plains all the way across Illinois, Wisconsin, and Minnesota, broken by occasional rough hills and rocks. Read *Of Human Bondage* in the train and am disappointed in it, having read it years ago. Am met at Minneapolis by Mrs. Murray and another woman. Two journalists come to see me. Get to bed at midnight.

February 14. More journalists & photographers in the morning, also a nice bookseller-cum-bibliophile man called Leonard Wells. Mrs. Murray collects me to lunch with the Women's Club. A very grand club-house. Lecture: "Modern Spirit in Literature." Go afterwards to see Mr. Wells' shop, and dispatch some of my own books, i.e., books I have read, back to myself at New York, to relieve my congested luggage. Leave Minneapolis at 5 for Des Moines. My train is nearly an hour late, so I don't get there till after 1 and am met by Mrs. Cowles, a small dark woman with a greasy skin and fuzzy black hair; not bad, downright & sensible.

February 15. Sleep late. Reporters in the morning and photographs. Lunch alone with Mrs. Cowles, & then lecture on "Novels & Novelists"; Women's Club. Have tea with Mrs. Kratsch, who has a rather prettily situated house among trees on a hill. Des Moines is quite prettily situated, for it is hilly and wooded; better trees than usual. Mrs. Kratsch has lovely Indian corn cobs from Arizona hanging in bunches outside her front door—golden, orange, dark red, purple, white, and even blue and white. A huge noisy tea party.

Dinner with the Cowles. A dinner party. Some men, actually; but not attractive specimens—hard, crude, Middle-West business men. I am very tired. Expect to find my sleeper waiting at the station, but it isn't there, so I have to wait at the station until nearly 1 o'clock. Fortunately I am tired enough to go to sleep on a wooden bench among my luggage, looking like an immigrant. My redcap is very sympathetic & says he saw my photograph in the paper. Such is fame.

After dinner they ring up from Cowles' office to say there has been an attempt to assassinate Roosevelt.

February 16. Arrive at Kansas City at 7:20 & am met by a dear little dump called Mrs. Doughty. She takes me to the Baltimore Hotel, where I am put into a complimentary suite consisting of two bedrooms, two bathrooms, a shower-bathroom, three w.c.'s, a hall, and an enormous sitting room, all filled with roses. A jolly view over the city & skyscrapers. Get a large post, including English letters, and read them in the intervals of seeing reporters. Write some letters. Mrs. Doughty comes again to fetch me for luncheon; she telephones up to my room saying "this is your friend Mrs. Doughty." I sign a lot of books in her room at the Women's Club. An enormous luncheon, where I sit between the president, an awful fat ill-tempered looking bedint [lower-class person, in Vita-Harold terminology] called Mrs. Bush, and an exceptionally nice, original intelligent person from Maine called Mrs. Martin. Like Mrs. Martin very much indeed; she is a real grown-up highbrow full of ideas. Am slightly disconcerted by having to lecture from the luncheon- table, with the front row of the audience about 3 feet from my nose, but it does very well & they seem delighted. "Modern Spirit in Literature" again. I am getting quite glib at it. Then I am taken for a drive by Mrs. Bush, Mrs. Doughty, & another enormously fat woman (Mrs. Hearst?) to see the city, War Memorial, and statues called the Pioneer Mother & the Scout. All rather good; the war memorial very modern; but it looks rather incomplete because they ran out of funds. The residential quarter is well & elaborately planned, with some very charming houses on hilly ground with trees. Have tea with Mrs. Hearst. Very tired. Dine at the Country Club, but am allowed not to change. The Country Club is charming, with an English looking room, a log fire, sofas and cretonne. A nice dinner; about 40 people. Sit between Mrs. Bush again & a nice old judge, but talk nearly all the time to the editor of the local paper, Mr. Haskell, a clever man who loves Hadji's book on his father. Met Ernest Hemingway's aunt. Nice people altogether. Mrs. Doughty drives me back to the station, which I leave at 10:30 for Chicago in one of those beastly sections.

February 17. Arrive at Chicago at 9:30 & go to Mrs. Fairbank's house. Find letters there & spend a peaceful morning, writing letters, re-packing, etc. Some men come to lunch, & then I go to Krock's bookshop to sign books, & ten to see Mrs. McNeil at Colston Leigh's. To be with Mrs. Houston Johnson who I don't like at all. Mrs. Fairbank who has arranged to collect me there at 5:15 doesn't arrive till 6—so I have to dress in a hurry & am late for dinner. Drive with Mrs. Manheimer, & dislike it extremely; for one thing I am very tired & for another they are all pretentious, pseudo-smart Jews. Go on with them to lecture at Book and Play Club; "Modern Spirit in Literature" again; a horrid audience, all Jews; can't capture them at all. Very tired & dejected. Leave Chicago at 1:55 A.M. for Madison.

It is much warmer, & Chicago is all slush and heaps of dirty snow.

[Ed. Note: I have left this entry intact, as I have all the others, so as not to censor Vita's opinions, which were typical of her time and social set.]

February 18. My train arrived at Madison at 6:35 but I did not wake till 8, as we got shoved onto a siding. I woke to find a bright sunny day, with a certain amount of snow. Took at taxi to the Hotel Loraine, where I got a room & had some breakfast. I avoided reporters by telling them Mrs. Miller was coming to take me out. She did, in fact, come at 10—a nice elderly woman with lovely eyes of powder-blue and grey hair, accompanied by another woman whose name I didn't discover, something like Schliedermann. They drove me round Madison in a large motor, showing me the University buildings first, & the Capitol & Observatory; then we went along the shores of Lakes Monona and Mendota. It must really be very pretty in summer. The lakes which are 5 in number are surrounded by low hills and trees, and one gets into the country much quicker than usual, Madison being only a small town. They have an interesting modern building which is an experimental place for woodwork, but the architecture of the small houses near the lakes was very poor, not nearly so good as Kansas City.

I lunched at 1 o'clock with the Civics Club at the Loraine Hotel—nearly 600 of them. I sat between Mrs. Miller & Mrs. Glenn Frank, wife of the president of the University. Didn't like her much, but beyond her was one George Middleton, who interested me—he is connected with some dramatic agency & knows a lot of people I know. After luncheon I gave my lecture ("Modern Spirit in Literature") from the high luncheon table; it went very well indeed; one of the best audiences I have had, so I recovered from the dejection of the Chicago meeting last night. They asked me to give a personal impression of Virginia afterwards, which I did, also to "explain" *Orlando!* Mrs. Frank then took me to her house where I met her husband, and then to tea with Mrs. Walter Franklin, a fair young woman who has just built a house on the edge of a lake, with rather nice rooms panelled in unstained wood. A large selection of the club members came, the plainest and dowdiest lot of women I have ever seen or ever wish to see. All very noisy and boring; I was made to stand by the door while they all filed past & were introduced.

I caught the train back to Chicago at 5. Glenn Frank appeared at the station to see me off, and gave me his book. I arrived at Chicago at 9 & went to Mrs. Fairbank's house where I am staying; they were all out at a party except Janet Fairbank whom I discovered dressed up as a little girl, with her hair down her back, a hair-ribbon, short skirts, black pumps, and white socks with an expanse of fat hairy leg above them. Not pretty, but she did give me a cocktail. I refused to go to the party, & went to bed instead in an empty house.

February 19. Had breakfast with Mrs. Fairbank & Janet, & left Chicago at 10. Got to Columbus at 6:50 after a long day over unspeakably hideous country, but had a pleasant surprise when the clocks were put forward an hour, so that I appeared to arrive at 5:50 instead of 6:50. Mr. & Mrs. Rockwood met me at the station & took me to the hotel (Dechler-Wallick) to get a room; then took me out to dinner with Mr. & Mrs. Wright, the latter an intelligent woman. More abuse of certain English lecturers, notably Margo Asquith, Oliver Baldwin, & Priestley; but they had liked Hugh [Walpole], Randolph Churchill, Yeats, & James Stevens.

I escaped early; found a reporter waiting for me at the hotel.

Janet Fairbank drove me to the station at Chicago by the "lower level" streets—most sinister tunnels, in which the unemployed are allowed to sleep. Through their arches I caught sight of the bare masts of Byrd's South Polar ship; an extraordinary effect of anachronism.

February 20. I had even more reporters than usual in the morning, including Eugenia Wolfe, who rang me up first on the telephone, when it sounded like "This is Virginia Woolf speaking." I also had a visit from Mrs. Wiggins wanting me to sign a petition for the repeal of the 18th Amendment, but I pointed out that this was scarcely my business. Another bore rang me up about the history of the Wests.

Mrs. Rockwood came for me after 12 and took me out to lunch at the Country Club with a very good-looking Mrs. Edmunds. There were other people there, of course. Quite a pretty club, out in the country, and actually built on a *hill.*

After lunch I was allowed to return to my hotel and tried to write to Virginia with only minor interruptions, such as a young man who said "Lady Victoria?" outside my door in a gentle voice, wanting me to sign my books for him, and a girl who came for an interview but ended by telling me how she longed to go to college only her parents could no longer afford it.

The Rockwoods collected me at 6:30 & took me to dinner at the Club house. We then returned to my hotel and I lectured in the ballroom there; "Changes in English Social Life." A very *dankbares publicum* [thankless public], and it went very well indeed. I was then introduced to hundreds of people, but was rescued by Mrs. Edmunds and taken away into a small room with a select few, and given a whiskey & soda. I liked Mrs. Edmunds, who is really lovely without a hat—lovely wide brows and a serene look; dark hair; a Madonna-like type. Then there was a ball—the elite of Columbus, I watched it from the upper balcony till after twelve, when I parted from the kind Rockwoods with expressions of gratitude, and from Mrs. Edmunds with every assurance that we would meet again, perhaps in England; went upstairs & did my packing, & then to bed.

February 21. Leave Columbus at 8:25 A.M. and reach Cincinnati at 11:20 A.M. where I am met by Mr. & Mrs. Scott Allen. [. . . .] Am driven to Miss Ruth Harrison's house, Weebetook, Grandin Road, G. Walnut Hills, where I am to stay. Old-fashioned house with heavy Victorian furniture and old family photographs, a winter garden, and a nice view up the valley of the Ohio & the Kentucky hills opposite. Miss Harrison herself is rather like Margaret Warrenden. Expect to find letter & tickets awaiting me, but they are not here, which rather worries me. Lunch with the Woman's Club, noisy and dull. Lecture afterwards, "Modern Spirit in Literature" to an overcrowded and indeed overflowing auditorium. A lady comes up afterwards, and tells me she has had a vision during my lecture, and that I was Balkis, Queen of Sheba in a previous incarnation. Try to look suitably grateful. The mayor of Cincinnati, Mr. Wilson, by whom I sat at lunch, introduced me in a great many ill-chosen words. They all seemed pleased, and one lady threatens to write to Virginia saying how well she interpreted *Orlando.* Return to Miss Harrison's where a lady strives to collect a specimen of my handwriting for the local graphologist, and another lady to present me with three anthologies of local verse.

Dine with Miss Harrison who has a dinner party. Am not allowed to go to bed before 1.

February 22. Hadji arrives from Georgia at 2:30. Spend the morning fussing about my reservations, as the post has failed to produce my tickets. Just when everything is fixed up the tickets arrive, with English letters too.

Hadji lunches out, I lunch with Miss Ellison & the American Pen Women. Ghastly entertainment. Then I go to the bookshop in the hotel to sign books; a nice shop, in a big panelled room like a library. Return to Miss Harrison's & go with her and Hadji to tea at the Scott Allens. We all dine with the English Speaking Union & Hadji lectures on "National Character & International Co-operation." Go home to change & pack, and leave alone for Philadelphia at 11:20.

February 23. Get to Philadelphia at 5 after a long day in a very hot train. I spend most of the day writing letters. We go through the Alleghenies, and along the valley of the Susquehanna. A dramatic piece of engineering called the Horseshoe Curve. Am met at Philadelphia by a stout bedint called Miss Lord who drives me out to Bryn Mawr, 15 miles away. She explains what a beautiful drive it is, and we then pass through endless suburbs black with cars. I stay at the President's House; the President, Miss Park, is away, so I am alone with Miss Lord who apparently shares the house with her. The local bookseller brings books for me to sign. Dine with Mrs. Manning—one of the faculty—and about ten of the students; nice pretty girls. Lecture in Goodheart Hall on D. H. Lawrence and Virginia, a vast hall like a cathedral. Meet Alice Smith there, and return with her to Miss MacGeorge's house where she is staying, after a supper party with the students who all bring books to sign. Meet a very nice Miss Ely, to whom I say "I am going to make a very personal remark." She replies: "I am going to make the same remark to you." I say "But you don't know what it was." She says, "You were going to say, What a lovely frock." She is quite right, so we get on like a house on fire, and she offers me the loan of her adobe house in Santa Fe.

I also meet Mrs. Hotson, wife of the professor who does research on Marlowe and Shakespeare.

February 24. Miss Lord motored me to the Widener house. We dropped Alice Virgin[ia] at her own house on the way, and collected Miss MacGeorge at the station, she being the person who had suggested the expedition. The Widener house is a large, white classical building surrounded by formal gardens of yew and box and shingle paths, on the outskirts of Philadelphia. The interior is far too rich and Ritzy; it is, in fact, very like a grand hotel, only the petit-point furniture is real, the black hawthorn vases are real, and the tapestry panels are real. Mr. W. [Widener] is away in Florida & we were taken over by his "art secretary,"

Miss Standen, an English girl,—the comfort of hearing an English voice! Her mother lives at Sevenoaks. There are not too many things, but all of the first quality. Rembrandt's Mill is there, and Sir Joshua's Mrs. Graham, & Hoffner's own children; two Ver Meers [*sic*], two Bellinis, a Donatello David in marble, Chinese porcelain, Cellini jewels, Isfahan rugs, and the finest Limoges plate I ever saw. Also Manet's dead matador, a curious, black & white, foreshortened picture.

Miss Lord drops me & Miss MacGeorge at the station. Miss MacGeorge from having been a rather dry, shy spinster, melts suddenly & becomes human. We eat chicken salad sitting up at a counter in a drug store, and do cryptograms meanwhile. I catch a train at 1:57 for Wilmington, which I reach in half an hour. I proceed to the Dupont Biltmore Hotel where I remain in blissful and unusual solitude till 7. Employ the time profitably in writing letters and washing some of my clothes; also myself. A motor comes at 7 to take me to Newark where I am greeted by Mr. Kase, a dear little man. I expect to be given dinner, but nothing is said about it, so I go empty onto the platform. "Novels and Novelists"; a rather heavy audience, and I have to put a lot into galvanizing them. They do end by waking up a bit. I am then taken to Mr. Kase's house, where I meet the faculty; also Mrs. Kase, an anemic little woman with a bad stye in one eye. Not much fun, in fact no fun at all, but there are some biscuits which I eat gratefully. Escape early and am motored back, passing an enormous poster on a boarding on the way: "They *hired* the money, didn't they?"

February 27. Arrive in Pittsburgh from Washington at 8 A.M. and drive to Hotel Schenley [?] where I engage a room for the day. Change, and lecture at 11:00, "English Social Life" at the XXth Century Club. Lunch with the Club. A large, elderly, Edwardian looking lady called Mrs. Thompson then drives me off to "see Pittsburgh, such a beautiful city." It reminds me of Sheffield. The actual situation is a good one, on hills rising steeply from the banks of two confluent rivers. When I have admired the factory chimneys and coal dumps sufficiently, Mrs. Thompson & Mrs. Kuhn say they will drive me out into the country. So we drive along an asphalt boulevard to a suburb called Sewickley, and am shown a number of vurry vurry beautiful country houses all rather like Park Grange, but fully exposed as usual to the road and to the windows of their neighbours. We then return to Pittsburgh & drive out to the Country Club for tea. The Country Club is really rather nice, with a large glassed-in patio and a pleasant view over grassy slopes and trees. It is being repaired, so we have to have tea in the gun-room which produces screams of amusement from the ladies. It is a perfect ordinary room, with sporting prints and a few guns on a rack, but Americans are easily and unexpectedly amused. I am shown a school, consisting of two or three red brick buildings of which they are immensely proud. On the way back to Pittsburgh I am promised a treat: I shall see Mr. Mellon's house. (Mr. Mellon & Mr. Carnegie are both natives of Pittsburgh.) Mr. Mellon's house is a pseudo-Tudor building of dirty brick, in the heart of the city. We also see a fine municipal building rather like the Strozzi palace in Florence. We drop Mrs. Kuhn, and Mrs. Thompson takes me to her own house where she wishes me to see the portrait of her husband. A gentleman with whiskers. I am more amused by the lift, which is a kind of bird-cage in the hall, running on two thin steel rods, the most fragile-looking object for the conveyance of Mrs. Thompson who suffers from heart disease and is exceedingly stout, crowned by an enormous coiffure and a plumed hat perched on the top of it. She produces, with evident pride, a particularly plain daughter called Doris. She gives me a book by Mark Sullivan, and her motor conveys me back to the hotel. I change, dine, and leave at 11:30 for Dayton.

February 28 Arrive at Dayton at 9:40 A.M. and am met by Mr. Frizell, Miss Margaret Smith, and reporters. They take me to an hotel. I create some confusion by assuming that Miss Smith is Mrs. Frizell. She takes me to see Orville Wright, an uncommunicative but agreeably modest little grey man who shows us some photographs of his brother and of their early flights. A photograph of Wilbur flying at Biarritz over the head of a very startled horse trying to trot with a landau. For the rest, the walls of his incredibly bleak little room are hung with bronze plaques from various societies, commemorating the achievements of the Wright brothers. I am then taken to luncheon with Mrs. Patterson, where I find about eight other women. The Pattersons are the manufacturers of National Cash Registers. A rich looking house, which they fear they may have to leave as half their factories are closed down. Mrs. Patterson is a dark, rather pretty woman in the thirties. We have cocktails. There is an intelligent woman called MacMurray who is a correspondent of the *New York Times.* After lunch we go over to see the Patterson factories, and are shown a movie describing chiefly how old Mr. P. provided cocoa at eleven for his workers and transformed the slums of Dayton into a garden city. The movie is designed on the Mickey Mouse system, showing how ivy and Virginia creeper covered the wooden fences and the brick frontages; the vegetation rushes up in a way to fill the heart of any gardener with envy.

Return to the hotel and watch a very fine conflagration from my window. Hadji arrives when I am already at dinner with the Nomad Club, & we lecture jointly about the modern spirit in literature. He feels ill & I am terrified that he may have flu.

March 2. Hadji & I go to cash a cheque in Cleveland, and to the bookshop in Hulle's store at 11 in the morning. Autograph books there, and meet a few people,

including the Hulle son. I leave for Indianapolis at 12:50 & Hadji leaves for Buffalo at the same time. Read Faulkner's *Light in August* in the train, a very strange
and unpleasant but striking book. Arrive at Indianapolis at 6:10 where I am met by
Mrs. Bingham & another woman. They break it to me gently that Mrs. Bingham's
cook is ill, so that they cannot have the dinner they had planned for me. I bear the
news well. They take me to the Columbia Club, where I dine alone, and write letters after dinner. There is a rather fine circular piazza, with a flood-lit war memorial in the middle—Civil War, not European—and many twinkling sky-signs. I go
to bed early and have the most appalling nightmares; also there is a fire somewhere
& sirens all night, so I don't sleep much.

March 3. Mrs. Bingham, her sister, and a reporter arrive together shortly after
10, and remove me to the lecture hall. A confusion arises, as I had expected
"Novels and Novelists" and they have billed me for "English Social Life." It is
put to the vote of the audience, who plump for the latter. But when I have finished, the minority which had asked for novels start asking me questions about
that, so that I practically give the second lecture too. Lunch with the Club at the
Columbia Club; am very tired, and the woman with the strident voice who sits
next to me and tells me all about Progressive Education does not know how near
to murder I feel. I discover to my dismay that after-luncheon questions are customary here. They keep me on my feet for nearly another hour. One woman
asks me what I think of *The Well of Loneliness.* I am so cross by this time that I
have a good mind to tell them exactly what I *do* think.

I then go to three bookshops to sign books. One shop is kept by Mrs. Nicholson, who was a Miss West; great jokes about this. Another bookseller keeps a
picture gallery & shows us some rather nice Lawrences. I then return to the
Club to pack, accompanied by Mrs. Bingham's sister who keeps up an incessant
flow of conversation. An old school friend of Anne rings me up and talks for
hours; she is ill, so cannot get to see me; thank God for that. Will I write to
Anne, she says, giving her this that and the other message? I say I am very sorry,
I have no time for letters & she had better write herself. Having packed, I rejoin
Mrs. Bingham downstairs & she takes me to tea with Mrs. MacCarthy, where
there are cocktails. Grateful for this, but am cautious not to drink too many.
Half a dozen young women there are less cautious. They sit on the floor round
me and explain how they buy alcohol for 4 dollars a gallon and make gin with
it. They say the young people think and talk of very little but drink, and that no
party is regarded as a success unless everybody gets tight. If that is the case, then
Mrs. MacCarthy's party is a howling success. The young women and two young
men carry me off, luggage and all, to the house of one of them, by name Mrs.
Eno, a dark untidy creature, who much to my delight says she didn't like *Fam-*

ily History. I change for dinner in Mrs. Eno's bathroom, while the rest of them sit in the bedroom next door shouting conversation at me all the while. One of the young men then drives me to dinner with Mrs. Woollen, who is cross (but pretends not to be) because she had expected me to change in *her* house. A ghastly woman who goes in for graphology, astrology, palmistry, and a belief that Egyptian mummies pursue people with vengeance. An Italianate house and a very good dinner, but Mr. Woollen has unfortunately gone off to New York with the key to the cellar in his pocket. I sit next to an old Dr. McCulloch who is a friend of Hugh; he is also deaf, so I have to shout. The conversation revolves mostly round the bank crisis. After dinner Mrs. Woollen tells my character from my hand-writing. In the middle, my young friends arrive to fetch me, at which Mrs. Woollen becomes more vinegary than ever. I return to the Enos' to change into travelling clothes. They all accompany me to the station, & I leave for Toledo more dead than alive at eleven.

March 7. Get to Greencastle at 9:20, having left Detroit at 11 last night. The express stops on purpose to let me off, and then rumbles away towards St. Louis. I am left standing on the wrong side of the line, opposite a station half the size of Staplehurst. It pours with rain. There are no redcaps, but a kind gentleman appears from nowhere and helps me with my luggage. I establish myself on a wooden bench in the station and prepare to wait there for five hours. I finish an article and write some letters, and every hour or so an express crashes through. At 1:30 the local taxi arrives to take me to the other station, about a quarter of a mile away. I find a minute cafe there, and have something to eat; very nasty. At 4:30 I arrive at Bloomington, very dirty, very cross, and rather tired. I am met by three girl students who insist on taking me to the local photographer, a most tiresome and dilatory man who says "Miss Sackville-West" three times in every sentence. I am then driven round the University buildings, one of which bears a suspicious resemblance to the front of Knole. My three little chattering guides are pleased when I tell them this. It is the tenth anniversary of their society, and they have never had an English speaker here before, so it is evidently an occasion. They are very sweet, very proud of their university (which is co-ed), and very full of questions. They escort me to my room in the Union Building which is really rather fine—Collegiate Tudor in grey stone—and I have some difficulty in getting rid of them. I achieve this at last by saying that I must have a bath. At six they return to fetch me for the banquet, bringing gardenias with them. A vast hall with about 400 students of both sexes already seated at tables, and some faculty sprinkled about. Everybody rises as we come in, which is embarrassing. I sit at a long table with the Society, which is very select (so they explain) consisting of only ten members. They are all extremely pretty, exquisitely dressed, and more made-up than any tart. Before dinner begins they all sing a song in praise of their university, and the Chairman Noemi Osborne reads an ode in my honour. At dinner we talk about American college life, "beaux," "dates," and what they intend to do when they have graduated. Most of them want professions, but then what about the beaux? They ask me if English girls make-up as much as they do, and I truthfully reply No. I say that they will spoil their complexions, and they look grave. One of them is quite lovely, one of the loveliest girls I have ever seen. They talk very freely, because there is no faculty at the table. I lecture after dinner from a high platform: "Novels & Novelists." I enjoy it. They ask hundreds of questions afterwards. Then there is a reception, with the usual autographing, and some of my Indianapolis friends turn up, having come down here on purpose. Flattered by this, but hope that they also have not had to wait 5 hours at Greencastle. After the reception I hope to escape, not a bit of it: they take me down to the cafeteria and we eat chocolate sundaes. Then we cross the campus to the *Daily Student* office—for they edit and print the local paper. I am introduced to a young man who has invented a machine which is to revolutionise photographic reproduction. He explains it to me at great length and I try to look as though I understood. It has stopped raining and is a bright starry night.

March 8. I have breakfast with three men undergraduates in a huge room at the very top of the building. Some of the professors are there too. Much talk about the crisis. I am made to sign endless copies of my photograph, which has now appeared in the local paper. They then drive me to the station where I leave at 11:17 for Chicago. Pretty country, very like England. Reach Chicago at 5:20 and leave again from another station at 6. An enormous and completely empty train; there is only one other person in the dining car. The redcaps say no one is travelling at all. Get a telegram from H. at Chicago saying he has managed to raise 500 dollars.

An American customs man comes and cross-examines me very closely, asks my business in Canada. When I say "lecturing" he asks if I lecture about religion or politics. I say neither: literature. Am I quite sure I preach neither atheism nor Communism? And who finances me? I reassure him by showing him my contracts.

March 11. Have to get up at 6:30 at Springfield and am confronted by a cold snowy morning and a Mrs. Cooley. I am taken in a large car to the house of Mrs. Dutton, through miles of residential suburb. There I have a bath and breakfast, and at 10 I am conducted (after seeing reporters) to the Women's Club where I lecture on English social life. Having no manuscript, I have to fall back on some very inadequate notes. I lunch afterwards with the Club Committee at the club house, an ugly yellow building in Sham Gothic. I then leave for New Haven, where I am met by Prof. William Lyon Phelps and Prof. Tinker, who discovered the Boswell papers at Lord Talbot's. We go to Phelps' house where I meet Mrs. Phelps. Phelps then takes me out on a tour of inspection, and it dawns on me that New Haven is really Yale. That idiot Leigh had never told me. Fine grey stone buildings in Collegiate Tudor, all very reminiscent of any large Wiltshire manor-house. A magnificent library with windows like a cathedral, all done in grey and silver. I then deliver the Bergen Lecture, "On Writing a Novel." Nice young undergraduates. Miss McAffee who edits the *Yale Review* takes me off to her rooms in the building, where I meet Pottle, who is carrying on with the Boswell papers in succession to Geoffrey. He describes Geoffrey's methods of work to me—all done on the backs of old envelopes. I dine with Phelps and others at an old club-house, nice, eighteenth century, and leave for New York after dinner.

March 12. Arrive at New York at 7:30 and go to the New Weston. Find letters there, and at 9:30 Hilda [Matheson] rings me up from Penn. Audibility about the same as from London to Sissinghurst. First the telephone rings and an American voice says "Is that Miss Sackville-West?" Miss Matheson would like to speak to you." An English voice says "You're th-r-r-r-ough.'" Then I hear Hilda. The American voice says "O.K.?" and I reply "O.K." We talk about Nigg's [son Nigel's] plans and about Sissinghurst. Very odd. Dottie [Dorothy Wellesley] speaks. Then Hilda again. Then we get cut off, and the Atlantic resumes its normal place.

Retrieve our luggage from the checkroom and re-organise our packing. The papers are full of the California earthquake. Go out to lunch with Mrs. Dana Gibson, who is a little less noisy than Lady Astor and much better-looking. She announces with pride that she is just on 60. She looks about 45. Dana Gibson is there, & Walter Lippman with a taciturn wife, Kermit Roosevelt who tells us about the shooting at Miami and two other men whose names I don't catch. One a doctor, Xian [Christian] name Dan. They all say the American banking system is crazy. One cocktail apiece, and then iced water. The men have whiskey & soda. Walter Lippman is going to California this week to lecture, & says he would rather see the moon through the Mount Wilson telescope than any sight in America. Kermit speaks with a new respect of the President, & they all praise his idea of broadcasting a simple explanation of the situation tonight.

I walk home. A lovely sunny day. Mrs. Springarn [?] & a Mr. Wright fetch me at 4 and take me to a music-hall in Harlem. Jules Bledsoe sings "Ol' Man River" among other things. Lovely dancing, & good knockabout fun. The audience is all black except ourselves. Ruth Reeves or Read who decorated the Roxy Theatre meet us there; a nice woman. They bring me home & I dress. Edward Tinker fetches me & we go to the Cosmopolitan Club for dinner. Sit between Tinker & a man (name unknown) who discusses Proust's homosexuality at great length and in much detail. We dine in a private room, about 20 or 30 people making more noise than the 800 in Montreal. Mrs. Frank Doubleday there, very friendly and proprietary & tiresome. Will we come & stay at Oyster Bay on our last night in the States? Effendi is so longing to see us. I say firmly that we have other plans.

March 17. Harold leaves early for New York. Mina Curtis takes me up to her farm in the Berkshire hills. On the way we pass through Old Deerfield, a rather self-conscious but very pretty New England village; elm avenues and white boarded houses. Clappered [*sic*], they are called, from clap-board. We disembark from the car at another village up in the hills, and change over into a Ford lorry, as the road is so bad. It is indeed. Snow and mud and ruts and bumps. Lovely wild woods though. I am delighted to be in the real country again. A nice, low, rambling wooden house with pigeons on the roofs, Jersey cows and hotses in the stable. The house is shut up, and we sit over the fire in the little guesthouse and Mina tells me about Bunny [David] Garnett with whom she was in love and who spent a month there with her writing *Pocahontas.* She had motored him all over Virginia collecting material. I stroll down the lane with her dogs while she gives orders to her men. Pines and white birches and a rushing stream. I like it & am happy.

Back at Northampton, I dine with Marion Dodd and Esther Dunn. Robert Frost there, a handsome man who goes in for good conversation. He has a professorship at Amherst. He pays me compliments about "The Land," which I return in kind. I lecture afterwards—not very well—to Smith College, "Modern Spirit in Literature."

March 18. Leave Northampton in a little chilly dawn, change at Springfield, and arrive at Boston, where I am met by Mr. Roland Hopkins. He drives me to his house, where I lecture at 11 A.M. on D. H. Lawrence & Virginia to an overcrowded room full of women. For the first time I find myself speaking with ease & fluency & without notes. A large luncheon party afterwards at the house. A Mr. Johnson and an extraordinary woman who has been sending me flowers & whom I met at the Scaifes come to fetch me & take me to see the [Isabella Stewart] Gardner Museum. Mrs. Gardner was a "character" who built herself a large house like a Venetian palace in Boston & collected things—half Italian primitives, half modern pictures—somewhere in the '80s and '90s. She must have been exactly like B.M. There is a Sargent portrait of her, and the Sargent of "El Jaleo." The centre of the house is occupied by a Venetian courtyard roofed over by glass and crammed with hot-house flowers. The smell of the hyacinths in that centrally-heated place is overwhelming. The house is an extraordinary jumble, but they dare not alter anything, because under her will the whole thing is given away if anything is changed. A bunch of marigolds is to be placed every day of the year under a certain picture, a bunch of violets under another.

The extraordinary woman, whose name I forget, takes me to tea with Mrs. Phillips. A large party there; all toadies. I escape and go to see Mrs. Carpenter from Berlin. The extraordinary woman insists on accompanying me, and waits patiently in the car outside. She then drives me to Miss McGlade's, where I have a very nice dinner. Dale Warren there. I find that I am also expected to dine with Mrs. Hopkins *and* the Scaifes, owing to a muddle of Leigh's. I stick, firmly to Miss McGlade, whom I like, and who is my own private arrangement.

After dinner I drive out to the Scaifes, where I stay.

March 20. Pasatiempo, Santa Cruz. Woke to find a slight fog, which quickly cleared off, leaving a brilliantly sunny day. I wrote a few letters, and at about eleven Miss Hollins came and fetched me, and we motored into the hills, up and down lanes so narrow that the buses scraped along both sides of the car. We went first to her racing stable, there were two foals in a paddock. Then up into completely uninhabited country, heavily wooded with medrone, ilex, and redwood. She lost her way once, and we came unexpectedly on a wood shack with a few puppies tumbling about, and a dark girl and a fair boy standing enlaced in the doorway. A most Arcadian pair. They re-directed us, and after miles of steep and muddy lanes we came to a vineyard whose proprietor was a friend of Miss Hollins. He led us into his "cave,"—a sort of barn,—and gave us wine out of vast barrels. An Englishman appeared, named Braithwaite—an odd-looking, rather faded man with blue eyes, who said he came from Lake Windermere, had been out here for years, and never intended to go back. There were about six bulldogs of all sizes and ages. Then we went on to lunch at the Golf Club. I felt rather fish-out-of-water among half a dozen golfing ladies in sweaters and tweed skirts. All very hearty. After lunch Miss Hollins & I set out for Monterey, about 60 miles away. We stopped in Monterey at an antique shop kept by Mrs. Elkins (David Adler's sister), which is the house where R.L.S. [Robert Louis Stevenson] lived for a time. A lovely old wooden house. Then to Mrs. Elkins' own house, old and wooden also; very good taste, rather Syrie Maugham-ish, bleached wood and Fantin-Latour arrangement of (sham) flowers. Then on to Carmel; white sand and cypresses. These cypresses are spreading, like cedars, instead of being pointed, and grow nowhere else but on that strip of coast. They are very dark and gnarled and lovely, with the white sand beneath them and the sea twinkling beyond. We found Robinson Jeffers' house, very rugged, on the edge of the sea. A curiously Cornish effect; great rocks, a grey sea, and alyssum all over the place. A notice-board on the gate says "Not at home," but an old lady in corduroy trousers who drives up at the same moment walks firmly in. Jeffers emerges, a tall, lean, handsome man in riding-breeches and a shirt with a Byronically open throat. Electric-blue eyes and greying hair. He is very taciturn, and very much aware of his good looks. He asks us in, but not very cordially. A dark untidy room roughly panelled in wood, with a window-seat overlooking the sea and lots of books. Conversation rather sticky till Mrs. Jeffers arrives, plump and voluble. Miss Hollins introduces me as Mrs. Nicolson, but Mrs. J. exclaims "Orlando!" and explains me to "Robin," who then thaws a little and talks about the Woolfs. Mrs. J. then says we must come over to tea with Mabel Luhan. Miss Hollins is sent off to look for the Jeffers twins at the barber's shop, and "Robin" takes me and Mrs. J. to Mrs. Luhan's house 200 yards away. Mrs. Luhan is plump and dark, dressed in black with a white jabot; her hair is cut square like a medieval page. She looks faintly Indian. There are large photographs of Tony [Luhan] on the mantelpiece. Brett [Dorothy Brett] is there, very untidy and chinless and deaf; her head tied up in an Indian handkerchief. Mrs. Jeffers says, "Now, Brett, put on your ears," and Brett obediently places a kind of telephone over her head, attached by flex to a black box like a Kodak which she holds on her knee. Every now and then she changes its little battery, like putting in a new film. Mrs. Luhan gazes with rapt and undisguised passion at Jeffers, who pretends not to notice. I talk to Brett. She has not been home for nine years, and asks with avidity after all her friends. How is Duncan [Grant]? Does he still fall in love with young men? Is it true that Carrington killed herself? How is Ottoline [Morell] ? How is Virginia? How are Gertler and Siegfried Sassoon? I shout answers into the Kodak. She is trying to get naturalised American, but has to pass an exam first about the American constitution. Mrs. Luhan asks with some acerbity about Frieda Lawrence. They all scream when I say that she has been lecturing at Oxford.

We leave finally and drive to Mr. McComus' studio at Monterey. A nice man with a wife like Consuelo Balzan. He shows us sketches of Arizona. It is dark when we leave, and we drive home, Miss Hollins stopped frequently at various houses on the way to collect a hat or a sweater; none of these are forthcoming, but she retrieves other lost objects instead, such as a baby Ciné. We drive through more cypresses, very lovely against the dark sea. We don't get home till 9:30.

PART V

CRITICAL WRITING

Vita took her job as an acknowledged and respected critic and responsible reader seriously. Both her lecture on modern English poetry and her perceptive and learned book on Andrew Marvell reflect that seriousness. That she could be light about such things in no way detracted from her power of judgment, as we see in her letter to her friend, Alvilde Lees-Milne (May 29, 1955), extolling her kindness and lamenting what she had just read: "I can't think how in the whirl and gaiety of your London life you remember things like your promise to send me Bonjour Tristesse. God, what a Waste Land of a book! It made me want to write a counterpart called Bonjour Bonheur."

From her early diary entry about the first fee she earned for writing a poem to her essays on other poets, her deep concern with matters of the mind is clear. She was no less renowned as a critic of literature and of poetry, no less celebrated as a lecturer on modern writing, than as an authority on gardens and country living.

In her small book on Andrew Marvell, one chapter of which is reprinted here, Vita takes the intricate details of his poems seriously, and uses her wide knowledge of literary modes to illuminate the subject under consideration.

Her lecture: "Some Tendencies of Modern English Poetry," given October 16, 1928 and her story called "The Poetry Reading," included elsewhere in this volume, reveal, perhaps as much as her own poetry does, her concern not just with that particular genre but with herself as exemplifying its traditions—no matter how against the current they were. As it happens, by one of those ironic twists of literary fate, the peculiar self-reflection of this story places Vita firmly in that very modernist tradition against which some of her more seemingly traditional writings seem to position themselves.

The titles for her lecture tour of 22 cities in the United States in 1933, from January to April—during which she was treated as a well-known scholar and writer—are indicative of the range of literary topics she could handle with ease. She spoke on "Novels and Novelists," "Changes in English Social Life," "The Modern Spirit in Literature," "Travels Through Persia," and "D. H. Lawrence and Virginia Woolf." Most of these lectures seem to have been great successes, according to all accounts.

Yet Vita's success as a fiction writer was at fault, I think, for overwhelming her critical writing. When she was young, she had always found herself "not clever," but it is in the long run she herself who best sums up her qualities as a critic: "Learned I am not; well-read only in scraps; polemical not at all; didactic: I hope not, but am not very sure." Her uncertainty as to whether or not she was didactic seems to me something of a fair testimony to her not being so.

LECTURE ON
MODERN ENGLISH POETRY (1928)

The following talk was given for BBC Radio, in London, in five parts, on five Tuesdays in the fall of 1928: October 2, 16, and 30, and November 13 and 27. It has not been previously published. In World War II, all the contracts between Vita Sackville-West and the BBC were destroyed, and no trace remains of the archives. My gratitude to Nigel Nicolson for permitting me to publish the talk, which is of great interest to those concerned with the reception of poetics and poetry in England at this period.

"SOME TENDENCIES OF
MODERN ENGLISH POETRY"

I have not come here today to make out a case for modern poetry. Neither have I come to make out a case against it. But we have been accustomed, in the past, to divide the poets roughly into two main groups, the Classical and the Romantic, and to those two groups we are now inclined to add on a third, which we call the Modern. We accept the addition, according to our temperaments, with distaste, mistrust, and apprehension, or with relief, interest, and sympathy; but be our attitude what it may, the classification has definitely taken its place in our critical jargon. Now, nothing in literary criticism is more difficult than to steer clear of jargon; it is a jargon not only of phrases but of the whole attitude that we have to avoid, if we are to keep the mind free and open, to think freshly, and not to become enmeshed in stale shibboleths. Literary criticism is responsible for more loose thinking than any other form of intellectual activity; the two words I used just now, Classical and Romantic, may stand as instances of what I mean. We all respond vaguely when these words are uttered, we contort our minds into a certain shape, getting them ready for what we are to hear next, but I doubt whether many of us, under pressure, could come forward with any very exact definition. And this is wrong. We ought not to be content to use words, and to think in terms that we are not prepared to probe to the last recesses of their significance. But such is the nature of literary or indeed any aesthetic criticism that we have constantly to call our minds back from wandering away into the mists of abstraction, the swamps of pseudo-scientific terminology; to get our feet on to firm ground, and discipline our unruly vocabulary into monosyllabic words of good concrete meaning. What have we, then, in mind when we so glibly speak of the modern spirit? Are we quite sure that any such thing exists? And if we come to the conclusion that it does exist, by what characteristics are we to define and recognise it? These are the questions which I have set myself to answer, and to consider further to what developments in poetry such a spirit may be expected to lead.

For my own part, I am one of those who believe that no innovation is quite so startling as it appears to its own contemporary generation, and that all poetry, at one time, went under the probably rather scornful designation of "modern." I believe, for instance, that Donne must have surprised his contemporaries just as much as Mr. Eliot, let us say, surprises us; but to us Donne wears a definitely seventeenth-century air, as the portraits in a picture-gallery have what we would call an Elizabethan face, or a Georgian face, though by what means we are so certain of our chronology we could not very easily tell. It is a question of perspective, of getting sufficiently far away. I believe that poetry is a continuous stream, rather than a series of lakes connected only by a tenuous trickle, or by a cataract which we call Blake, or Mallarmé, or Walt Whitman, as the case may be. A stream with windings certainly, flowing through various landscapes: now past broad lawns and Palladian mansions, now through dark ravines overhung by ruined castles and ivy-mantled towers, now widening out again between calm pastures, but always the same stream, though fed by many tributaries. This is probably only another way of expressing a belief in action or reaction, the swing of the pendulum, the positive & the negative, or whatever term we may choose for the sake of convenience, and to go further into the situation would involve an examination into the old dispute as to what poetry really is, in what quality and degree it differs from prose, even so-called poetic prose, an examination for which we have no time, even though they would not be wholly irrelevant to the purpose of my argument and inquiry. I am assuming, therefore, that we are more or less agreed upon the nature of poetry—that we speak in fact, the same language when we speak of poetry—and I am assuming also, as the very title of my essay indicates, that we are to work on the assumption that poetry *has* some future before it, a point upon which opinion does not appear to be always unanimous. But it must be admitted from the start that the field of poetry has recently been so much enlarged that we are now compelled to recognise as poetry—or at least as subjects which the poets themselves deem proper material for the exercise of their craft—many regions of human experience, many subtleties of human perception, which would have caused our forefathers to shudder and to exclaim. We have come to recognise that no subject is, in itself, more "poetic" than any other subject and that to talk about the province of poetry is nonsense.

No subject, however rough, however slight, however common, and above all however intellectualised, is to be rejected; all is to be grist to the poetic mill.

This, I think is one of the first differences to be observed; one of the first, and perhaps one of the best, one of the best, I mean, in the sense of being one of the most enriching; and if we are to regard poetry as a living thing, as a growing thing, and not as a mere hobby for the student and the dilettante, we cannot do otherwise than welcome any tendency to push back the frontiers of the poet's estate, to vary the landscape though which the stream of poetry flows. It must however be confessed that what we have gained upon the one count we have lost upon another. I am not now speaking of what many people consider the loss to poetic diction; not of the uncouth phraseology and halting metres which grate upon so many ears. Of diction—that is to say, of the surface texture of modern poetry—I shall have to speak presently, though briefly; what I am most concerned with is something far more fundamental; it is the very stuff out of which that poetry is to be made. Against our gain must be set a loss. It is true that many humbler and many subtler aspects of life now find their expression in poetry, but there is one aspect which is, today, entirely omitted, and that is, unfortunately, the aspect which has given us, in the past, the noblest poetry of our language. It is impossible to imagine, even after allowing for changes of diction, a Gray's "Elegy" or an "Ode on the Intimation of Immortality," still less an "Excursion" or a *Paradise Lost,* as the product of the early twentieth century. It may be argued that we have no great poetry today because we have no great poets; that is a perfectly definable argument. Still, I do not believe that even a great poet, were one to arise, could or would move upon the plane or breathe the air of Milton and of Wordsworth. This is simply another way of saying that sublimity has gone out of fashion. Or I might say, again, that we have no passion because we have no convictions. And it is very difficult to see what is to take the place of that passion which in the past, and according to the temperament of the writer, has clothed itself in the garments of reverence, awe, and faith. We have nothing but doubt and uncertainty, both negative forces; and above all we have, overdeveloped, that destructive sense of proportion—destructive to poetry, I mean—which we are pleased to call our sense of humour. It has been frequently suggested of late, indeed, that science might provide some material for poetry, but although this idea seems plausible and fertile enough at first sign, on second thought it is apparent that it represents only a very journalistic conception. I allude to it, and to the fact that such a suggestion has been made, merely to support my contention that something, some constructive meaning, some ideal, if you like to call it that, is lacking in the poetry of today, and that the critics have felt the lack of it, and are casting round for something which may take the place of the quality which I have characterised as reverence, awe, and faith. And when I say faith, I do not, necessarily, mean a religious faith; I mean what I can only call passion, that sense that some things *are* more important than other things and by that I do not mean, again, the fine frenzy, but a quieter, deeper thing, which is unaffected by our sense of humour, and expresses itself without the deterrent fear of ridicule.

It is precisely this, I think—this fear of ridicule, this absence of passion, this almost morbid dread of seriousness—which is driving the poets towards trivial, commonplace, or over-intellectualised subjects. The excuse often offered for the trivial and the commonplace is that the poets want to bring poetry nearer to the average human comprehension but I do not believe that there is any honesty in that excuse. No poet worthy of the name cares whether the man in the street understands him or not; he knows only too well that the man in the street doesn't read him, whether he writes about the immortality of the soul or about a workman throwing his boots at his wife. The intellectualisation of poetry is another thing, and I want to deal with that under my next heading.

So much, then, for the question of subject matter, which although important enough is by no means all-embracing; for a writer, if he be truly a poet—and in saying "if he be truly a poet" I mean if he be capable of putting his raw emotion into the crucible of his mind, so that it emerges a finer and more shapely thing; if he be truly a poet, I say, we will grant him the right to use any subject matter he think fit; and especially in this question of modern poetry, we shall be less interested in his subject than in the angle from which he approaches it. This brings me to my second point of difference between modern and what we may call traditional poetry, though I am aware that in using the words "traditional poetry" I am slipping into one of those loose expressions I most want to avoid. Still, for purposes of differentiation, we will let it stand.

My second point of difference concerns the question of focus, and herein lies probably the principal contribution of modern writers to literature. It is a platitude, but also a necessity, to insist upon the change which has taken place in our attitude towards all the arts: painting, sculpture, music, poetry, prose—those who practice these arts today tend, more and more, to dispense with conventional representation, and to inspire their work with something less life-like certainly, but aesthetically, psychologically, and emotionally even, more significant. Of course, as regards some of the other arts, there is nothing new in this; one has but to instance early Chinese pottery, for example, or certain primitive paintings and sculptures, but I am not speaking of the other arts, I am speaking of literature, and more especially of poetry, and so far as literature is concerned I do believe that a very real though, perhaps not a very profound, innovation has been introduced. It was born in France, where Mallarmé and Rimbaud, no less than Cézanne, began to see life from a queer, unfamiliar, oblique angle, something like a caricature, which surprises us first by it unlikeness and then by its likeness to the object. What this angle exactly is, and what this trick of focus, I find difficult to define; it varies, naturally between poet and poet, though in its total impression, it is always recognizable; it has, merely, different manifestations. Very often it manifests itself by a trick of phraseology, by allusion, by ellipses; by noun and adjective placed together in unfamiliar juxtaposition; by mannerisms of every kind. It is an attempt to view things with a fresh and different eye, even if the view is to produce something ungainly as a result; and again, in this respect. The mind is drawn irresistibly to the obvious analogy of modern painting. In a more fundamental sense, their attitude is less difficult to define. It springs, let us say, from the modern disgust with life, from the sense that the squalor of life is at least as evident as its beauty, and the consequent desire to rough-handle these conflicting elements, in an attempt to bring them into some sort of co-relation, an attempt which occasionally lands the poet in a setting-down of contrasts of almost incredible crudity. So we may say, that the principal points seem to be the discarding of conventional beauty and of reality (that is, representation), in favour of *interest*. No representation is no longer interesting to us, if interesting it ever was; for what it is worth, it has been done over and over again, and brought to such perfection that its achievement, to us, with the example and experience of our ancestors behind us, has become a matter of mere technical skill, an exercise in ingenuity. Conventional beauty is rapidly going the same road; to apprehend it has become a matter of thinking at second-hand, a thing intolerable to any truly creative mind. No, it is a fresh perception that we demand, the expression of states of mind, and a more revelatory interpretation of life, of object, of the universe, are the topics which set out to capture our interest and stimulating response. It follows, automatically, that poetry is becoming more and more abstract, allusive, intellectual—and indeed I am not at all sure that the 17th century metaphysical poets were not as truly our precursors as were the nineteenth-century symbolists.

I do not think that I am contradicting myself in anything I said before. I said that modern poets were afraid of seriousness, and I adhere to this, with the qualification that this intellectual attitude is the only thing about which they dare to be serious at all, and even that is frequently presented under an apologetic, sarcastic, or paradoxical guise. Nor is it precisely a breeding-ground for passion, but rather an anatomical, desiccated thing. It has called down, among other accusations, on modern poetry the charge of being introspective (though why poetry should not be introspective on occasion I do not know), but it seems to me that this is a false, short view. It is true that if we are interested in states of mind, those states of mind are mostly likely to be our own, since our own mind is the one we know most intimately; but this intellectual poetry is not concerned solely with psychological freakishness: it is concerned also with objects in the internal world, and with the significance that may be extracted from a fresh view of them. Indeed, one of its merits is that it endeavours to see the world, and the objects in the world, in a fresh unprejudiced way, and although the result is often ridiculous, it is also occasionally illuminating.

It goes without saying that many absurdities are perpetrated in the name of these new aspirations, even by those whose intention is sincere. But it must be remembered that this aspect of modern poetry is not only at the experimental stage, but also that the poets are experimenting with very difficult and ticklish material. If so small a proportion of poems in this new manner are successful as works of art, it is because the balance is so excessively precarious, the line between success and failure so perilously narrow. It is very difficult indeed to deal with the fine shades of perception in so inadequate a medium as words. Only when the moment of clearsightedness has been peculiarly intense, does something come through to us of the vision the writer is trying to render; and if this is true of all poetry, how much truer must it be of poetry which is dealing with experiences so fragile and so elusive. The pity is that so many of those experiments should appear in print, when they ought more properly to have gone into the waste-paper basket. They exasperate the reader, and blind him to the really interesting development which is taking place; they can serve no other purpose.

There remains the third point of difference, which to my mind is the most superficial of the three, though the most immediately apparent, and that is the question of form. A great deal has been written and said about free verse; a great deal more, I think, than the subject deserves. For one thing, it is not quite new, though it is certainly more generally practised today than heretofore. But it is easy to understand why this controversy should rage: it is because the practice of free verse provides a very dangerous trap, both for the writer and the reader, for the writer because it may enable him to escape many of the exactions of his craft, and for the reader because it is not always easy to distinguish between charlatanism and the genuine article. I want now, however, to discount the work of those charlatans who have brought discredit upon a perfectly genuine and laudable attempt to render the language of poetic diction more pliable and more elastic, and to concentrate only on free verse at its best. I will say at once, and without hesitation, that free verse properly used is as powerful and delicate an instrument as any that has been devised for the poet's art. I would go further, and say that it is a more civilised form than the regular stress and the recurrent rhyme; more civilised, in that it is further removed from the facile beat and jingle which for obvious reasons please children and unsophisticated people. It demands, for one thing, a finer ear; and this is no paradox, for free verse, in skillful hands, allows of modulations, subtly fitted to the sense, which are denied to all the accepted English forms with the exception of blank verse, its nearest relative. Mr. Robert Graves, with whom I don't always agree, puts it neatly when he says that "the claim of free verse is that actually each line, not only each stanza or passage, may be subject to a new musical change." It follows naturally enough that, whereas bad free verse is easy to write—anybody can do it—good free verse demands a sensitiveness and technical skill at least as great as those necessary for writing in a metre which helps the poet with its adventitious advantages, rather than hampers him with its more rigid laws.

There is a great deal more which I should like to say about free verse, and many illustrations which I should like to give, but time forbids; one comment, however, I must make lest I be misunderstood, and that is, that I do not believe that free verse can ever take the place, for certain purposes, of the recognised poetic forms. The greatest disability, I think, under which free verse labours is that it is less pleasing and consequently, above all, less memorable than its metrical rivals. It may be as satisfying to a well-developed aesthetic sense, but it does not, especially in its more exaggerated forms, take the same hold on the heart. A fine taste, as well as a fine ear, is essential to the poet; he must have a sense of what is suitable, and he must know with a right instinct what is suitable to free verse and what is not. Without wishing to be dogmatic, I would say that much metaphysical, narrative, dramatic, and descriptive poetry might well be cast in free verse, but lyrical poetry never.

Then there are side-issues on which I have not touched at all, tempting though they are. Every age has had its own poetic fashions, and ours is no exception. Every age has its own vocabulary, and its own flora and fauna; its overworked adjectives, and its favourite words; these things might form the subject of a diverting study, but are of course no more than the ornaments or blemishes of the surface texture. We tire of them as quickly as we tire of every fashion, and look round for something else. Thus already today, merry-go-rounds and harlequins, zinnias and unicorns, bore us as something merely out of date. I might speak too of the modern trick of reference to some detail which is charged with meaning in the poet's experience, but which has no meaning in ours; it is made to stand as a symbol for unutterable things, but we are given no plank with which to bridge the gap. But these furbelows have no real bearing on the subject we have been discussing, and I shall turn from them to the second part of my problem.

This was, if you remember, to what developments in poetry may the modern tendencies be expected to lead? And that is a question which no one, unless inspired with the gift of prophecy, can properly answer. I think it will be more useful to sift and summarise what I have said hitherto, and to see what proportion of the desirable and the undesirable we shall get out of such a sifting.

We have seen—if I have been so fortunate as to get you to agree with me— two principal differences between contemporary poets and their predecessors; firstly, that no high seriousness is allowed to inspire their verse, and secondly, that they endeavour to approach the world, both external and intellectual, from a new angle. There are minor differences, with which I have dealt, but we will ignore them for the moment. Let us call the two principal differences by convenient names: the difference of seriousness, and the difference of focus. In the first lies, according to my view, the loss, the disastrous loss; and in the second the gain. The point, you see, is whether the compensation is adequate. I submit that it is not. I am as interested as anyone in this difference of focus, and I respect it when I come across it, but I cannot believe that it is weighty and sufficient enough to fill permanently the room of the qualities it is trying to oust. It is interesting up to a point, as being representative of an age in which the old values are no longer stable, and in which we are casting round for an expression, almost a formula, of our perplexity and distress; but the whole attitude is, intrinsically, too negative, too limited, surely, to prove anything but a blind alley. To seek, in a new angle of approach, a substitute for the seriousness we have discarded, is surely nothing but a wanton evasion, a begging of the question. This attitude may provide an enrichment to literature, in the sense that it requires an angle of vision which has never been expressed before, but it is an enrichment which should be used sparingly—sparingly and suitably—not put forward as the foundation on which the great weight of literature may safely repose. The attitude fails, moreover, because it is incomplete; this vague discontentment is a thin, peevish thing, without the dignity of true pessimism; it is simply a confession of our inability to grapple with the problems that beset us today. It has not the bite of cynicism on the grand scale, such cynicism as Swift's or Voltaire's. Everything has been taken from us, our belief in continuity, in usefulness, in stability; we are disgusted with civilisation; we are bewildered by the pronouncements of science. And to oppose these catastrophes, we can produce nothing but a whimper of discouragement, and a trick of manner by which we hope to carry off and disguise the emptiness beneath.

> "What are the roots that clutch, what branches grow
> Out of this stony rubbish? Son of man,
> You cannot say, or guess, for you know only
> A heap of broken images, where the sun beats,
> And the dead tree gives no shelter, the cricket no relief,
> And the dry stone no sound of water. Only
> There is shadow under this red rock,
> (Come in under the shadow of this red rock
> And I will show you something different from either
> Your shadow at morning striding behind you,
> Or your shadow at evening rising to meet you:
> I will show you fear in a handful of dust."

Now those are fine lines, and the exactly convey the mood which I have been trying to describe; they say something which is worth saying, but although it is worth saying once in a way, I maintain that it is insufficient. It is too limited. Our attention is arrested for a moment by this frame of mind, partly because we are always more easily arrested by destruction and denigration, but we very quickly come to an end of it, and want to go on to something else. We say, "Very well. You have shown us the stony rubbish, the heap of broken images; we have looked, and admitted the existence of these things; now we must have something to put in their place." But so far the poets have nothing to give us; they reject the old, quite rightly, and we, quite rightly, are dissatisfied with the new.

This brings me back to the original question, what is to become of poetry? What becomes of poetry must depend very much on what becomes of men's minds; it is absurd to think of poetry as something separate from current life, shut away in an air-tight compartment. Literature must always, to a certain extent, hold the mirror up to general tendencies of thought. It is possible of course that we may witness, or that our children may witness, a return to the perennial problems which occupy men's minds; it is also possible that when we have absorbed the new values of science, when they have become a part of our consciousness, ceasing to be, as today, merely honoured in the intellect, our enlarged conception of Time and the Universe may reflect itself in serious and steadfast poetry. It is impossible to tell. But if our descendants do ever emerge, after this sad age of empty darkness, into a fuller light, they will surely look back on us,

> "Remember us—if at all—not as lost
> Violent souls, but only
> As the hollow men."

FROM *ANDREW MARVELL* (1929)

Vita's small book on Andrew Marvell might not seem at first glance a very likely place from which to single out her way of judging, for herself and her contemporary reading public, the poems of another writer and poet. For Marvell was, of course and to understate the case, of a style and outlook totally different from her own. And yet her writing here shows both her certain grasp of English poetry of that period and her sureness of judgment and fairness of outlook. What she calls the "preposterous rubbish" of the side-splitting "Upon the rock" passage she quotes, and her comments on his metaphors when they are particularly exaggerated or indeed splendid, as she says, seem as convincing as those of many literary critics preceding and following her, who were far better known than she was.

If her own poetry is uneven in what we might generally, at present, evaluate as its qualities and shortcomings, her taste is remarkably sure, and her assessments incontrovertibly learned. So she discourses on the Horatian ode, the pastoral tradition, and the like, quoting relevant passages as she goes along. What makes her essays particularly engaging is her unfailing eye for the outlandish passages, such as the one below on the Caesarean section, and her stylistic parody, as in the question: "Saw Marvell Cromwell?"

ANDREW MARVELL

VII

It is necessary, however, to turn to that other Marvell—the Marvell who had read too much of Donne, and who exercised his wit either upon ethical questions, or upon love, or even upon religion. It is not to be denied that this Marvell suffered from the faults of his contemporaries. He was capable of writing such preposterous rubbish as the notorious

> Upon the rock his Mother drave,
> And there she split against the stone
> In a Caesarian section;

he took pleasure in the metaphors drawn from cosmography or geometry which were so fruitful a source of disaster, and, like all his fellows, sometimes he managed them successfully and sometimes he came to grief. Sometimes, again, the question of his success or failure is debatable, and must be resolved by personal taste. What are we to say, for example, of these two verses:

> Unless the giddy Heaven fall,
> And Earth some new convulsion tear,
> And us, to join, the World should all
> Be cramped into a planisphere.
> As lines so loves oblique may well
> Themselves in every angle greet
> But ours so truly parallel,
> Though infinite can never meet?

or of this, where the beauty of the first two lines almost redeems the extravagance of the two following:

above Harold Nicolson, Vita, Rosamund Grosvenor, and Lord Sackville on their way to court, for Vita to testify in the celebrated case over Seery's (Sir John Murray Scott's) will, in which Lady Sackville was the chief beneficiary, 1913.

right Vita playing Portia in *The Merchant of Venice*, early 1900s. Photo by the Court Studio.

1913 painting of Vita by William Strang

Violet Keppel (Violet Trefusis) in the early 1920s

right Gwen St. Aubyn (Lady St. Levan) with the dog Martin, circa 1934

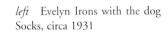

left Evelyn Irons with the dog Socks, circa 1931

right   Mary Campbell, circa 1927

left   Hilda Matheson, circa 1929.
Photo by Howard Coster.

left Vita and dogs at Long Barn, 1928. This photograph was used as the model for the image captioned "Orlando at the present time," in *Orlando,* Virginia Woolf's "love letter" to Vita. Photo by Leonard Woolf.

right Virginia Woolf at Rodmell, June 1926. Photo by Vita.

Vita and Harold on the steps at Sissinghurst

Harold and Vita by the mantle at Sissinghurst

Vita and her dog Rollo in the orchard at Sissinghurst, circa 1940

Vita in France, September 1928. Photo by Virginia Woolf.

left   Vita and Harold at Smoke Tree Ranch, California, 1933

right   Vita at Sissinghurst in 1955, at age 63

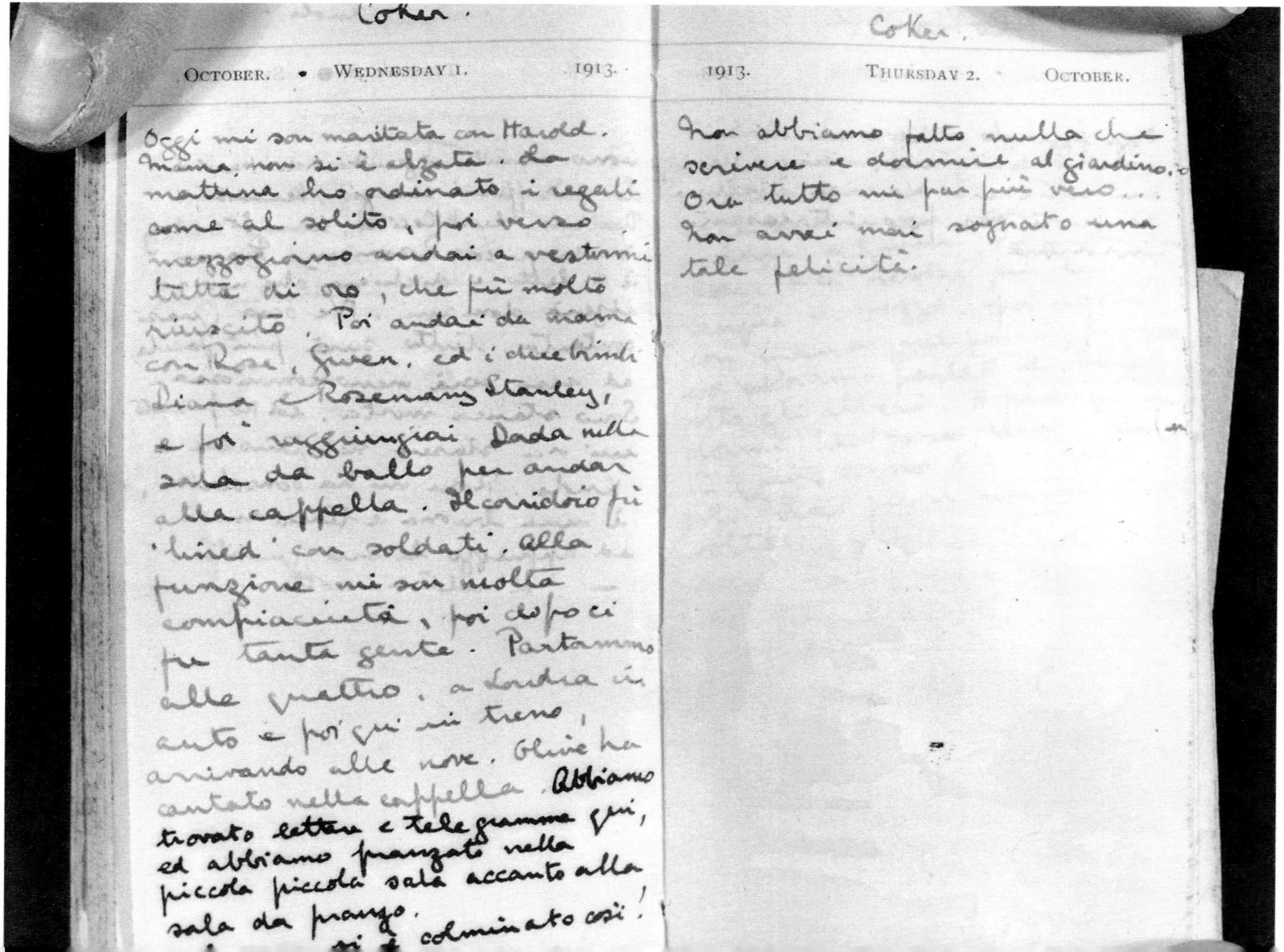

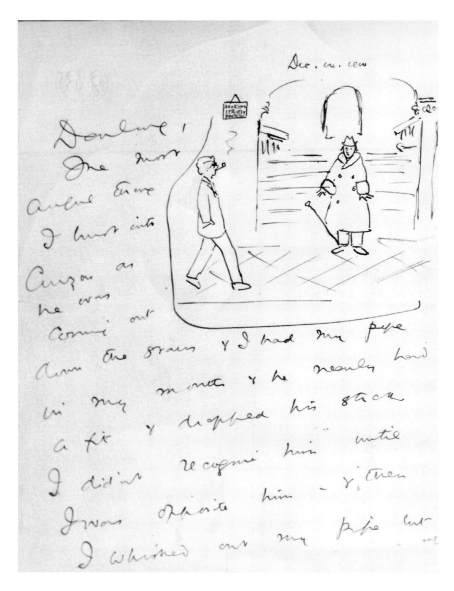

above Letter (date unknown) from Harold to Vita, about running into Lord Curzon (whose biography Harold was writing), startling him so that Curzon dropped his walking stick and Harold rapidly "whisked out" his own pipe. (courtesy of the Lilly Library at Indiana University)

left Vita's diary page, written in Italian, from October 11, 1913. It begins, "Today I married Harold. Mama didn't get up. In the morning I arranged for all the meals as usual, . . ." and concludes, "I would never have dreamed of such happiness." (courtesy of the Lilly Library at Indiana University)

The Saluki, or Gazelle-Hound, from Vita's last book, *Faces* (London: Harvill Press, 1961). Photo by Laela Goehr.

Collie dog from *Faces*. Photo by Laela Goehr.

above   VITA tiles in Vita's Writing Tower. Photo by Mary Ann Caws.
below   Nigel Nicolson and Mary Ann Caws at Sissinghurst, 1999.

> How wide they dream! The Indian slaves
> That sink for pearl through seas profound,
> Would find her tears yet deeper waves
> And not of one the bottom sound?

If we except *Appleton House* it is, generally speaking, noticeable that Marvell's use of injudicious conceits occurs most frequently in poems which we may presume him to have written round a deliberate thesis—such poems as *Eyes and Tears, The Match,* and *Upon the Hill and Grove at Billborow.* There are other poems which I am reluctant to include. Is *On a drop of dew* to be condemned? or *The Coronet?* or *The Gallery?* or *The Fair Singer?* or the *Definition of Love,* characteristic of the metaphysical school though it is, with its splendid opening?—

> My love is of a birth as rare
> As 'tis for object strange and high:
> It was begotten of Despair
> Upon Impossibility.

Surely not. Conscientiously though one may search through the pages of Marvell's lyrics, the worst offences are not to be found in him. It is impossible to imagine Marvell writing such a set of verses as Cleveland's *Fuscara.* Moreover, the true poet bursts out in the most unexpected places, as:

> Near this, a fountain's liquid bell
> Tinkles within the concave shell.
> Might a soul bathe there and be clean,
> Or slake its drought?

or—the shallower but still charming Marvell:

> Through every garden, every mead,
> I gather flowers; (my fruits are only flowers,)

or, most unexpected of all, the "old honest countryman," the garden-poet, suddenly interposing himself in the midst of an Horatian ode upon Cromwell:

> So when the falcon high
>   Falls heavy from the sky,
> She, having killed, no more does search,
>   But on the next green bough to perch.

The poet in Marvell died hard, whether he tried to stifle that poet under the weight of fashion or under an absorption in public affairs. And this mention brings me to yet another aspect of Marvell, which must not be forgotten.

We have considered him as a nature poet, as a pastoral poet, and as a poet of the school of wit; to consider him as a satirist lies outside the scheme of this essay, but there is a group of poems which straddles across the frontier between lyricism and politics. This group includes the *Horatian Ode upon Cromwell's return from Ireland, The First Anniversary of the government under O. C.* and *The Poem upon the death of O. C.* The Horatian ode is almost too well known to admit of quotation, but it throws so revealing a light upon Marvell's eminently reasonable and impartial attitude about public events that a few excerpts may be allowed. I have already quoted a passage from the *Rehearsal Transprosed* in defence of Marvell's alleged political inconsistency; the Horatian ode will bear out the opinions expressed therein, not so much in the famous lines upon the execution of Charles I,

> He nothing common did or mean
> Upon that memorable scene:
> But with his keener eye
> The axe's edge did try,
> Nor called the gods with vulgar spite
> To vindicate his helpless right,
> But bow'd his comely head
> Down, as upon a bed,

as in these four significant lines:

> Though Justice against Fate complain,
> And plead the ancient rights in vain:
> But these do hold or break
> As men are strong or weak,

a fatalistic creed which foreshadows his later words: "Men may spare their pains where Nature is at work, and the world will not go faster for our driving." The time was ripe for Cromwell, and, though Marvell did not approve of civil war, and thought on the whole that men "ought to have trusted the King," he recognized that according to the laws of nature the weak man must be broken by the strong,

> For to be Cromwell was a greater thing
> Then aught below or yet above a King.

But what has he to say of Cromwell himself since our concern here is less with Marvell's political convictions than with his vision as a man and a poet. The poem upon the death of Cromwell opens with an account of Cromwell's affection for his daughter and grief at her death, all in conventional strain; but the poet in Marvell, as has been said, was liable to burst the conventional fetters:

"All, all is gone,"

he exclaims suddenly,

"All, all is gone of ours or his delight
In horses fierce, wild deer, or armour bright,"

and from convention the poem swings to actual experience and interpretation:

I saw him dead. A leaden slumber lies
And mortal sleep over those wakeful eyes,
Those gentle rays under the lids were fled
Which through his looks that piercing sweetness shed;
That port which so majestic was and strong,
Loose and deprived of vigour, stretched along,
All withered, all discoloured, pale and wan,
How much another thing, no more that man?
Oh, human glory, vain; oh, death, oh, wings,
Oh, worthless world; oh transitory things! . . .

Saw Marvell Cromwell dead? Saw Milton Marvell ever? Poetry is a cynically lying jade, and her evidence is of no account.

A NOTE ON *THIEVES' CANT* (1947)

Vita's fascinations extended to philology, as witnessed by this piece on the differentiation between cant, the "tight and correct" opposite of the "loose, expressive, and metaphorical" slang that creeps into language. Specialists of the medieval French poet François Villon have made a study of the thieves' cant he uses, but it is not exactly a common focus of study. I include Vita's piece, found so strangely placed as an appendix to the 1947 edition of Knole and the Sackvilles, *as a further demonstration—should one be needed—of her widespread curiosity for language as for learning of all sorts.*

. . . I think few people, apart from students of philology, realize the existence of that large section of our language in use among the vagabond classes. Cant and slang, to most people's minds, are synonymous, but this is an error of belief: slang creeps from many sources into the river of language, and so mingles with it that in course of time many use it without knowing that they do so; cant, on the other hand, remains definite and obscure of origin. Slang is loose, expressive, and metaphorical; cant is tight and correct; it has even a literature of its own, broad and racy, incomprehensible to the ordinary reader without the help of a glossary. Its words, for the most part, bear no resemblance to

English words; unlike slang, they are not words adapted, for the sake of vividness, to a use for which they were not originally intended, but are applied strictly to their peculiar meaning.

Although the origin of cant as a separate jargon or language is obscure—it does not appear in England till the second half of the sixteenth century—the origin of certain of its words may be traced. Of those included in the vocabulary, for example, *ken,* for house, comes from *khan* (gipsy and Oriental); fogus, for tobacco, comes from fogo, an old word for stench; *maund,* or *maunder,* to beg, does not derive, as might be thought, from *maung,* to beg, a gipsy word taken from the Hindu, but from theAnglo-Saxon *mand,* a basket; *bouse,* to drink (which of course, has given us booze, with the same meaning, and which in the fourteenth century was perfectly good English), comes from the Dutch *buyzen,* to tipple. *Abram,* naked, is found as *abrannoi,* with the same meaning Hungarian gipsy; *cassan,* cheese, is *cas* in English gipsy; *diniber* survives for "pretty" in Worcestershire. *Cheat* appears frequently in catit as a common affix.

As for *autem mort,* I find it an early authority thus defined: "These *autem morts* be married women, as there be but a few. For *autem* in their language is a church, so she is a wife married at the church, and they be as chaste as a cow I have, that goeth to bull every moon, with what bull she careth not.

PART VI

HOUSE, GARDENING, AND NATURE

Vita's enlightened interest in specific place and landscape was matched by her equal interest in architecture and its history. Buildings of many sorts of locations elicited her enthusiasm, as did their history. She was no less eager to reflect on the ways in which the human imagination could shape from diverse materials in the natural world such an enormous variety of arrangements. Her knowledge seems endless on an endless variety of topics.

The multiform intertwinings in the human construction of material both artificial and natural supplied her with a continual source for her poetry and prose. In her writing about these vast topics, we sense both pattern and passion.

From *Knole and the Sackvilles* (1922)

*Perhaps Vita's most celebrated book, about history, house, and herself, concerns her
dearly loved and hard-lost Knole. Her relation to her colorful ancestors infuses the book
with nostalgia and beauty. Yes, she hated growing old, but the age of this house marks
it as venerable, and her relation to it as no less so. Vita's passion for and knowledge of
architecture was founded on her love of her house at Knole (its construction ranged from
King John to King James), well documented in this history of that "great Elizabethan
pile"[1] and its—and her—ancestry.*

There are further reflections on Knole and the adjacent property in her book Eng-
lish Country Houses. *Knole House itself is illustrated in this small volume, and details of its construction and appearance abound. In her other descriptions, as in these,
her writing feels lived, whether she is describing the black-and-white "startling and
stripy" timber houses of thick beams placed in plaster of a pale coloring contrasting with
the black beams, such as are found in Cheshire, or the brickwork of East Anglia, or
then the buildings of Nicholas Hawksmoor. However, because of her personally intense
connection to Knole, we are especially held by her description of it, the palace of the
Archbishop of Canterbury—the leader of the Anglican church—then a royal palace,
later in its "fulfilment as the home of an English family in whose hands it has remained ever since 1586." It feels organic, in spite of its five acres with its seven courtyards, gray and green, "quiet as a college; the garden paths suited to the pacings of
scholars as well as of courtiers; its 'stately and tempered medievalism lacks all taint of
the nouveau riche.'" History speaks loudly from its Elizabethan and Jacobean interiors
so richly decorated, with its long galleries and large fireplaces and big curtained bed (as-
signed to the King or the Venetian ambassador, or a poet or archbishop "or to Charles
the Second spending a night there with Nell Gwyn").[2]*

But it is in Knole and the Sackvilles, *with its intricate and nostalgic recount-
ing of the intimate connection between her adored house and her ancestors, that Vita's
impassioned and intense reflection has the feeling of an entire heritage to which she is
entitled both completely understood and irretrievably lost. Her childhood memories and
her adult's comprehension mingle here, as nowhere else. This is the nostalgic and
melancholy Vita, who may have lost her heritage, but who has earned our respect by
the detailed and careful delineation of her lineage and its place.*

When, in 1957, Alvilde Lees-Milne visited Eddy Sackville-West, who was living in Ireland, Vita lamented: "Drip, drip, drip; and all so green, and Eddy mouldering away towards old age when Knole . . . coud be his—and he doesn't want it, and I who would have given my soul for it."[3] Knole was taken over by the National Trust in 1947 and Vita wrote a new guidebook to the property at that time. Probably her last visit to the property was in 1958, when a letter to Harold expressed her continuing regret that the estate could not be hers. Vita opened Knole and the Sackvilles *with a poem by Christopher Smart.*

KNOLE AND THE SACKVILLES

The dome of Knole, by fame enrolled,
The church of Canterbury,
The hops, the beer, the cherries there,
Would fill a noble story.

Let Se'noaks vaunt the hospitable seat
Of Knoll [sic] most ancient; awfully my Muse
These social scenes of grandeur and delight,
Of love and veneration let me tread.
How oft beneath yon oak has am'rous Prior
Awakened Echo with sweet Chloe's name,
While noble Sackville heard, hearing approv'd,
Approving greatly recompens'd.

—Christopher Smart

CHAPTER I

THE HOUSE

i

There are two sides from which you may first profitably look at the house. One is from the park, the north side. From here the pile shows best the vastness of its size; it looks like a medieval village. It is heaped with no attempt at symmetry; it is sombre and frowning; the grey towers rise; the battlements cut out their square regularity against the sky; the buttresses of the old twelfth-century tithe-barn give a rough impression of fortifications. There is a line of trees in one of the inner courtyards, and their green heads show above the roofs of the old breweries; but although they are actually trees of a considerable size they are dwarfed and unnoticeable against the mass of the buildings blocked behind them. The whole pile soars to a peak which is the clock-tower with its pointed roof: it might be the spire of the church on the summit of the hill crowning the medieval village. At sunset I have seen the silhouette of the great building stand dead black on a red sky; on moonlight nights it stands black and silent, with glinting windows, like an enchanted castle. On misty autumn nights I have seen it emerging partially from the trails of vapour, and heard the lonely roar of the red deer roaming under the walls.

ii

The other side is the garden side—the gay, princely side, with flowers in the foreground; the grey walls rising straight up from the green turf; the mullioned windows, and the Tudor gables with the heraldic leopards sitting stiffly at each corner. The park side is the side for winter; the garden side the side for summer. It has an indescribable gaiety and courtliness. The grey of the Kentish rag [slates] is almost pearly in the sun, the occasional coral festoon of a climbing rose dashed against it; the long brown-red roofs are broken by the chimney stacks with their slim, peaceful threads of blue smoke mounting steadily upwards. One looks down upon the house from a certain corner in the garden. Here is a bench among a group of yews—dark, red-berried yews; and the house lies below, in the hollow, lovely in its colour and its serenity. It has all the quality of peace and permanence; of mellow age; of stateliness and tradition. It is gentle and venerable. Yet it is, as I have said, gay. It has the deep inward gaiety of some very old woman who has always been beautiful, who has had many owners and seen many generations come and go, smiled wisely over their sorrows and their joys, and learnt an imperishable secret of tolerance and humour. It is, above all, an English house. It has the tone of England; it melts into the green of the garden turf, into the tawnier green of the park beyond, into the blue of the pale English sky; it settles down into its hollow amongst the cushioned tops of the trees; the brown-red of those roofs is the brown-red of the roofs of humble farms and pointed oast-houses, such as stain over a wide landscape of England the quilt-like pattern of the fields. I make bold to say that it stoops to nothing either pretentious or meretricious. There is here no flourish of architecture, no ornament but the leopards, rigid and vigilant. The stranger may even think, upon arrival, that the front of the house is disappointing. It is, indeed, extremely modest. There is a gate-house flanked by two square grey towers, placed between two wings which provide only a monotony of windows and gables. It is true that two or three fine sycamores, symmetrical and circular as open umbrellas, redeem the severity of the front, and that a herd of fallow deer, browsing in the dappled shade of the trees, maintains the tradition of an English park. But, for the rest, the front of the house is so severe as to be positively uninteresting; it is quiet and monkish; "a beautiful decent simplicity," said Horace Walpole, "which charms one." There is here to be found none of the splendour of Elizabethan building. A different impression, however, is in store when once the wicket-gate has been opened. You are in a courtyard of a size the frontage had never led you to expect, and the vista through a second gateway shows you the columns of a second court; your eye is caught by an oriel window opposite, and . . . by the clock tower which gives an oddly Chinese effect immediately above the Tudor oriel. Up till a few years ago Virginia creeper blazed scarlet in autumn on the walls of the Green Court, but it has now been torn away, and what may be lost in colour is compensated by the gain in seeing the grey stone and the slight moulding which runs, following the shape of the towers, across the house.

On the whole, the quadrangle is reminiscent of Oxford, though more palatial and less studious. The house, built round a system of these courtyards: first this one, the Green Court, which is the largest and most magnificent; then the second one, or Stone Court, which is not turf like the Green Court, but wholly paved, and which has along one side of it a Jacobean colonnade; the third court is the Water Court, and has none of the display of the first two: it is smaller, and quite demure, indeed rather like some old house in Nuremberg, with the latticed window of one of the galleries running the whole length of it, and the friendly unconcern of an immense bay-tree growing against one of its walls. There are four other courts, making seven in all. This number is supposed to correspond to the days in the week; and in pursuance of this conceit there are in the house fifty-two staircases, corresponding to the weeks in the year, and three hundred and sixty-five rooms, corresponding to the days. I cannot truthfully pretend that I have ever verified these counts, and it may be that their accuracy is accepted solely on the strength of the legend; but, if this is so, then it has been a very persistent legend, and I prefer to sympathize with the amusement of the ultimate architect on making the discovery that by a judicious juggling with his additions, he could bring courts, stairs, and rooms up to that satisfactory total.

. . .

vi

There are other galleries, older and more austere than the Cartoon Gallery. They are not quite so long, they are narrower, lower, and darker, and not so exuberant in decoration; indeed, they are simply and soberly panelled in oak. They have the old, musty smell which, to me, wherever I met it, would bring back

Knole. I suppose it is really the smell of all old houses, a mixture of woodwork, potpourri, leather, tapestry, and the little camphor bags which keep away the moths; the smell engendered by the shut windows of winter and the open windows of summer, with the breeze of summer blowing in from across the park. Bowls of lavender and dried rose-leaves stand on the window-sills; and if you stir them up you get the quintessence of the smell, a sort of dusty fragrance, sweeter in the underlayers where it has held the damp of the spices. The potpourri at Knole is always made from the recipe of a prim-looking little lady who lived there for many years as a guest in the reigns of George I and George II. Her rooms open out of one of the galleries, two of the smaller rooms in the house, the bedroom hung with a pale landscape of blue-green tapestry, the sitting-room panelled in oak; and in the bedroom stands her small but pompous bed, with bunches of ostrich-plumes nodding at each of the four corners. Strangers usually seem to like these two little rooms best, coming to them as they do, rather overawed by the splendour of the galleries; they are amused by the smallness of the four-poster, square as a box, its creamy lining so beautifully quilted; by the spinning-wheel, with the shuttle still full of old flax; and by the ring-box, containing a number of plain-cut stones, which could be exchanged at will into the single gold setting provided. The windows of these rooms, furthermore, look out on to the garden; they are human, habitable little rooms, reassuring after the pomp of the ball-room and the galleries. In the sitting-room there is a small portrait of the prim lady, Lady Betty Germain, sitting very stiff in a blue brocaded dress; she looks as though she had been a martinet in a tight, narrow way.

The gallery leading to these rooms is called the Brown Gallery. It is well named: oak floor, oak walls, and barrelled ceiling, criss-crossed with oak slats in a pattern something like cat's cradle. Some of the best pieces of the English furniture are ranged down each side of this gallery: portentously important chairs, Jacobean cross-legged or later love-seats in their original coverings, whether of plum and silver, or red brocade with heavy fringes, or green with silver fringes, or yellow silk sprigged in black, or powder-blue; and all have their attendant stool squatting beside them. They are lovely, silent rows, for ever holding out their arms, and for ever disappointed. At the end of this gallery is a tiny oratory, down two steps, for the use of the devout: this little secret place glows with colour like a jewel, but nobody ever notices it, and on the whole it probably prefers to hide itself away unobserved.

There is also the Leicester Gallery, which preserves in its name the sole trace of Lord Leicester's brief ownership of Knole. The Leicester Gallery is very dark and mysterious, furnished with red velvet Cromwellian farthingale chairs and sofas, dark as wine; there are illuminated scrolls of two family pedigrees— Sackville and Curzon—richly emblazoned with coats of arms, drawn out in

1589 and 1623 respectively; and in the end window there is a small stained-glass portrait of "Herbrand de Sackvilic, a Norman notable, came into England with William the Conqueror, A.D. 1066." (*Ilerbrandus de Sackville, Praepotens Normanus, intravit Angliam cum Gulielmo Conquestore, Anno Domini MLXVI.*) There is also a curious portrait hanging on one of the doors, of Catherine Fitzgerald, Countess of Desmond, the portrait of a very old lady, in a black dress and a white ruff, with that strange far-away look in her pale eyes that comes with extreme age. Bernard Berenson, somewhat to my surprise, once told me that in his opinion it was by Rembrandt. Tradition says of her that she was born in the reign of Edward the Fourth and died in the reign of Charles the First, breaking her leg incidentally at the age of ninety by falling off a cherry tree; that is to say, she was a child when the princes were smothered in the Tower, a girl when Henry the Seventh came to the throne, and watched the pageant of all the Tudors and the accession of the Stuarts—the whole of English history enclosed between the Wars of the Roses and the Civil War. She must have been a truly legendary figure in the country by the time she had reached the age of a hundred and forty or thereabouts.

It is rather a frightening portrait, that portrait of Lady Desmond. If you go into the gallery after nightfall with a candle the pale, far-away eyes stare past you into the dark corners of the wainscot, eyes either over-charged or empty—which? Knole is not haunted, but you require either an unimaginative nerve or else a complete certainty of the house's benevolence before you can wander through the state-rooms after nightfall with a candle, as I used to do when I was little. There were no electric torches in those days. The light gleamed on the dull gilding of furniture and into the misty depths of mirrors, and started up a sudden face out of the gloom; something creaked and sighed; the tapestry swayed, and the figures on it undulated and seemed to come alive. The recesses of the great beds, deep, might be inhabited, and you would not know what might watch you, unseen. The man with the candle is under a terrible disadvantage to the man in the dark. But I was never frightened at Knole. I loved it; and took it for granted that Knole loved me.

vii

As there are three galleries among the state-rooms, so are there three principal bedrooms: the King's, the Venetian Ambassador's, and the Spangled Room. The so-called King's Bedroom has long been a subject of dispute. Fanny Burney, writing to her sister Susanna in October 1779, remarks that one of the state-rooms had been fitted up by an "Earle of Dorsette for the bedchamber of King James I when upon a visit to Knowle [*sic*]; it had all the gloomy grandeur and solemn finery of that time." Fanny Burney made a terrible muddle over the state-bedrooms at Knole, and is a most unreliable witness. It was she who originated the tradition perpetuated in my family that the King's Bedroom was prepared for King James I. I used always meekly to repeat this legend, but in wiser and better-informed years have come to the conclusion that it is without foundation. For one thing, there is no mention of any visit to Knole in the detailed account of the *Progresses of James I.* This, in itself, although negative, would seem to be conclusive. Then, for the second thing, there is the further indisputable contention that the sumptuous character of the carving and upholstery suggests a later date, more like Charles II than James I. I fear, therefore, that the idea of James I ever laying his ugly head on those bumpily embroidered pillows, or being enclosed within those coral-coloured bed-curtains at night, must be forever discarded. I am sorry about this, because the immense bed with its canopy reaching almost to the ceiling, decked with ostrich feathers, the hangings stiff with gold and silver thread, the coverlet and the interior of the curtains heavily worked with a design of pomegranates and tiger-lilies, the royal cipher embossed on the pillows, should have been a bed for a King, even so unattractive and uninspiring a King as James I.

I don't know what else to say about the King's Bedroom, otherwise sometimes called the Silver Room. I know it is very famous, but I have never liked it, and it is no good writing a book like this unless one states one's own feelings and prejudices. I think it is the only vulgar room in the house. Not that the great bed is vulgar; that is magnificent in its way, and beautiful too. What is shockingly vulgar is the set of furniture made of embossed silver: the table, the hanging mirror, the tripods—all the florid and ostentatious product of the Restoration. Charles Sackville cannot have known when he had enough of a good thing. He did not have it all made for himself; the silver table, for instance, bears the initials in a monogram F.D.H.P. which can be interpreted as meaning Frances Dorset (Charles Sackville's mother) and Henry Powle, her second husband. It has been suggested that the silver furniture at Knole was copied from similar sets made for Louis XIV at Versailles, all of which was melted down to meet some of the expense of the wars against England. If this is true, the set at Knole would thus be the only reproduction still in existence.

There is a lot more silver in the King's Bedroom—there are silver sconces on the walls, ginger-jars, mirrors, fire-dogs, rose-water sprinklers, and a whole dressing-table set of hairbrushes and boxes, even to a little tiny eye-bath, all in silver. I often longed to brush my hair with what I wrongly supposed to be King James' brushes, but having been strictly brought up not to touch anything in the show-rooms I didn't dare.

It is almost a relief to go from here to the Venetian Ambassador's Bedroom. Green and gold; Burgundian tapestry, medieval figures walking in a garden; a rosy Persian rug—of all rooms I never saw a room that so had over it a bloom like the bloom on a bowl of grapes and figs. I cannot keep the simile, which may convey nothing to those who have not seen the room, out of my mind. Greens and pinks originally bright, now dusted and tarnished over. It is a very grave, stately room, rather melancholy in spite of its stateliness. It seems to miss its inhabitants more than do any of the other rooms. Perhaps this is because the bed appears to be designed for three: it is of enormous breadth, and there are three pillows in a row. Presumably this is what the Italians call a *letto matrimoniale*.

viii

In a remote corner of the house is the Chapel of the Archbishops, small, and very much bejewelled. Tapestry, oak, and stained-glass—the chapel smoulders with colour. It is greatly improved since the oak has been pickled and the mustard-yellow paint removed, also the painted myrtle-wreaths, tied with a gilt ribbon, in the centre of each panel, with which the nineteenth century adorned it, when it was considered "very simple, plain, and neat in its appearance, and well adapted for family worship." The hand of the nineteenth century fell rather heavily on the chapel: besides painting the oak yellow and the ceiling blue with gold stars, it erected a Gothic screen and a yellow organ; but fortunately these are both at the entrance, and you can turn your back on them and look down the little nave to the altar where Mary Queen of Scots' gifts stand under the perpendicular east window. All along the left-hand wall once hung the Gothic tapestry-scenes from the life of Christ, the figures, ungainly enough, trampling on an edging of tall irises and lilies exquisitely designed; and "Saint Luke in his first profession," wrote Horace Walpole irreverently, "holding a urinal." There used to be other tapestries in the house; there was one of the Seven Deadly Sins set, woven with gold threads, and there was another series, very early, representing the Flood and the two-by-two procession of the animals going into a weatherboarded Ark; but these, alas, had to be sold, and are now in America. So is the tapestry from the chapel, which now hangs in the [Fine Arts] Museum at Boston, Massachusetts.

The chapel looks strange and lovely during a midnight thunderstorm: the lightning flashes through the stone ogives of the cast window, and one gets a queer effect, unreal like colour photography, of the colours lit up by that unfamiliar means. A flight of little private steps leads out of my old room straight into the family pew; so I dare to say that there are few aspects under which I have not seen the chapel; and as a child I used to "take sanctuary" there when I had been naughty: that is to say, fairly often. They never found me, sulking inside the pulpit. I used to think of John Donne, who sometimes preached there when he was Rector of Sevenoaks, reducing Lady Anne Clifford to tears.

ix

There would, of course, be many other aspects from which I might consider Knole; indeed, if I allowed myself full license I might ramble out over Kent and down into Sussex, to Lewes, Buckhurst, and Withyham, out into the fruit country and the hop country, across the Weald, over Saxonbury, and to Lewes among the Downs, and still I should not feet guilty of irrelevance. Of whatever English county I spoke, I still should be aware of the relationship between the English soil and that most English house. But more especially do I feel this concerning Kent and Sussex, and concerning the roads over which the Sackvilles travelled so constantly between estate and estate. The place-names in their letters recur through the centuries; the paper is a little yellower as the age increases, the ink a little more faded, the handwriting a little less easily decipherable, but still the gist is always the same: "I go to-morrow into Kent," "I quit Buckhurst for Knole," "my Lord rode to Lewes with a great company," "we came to Knole by coach at midnight." The whole district is littered with their associations, whether a village whose living lay in their gift, or a town where they endowed a college, or a wood where they hunted, or the village church where they had themselves buried. Sussex, in fact, was their cradle long before they came into Kent. Buckhurst, which they had owned since the twelfth century, was at one time an even larger house than Knole, and to their own vault in its parish church of Withybarn they were invariably brought to rest. Their trace is scattered over the two counties. But this was not my only meaning; I had in mind that Knole was no mere excrescence, no alien fabrication, no startling stranger seen between the beeches and the oaks. No other country but England could have produced it, and into no other country would it settle with such harmony and such quiet. The very trees have not been banished from the courtyards, but spread their green against the stone. From the top of a tower one looks down upon the acreage of roofs, and the effect is less that of a palace than of a jumbled village upon the hillside. It is not an incongruity like Blenheim or Chatsworth, foreign to the spirit of England. It is, rather, the greater relation of those small manor-houses which hide themselves away so innumerably among the counties, whether built of the grey stone of southwestern England, or the brick of East Anglia, or merely tile-hung or plastered like the cottages. It is not utterly different from any of these. The great Palladian houses of the eighteenth century are in England, they are not of England, as are these irregular roofs, this easy straying up the contours of the hill, these cool coloured walls, these calm gables, and dark windows mirroring the sun.

. . .

Appendix 2[4]

I have to record with sorrow that Knole was given over to the National Trust in 1947. It was the only thing to do, and as a potential inheritor of Knole, I had to sign documents giving Knole away. It nearly broke my heart, putting my signature to what I couldn't help regarding as a betrayal of all the tradition of my ancestors and the house I loved.

I deeply respect and admire the National Trust and all that it does for the salvation of properties. I don't know where we should be without it. I should, however, like to reprint an article I wrote in the Spectator which will perhaps reflect the feelings of many other people who have had to hand over their home because they were no longer able to afford to keep it up:

In times when the esteem of beauty and the humanities hides like an un-honoured nymph from the eyes of men; times when expediency, convenience, and economy demand and hold our entire and sole consideration; times when pressure compels us to forget that "Beauty being the best of all we know. Sums up unsearchable and secret aims"; times when beauty and all that stands for culture make no more impact on men's ears than the unreality of a dead language—in such times it comes as a plumb luxury to indulge even for a moment in the contemplation of something so very different, something so unnecessary, so inordinate, prodigal, extravagant, and traditional, as the great houses of the past. Of the past they are indeed, not only in century but in spirit; anachronisms both in time and in tenure. Yet in their growth they were organic, and in their creation they involved the completion of many a human life, the life of the craftsman who laboured, the stone-mason, the carver, the carpenter, the builder of chimneys, and the life also of those who ordered and enjoyed, the obscure "Richards, Johns, Annes, Elizabeth, not one of whom has left a token of himself behind him, yet all, working together with their spades and their needles, their love-making and their child-bearing, have left this."

FROM *COUNTRY NOTES* (1940)

Vita's wide reading informs her best writing. The initial essay in Country Notes, "January," begins with a reflection on Arthur Rimbaud's sonnet about the colors of the vowels, which she extends to the months of the year. January, she says, "is a large pewter plate stained with the reflection of a red sunset." It is not a month in which enough happens for her: It is too stationary. "I like the evidences of life, and in January there are too few of them." But, she continues, it is a perfect month for walking under the "bare trees, the wild, wet sky, even the car-ruts full of water, and the seagulls settling on the plough. . . . Damp and disheveled, January is the month for thick shoes, a dog at our heels, and the wind in our faces."⁵ May, she observes in her essay on that month, when so much happens too quickly to be seized in words, is the exact opposite of this winter feeling and demands a totally different reaction, no less vivid.

Vita's personality and her life imbue every piece of her country writing, yet she leaves no impression of someone dwelling in a castle, writing in a tower: Here she feels as present as your next-door neighbor, who might just have come in from a walk, able to tell you exactly what she saw, felt, thought. Like a neighbor who might ruminate at length on "Gardens and Gardening," she tells you how she took up gardening (as she did at 22), with a strip known as "Vita's garden," which she neither tended nor loved, or how she hates gadgets of all kinds and the names for them. A brief essay on gardeners follows later, relating how disconcerting she finds such people. In this book, as in most of Vita's writings, there is a reflection on the land she loves: Kent; often it is "looking absurdly like itself," and almost always it is quickly forgotten by the foreigner passing by in his train, although "we who live in Kent do not forget about it and have no wish to do so."⁶

Most of these essays were originally written for the New Statesman, a British periodical.

COUNTRY NOTES

A Country Life

Living in the country as I do, I sometimes stop short to ask myself where the deepest pleasure is to be obtained from a rural life, so readily derided as dull by the urban-minded. When I stop short like this, it is usually because some of my metropolitan friends have arrived to ruffle my rustic peace with the reverberations of a wider world. They ask me if I have seen this or that play, these or those pictures, and always I find myself obliged to reply that I have not. This makes me appear, and feel, a boor. Then after this most salutary visit they drive off, back to London, and the peace and the darkness close down on me once more, leaving me slightly disturbed but on the whole with an insulting sense of calm superiority. They leave me feeling that I am getting more out of this short life than they for all their agitations, an attitude of mind which strikes me as intolerably self-righteous. How can I possibly justify it? Should I not believe that it is more important to concern oneself with the troubles and interests of the world, than to observe the first crocus in flower? More important to take an active part wherever one's small activity would be most welcome, than to grow that crocus? How, then, to explain my backwater's deep source of delight?

I suppose the pleasure of country life lies really in the eternally renewed evidences of the determination to live. That is a truism when said, but anything but a truism when daily observed. Nothing shows up the difference between the thing said or read, so much as the daily experience of it. The small green shoot appearing one day at the base of a plant one had feared dead brings a comfort and an encouragement for which the previous daily observance is responsible. The life principle has proved unconquerable, then, in spite of frost and winds? The powers of resistance against adversity are greater than we thought; the germ of life lies hidden even in the midst of apparent death. A cynic might contend that nothing depressed him more than this resoluteness to keep going; it depends on the angle from which you regard this gallant tenacity. For my own part I find a singular solace in the renewal and reality of even the most monotonous of natural processes; I welcome the youth of the new season, whether it comes with the first lambs to be born in a snowstorm or with the new buds of the hornbeam pushing the old brown leaves off the hedges. If you have a taste for such things, no amount of repetition can state them; they stand for permanence in a changing world.

Country Speech

How much one regrets that local turns of speech should be passing away. There was a freshness and realism about them which kept the language alive and can never be replaced. Imported into prose they become fossilised and affected, for accurately reported though they may be in those novels of rural life of which one grows so tired, the spontaneity and even the accent are lacking; imported into poetry, they instantly sound like the archaisms of a poetic convention. If I read the phrase, "The cattle do be biding in the meads," it gives me no pleasure at all, but if a cowman says it to me (as he once actually did) it fills me with delight. I like also being informed that the rabbits are "interrupting" or "interfering with" the young trees; at least, I do not like the fact, but the way in which it is conveyed does much to mitigate my annoyance. I resent the mud less when I am told that the cows have "properly slubbed it up." Then sometimes comes a proverbial ring: "He talks too much, talk and do never did lie down together." I do not see where we are to find such refreshing imagery in the future, unless, indeed, we look to America where the genius of the vivid phrase still seems to abide.

The Knitter

I have a friend who knits. She sits on the floor, the firelight glancing on her hair, her tartan scarf thrown over her shoulders. She and the wide brick fireplace and the clicking needles and the balls of wool heaped on the floor beside her would compose a complete Dutch-school picture, were it not for the tartan scarf which suggests a crofter's cottage. She, oblivious of such objective considerations, continues to knit. She does not care whether she looks Dutch or Scottish; whether she fits into the tiled interior rosy as a pippin, or into the shieling. Nor do I care either. All that I know is that whenever she condescends to visit me, she, with her scarf and her wools, adds colour to the warm evening hour, when it has grown too dark to go out and one sits over the fire and talks.

Talks. . . . There is the snag. One cannot, I find, talk to a knitter. Conversation may seem to be going in that greased, easy way essential to all good conversation; starting hares [broaching topics] too lavishly to follow them up; allowing pauses for rumination; bursts for sudden eagerness in digressions, returns, new departures, discoveries of rooted creeds or new ideas—sooner or later the challenge is bound to come: "Don't you agree?" or "What do you think?" "Yes?" says the knitter, startled but polite, "seventy-five, seventy-six—just a moment till I get to the end of my row—seventy-seven, seventy-eight—yes," she says, looking up brightly, "it's all right now. What were you saying?" But of course one has forgotten or no longer cares.

All the same, everyone who wants to add a coloured domestic touch to that pleasant idle hour which comes between tea and dinner should engage a permanent knitter, dumb if necessary but ornamental. There is something soothing to the nerves about the monotony of the long needles travelling up and down the line; something satisfying to the eye about this primitive craft so closely allied to netting and weaving. A lace-maker rattling the bobbins on her pillow would make too much noise, and the whiteness of her work would jar too crudely on the hush and dimness of the room. The knitter with her wools, curled up beside the fire, is precisely what is needed. So long as you do not expect her to talk.

Small but Vigorous

Certain small animals seem to have been created with a fury of energy enough to do credit to any dictator. On another plane of life they might have accomplished anything. Luckily for humanity, they are limited by their size to relatively harmless activities. One of them, indeed, the common shrew, which may be heard squeaking either with excitement or temper in the long grasses, is one of the smallest mammals in existence, but his minute framework in no way limits the ardour with which he sets about his business. This business is usually concerned with the obtaining of food, for the shrew is one of those unfortunate creatures who must eat continuously and enormously. It is not so much that he is greedy, as that if he neglects his appetite he simply dies. No wonder that he is in so desperate a hurry when he knows that his last meal must be followed by another one within the hour, and that his long nose must lose no time in smelling it out. Even at night he cannot rest, for he cannot stoke himself up for the hours of darkness with a particularly large and late dinner: he is so constituted that he must eat often. Six times his own weight in food will see him safely round the clock, but any deprivation or delay will soon reduce him to a pathetic little corpse. If you have the time and inclination to spend most of the day hunting for worms and insects, you may keep a tame shrew and impress your friends by the readiness with which he will snatch food from your hand, but be under no delusion: this is not because he loves or trusts you, it is merely his extreme urgency leaving no room for fear.

Another hearty eater who is afflicted with a similarly precipitate temperament is that bane of gardeners, the mole. Larger and heavier than the shrew, he still demands at least the equivalent of his own weight in food each day. But consider the exercise he takes, and the violence he displays in taking it. It is enough to make anybody hungry. Semi-blind as he is, we might expect him to go about his work half-heartedly as a sluggard, but on the contrary he rushes at it as though a troop of devils were after him. Digging furiously, his track may often be watched rising in weals and mounds across the newly-raked seedbed, tracing his progress underground. Physically the little miner is beautifully adapted for his curious mode of life; his front paws are amazingly strong and provided with sharp claws and an extra bone; his ears non-existent though his whole body is, one might say, an ear; his eyes so deeply buried in his fur that they can come to no harm while he tunnels; his fur so disposed that there is no "wrong way" in which it can be brushed up, a very useful asset when its owner may have to retire backwards along a narrow passage. His teeth are sharp and numerous, as you will learn if you attempt to pick him up; his nose pointed and well-designed for use as a kind of trowel; in fact, the only weak point in his whole equipment lies in the fact that he dies immediately from a rap on that useful snout.

Eclipse

Many, if not most, people must have observed how frequently happenings occur in series. There exists a superstition that things happen in threes—you break one object and then immediately break two others, although you may not have broken anything for years. I do not know on what ground this superstition is based, but although I try (unsuccessfully) not to be superstitious, there are still certain beliefs to which I pay attention. One of those beliefs, corroborated by experience, is that although for weeks and even months one's own personal life may have remained uneventful, it will suddenly and without warning produce event after event, all in a rush, all in one day. That these events should be on a big scale or small does not affect the question. The point is that a number of things happen suddenly within twenty-four hours. Doves enter the window at dawn and sit cooing on the windowsill; a girl gets engaged; a boy gets a job; one hears the cuckoo for the first time this spring; the swans lay eggs; two partridges are discovered to be nesting in the orchard; eighteen bantam chicks hatch out; green woodpeckers carve a hole in an apple-tree; a puppy chews the Greek tortoise, and the sun goes into eclipse.

A busy day for those who enjoy a quiet life.

The sun went gently, not dramatically, into his eclipse. There was none of that darkened drama which attends the total phenomenon. The sun merely crept, rather cautiously on this occasion, behind the moon's shadow for three-quarters of an hour, allowing his sinking majesty to be impaired by no more than a bite out of a schoolboy's slice of bread-and-butter or the Mad Hatter's out of his teacup. It was not an impressive eclipse, as eclipses go. But even a partial eclipse, I discovered, may offer unexpected effects. I was thankful that unlike the Chilcotin Indians I need not feel obliged to tuck up my robes and, leaning on a stave, walk round in circles until the sun was once more in safety. I was thankful that I might squint simply through a smoked glass, standing outside the kitchen door, sharing the glass with other members of my small household. We passed it from hand to hand, from eye to eye. Looking westward at the sinking bitten sun, other objects came strangely into our darkened view: a flowering tree of red prunus, transmuted into a tree of a sinister loveliness unknown to any earthly botanist; and Kentish oast-houses coming into the small dark picture too—those oast-houses which always suggest witches' hats even in ordinary daylight, but which seen through a smoked glass with an eclipse of the sun going on behind them take on an alarmingly Sabbatical character. The visiting moon did indeed leave something remarkable that day.

May

At this season of the year, when so much in nature happens so quickly, I find it difficult to keep my head. I surmise that such a phrase may read as an affectation;

yet I protest with all my sincerity that I do try to set down on paper as simply and directly as possible the feelings by which I am moved. It is a hard thing to do; hard not to appear either exaggerated or mawkish, precious or inexact. It is very difficult indeed to write about nature and the natural processes without getting bogged in morasses of sentimental language. It is difficult for any honest writer to express his feelings in a way which will convince himself, let alone his readers, of his original sincerity; and if it is hard enough to be starkly honest towards ourselves even in our own private thoughts, to arrive without embellishment or gloss at what we really mean, the writer alone knows how far harder it is to be faithful on paper. Something comes between the writer and his pen; the passionate feeling, the urgency to record, emerge as a blob of ink, a smudge, a decoration. As Orlando discovered, green in nature is one thing, green in literature another. Thus if I set down that I have today seen apple-blossom strewn by wind on grass, I am stating a fact, and if I should happen to re-read my own words in future years (which is unlikely) they will probably recall that vision, as fresh and bright in memory as on that morning in the month of May. If, on the other hand, I start to expand my statement, in the hope of evoking a similar vision in the mind's eye of another, I shall immediately find myself drawn into semi-falsities, into truth wrapped round with untruth; I shall immediately begin to search for what the apple-blossom was like. I shall find confetti or snowflakes as a convenient comparison; I shall hit on the word shell-pink to express the delicacy, the papery delicacy of the scattered petals; I shall begin to "write"; but really, if I can be sufficiently severe with myself, I shall put my pen through all those blobs of ink, those wordy words, and cut myself back to the short phrase about apple-blossom strewn by wind on grass. It ought to be evocative enough, without amplification; but such is the impuissance of the human mind that it requires expansion before the experience of one person can be communicated to another. Or, at any rate, it requires a magic which mere prose is unable to provide. This is where poetry comes in; where poetry is, or should be, so far more evocative, more suggestive, than prose. Prose is a poor thing, a poor inadequate thing, compared with poetry which says so much more in shorter time. Writing, is indeed a strange and difficult profession.

Gardeners

Gardens have behaved in an extraordinary way this year (1938). Looking back upon my garden-diary, I find that on January 26th the blue primroses were in full flower, thus preceding their ordinary flowering period by about two months. Primroses, even the blue ones, have no right to start flowering in profusion until March or April. Then, on March 9th I find a note saying "all primroses flowering in earnest," and towards the end of the month another note to the effect that the garden appears to have gone mad, and that the pink clematis montana is out in company with tulips, hyacinths, anemones, and even a few of the flag irises. By April 1st we were eating asparagus from the open; by Easter I was picking roses. But there is no need to go on with the tale. Everyone knows that gardeners invariably say the season has been exceptional, only this year it happens to be true.

I find gardeners disconcerting people. Either they know infinitely more about the subject than I do, or else they know infinitely less. Seldom do I encounter one with whom I can discuss our common topic on equal terms. The gardener who knows more is impossibly highbrow, and makes me feel as small as a board-school child trying to discuss mediaeval Latin literature with, say, Miss Helen Waddell; the gardener who knows less makes me feel as though an earnest culture enthusiast said: "Do tell me something about *The Shropshire Lad;* it's a play, I know, but I've never seen it." This, by analogy, is what happens when somebody points to a delphinium and says "How they have improved lupins recently, haven't they?" How should one reply? To correct the speaker sounds patronising; to pass over the slip in silence destroys the possibility of further comment.

The Kentish Landscape

At the moment of writing these words, Kent is looking absurdly like itself. Cherry, plum, pear, and thorn whiten the orchards and the hedgerows; lambs frolic; the banks are full of violets and primroses; the whole landscape displays itself as an epitome of everything fresh and innocent which has drawn ridicule upon the so-called school of Georgian poets. It is a simple delight which pleases everyone, from the unsophisticated to the sophisticated. Why affect to despise it? Year after year I enjoy it more, and reflect with pride that my own county offers a fair presentment of the English scene to the foreigner travelling in his Pullman between Dover and London.

He, of course, cannot know it as we know it, though on his way up to London he is accorded a generous glimpse of the valleys of the Beult and the Medway. He sees the orchards and the hop-gardens; orchards he has seen before in his own Normandy, but the hop-gardens strike him as very peculiar and individual, opening and shutting as they do while the train flashes past. If he does not already know what they are, he is reduced to asking an obliging stranger for the explanation. Those tall bare poles, that elaborately knotted string, those ploughed acres—what does it all mean? The explanation is forthcoming: it is English beer. Of course: this is Kent. He looks out again with renewed interest, he remembers that this is called the garden of England.

Then his train slides into London, and he forgets about Kent.

But we, who live in Kent, do not forget about it and have no wish to do so. Intimately, not dramatically, it unfolds itself month by month. There are other landscapes more sensational, more romantic, more picturesque. This is a countryside which needs knowing. It needs a close and loving knowledge of the woods, the lanes, the villages, the changes of light, and the lost places. It needs, perhaps, a spirit far removed from the speed and competition of modern life to know and love it completely. One must be satisfied with small and subtle things. One must have time to absorb. Otherwise one is in very much the same position as the man in the train, flashing through, registering merely the passing comment: "Very pretty, yes, very pretty indeed."

Living here, we realise more than the prettiness, the tenderness, the intimacy, we realise also the variety which can be ours for a little trouble. I wonder what picture the word "Kent" evokes most readily in the minds of its lovers. For one of us, it will be acres and acres of blossoming trees; for another, the short sunny slopes of the chalk hills; for another, the wide skies and lush meadows of Romney Marsh; for another, the seacoasts; for another, a bluebell wood and the sunlight falling through the young green of the beeches. There are the slow streams and the stone bridges, composing exquisitely with the tower of the village church-beyond. There are the villages themselves, many as yet unravished—Yalding, Smarden, Chiddingstone, Brenchley; the little towns which preserve their charm and dignity such as Tenterden with its wide main street and the decency of its small Georgian houses, Cranbrook rocketing up and down hill, crowned by the white windmill and its noble sails. There are the dens and the hursts, with the miles of pleasant country in between, and the pink cottages tucked into odd corners, bright as a painter's palette with their jumble of flowers. All this is Kent, and all indubitably English.

Sentimentally, we may linger over some of the lovely place-names: Sutton Valence, Appledore, Stone-cum-Ebony, Capel-leFerne, Damian in the Blean, and the three Boughtons, Aluph, Malherbe, and Monchelsea. Historically our associations need fear competition with no other county: four of the Cinque Ports are ours, the Pilgrims' Way, and majestic Canterbury. We have plenty of food for pride, either as men of Kent or Kentish men.

But how true, in actual fact, is this idyllic picture? We all know the optimistically misleading style of the average guidebook, in which we are conducted by the enthusiastic author from one enchanted spot to another, little paradises of rural retirement, as secluded as when Cobbett passed between our meadows on his famous rides. Here is nothing, if the author is to be believed, to mar the prospect or rudely to jerk the dreaming mind. Every now and then, of course, the author gets confronted by some evidence of ugly utilitarian modernity to which he can blind neither himself nor his readers, and then in a fine indignation he lets himself go in several pages of lamentation, leaving us with the impression that these eyesores are of rare and strictly local occurrence, restricted to a few square miles or acres of victimised landscape, unlikely to impose themselves on a smaller scale on the happy wanderer who has the privilege of following his guidance down the byways. How far, I wonder, have I been guilty of giving the same misleading impression? One must be strict in these matters, even at the cost of some nasty truths.

Let me admit, then, that I have dwelt on the favoured corners and have left unmentioned those which one would rather pass with averted eyes. There is no denying that parts of Kent are dangerously near to London, and that the progressive spirit of the Southern Railway has brought them within a point of accessibility which can only be called suburban. The railway company, the road-makers, and the building societies have worked together in a morticed harmony which, applied to international problems, would soon produce a desirable settlement of world affairs. The owners of the land, acting either under the stress of financial compulsion or allured by the temptation of a quick and certain profit, have lent their co-operation by large sales of property to enterprising speculators. On the part of all concerned there has been a general agreement to "develop" the residential possibilities of one of England's loveliest counties. The only pity is that under this process of development the country should so rapidly be ceasing to be lovely.

It is necessary, today to find exactly where to go in order to find the unspoilt beauty where the true country-lover may rest his soul. My only plea in defence of my own veracity is that such retreats do still exist in Kent, more generously than the frequenter of main roads could possibly imagine.

We who care about such things view with alarm the spread of what we can only regard as damage. Daily, we see our fine trees being felled and their place taken by concrete posts slung with chains in front of shoddy buildings. Screaming red roofs and half-timber (no more solid than plywood) spring into being amongst our mellow cottages. Small wonder that we ask ourselves where it is going to stop, or, in a more practical spirit, what can possibly be done about it.

We do not wish to be reactionary or to deny the necessity of modern demands. Accommodation must be found, both for the working-man whose legitimate business keeps him to the district and for the daily-breaders and the weekenders whose desire is for a "cottage in the country." The natural consequences of these needs appear respectively in the form of council cottages and the small villa or bungalow. To the credit of the local councils it must be said that their productions are frequently of decent design, workmanlike construction, and aesthetically quite creditable. They could be better, of course, but they could also be a great deal worse. The same credit can scarcely be given to the large-scale contractors who supply the myriads of small "homes" so temptingly offered on easy terms, nor to those members of the public who snap them up so quickly that the advertisement board which was there yesterday will be gone by to-morrow. For this standardised trash I could wish only one fate: that it should all be miraculously transported and dumped as one large new city in the plumb Middle West of America.

Let me not be misunderstood. I recognise fully that "development" must take place; that sellers of land and contractors must make their profits; that the new owner and occupier must be satisfied as to convenience and cheapness. But still I wonder whether the outcome of all these separate requirements need be of such unexceptionable hideousness? I have heard it said that the whole trouble arises because there is no central control, and that the present haphazard system can produce only what it does actually produce. I have even heard it suggested that an official committee of supervision for the whole country should be appointed under the auspices of the Office of Works. The men whom I privately heard making this suggestion were Lord Curzon and Mr. Ramsay MacDonald, two very different types of men, the patrician and the politician, yet both inspired by the same wish to preserve the beauty of their country. There is much to be said for such a scheme, but there are also a great many obvious objections to raise against it. In its favour it may be said that the taste and experience of an expert advisory board would in the aggregate be better and more valuable than the taste of the average builder and of the public for whom he caters; against it may be said that in matters of taste few men with strong prejudices agree (and from such men the advisory board would presumably be drawn) and that one generation would almost certainly condemn the voice of the other. It is also evident that the indignation aroused by the restrictions necessarily imposed by such a board would be extreme, for our national character comprises a strong dislike of interference in our private affairs, and in a non-totalitarian state it is difficult to believe that a man would tolerate dictation in so private and personal a matter as the choice of his own home. If he likes bow-windows with stained glass, sham beams, or scarlet roofing, what authority can venture to forbid him to have it? The only appeal is to his own discretion and sense of fitness; but the sad truth is that the taste of the public is demonstrably bad. It prefers the ornate to the simple, the pretentious to the modest, and the consequence is that the small margin available in the estimate goes into something showy rather than into the honest domestic architecture whose survivals provide one of the minor beauties of our country. It seems only a foolishly Utopian dream to hope to raise the standard by even the most tactful methods of propaganda, yet the fact remains that a change of heart in the public alone would produce a change of method in the builder.

It appears to me that something might be done by organising open competitions among the regional architects. As men familiar with the district they would have a good chance of understanding its needs, both practical and aesthetic: the treatment of brick, stone, plaster, tiles, or thatch, as the case might be, would come naturally to them as part of their daily life. The winning entries in these competitions should be displayed as a kind of bait to the public in several ways, either by photographs of the design in local papers, or exhibited in the post offices, or, best of all, as actual constructions to be let or sold. It is conceivable that with a *de facto* example before their eyes, some prospective purchasers might turn from the monstrosities to which at present they are offered no alternative, and where some lead the way others might follow. There is no real reason why a presentable house or cottage should not be erected conveniently and inexpensively, nor should the solution unduly tax the ingenuity of the designer. His scope would indeed be varied and extensive, for apart from private dwellings the public requirements are great, and in the creation of new streets, new suburbs, even new villages, I can imagine a lively excitement to an inventive man. There is nothing necessarily to be said against the garden-city, of which indeed one has appreciated some attractive examples; the garden-village, in the country, complete with church, school, shops, and even a central community garden as well as gardens to the individual houses, might invite the envy of strangers from miles around and cause us to forget the shudder usually aroused by the mere sight of the words "building developments." It should also be possible, by the extension of such schemes, to concentrate activities in more definite areas, instead of letting them straggle in their present happy-go-lucky fashion all over the place.

The isolated bungaloid effort, admittedly, is difficult to cope with, since you cannot prevent a man from buying a plot of ground where he likes and putting up whatever he likes on it. It seems very strange that a man who has the taste and sensibility to wish to live among beautiful surroundings should not also have the taste to see that his own abode is probably the one thing which ruins them; but so it is. Here, again, the bait of a suitable, non-discordant sample might do more than many pages of written exhortation and entreaty. Many people, small blame to them, prefer the convenient modern dwelling to the picturesque but earwiggy old creeper-covered cottage where the alternative is either to crawl about bent double or else to bang your head on every lintel. There is no reason why they should not have it; there is also no reason why they should make it impossible to look across miles of country where nothing breaks the eye's delight.

Owls Brood

I find something curiously touching in the quiet patience of a nesting bird. Day after day, at whatever hour one visits the nest, she is sitting there, close, warm, and lonely. One wonders what her thoughts may be; what fears may assail at the approach of footsteps; what deep instinct informs her of the final reward of her perseverance. The courage of some of these small creatures is indeed remarkable; I have inadvertently put my hand right on to a thrush, and had my finger sharply pecked by a blue-tit in a drainpipe. Not so a Little Owl, nesting in a hollow apple-tree I pass every morning on my way to breakfast. Long before I have reached the tree she is out and away, flying off with the peculiarly noiseless flight which suggests twilight far more than the dews of summer morning. Once or twice I have deceived her; crept up to her tree, and seen her cowering, head drawn back, ready to strike, a wicked eye looking up at me from the darkness. I was afraid she might desert her nest, a squalidly messy affair, but she shows no sign of doing so, and I look forward to the day when five recoiling babies will huddle at the bottom of the hollow trunk.

Fog

Leaning over the parapet of the Pont Neuf, I watched a few swirls of vapour drift above the river, so ethereal and milky that they really only added to the cleanliness and elegance of Paris. A Frenchman beside me thought otherwise. "Voilà," he observed gloomily to his companion, "*voilà ce qu' à Londres on appelle le fog.*"

I was amused by this remark, having a sudden vision of a midnight darkness descending on London at midday, diabolical with flares, congested with crawling traffic. There is a certain beauty in this black-and-red effect, however, although it may be denied to the choking yellow variety; and considerable beauty also in the white country fog, so long as it is not too thick. It must be transparent enough for us to discern the shapes of trees, their trunks cut off, so that nothing but the finely veined heads remain, untethered, as sometimes in a desert mirage the tops of mountains appear to float suspended above the solid earth. In this thin fog, familiar objects become invested with a new unreality: it is as though we were seeing them for the first time. *Dissimili non sono che nei sembianti*—a most profound remark. Even houses, the homes of men, become as suggestive as the unknown lives moving inside them. A side-road, opening and vanishing as we creep past, might lead into another and more desirable world. It is only when the shroud really comes down and we know that the thickening must deepen with the failing daylight, that fog turns into the enemy, obliterating, instead of enchanting, our way.

Since such disadvantages are likely, indeed certain, to overwhelm our island at intervals during six months of every year, upsetting the arrangements of thousands and even throwing them into actual danger, why may we not be given white kerb-stones along our country roads? The device is obvious and relatively inexpensive. There would be no need for the extravagance of a running kerb everywhere; white, painted, upright stones, like miniature milestones, placed every few yards would be of enormous value to the motorist in fog. One knows the difficulty of trying to follow a grass verge; one knows also with what relief one hails a mere white central line. Now in Italy, where the peril of fog is practically nil, many of the main roads and bridges are ornamented by black and white striped stones, running for miles, for no reason that I can see except pure bravura. If Italy can afford this luxury, why can we in England not afford a similar necessity?

Gadgets

I mistrust gadgets, generally speaking. They seldom work. The proved, old-fashioned tool is usually better and it is safer to stick to it. I thus make a rule of throwing all tempting catalogues of gardening gadgets straight into the wastepaper basket, not daring to examine them first, because I know that if I examine them I shall fall. It will mean only that I shall with some trouble obtain a postal order for 10s. 6d., to acquire an object which will speedily join similar objects rusting in the tool shed. It should be clear from this that my mistrust of gadgets is equalled only by my weakness for them and that no amount of experience can make me find them anything but irresistible.

Nevertheless this attitude may be ungrateful, for there are certain gadgets which have been my companions for so long that I have ceased to think of them under that name. There is the walking-stick shaped like a golf-club with a cutting edge to slash down thistles; you can do it without pausing as you walk, and not only does it control the thistles but provides a harmless outlet for ill-temper. Then there is the long narrow trowel of stainless steel and its associate the two-pronged hand fork, both unrivalled for weeding in between small plants, though perhaps there is no tool so well adapted for this purpose as the old table knife with the stump of a broken blade. There is the little wheel on the long handle, like a child's toy, which you push before you and which twinkles round, cutting the verge of the grass as it goes. Above all, there is the widger, the neatest, slimmest, and cheapest of all gadgets to carry in the pocket. Officially the widger is Patent No. 828793, but it owes (I believe) its more personal name to the ingenuity of Mr. Clarence Elliott, whose racy gardening style ought to be more widely appreciated. He invented the widger, its name, and the verb to widge, which, although not exactly onomatopoeic, suggests very successfully the action of prising up—you widge up a weed, or widge up a caked bit of soil for the purpose of aerating it—all very necessary operations which before the arrival of the widger were sometimes awkward to perform. This small sleek object, four inches long, slides into the pocket, no more cumbersome than a pencil, and may be put to many uses. Screwdriver, toothpick, letter-opener, widger, it fulfils all functions throughout the day. Its creator, Mr. Elliot, I observe, spells it sometimes with a y: wydger, no doubt on the analogy of Blake's Tyger, just to make it seem more unusual. Whatever the spelling, it is the perfect gadget.

What an odd little word "gadget" is, almost a gadget in itself, so small and useful. Its origin is obscure and it is believed not to appear in print before 1886. Yet it is not, as might be thought, an Americanism. It appears as an expression used chiefly by seamen, meaning any small tool, contrivance, or piece of mechanism not dignified by any specific name; a whatnot, in fact, a chicken-fixing, a gill-guy, a timmey-noggy, a wim-wom. I commend these agreeable synonyms to Mr. Clarence Elliott's notice, and at the same time record my gratitude for his revival of that other sea-faring word, manavelins. I wonder how many English-speaking people are familiar with its meaning?

Note from another country: Tuscany

Once when I made the mistake of living in London somebody wrote to me in a charmingly old-fashioned writing, with a great many capital letters and underlinings, saying: "What a Torment it must be for you to live in a Town, seeing nothing but Houses and Advertisements." This might seem to be a simple saying, but it sank into me and made a stain, so that I wondered about people: how many of them, who lived in towns, really saw nothing but houses and advertisements? and how many of them who led a more retired life, built up for themselves a whole inner existence out of tiny but immensely significant occurrences—Montaigne, for instance, was obviously such a one, to whom even a new thought was an event; and in the permanent mood of an intense inward excitement he took to his essays, as the daily purgation of a mind which must find some outlet, so intoxicating were the discoveries made in solitude, and came to the conclusion that it is exceedingly difficult to say what one means. My copy of Montaigne says on the fly-leaf: "Mary Jones, her Husband's Gift 1751, price 14s. the three Volumes." I like to reconstruct that Mary Jones. To her, her husband, spelt with a capital letter, was a fact; and his gift, also spelt with a capital letter, was an event: Her Husband presented her with the Gift of Montaigne's Essays, nicely bound in brown leather, but on what occasion she does not say: not an anniversary, surely, or the appended date would have been more specific than merely 1751: no, it must have been an occasional gift, an unbirthday present, on a stray day of the year; perhaps he had been cross to her in the morning, and, sensible of remorse, returned home in the evening with the gift under his arm, who knows? And the cost of the gift, he must have told her that; let it drop, as it were: fourteen shillings! else how should she have known, as know she evidently did, for the sum is entered in the same handwriting. Or was that writing his, not hers? We shall never know, nor shall we know whether the acquisition or the perusal of that Montaigne represented an adventure, a milestone in the life of Mary Jones; all that we can know is that the gift at some time, perhaps at her death, passed from her possession into that of Thomas Sedgwick Whalley, of Rendip Lodge, whose bookplate adorns the end-paper and then comes my name, with that of the friend who gave me the book: a whole little palimpsest of lives, superimposed one on another in the foxed old volume: Montaigne himself, Mary Jones, Mr. Whalley, and then finally me.

Such speculations are possibly not worth pursuing, and the psychoanalysts, indeed, definitely disapprove of daydreams; they give them a terrible name, uncoordinated thought or something like that, and tell us to practise a useful concentration. But the truth is that the adventures which happen in the mind are more dangerous and important than those which happen outwardly in the open air; they have a habit of fermenting, and all sorts of toadstools sprout in the halflight of our underground cellars. Shall we then listen to the psychoanalysts and their warnings? The toadstools have their beauty. Scarlet, speckled, grotesque, they glow in the obscure corners. It is not safe to explore underground: you do not know what you may meet.

There was an adventure which happened to me once, and which, although it will lose everything in the telling, I will tell. It did not take place among houses and advertisements, and those who saw me pale with terror—those, that is, who saw the effect without having shared the experience—laughed at me in a kindly way. I was annoyed that they should have found me out, for what had happened concerned me and me only, but there was no help for it—my looks had betrayed. Had I seen a ghost? No, I had seen nothing so palpable as a ghost; I had in fact seen nothing at all; I had only felt. I was careful not to tell them this; I simply said that I felt ill and wanted air. So I did. But what I wanted most was time to absorb something which I already knew I should never forget.

The place was an old Italian castle, situated down in a valley among cypresses. The slopes of the hills, in rough terraces, were covered with vines; and as the month was October the leaves had turned to a brilliant red, so that the hillside in the level rays of the sinking sun appeared to be on fire. It was a remote place in the country, a deep bowl of a place, scooped in the hills; and that old castle, among the black trees, scarcely visible, seemed to be trying to burrow its way even more deeply into the heart of the earth. I am not saying that it was sinister, for it was not; only it was like a great piece of rock that had got lodged among the cypresses at the bottom; that had rolled itself down from the top of the hills and would have liked to go deeper had the earth not stopped it. There were no other dwellings within sight; it was alone with the red vines and the black cypresses and the circle of blue sky overhead; nor could it rightly be called a dwelling, for the peasants used it only during the daytime and deserted it for the night when their labour was done. It was deserted when we came to it, but the great gate was open to a push in the thoughtless trusting way of remote country districts, and our footsteps rang unchallenged on the stones of the inner courtyard. We penetrated into the rooms; they were put to purely useful uses; hung with grapes, that is to say, grapes that were not to be pressed into wine, but dried into raisins, so that they were hung, bunch after bunch, along osier wands where the maximum of sunlight would strike upon them. Even now the afternoon sun was on them, making them transparent as they hung, the veinings and even the pips visible, as the veins of a hand held against the fire. We exclaimed, and thought them lovely. But there were deeper recesses within the castle: a flight of stone steps, leading down, less attractive than the old banqueting rooms hung with grapes, but more attractive because more mysterious, less obvious, more frightening. I slipped away and went down alone.

Upstairs I left the courtyard, with the late sun striking into it, and the voices of my friends; the steps led me down into an increasing darkness, so that I reached out my hand to touch the wall lest I should stumble. I could just see that the bottom of the steps opened out into a cellar. There was a gleam of light from a cobwebbed window opposite. A dim aroma came up to me, but I thought nothing of it, and trod light-heartedly down into the cellar, and stood there among the enormous barrels, like vats, ranged on either side of the vault. I stood there, pleased to be alone in that queer place, looking at the vats, and snuffing the curiously scented air. I did not at first understand how insidious the scent was; at first, it was sweet and heavy, neither pleasant nor unpleasant, but just different from anything I had ever smelt before. I snuffed it, interested, as one might play with a new idea. I was down there, I suppose, for two minutes before I was overcome. I had not realised that the barrels were full to the brim with fermenting juice. Even as I was seized with panic—panic in the classical sense of the word, panic in the sense of a spirit sprung from nature and stronger than myself—I did not realise it. I knew only that I must reach the air or I should fall. Blindly I turned and staggered for the steps, gasping for air, gasping above all for sanity, struggling to escape the cellar where such irresistible forces had nearly taken possession of me. I reached the top, and the hands of my friends pulled me into the light.

But what I still want to know is, what happened to Mary Jones and Mr. Whalley when they went down into the darker places?

From *A Joy of Gardening* (1958)

It is widely agreed that Vita's writing and talks on the art of gardening, along with her travel writing, count among her best works. Her involvement in and knowledge of the many aspects of choice: what goes with what and why, and care: how to best control and tend, are in full evidence. She waxes lyrical, plays with nomenclature, and demonstrates a complete scale of emotions in relation to this art. Included here is a reflection on sight and colors, in which a pair of amber-colored spectacles intensify the vision, and remind us of the rose-colored spectacles that give rise to the plot of her novella Seducers in Ecuador.*

These musings are divided by seasons: "Lilacs of loose delicacy," in the Autumn selection, begins with a rousing introduction: "In the last-minute scramble to order the shrubs we had made note of in those far-away happy months of May and June, and have since forgotten, let us now remember the Preston lilacs, Syringa prestoniae, before it is too late." There is often a sense of urgency in her tone and subject. Often it is called upon to discuss how to redeem various neglected gardens; she takes those "redemptions" seriously. "Good gardeners take trouble," she entitles one of her essays, distinguishing between "most of us amateur gardeners," and good gardeners, those who know their job. She knows the job of writing, as of gardening, despite her modesty.

In her "French Idea of Gardening," Vita draws a horrific contrast between the charm of the villages with their pots of flowers in the street and the ghastly formal public gardens with the names of towns spelled out in flowers. In her reflection on Alpines, she counsels on the varied heights at which certain flowers and bushes should be planted, according to the landscape. Here, as elsewhere, she shows an abounding curiosity about small details, such as the items in a catalog. Her strong advocacy in simplicity in everything has no feeling of outdatedness; rather, like her own carefully tended garden at Sissinghurst, it is of lasting value. She is perhaps at her verbal best in these garden variety of reflections.

A Joy of Gardening

Summer

. . .

Full-bosomed trollop of a rose

The other day I encountered a gentleman wearing amber-colored spectacles. He was kind enough to say that I had a well-chosen range of color in my garden. I expressed some surprise at this, since it was obvious that he could not be seeing any colors in their true color, but must be seeing them in some fantastic alteration of tincture. Yes, he said, of course I do; it amuses me; try my glasses on, he said; look at your roses; look also at your brown-tiled roofs; look at the clouds in the sky. Look, he said, handing them to me. I looked, and was instantly transferred into a different world. A volcanic eruption, or possibly an earthquake, seemed imminent. Alarming, perhaps, but how strange, how magical.

Everything had become intensified. All the greens of turf or trees had deepened. All the blues were cut out, or turned to a blackish brown. The whites turned to a rich buttercup yellow. The most extraordinary effect of all was when you switched over to the pink variations of color. There has been some correspondence in the press recently about that old favorite rose, Zéphyrine Drouhin. Dear though she was to me, perfect in scent, vigorous in growth, magnificent in *floraison* (a lovely and expressive word we might well import from French into English, since we seem to have no equivalent in our language), and so kindly and obliging in having no thorns, never a cross word or a scratch as one picked her—dear though she was, I say, I had always deplored the crude pink of her complexion. It was her only fault. Seen through the magic glasses, she turned into a copper orange; burnished; incredible.

Zéphyrine Drouhin has a romantic history, worthy of her breeze-like name. She derives from a hybrid found growing in 1817 in a hedge of roses in the Ile de Bourbon, now called Réunion, off the cast coast of Africa. This hybrid became the parent of the whole race of Bourbon roses, which in their turn have given rise to the modern roses we call Hybrid Perpetuals and Hybrid Teas. This is putting it very briefly, and seems to bear no relation to the great pink bush flowering in the summer garden under the name Zéphyrine Drouhin. Who was Zéphyrine? Who was Monsieur Drouhin? These are questions I cannot answer. They sound like characters in a novel by Flaubert. I know only that this gentle, thornless, full-bosomed, generous trollop of a rose turned into a fabulous flaming bush under the sorcery of the tinted glasses.

. . .

Autumn

. . .

The French idea of gardening

I have recently returned from a wandering holiday in southwestern France, and have been observing with interest the French idea of gardening, as compared with our own. I do not mean the grand formal gardens in the style of Le Nôtre, at which the French with their wonderful sense of architectural symmetry excelled, but the public gardens and the efforts of villagers along the roads.

The villagers produce an altogether charming effect, comparable with our own cottage gardens at home. The village street is lined with pots, standing grouped around the doorways or rising step by step up the outside staircase when there is one, pots filled with pink geraniums, zinnias, begonias, nasturtiums, carnations, marigolds, all mixed and gaudy. Clouds of the Heavenly Blue morning glory drape all the little balconies, and the orange trumpet creepers ramble everywhere. Especially enviable are the ancient bushes of hibiscus, which in the southern sunshine flower far more luxuriantly than with us, both the blue one and the red one, and that pretty creamy one with a whiskery maroon blotch on each flower, which is like a chintz, *Hibiscus syriacus.* They are usually grown as standards, with a huge head smothered in blossom. Nothing could be gayer or lovelier or, in its way, simpler than this garish exuberance of the village street. It is the natural expression of a desire for color, and I wish our own villages would all copy it.

The public gardens, alas, provide a different story, and bear only too distressing a likeness to many of our own municipal layouts. It seems impossible, even in these days, for the professional municipal gardener to get away from the Victorian and Edwardian passion for bedding-out. Why can he not, in this country, take a hint from the London parks, wellnigh irreproachable in the good taste of their flower arrangements? But no. In France he goes just as bad, and just on the same lines. Horrible lozenges and kidney-shaped and shamrock-shaped beds, laboriously filled with scarlet salvia, cannas, coleus, and nameless monstrosities of variegated foliage; regimental edgings of rosettes like flattened artichokes; vast leaves of not-very happy bananas in the center; and dreadful little conifers stuck meaninglessly about. The French are also very fond of writing the name of the town in lobelia and white alyssum. Such ingenious practices may please children, but they should not please grown-ups.

Nothing but my intense admiration for the incomparable French taste and civilization could provoke such surprise and dismay. It is all very odd, very odd indeed. One is left wondering why.

A ribbon of Alpines

A most pleasing and original suggestion reaches me in a nurseryman's catalog. It is the sort of suggestion which could provide extra color and interest in a small garden, without taking up too much space and without involving too much labor. It is, simply, the idea of growing low Alpines in a narrow border on both sides of the path running from your gate to your door, or, of course, on both sides or even one side of any path you may find suitable.

By "low" Alpines I do not mean those plants which occur only on the lower slopes of mountains, a technical term in horticulture, as opposed to the "high" Alpines. I mean flat-growing; close to the ground; the sorts that make little tufts and squabs and cushions and pools of color when in flower, and neat tight bumps of gray or green when the flowers have gone over. The range of choice is wide. Saxifrages, silene, stonecrops, thrift, acaena, androsace, aubretia in moderation, thyme, *Achillea argentea, Erinus alpinis, Tunica saxifraga, Bellis* Dresden China, sempervivurm or houseleeks, some campanulas such as *C. garganica,* so easy and self-sowing—the list is endless, and gives scope for much variety.

I would not restrict it only to the rugs and mats and pillows, but would break its level with some inches of flower stalks, such as the orange Alpine poppy, *Papaver alpinum,* and some violas such as *V. gracilis* or *V. bosnaica,* and some clumps of dianthus such as the Cheddar pink, and even some primroses specially chosen, and any other favorite which may occur to you. This list is not intended to dictate. It is intended only to suggest that a ribbon or band of color, no more than twelve inches wide, might well wend its flat way beside a path in even the most conventional garden.

But if you had a garden on a slope, in a hilly district, what an opportunity would be yours! Then your flat ribbon would become a rill, a rivulet, a beck, a burn, a brook, pouring crookedly downhill between stones towards the trout-stream flowing along the valley at the bottom. I suppose some people do possess gardens like that. Let those fortunate ones take notice, and, dipping an enormous paint brush into the wealth offered by the autumn catalogs, splash its rainbow result wherever their steps may lead them.

Lilacs of loose delicacy

In the last-minute scramble to order the shrubs we had made a note of in those far-away happy months of May and June, and have since forgotten, let us now remember the Preston lilacs, *Syringa prestoniae,* before it is too late.

I must confess I don't know anything about Miss Isabella Preston of Ottawa, beyond her name and her reputation as a hybridizer of lilies and of lilacs (*syringae*) and the exciting crosses she has made between *Syringa villosa* and *Syringa reflexa.* I wish I did know more. She must be one of those great gardeners, a true specialist devoting a whole life to the job—how enviable a decision to take, how wise to concentrate on one subject and to know everything about it instead of scattering little confetti bits of information over a hundred things. Such thoroughness and such privity of knowledge carry one back to medieval dates when leisure was the norm. I picture Miss Preston to myself as a lady in a big straw hat, going round with a packet of labels, a notebook, and a rabbit's tail tied to a bamboo stick.

Perhaps this is all wrong, but there can be nothing wrong about my impression of Miss Preston's lilacs. Elinor is a most beautiful shrub with tall erect panicles of a deep rose color, opening to a paler shade as is the habit of the whole syringa family. Elinor is the only one I have hitherto grown, and can give a personal testimonial to; but Isabella is well spoken of, and so is Hiawatha, reddish purple to start with, and pale rose to end up.

All the Preston hybrids are said to be strong growers, and are also entirely hardy as one would expect from the harsh climate in which they have been raised. Whether you prefer them to the old garden lilac, in heavy plumes hanging wet with rain, or whether you will reject their looser delicacy in favor of those fat tassels with their faint scent associated with one's childhood, is for you to say.

Simplify

Down in the West Country stands a castle, savage, remote, barbaric, brooding like a frown across the jade-green water meadows towards the hills of Wales. This castle has always preserved its secretive quality. It is nearly 1000 years old. It has played its part in English history. It comes into Shakespeare, an honor accorded to few private dwellings by our national poet:

> How far is it, my lord, to Berkeley now?
> I am a stranger here in Gloucestershire,
> These high wild hills, and rough uneven ways, . . .

A stranger myself in Gloucestershire, I had been asked by the present owner to discuss with him the redemption of the neglected garden. It is not everyone who can dispose of terraces falling away beneath towering walls and buttresses, apparently constructed of porphyry and gold—such is the nature of the local stone—but the problems of taste and upkeep affect all of us, in castle, manor house, cottage, villa, or bungalow. The problems vary in degree, but in principle are the same. What will look right? What colors will agree with the fabric, be it this ruddy rusty splendor of Berkeley or the raw red brick of the housing development? What shall we avoid, and what select? Harmony must be achieved somehow. And, as a last imperative consideration, what will give least trouble in maintenance?

We have reached the era of simplification in gardening; and, so far as one can ever feel sure about any question of taste, always a dangerous venture, I feel almost sure that we are now traveling along the right lines. We are gradually abolishing the messy little bedding-out system, and are replacing it by generous lawns of our good green turf. We are replacing our bad herbaceous borders, hitherto stuffed with poor specimens of lupine and what-have-you, by flowering shrubs which entail far less work and are far more interesting to grow and to observe.

There was a terrace at Berkeley, under one of the great walls. It was a wide terrace, and it had been used to provide a herbaceous border. In the old days when many gardeners were employed, staking and weeding, it probably made a good effect. Not so today. "Dig it all up," we said. "Scrap it. Simplify. Make a broad green walk, quiet and austere, to be mown once a week. And on no account smother the walls with climbers. Whatever there is must be special and choice. Simplify."

It is a counsel to be applied to all gardens, whether majestic or modest.

PART VII

STORIES

Vita's stories have the immense and instantly sensed advantage over her novels of concise and unflowery clarity. Some, like "The Engagement," have a fierce lucidity about them, giving no quarter to digression or to description that does not move the plot along. Some, like "The Poetry Reading," show Vita from her own point-of-view, but, if it were possible, from the outside. They are frequently angled in a way that lends them a particular relevance to the picture of Vita Sackville-West as a fiction writer.

They seem to fit more closely to the interest of a present-day reader, perhaps impatient with the details of large houses, Edwardian families, and plot complications often found in Vita's novels. Her stories are generally terse and to the point, and often distressing.

"THE ENGAGEMENT" (1930)

This is a terrible and quiet story, never published. From the beginning, with the perfect order of the tea table, cloth, and mind of the waiting woman, so sure that all will be as it was, to the distressing end, it is as ordered as the tea table. Any reader is of course bound to be far less sure that the hostess of the outcome, sensing the desperately neatness of the waiting woman's life, her plans, and her surroundings, fearing the tragedy invited by the very Jamesian postponement she has engineered in her romance. In the focus upon the arrangement—which is then capsized by the exterior intrusion of the unexpected—it is the diametrical opposite of Edith Wharton's teatime story of an arrangement, "The Other Two," with which it makes a brilliant contrast.[1] In the Wharton story, three gentlemen who have shared the tea-serving lady's favors are invited to sit down around the perfectly laid-out table, too easy by far.

In the Sackville-West story, the upset of the teatime is all the more drastic in being unpictured.

"THE ENGAGEMENT"

She sat alone in her little room that was so pretty in the evening, when the curtains were drawn and the skillfully disposed lamps were lit in their different corners, touching up both the real flowers in the vases and the printed flowers on the chintz, and suggesting by the background they left unlighted a warm enveloping intimacy which, again, was furthered by the purring kettle on the tea-table and by the fire glowing comfortably in the low grate.

She sat on the sofa before the tea-table, very acutely aware of this brooding intimacy, her hands lying loosely joined in her lap and a vague smile full of a pleasurable expectation on her lips. Her eyes, though they took in nothing consciously of what they saw, rested on the bright order of her tea-table, the white cloth edged with lace, the tiny flame under the kettle, and the thread of steam that came from the spout. These things pleased and satisfied and caressed her; altogether, the trend of her mind that evening was full of harmony and repose;

she was not even excited, as many people in her circumstances might have been; no, it was rather a sense of arrival that she experienced, with its accompanying relief, arrival after a long, unsatisfactory, desultory period of existence, arrival at a home, where she might be sure of welcome, of safety, of protection, with no further necessity for departure. She had always tried to stave off the burden of her loneliness by surrounding herself with all the appearances of comfort, witness the pretty room, the lamps, and the speckless tea-table; knowing all the while without admitting the knowledge, that such parade was fictitious, and fulfilled most inadequately its purpose of lessening the void within. But now—*now* she was glad that her room should be so pretty, and her silver kept so bright, since such grace could not fail to please, but must surely steal seductively upon the senses, especially upon the senses of one who after months of exile had grown unaccustomed to these gentle refinements, and to whom they must surely represent all that she herself represented—femininity, domesticity, home.

With the smile still upon her lips and her hands still lying loosely joined in idleness she sat waiting for the brisk ring at the door-bell which would vibrate through the little house. It would come punctually at five; she had never known him to be either a minute in advance or a minute behind the appointed hour. She had still five minutes to wait. She liked his punctuality, it was so well in keeping with her idea of him: calm, reliable, unperturbed. As she thought of him thus the smile softened on her lips, and even a little tenderness crept into her eyes, a little tender amusement, the proprietary indulgence of one who knew him so well, that he could have no surprises up his sleeve for her. That was exactly what she liked about him: his rock-like reliability. Not a very romantic feature, perhaps. But so comforting. She must not expect romance from him—and yet, wasn't it rather romantic after all, his devotion to her throughout all those years? his fidelity to her even though she gave him no hope, and his quiet persistence that had at last bored its way through her indifference, culminating in this day when after eight years she was really going to put both her hands into his and tell him he was to attain the wish of his heart? Wasn't it perhaps after all rather romantic? How faithful he had been! She looked back upon the eight years, and upon his programme that had been so regular, so unvarying; it had grown to be like some natural law, like the return of the seasons, for instance, or the cycle of night and day, something that one depended upon and took for granted, and whose disarrangement would utterly astonish. A sailor, he had always been absent for eleven months out of the year, and at a given moment his letter had always come, announcing his return when she was'nt in the least thinking about him. "My leave is due, dear, and I reach London on the fifth of July," or whatever the date might be, "so if convenient to you I will call on you at five o'clock on the sixth, and I hope you will keep some days free for me dur-

ing the month I am on leave." She had always experienced a slight droop of
boredom when this letter arrived. Then it would be followed by its writer, and
she would be surprised to find him, on the whole, rather more attractive than
her recollection of him, and they would spend good companionable days together; and although she never felt herself tempted to yield to his pleading she
was always quite sorry when the time came for him to go away.

He was a sort of joke to her friends. "How's old James?" they would ask her,
"Are you going to tell him you'll marry him next time he comes on leave?" and
she would laugh constrainedly, because although her friends all liked him she
knew they couldn't fail to think him dull. She used to wonder whether she
would be ashamed of him if he were her husband. She knew that she ought to
be proud; he was such a good fellow, such a splendid fellow; it was only the silly
part of her that was conscious of a sneaking shame. His hands were too large,
his manner too bluff, his clothes too stiff and ill-fitting, his hair too scanty . . .
Thus she had thought; for she had had plenty of time for thinking. But now she
thought thus no longer; for she had transformed her ideas so well that she had
effectually stamped on that sneaking shame. She dwelt only on the excellent side
of him, the firm steadfastness of him, that ever since she had reached her final
decision had given her that reassuring sense of arrival. She might feel, perhaps,
a little defiant about him; might be a little on the defensive when she took him
amongst her friends; but she informed herself stoutly that it was because they
couldn't appreciate his good qualities; he didn't betray his real self to most people; she alone had had the perception to appraise his worth. And she went a little further now: she looked forward to seeing his kind eyes bent upon her, and
to hearing his big laugh, and above all she looked forward to his assumning
complete control over her and her existence, as she knew he would do in his
large, calm, competent way, directly she had told him he might have the right.
How gladly she would hand everything over to him! no more loneliness, no
more battle; yes, she was happy to have reached this decision, and only regretted that she had been so curiously obstinate in not reaching it years before.

The clock on the mantelpiece began to wheeze, and then struck five on a
clear little bell, and almost immediately afterwards came the ring at the door, as
she had known it would come.

Very tall and powerfully built, he looked enormous in the small room, among
her little tables and ornaments, and she herself felt dwarfed by his stature, but it
was a pleasant sensation, and she was conscious, with an instinct suddenly disturbed, of wishing very much to be gathered up and shielded within his arms,
once for all, and to have her mind made up for her, quite firmly, upon all matters. Well, no doubt, before many minutes had elapsed, that would happen; and
she began to tremble a little, and to talk without permitting any pauses, asking

him whether he had had a good journey, and whether he did not notice the cold in England after coming from the tropics. The tea-things came to her assistance, too, enabling her to keep her eyes away from his, for she felt that as he stood there he was watching her, and it was a relief to keep her head bent while she picked up and set down busily the utensils for making tea, maintaining meanwhile the chatter at which she was an adept.

At last she looked up, and saw that his eyes were particularly bright, and that although silent he seemed to be animated right through his being by a suppressed excitement. She turned suddenly faint with the delicious apprehension. "Come and sit here," she said, patting the sofa, "I've got such heaps of things to talk to you about."

"So have I," he said, and sitting down beside her he laid his large hand over hers; it was strong and heavy, and at his touch her heart turned slowly over. "My dear," he said, "you're the very best friend I've got, although you could never care for me in any other way, so I wanted you to be the first person to know of my happiness. Yes; I see you've guessed. I met her out there, and I used to talk to her about you, and about my hopelessness—you know the sort of thing. That's how it began. And although of course no one can ever quite take your place . . . but I needn't tell you that. We hope to be married quite soon: while I'm on leave this time, in fact. She arrives in England next week, and I want you to meet her; I know you'll love her; everybody does: she's that kind of person."

"Oh, how splendid!" she replied, "how perfectly splendid, and how nice of you to tell me at once, and you must bring her to see me the moment she arrives, won't you?"

"THE POET" (1930)

The story "The Poet"² is of particular interest because of our contemporary fascination with appropriations. In addition, it reads like a prefiguration of an incident in Vita's own life.

In February of 1949, just before leaving for Spain, Vita sent to the Poetry Review a poem called "The Novice to her Lover"; the poem was published in the June/July issue. Then in November, she recommended Poems 1935–48, by Clifford Dyment, for the King's Medal for Poetry, and therein she found a poem very like her own. It may be that she had read his poem, "St. Augustine at 32," previously in 1934, in St. Martin's magazine, and she certainly had read it later, in 1944, when he had included it in his book The Axe in the Wood, for she commented on it then approvingly. John

Gawsworth, the editor of the Poetry Review, *mentioned this to the* New Statesman. *They followed up on the peculiar incident, much to Vita's distress: this "odd story,"*
she called it. Clifford Dyment's poem and hers appear almost identical except that, in
Vita's poem, a nun is writing rather than a monk. There was consternation on both
sides, quite understandably, and the story becomes all the more interesting in consider-
ing the gender shift within "The Poet." In any case, it reads like a forewarning of how
she was likely to absorb the words of another poet unconsciously.[3]

The Dyment affair seemed very mysterious to Vita, who wanted to give it a roman-
tic twist, and it is of no less interest to the contemporary reader, whatever explanation
can be given.

"THE POET"

I first saw him sitting at a little table outside a cafe in Italy. He was alone, and I
knew him instantly for a poet by his wild eyes, his tumbled hair, his sensitive
nostrils, and his weak but beautiful mouth. He wore a faded blue shirt and a pair
of blue linen trousers, with his bare feet thrust into heelless espadrilles. At the
moment when my eyes first fell upon him he was gazing sorrowfully into a glass
of beer. I imagined that in those translucent amber depths he sought, perhaps,
some simile for a mermaid's hair—the cafe was situated on the shores of the
Mediterranean—but after a prolonged contemplation he beckoned to the waiter
and said in Italian: "There's a fly in this beer. Take it away."

I was disappointed. I had been so certain he was a poet and that he was English. His appearance was so romantic, the lonely fishing village was so romantic,
too: just the place for a poet, with its little harbour and the painted boats swaying softly on the dark green water, and the Mediterranean beyond, and the fish-
ermen's houses in a semicircle, the colour of tea roses and tulips, and the nets
hung out to dry, and the lovely hills rising behind, silvery with the olive trees.
Now it seemed that he was a native, a native, a peasant perhaps, come down
from the hills to catch the evening coolness of the port and to drink his glass before climbing back to bed: a native, a peasant, unlettered, and a materialist into
the bargain. As I watched him, he rose, and slouching away he vanished through
a little green door into a neighbouring house. I heard him coughing as he went.

On the following evening I saw him again in the same place. His glass of beer
stood beside him, his elbow was propped on the table, his cheek was propped
on his hand, and he was reading in a small book bound in calf, the pages slightly
foxed. I passed behind him and looked over his shoulder. He was reading Sir
Thomas Browne's *Religio Medici,* in a seventeenth-century edition. My spirits revived. I felt that my assumption had been justified.

As I sat down at another table and ordered my vermouth and seltz[er], unfolding my *Daily Mail* meanwhile rather ostentatiously, I felt rather than saw that he had raised his head and was glancing in my direction. I bided my time, paying no attention. Presently I heard, as I had known I would hear, the scraping of his chair on the tiled floor. He was edging himself towards me. He wanted to enter into conversation. I cursed myself for a brute as I heard his first apologetic cough develop into a terrible, a heartrending attack of coughing. I flung my *Daily Mail* aside, and hastily poured him out a glass of water. "By God, you're ill," I said.

He put his handkerchief to his lips and brought it away stained with red. "Ill?" he said, and stretched out a shaking hand. "There's death in that hand," he said with a twisted smile.

That jarred me. I had dramatized him to myself, heaven knows, but that he should dramatize himself was more than I could bear. I was divided between distress at his ill-health and disgust at his exploitation of it. In consequence I spoke rather briskly, asking him what ailed him—though it was clear enough.

He was ready to talk. He hadn't spoken his own language for three months, he told me. He had come to Santa Caterina to die. He thought it couldn't be long now, but he didn't mind: he didn't care for life, so long as it gave him time to accomplish that which he must accomplish. He thought he had done his best by now and was quite ready to go.

And what, I asked, was he so anxious to accomplish?

"I write poetry," he said, quite simply this time.

He was twenty-five years of age, he told me, and his name was Nicholas Lambarde. That seemed to me a good name for an English poet, in the tradition of Kit Marlowe, Robert Herrick, Richard Lovelace, and the rest. English poets had nearly always been endowed with good names, and Nicholas Lambarde might figure as honestly in an alphabetical index as the others. But, although I keep an eye on poetry, I had never heard of him. A mere name was not enough to make me take him on trust. What poetry, I asked, had he written? Had any of it been published?

No, he said, he had never bothered about publication. He cared nothing about contemporary fame. Posterity was the only thing that counted, and about posterity he had no doubt at all. He began then to talk of his poetry, dashing his hands through his hair; he talked extravagantly, lyrically; but somehow—although I am skeptical, I think, by nature, and not readily impressed—I couldn't feel that he was boasting in a void, or that the claims he made were in any way in excess of their justification. I couldn't explain to myself why he thus immediately convinced me. Perhaps his very scorn for present fame did its part, a scorn so rare and so manifestly genuine. At any rate, when he told me that he had that morning written a real poem, a true contribution to English literature, I believed him. And, in a way, as my story will show, I was right. He had.

He held very definite and vigorous views about poetry. He couldn't abide the modem school of *défaitisme* and despair. He couldn't feel—dying man though he was—that life was little more than the sloughed skin of a snake, or a rustle of dry leaves, or a parched land without water, or whatever the metaphor might be. Nor did he feel that poetry was the proper vehicle for metaphysics, any more than fiction was the proper vehicle for propaganda, sexual or sociological. He held that poetry ought to spring from its own soil and break freely into leaves, like a tree, with a suggestion of sky above and of roots beneath, drinking deeply in the earth. He believed profoundly in the technique of the craft, and held that the first use of technique was to suggest, by association, far greater riches than were actually stated by the words. In fact, rapturously though he expressed himself, he displayed a considered judgment and talked a great deal of sense.

He never read poetry nowadays, he said, for fear of being influenced, though, of course, he added, he had read through the whole of English literature in his early youth.

Every now and then he broke off to cough and to dab his handkerchief against his mouth.

Well, I stayed on at Santa Caterina. Nicholas Lambarde, invisible in the daytime, appeared regularly every evening at the café, ordered his glass of beer, joined me at my table, and talked poetry to me, while the stars came out, and the lights of the harbour dropped their plummets into the water. I watched him growing a little paler, a little thinner every day. His fits of coughing became more frequent and more violent. Still, when I exhorted him, he impatiently brushed aside my importunity and went on with what he was saying. The only important thing in the world to him was poetry. Death did not matter, health did not matter, nor time, nor fame, nor money: I never met anyone who lived so intensely or so continuously the life of the spirit. I can see him now, with his burning eyes, his unshaven chin cupped in his hands, and the stained handkerchief crumpled between his fingers, as he leant across the table, talking, talking.

One evening he said that he would like to ask me a favour. He had no friends and no relations, he said, and the only thing that bothered him was the disposal of his manuscripts after he was dead. He had thought of consigning them all to a literary agency, but that seemed an insecure thing to do, for who could guarantee that any literary agency would find him a publisher? Poetry did not pay— he knew that—and he feared that the eventual fate of his poems might be the waste-paper basket. On the one hand, you see, he was curiously sane. On the other, he was absolutely confident that in, say, a hundred years' time he would be recognized as the head of English song. He made a possible exception in favour of Shakespeare, but admitted no other rivals. If, that is to say, he had his chance, and that must be my business. In short, he asked me to act as his literary executor.

Of course, I accepted. No one could have refused him, and I was, as you may imagine, consumed with the desire to read these poems of which I had heard so much. Often though I urged him, he would never show me a line, but putting on an expression at once arrogant and secretive, would reply: "All in good time! You'll see, you'll see."

It was on a morning in early May that a fisher boy came breathlessly to find me, saying that the Englishman had died during the night: would I please come at once? I had never before penetrated into Lambarde's lodging, and it was with an uncomfortable sense of intrusion that I mounted the rickety stairs and stood upon the threshold of his room. I had not expected to find him surrounded by many possessions, but neither had I been prepared for such utter barrenness and poverty. He himself lay upon, not in, the bed, dressed as usual in his faded shirt and trousers, as though he had flung himself down in the last fatal access of coughing—for the sheets and counterpane were stained with a deeper flood than ever had been stained his pitiable handkerchief. One glance round gave me the complete inventory of the room. A pair of brushes, a comb, a razor; a bunch of wild jonquils stuck in a bottle, some shoes, a few books, mostly tattered. That was all I could see. But there were papers everywhere strewn over the bed, over the one table, and even over the floor—separate sheets of foolscap, some closely covered, some scrawled with but a single line, tossed aside, blown by the breeze into some neglected corner. His landlady, who had followed me upstairs, doubtless thought that she read criticism in my glance.

He would never allow her to tidy, she said; sometimes for weeks together he had locked the door and she had been unable to enter his room; and once, when she had ventured to pick up some of his papers and place them on the table, he had flown into the most terrible rage, so that she thought he would expire on the spot. It was comprehensible, she said, with the Latin peasant's understanding of the artist: the poor young man was a poet, and poets were cursed with that kind of temperament; one could not expect a stag to browse mildly like a cow. And she looked at him, lying upon the bed, with a compassion that forgave him all his trespasses.

But now he could prevent nobody from picking up his papers and arranging them on the table. It was, indeed, precisely what he had asked me to do, yet I did it with a sense of guilt, induced, no doubt, by my own knowledge of my own curiosity. Outwardly I was executing the wishes of a dead compatriot: in reality, I was gratifying the meanest of our instincts. Yet why should I blacken myself unduly? I love letters, I respect genius; I had lent a sympathetic ear to an unknown poet for weeks past; I had upset all my plans on his account. It was only fair that I should have my reward.

And yet, I swear, it wasn't only my reward that I thought of—the reward of discovering a new master of English verse. I honestly wanted to do my best by that proud, lonely, flaming creature who had lived for nothing but his art.

I persuaded the good wife to leave me, and, alone with the dead man, I fell to my task. You must believe me when I say that I have seldom been more excited. At first I was puzzled, for many of the writings were so exceedingly fragmentary; there were scraps of scenes from plays, whose characters bore names in the Elizabethan tradition—Baldassare, Mercurio, and the like; there were a few verses of what appeared to be a ballad; there were some ribald addresses to Chloe and Dorinda; there was the beginning of a contemplative poem on solitude. I fancied from all these that he had been practising his hand at the art of parody, for he had hit off the Elizabethan manner exactly, and the manner of the ballads, and of the Restoration, and of the early nineteenth century. Whatever else he had been, he was certainly a skilful parodist; I was sure that I had read something very like his play-scenes in some minor work of Kyd or Shirley, I couldn't remember which. But I turned over his poor papers impatiently, in the hope of coming on one of those poems of which he had said to me, "Lord! I'm tired, but I did something good today, something really first class. I'm pleased."

And I found them. I found the really first-class things. He was quite right: they really were first class. He had taken an enormous amount of trouble, putting his pencil through word after word, until he got exactly the word he wanted. That was the extraordinary thing: the amount of trouble he had taken in his search for perfection, carving each phrase laboriously from his brain, working it out like a puzzle; I could imagine him sitting there at that same table, concentrated, rapt, dissatisfied at first, and finally triumphant; I could imagine him springing up at last with a cry of triumph and pacing about the room declaiming the magnificent stanzas to himself. It had been a terrific effort, but he had always got it right in the end.

One of his first drafts ran thus:

> Fair star! I would I were as faithful as thou art,
> Not in sole glory piercing through the night,
> But watching with unsleeping lids apart
> eremite
> The restless ocean at its patient task
> Of slow erosion round earth's aged shores.

The pencil had been dashed through the last two lines, and he had substituted with scarcely a check:

> The moving waters at their priest-like task
> Of pure ablution round earth's human shores.

Yes, I thought, no wonder he was pleased with that; no wonder he had come down to the café to tell me had had done something really good!

And there were other passages which had worried him considerably:

> But after me I seem to hear
> The wheels of Time near
> A fiery spirit? bright and swift
> The Earth like Danae
> Like Danae the Earth
> Under the stars the Earth like Danae lies.

But he had got that right, too, nearly the whole of it; except one line, for which he had left a blank.

I sat back and stared at his papers. What had gone wrong in that poor muddled brain? What fantastic trick had memory played upon him? I remembered how he had told me that he had quite given up reading the poets now, "for fear of being influenced," though he had read them extensively as a boy. Influenced, indeed! the irony of it!

And yet, you know, I still maintain that a poet was lost in him. I found among his papers one sonnet, which, with the obvious though partial exception of the first line, I have so far been unable to trace to anybody else. It is not the kind of poetry which brought him downstairs to tell me that he had done something "really good"; it is, indeed, only a sonnet of a type which could be turned out in dozens by any competent rhymester, soaked in the conventions of English literature; the octet may pass muster, but the sextet is poor, as though scribbled down in a hurry; and probably I exaggerate the merit of the whole, being privy to the absolute truth which inspired it; but such as it is, it may very well stand as his epitaph:

> When I am gone, say only this of me:
> He scorned the laurels and the praise of men,
> Alien to fortune and to fame; but then
> Add this: he plunged with Thetis in the sea;
> Lay naked with Diana in the shade
> He knew what paths the wandering planets drew;
> He heard the music of the winds; he knew
> What songs the sirens sang; Arion played.
> Say this; no more; but when the shadows lengthen
> Across the greensward of your cloistered turf,
> Remember one who felt his sinews strengthen

And tuned his hearing by the line of surf.
One who, too proud, passed ease and comfort by,
But learned from Rome and Hesiod how to die.

"The Poetry Reading"

One of the oddest documents in Vita's own self-imagination, self-creation, and self-portraiture is the story called "The Poetry Reading," written in June 1944 but never published, in which Vita pictures herself giving a lecture. A dynamic figure in her black dress with matching scarlet scarf and shoes, she shows herself making an immense impression on two sisters who have come to hear her read:

> *Charlotte was also surveying Sackville-West; she saw the dark felt hat, the heavy cream lambskin coat, black dress, scarlet earrings, scarf, and shoes, yet apart from these externals the quality that held the audience and Charlotte in particular was not the beauty of the rather tired face, but its exceptional sincerity.*
>
> *Charlotte was interested in her personally, what did such a face reveal? So many things, almost everything that is save happiness; it was passionate, instantaneously receptive, sometimes childish, discontented, shy, imperious.*

Vita sees herself in extraordinary detail, as elegant, poised, humorous, and a bundle of other interesting qualities, which of course she was. She pictures herself as "remarkable" and courageous in the description that Dr. Watson hands Charlotte, along with one of her books: "This woman has that rare quality, courage; it breathes from every stroke of her pen." And at the reading, she hears her own voice: "How clear, how luxurious, how rich"(!)

The Vita who is pictured here is quite like the one we have learned to recognize, but it feels strange to be given the picture by the object of our gaze. Vita, both admiring and admired, was adventuresome to the extreme, in both her way of living and writing.

"THE POETRY READING"

The agitation in the Pringle household was such that the usually imperturbable black cat had found it necessary to arise from his accustomed place by Miss Amelia's workbasket and stroll in a state of dazed dignity in and out of the legs of the dining room table; pausing occasionally, with a slight twitching of the right ear but an otherwise Oriental inscrutability when a tassel from the red plush tablecloth interfered with the undulation of his tail.

Though his inherent pride would not allow him to flicker an eyelid in the direction of the equally perturbed canaries, it could be noted that the radius of his activities was sufficiently near his feathered companions to conclude that his thoughts must lie in that vicinity also. But the birds it seemed either from long custom or the excitement of the Misses Pringle appeared quite indifferent to the menace of Silas, and shafted like bright splashes of golden rain from one side of the cage to the other, giving forth bright trills of song.

"It was most thoughtful of Dr. Watson to remember us, when there are so many people he could have given them to," said Amelia Pringle, and her hand as she smoothed on the third finger of her grey cotton glove could be seen to tremble slightly. With two further fingers waiting to be enveloped, she paused and looked at the white printed card which lay on the dressing table next to her handkerchief sachet.

"He is always thoughtful," said Charlotte with equally warm emphasis and a half blush. Stepping down from the chair on which she had been standing to reach the hat box on top of the wardrobe, she unwrapped the contents of the box and placed one in each hand.

Amelia was still fluttering with her gloves, this nervous tip-toe quality of hers gave a rustling atmosphere which infected the whole house as if it were a poplar tree battling against the wind; in features the two sisters were similar but Charlotte's face was firmer, not having fallen into the timid disintegration of Amelia who was her senior by some nine years.

The younger woman came nearer to the dressing table; she first tried on the grey straw hat and then decided in favour of the black straw trimmed with pink and black ribbon. She leaned a little forward towards the mirror and surveyed herself; the picture was not displeasing; her eyes held life and depth, and faint sparks of rebellion lurked in her soul.

Amelia who was almost ready with her toilet caught her sister in this act of reflection and felt unreasonably irritated. In such moments she glimpsed a Charlotte which she had long hoped to erase.

Amelia asked nothing more of life than to live peaceably with her sister whom she had mothered for so many years, and to whom she was inordinately if narrowly devoted. Affectionate, kindly, almost sexless, she found it difficult to imagine that this mode of existence might possibly have its limitations and insufficiencies; yet there were moments such as the present when her sister seemed to threaten such security by her unconscious individualism.

"It makes you look far too young. We shall be late," she added as her sister, still facing the mirror caught the brim of her hat in each hand and pulled it becomingly in an arch across her face; she looked down at her dress.

"How shabby I am, it must be two years since I had a new dress. Amelia, perhaps if there's time we can look at the shops at Victoria," and then as if there was some connection between a new dress and the doctor she continued, "Dr. Watson said if he had time he would call in tonight to know how we shall have enjoyed ourselves this afternoon."

"Why there's nothing the matter with it at all," and Amelia fingered her sister's dress and then her own. "I've had mine for over five years and it's still as good as new."

"Oh but one grows so tired of the same old things, but we'll see," and she gave her rich infectious smile to Amelia, which left her little to say. Amelia moved about the room fussing a little over the hang of the curtains, and pushing the coat-hangers into position in the wardrobe.

"He doesn't seem to be bothering about his housekeeper leaving next month, has he told you what he intends to do?" and Amelia looked searchingly at her companion, but Charlotte appeared intent upon the two white cards that the Doctor had given them.

"Sackville-West? It sounds so familiar yet I can't think what I can have read of hers. Nice name isn't it? Sounds powerful."

Amelia joined her and once again they both read the invitation cards.

Royal Society of Literature
The Annual Lecture on Poetry will be given by V. Sackville-West
Her subject will be Wordsworth especially in relation to Modern Poetry.

To the two rather quiet ladies this small pasteboard square represented a world which had scarcely ever been formulated within them, a place of delicacy and romance, of secrecy and great glamour.

Amelia could not fail to be drawn by the compliment Dr. Watson had paid to their intelligence by given them the cards, but she had a slight suspicion that poetry and particularly poets were dangerous and not a little mad; she had her exceptions of course, she liked the stolidity of Tennyson, so safely folded within the swaddling clothes of Victorianism, this too applied to Wordsworth; she felt sure such men were good men, leaving an aura of gentle piety wherever they dwelt. How fortunate Dorothy Wordsworth was to possess and be in constant attendance on such an uplifting personage; she, Amelia, felt that if, only if, she had ever contemplated such a thing as matrimony then the worthy Alfred or William would have been the type selected by her.

"I wonder what she's like. If only he had brought these before we might have read up something," and Charlotte picked up a book of Sackville-West's poems and opened the page.

But Amelia moved impatiently towards the staircase. "We really haven't time."

Automatically her sister followed whispering the words she had just glimpsed, "The country habit has me by the heart." Could anyone, she thought, have expressed more feelingly yet more simply that innate love of country life. She paused on the landing and looked down into their little Clapham garden with its margin of pink and lavender and dark flopping roses, but she only half saw this little treasured spot; instead she seemed to see the woman who had the power to make other eyes see these things also.

Amelia was calling Silas into the kitchen away from the birds; when she had shut the door and poked a finger into the canaries cage with a loving coo, she came into the hall.

"To be an artist must surely be one of the loveliest things in the world," said Charlotte dreamily.

"Why?" and Amelia had opened the front door, seen a few lazy billows rolling over the very blue sky, and had picked up her umbrella.

"It must be like having a religion, you impart something of value, of great value."

But Amelia was not particularly interested. She gave a final roll to the sleek coil of her umbrella as they walked down the street, and gave another glance to the one creamy cloud above her head as if she suspected it of following her. "It's best to be on the safe side, you never can tell with this climate."

"Yes" and Charlotte gave an imperceptible touch to the book in her hand.

"I don't think we've ever seen a poet in the flesh before, have we?"

"Yes we have, there was Mr. Coutes, the Vicar of St. Gilda, you remember, he always looked so poorly."

"And wrote poorly too I thought," said Charlotte ironically.

"He was a very good influence in the parish, the church was always crowded."

"Yes but only with a certain type, the sort that have to lean on something or other. He was such a blind egoist that he could always attract a crowd, but as for being a poet!" Charlotte's sudden termination was eloquent.

"I sometimes think you are too exacting, Charlotte, you should learn to accept without question." Amelia had adopted the tone of correction which had impressed her younger sister so often.

"Perhaps you're right," replied Charlotte, feeling vaguely troubled and lonely, for Amelia seemed to be of one complete pattern—so free from doubt or desire—whereas Charlotte was unsettled and constantly torn between loyalty and genuine love for her sister and other restless qualities which Amelia refused to recognize or comprehend.

When comfortably settled on the bus, each opened their book, Amelia her Wordsworth and Charlotte the poems that Dr. Watson had given her that day. She remembered his words as he put the gift into her hands, pressing her finger tips. "This woman has that rare quality, courage; it breathes from every stroke of her pen." Why had his words seemed so significant? Why had he looked at her so intently, so eagerly? And why had she avoided him? But Charlotte was confused and did not wish to think clearly, it was too difficult; she concentrated on the book, opening it at a chance page she read—

> "What have I gathered, packed into old bales
> Stuffed into chests, or dusty on my shelves?"

She allowed her arms to fall limply against her body, she read no more. What conspiracy was afoot today, that everything seemed directed at her own tentativeness.

"What have I gathered?" Yes what indeed have I gathered, she thought with unaccustomed bitterness. I am thirty-six and all I have acquired is a reflection of my sister, a fusing of her mentality with my own, so that I never think separately, never act separately. I deliberately obliterate my own life so that it will comply with hers. As she continued with such thoughts her qualms were many. She seemed to be tearing up so much that was inrooted, it almost hurt; she felt she could not let such thoughts continue or ripen—where would it lead? There was Amelia that grey gloved finger placed upon the pages.

> "It is a beauteous evening, calm and free,
> The holy time is quiet as a Nun."

How serene the poems, how serene Amelia; her very breathing gentle and even bespoke her whole character; grey gloves, grey dress, grey mind; then the guilt of such criticism fell like a flood upon poor Charlotte, she was glad they had reached their destination.

"I wonder if Mr. Coutes ever recovered; they nearly always have poor health, these poetical persons, I mean I suppose it is that they don't eat the proper foods," said Amelia when they had alighted at the terminus.

"I don't suppose they let such things bother them," replied Charlotte carelessly.

"But they should that's the trouble, a little more discipline and diet and they would probably have lived to a proper age," came the emphatic reply.

"They didn't all die young," said Charlotte with amusement. "In any case perhaps they didn't wish to live to a ripe old age."

"Charlotte! How wicked! no one should wish their death. God was merciful enough to give us life, we should be grateful."

Exercising great tact Charlotte discontinued the discussion. "Do let us stop," and she took hold of Amelia's arm and drew her towards a shop window in which was a display of dresses. "I love the red one, isn't it a lovely shade?"

"It would be all right on a young person, now that's nice, and very much more serviceable," and she pointed to a navy blue dress in the far corner of the window.

"Yes I suppose it would be," said Charlotte. "If not today perhaps some other time I can try them on."

"I do think you're extravagant," said Amelia, determined to have the last word on the subject.

"You must take care of that, it would show such ingratitude to give him back a soiled book," she said later when they were on their way to Bloomsbury Square.

"But he doesn't want it returned," came the quiet reply.

"You mean he's given it to you?" Amelia was astonished.

Charlotte merely nodded and remarked upon the passing traffic, but silence came between the two sisters, the silence of separateness.

Nearing the lecture hall, however, they were drawn together by common excitement and were faintly relieved to see the commonplace building in the now dilapidated square where only a few large leafy trees appeared to show any evidence of freshness.

Charlotte remarked to herself how like the visitors were to Amelia, rather wrinkled, colourless, but no doubt infinitely wise. Could any of these be her poet? And she smiled inwardly at the thought of how she had already adopted Sackville-West as someone not remote like Milton or Homer or Dante, lofty and somewhat removed from the variety of complexes that seemed to be her experience of human natures, but she thought of her poet as primarily a human being, vivid, effulgent and quite universal.

By now they had entered the building. A quiet voice and hand indicated the direction they must follow up the wide circular staircases and further kindly verger-like forms ushered them into the hall.

"We'd better not sit too near the front," said Amelia in her most timid state.

"Will this do?" and they edged their way into two center seats halfway down the small panelled room. When settled, they looked around. Amelia began to regain confidence for the atmosphere was warmly parochial. Age and modification was strictly in evidence for no apparent reason. Charlotte was reminded of her sister's bedroom with its faint but perpetual odour of lavender and mothballs; and then she looked at the numerous photographs upon the walls. How similar they were to the occupiers of the seats. It might almost have been that at some former occasion the visitors had merely left their imprints upon those walls. She studied the portraits with mixed feelings, for however aware one might be of the restrictions of the Victorian and early Edwardian periods there was an integrity in those faces that the present age for all its emancipation could never produce; stodgy they might be but nevertheless disciplined and somehow refreshing in their purposefulness. Now, it is true, reflected Charlotte, we are emancipated but to what ends are we travelling when God himself seems to be an anachronism?

Her meditations were interrupted, however, by two visitors who were standing in the doorways: one a short rather insignificant woman in green and beside her a tall remarkable person in black and scarlet; Charlotte knew at once that this was the person she was waiting to hear.

"That is she," she exclaimed involuntarily to her sister.

Charlotte was also surveying Sackville-West; she saw the dark felt hat, the heavy cream lambskin coat, black dress, scarlet earrings, scarf, and shoes, yet apart from these externals the quality that held the audience and Charlotte in particular was not the beauty of the rather tired face, but its exceptional sincerity.

Charlotte was interested in her personally, what did such a face reveal? So many things, almost everything that is save happiness; it was passionate, instantaneously receptive, sometimes childish, discontented, shy, imperious.

They watched her take a seat beside her friend in the audience.

"Perhaps it isn't her, she hasn't gone to the front," said Amelia.

"Oh but it is," came Charlotte's voice of certainty in response to her sister's whisper.

The hall by now was almost full. Many glances were passed towards the woman in black and scarlet; the chairman had entered and she rose with a word to the friend beside her and a few remarks to several people in the audience and then made her way to the platform.

"I wonder who the friend is, they seem to understand each other rather well?"—and Charlotte glanced at the woman in green who was intent upon the poet. "I should think she was devoted to her," and the younger sister did not care especially whether this half soliloquy was understood or not.

The chairman opened the lecture with a charming and most complimentary speech in which he declared that he had heard the poet eighteen years before in that same hall and could still remember every detail of her dress.

"I'm not surprised," thought Charlotte with genuine affection and reverence for Sackville-West. This speech, flattering as it was, seemed a trifle too long, it being a common error of chairmen to mistake themselves for the lecturer.

Then the poet herself arose amid great applause and from that moment, fidgeting ceased, a leaf could be heard to drop from the elm tree in the square, and Amelia's nervous fingers omitted to pinch the opposite fingertips of her glove.

How clear, how luxurious was the voice now speaking. It held the richness of long matured wine, yet there was no hesitancy either in the delivery or in the content. Though the speech was written, the speaker had that fortunate faculty of giving the merest glance at the page upon the lectern, and with head raised and in the easy eloquence that springs from the most natural yet most profound truths she continued to absorb her audience.

Charlotte was but one of the many who said within themselves, "Ah, that's what I have always thought but never been able to express."

"I think Dorothy must have been something of a bore."

"I have a theory that if Wordsworth had lived at the present time he would have been a greater poet, for he was the victim of an age which was superficially moral."

"William must have been tiresomely dictatorial."

Oh how startling, how deliciously refreshing were such words, such views. Charlotte was delighted, more delighted than she could ever remember. She felt like a bird who suddenly sees the door of its cage wide open and infinite regions of space lying ahead.

Every word that came from the lips of this woman was born of supreme divine independence; she seemed to dwarf all the listeners. Charlotte had difficulty in maintaining her accustomed calm; she wanted to shout her freedom. Oh how little Amelia now seemed, she who had been a fortress hiding the light and the truth. Then she forget herself in listening again to the speaker. Someone at the back of the hall was laughing heartily at the subtle references to William's periodic disappearances and his corresponding silences upon such excursions, and a woman seated in front of the two sisters nodded approval to the friend beside her at almost every third word of the lecturer's until she, the nodding woman, became as automatic as a clockwork figure.

Then the full weight of applause broke . . . even Amelia took off her gloves so that it could resound the more. On it went, delivered with that fervour so rare yet so delicious in an English audience. Sackville-West was partially hidden from view as she sat down behind the lectern, but Charlotte watched closely and with ever increasing devotion that elusive face now transfused with a certain pleasure.

Then the younger sister looked again at the woman in green and was reminded anew of the absorption in this particular face for the woman who had just been speaking.

With regret they found the lecture was finally concluded, the crowd was dispersing and hung in clusters by the doorway.

Sackville-West was talking animatedly with innumerable admirers and signing autographs and often being completely obscured from view by such persons. Once Charlotte noticed she gave one brief yet curiously intense glance at the friend in green who seemed to be apart from the enthusiasts.

"I'm so very glad we came, she seems so human, doesn't she," said Amelia, giving a last glance at the poet as they moved away.

"I wish I knew her," said Charlotte.

"Why don't you ask for an autograph?" and Amelia was surprised at her own audacity.

"No, that sort of thing doesn't interest me."

The sky being clear and the sun brightening the thronged streets, the two sisters walked to Victoria.

Charlotte was once more looking at the red dress. "If it fits me I shall have it," she said with such unusual conviction that Amelia could not easily find the correct phrase.

"When do you think you will have an occasion to wear a scarlet dress," said she with sufficient acidity as they entered the store.

"When I marry Dr. Watson."

"Charlotte!" said the horrified Amelia.

PART VIII

NOVELS

The two works excerpted (Challenge, All Passion Spent) and the one given complete (Seducers in Ecuador) are of such importance within Vita Sackville-West's oeuvre that they seem to warrant star billing: Challenge *for its picture of Vita as a romantic young man,* All Passion Spent *for its message about the independence of women and the importance of their careers, and* Seducers in Ecuador *for its modernist style, theme, and realization.*

From *Challenge* (1924)

Written between May 1918 and November 1919, published in America in 1924 and in England finally in 1976, Challenge *has a background and a publishing history as interesting as the novel itself. Since it is impossible to find now, it has seemed fully worth reprinting much of it in this volume—the last part by far the most crucial to the story and to the Vita and Violet Trefusis story as well.*

The first paperback publication of Vita's second novel appeared in the United States in 1975 with little fanfare save that which its cover blurbs attempted to create. Its front cover pictures, in a languorous semi-reclining position, an elegantly dressed woman in a Chinese jacket and long silk frock, looking up and back over her shoulder at a demure woman in a drab gown with her hand under her chin. A rich tapestry serves as a proximate backdrop; the women are framed by an Oriental screen and a yet taller gilt-framed painting behind—the entire cover hints at layer upon layer of rich meaning. Directly under the title and the author's name we read: "Her famed, long-suppressed novel of consuming love and reckless passion." Suppressed, says the explanatory text on the back cover, because it told the truth about her "illicit love affair with Violet Keppel, the childhood friend for whose sake she was prepared to outrage convention by abandoning her husband Harold Nicolson, her family, and all that England meant to her." It continues with a quotation from Nigel Nicolson's foreword: "Seldom can a novelist have expressed so clearly, in the different characters of her hero and heroine, her conception of the capacity of the human spirit."

Initially it was not a single-authored text, for the two lovers, Vita and Violet Keppel (Trefusis), herself an accomplished writer, intended to write the novel together. In fact, Vita wrote it with Violet's input. Upon examination of the manuscript it becomes clear that very few substantial changes were made, and that the style is pure Vita in its effusiveness. B. M., Vita's mother, was firm about the novel's not appearing—in order not to embarrass the family—and Vita ultimately capitulated to her demands, halting publication despite her own anger and dismay.

The original manuscript of the novel is dedicated to Violet, but for the 1924 publication Vita thinly veiled this dedication by substituting a quotation in the Romany language—bearing out Vita's gypsy longings—from George Borrow's novel The Zimbali:

"This book is yours, honored witch. If you read it, you will find your tormented soul changed and free." The dark male hero, Julian, is presented first as a "tall, loose-limbed boy, untidy, graceful. . . . A single leap might carry him at any moment out of the room in which his presence seemed so incongruous" (p. 20). The women look at him with interest, the tall mirrors reflect the candles and the group of guests, and the one figure all eyes are concentrated upon is, of course, Julian, Vita's alter ego, not much disguised. He is bound up in politics and adored by the feminine other, Eve—Violet herself. Vita, in her escapades with Violet, called herself Julian, darkened her skin, donned men's clothers, and wore a khaki bandage as a turban around her hair. Violet was called Eve ("Lushka or "L" in their letters, and Vita's diary).

So inspired by her very long, passionate, and celebrated love affair with the seductive Violet Trefusis, Challenge is a fruity, melodramatic, superheated work, continually out of print. This book is the poof that Vita, at this point and also later, was capable of writing very purple purple-prose. From the novel now named Challenge but which had other names—light ones like "Foam" and heavy ones like "Rebellion" and "Endeavour"—the last chapters are included. Here and throughout, Julian (Vita) and Eve (Violet) are often all atremble, as is the writing. In these pages Julian is dramatically and romantically torn between his love for his lovely cousin Eve—who does not want to marry him but wants to love in freedom with him—and his passion for the Greek island of Aphros, where he is leading a revolution. These passions are, in his mind, both opposed to each other and confused with one another ("'Eve,' he murmured exultantly, 'Aphros!'"). By his side, Eve's opposite, the Greek Anastasia Kato, is pledged to the same revolutionary politics as Julian.

The plot of Challenge revolves around an island, politics, and the doom of lovers. Julian loves Aphros, his island, from which he will refuse to be separated, except at the price of giving up his dreams, escaping, settling down in—horror of all horrors—marriage. He is in love with the gentle but strong Eve, who has been, until now, his partner in everything personal and political. The lovers have a boat waiting for them, and Julian is willing to give up his ideals, go to Athens, and even marry Eve, but she, terrified by that idea, only wants to dance madly with him in true gypsy fashion. Finally, he leaves with Anastasia Kato, doomed as they are for having failed in their revolution, not by their fault but by Eve's betrayal. Eve will expiate the crime of not wanting to separate him from his fate by plunging herself into the dark waters, tied as absolutely to her fate as Julian is to his.

The setting of Herakleion, with a political revolution raging over the nearby archipelago, lends local color with its Greek names and costuming, but serves mainly as a backdrop to the presentation of Julian, the dark diplomat, a romanticized version of Vita.

Julian awakens from his passivity in the final chapter, when his passion overcomes his previous control. This is the antibourgeois point of the novel, completely in accord with the real Violet's disparagement of everything societal and staid, and with her dis-

dain for those elements that warred with the romanticism in Vita's heart and life. Julian's "rough head and angry eyes" match his erotically charged statements. "'I shall break you,' he says, like a man speaking to a wild young supple tree." Eve, in her dime-store-novel-styled desire ("she wanted him for herself alone") has waited for, schemed for, and battled for Julian. The gypsy melodies sweeping them up heighten the pitch of sacrifice: that of Julian's love for his land ("you'd sacrifice Aphros to me?") and that of betrayed faith ("where can one find fidelity?") The rebellion has been betrayed, and Eve's one-dimensional love of love is a betrayal also.

The plot will be picked up again in one of Vita's other romantic fictions, the gloomy and brooding 1934 novel, The Dark Island, *in which Venn, the hero attached to love, standing like Julian for Vita herself, will be more in love with the island than with life or with the love of another.*

The final chapters—the highlight of Challenge—*are reprinted here.*

CHALLENGE

PART III: APHROS

. . .

Four

The lyric of their early days of love piped clear and sweet upon the terraces of Aphros.

Their surroundings entered into a joyous conspiracy with their youth. Between halcyon sky and sea the island lay radiantly; as it were suspended, unattached, coloured like a rainbow, and magic with the enchantment of its isolation. The very foam which broke around its rocks served to define, by its lacy fringe of white, the compass of the magic circle. To them were granted solitude and beauty beyond all dreams of lovers. They dwelt in the certainty that no intruder could disturb them—save those intruders to be beaten off in frank fight—no visitor from the outside world but those that came on wings, swooping down out of the sky, poising for an instant upon the island, that halting place in the heart of the sea, and flying again with restless cries, sea-birds, the only disturbers of their peace. From the shadow of the olives, or of the stunted pines whose little cones hung like black velvet balls in the transparent tracery of the branches against the sky, they lay idly watching the gulls, and the tiny white clouds by which the blue was almost always flaked. The population of the island melted into a harmony with nature like the trees, the rocks and boulders, or the roving flocks of sheep and herds of goats. Eve and Julian met with neither curiosity nor surprise; only with acquiescence. Daily as they passed down the village street, to wander up the mule-tracks into the interior of Aphros, they were greeted by smiles and devotion that were as unquestioning and comfortable as the shade of the trees or the cool splash of the water; and nightly as they remained alone together in their house, dark, roofed over with stars, and silent but for the ripple of the fountain, they could believe that they had been tended by invisible hands in the island over which they reigned in isolated sovereignty.

They abandoned themselves to the unbelievable romance. He, indeed, had striven half-heartedly; but she, with all the strength of her nature, had run gratefully, nay, clamantly, forward, exacting the reward of her patience, demanding her due. She rejoiced in the casting aside of shackles which, although she had resolutely ignored them in so far as was possible, had always irked her by their latent presence. At last she might gratify to the full her creed of living for and by the beloved, in a world of beauty where the material was denied admittance. In such a dream, such an ecstasy of solitude, they gained marvellously in one another's eyes. She revealed to Julian the full extent of her difference and singularity. For all their nearness in the human sense, he received sometimes with a joyful terror the impression that he was living in the companionship of a changeling, a being strayed by accident from another plane. The small moralities and tendernesses of mankind contained no meaning for her. They were burnt away by the devastating flame of her own ideals. He knew now, irrefutably, that she had lived her life withdrawn from all but external contact with her surroundings.

Her sensuality, which betrayed itself even in the selection of the arts she loved, had marked her out for human passion. He had observed her instinct to deck herself for his pleasure; he had learnt the fastidious refinement with which she surrounded her body. He had marked her further instinct to turn the conduct of their love into a fine art. She had taught him the value of her reserve, her evasions, and of her sudden recklessness. He never discovered, and, no less Epicurean than she, never sought to discover, how far her principles were innate, unconscious, or how far deliberate. They both tacitly esteemed the veil of some slight mystery to soften the harshness of their self -revelation.

He dared not invoke the aid of unshrinking honesty to apportion the values between their physical and their mental affinity.

What was it, this bond of flesh? so material, yet so imperative, so compelling, as to become almost a spiritual, not a bodily, necessity? so transitory, yet so recurrent? dying down like a flame, to revive again? so unimportant, so grossly commonplace, yet creating so close and tremulous an intimacy? this magic that drew together their hands like fluttering butterflies in the hours of sunlight, and linked them in the abandonment of mastery and surrender in the hours of night? that swept aside the careful training, individual and hereditary, replacing pride by another pride? this unique and mutual secret? this fallacious yet fundamental and dominating bond? this force, hurling them together with such cosmic power that within the circle of frail human entity rushed furiously the tempest of an inexorable law of nature?

They had no tenderness for one another. Such tenderness as might have crept into the relationship they collaborated in destroying, choosing to dwell in the strong clean air of mountain-tops, shunning the ease of the valleys. Violence was never very far out of sight. They loved proudly, with a flame that purged all from their love but the essential, the ideal passion.

"I live with a Maenad," he said, putting out his hand and bathing his fingers in her loosened hair.

From the rough shelter of reeds and matting where they stood then among the terraced vineyards, the festoons of the vines and the bright reds and yellows of the splay leaves, brilliant against the sun, framed her consonant grace. The beautiful shadows of lacing vines dappled the ground, and the quick lizards darted upon the rough terrace walls.

He said, pursuing his thought—

"You have never the wish of other women—permanency? a house with me? never the inkling of such a wish?"

"Trammels!" she replied, "I've always hated possessions."

He considered her at great length, playing with her hair, fitting his fingers into its waving thicknesses, putting his cheek against the softness of her cheek, and laughing.

"My changeling. My nymph," he said.

She lay silent, her arms folded behind her head, and her eyes on him as he continued to utter his disconnected sentences.

"Where is the Eve of Herakleion? The mask you wore! I dwelt only upon your insignificant vanity, and in your pride you made no defense. Most secret pride! Incredible chastity of mind! Inviolate of soul, to all alike. Inviolate. Most rare restraint! The expansive vulgarity of the crowd! My Eve . . ."

He began again—

"So rarely, so stainlessly mine. Beyond mortal hopes. You allowed all to misjudge you, myself included. You smiled, not even wistfully, lest that betray you, and said nothing. You held yourself withdrawn. You perfected your superficial life. That profound humour . . . I could not think you shallow—not all your pretence could disguise your mystery—but, may I be forgiven, I have thought you shallow in all but mischief. I prophesied for you,"—he laughed—"a great career as a destroyer of men. A great courtesan. But instead I find you a great lover. *Une grande amoureuse.*"

"If that is mischievous," she said, "my love for you goes beyond mischief; it would stop short of no crime."

He put his face between his hands for a second.

"I believe you; I know it."

"I understand love in no other way," she said, sitting up and shaking her hair out of her eyes; "I am single-hearted. It is selfish love: I would die for you, gladly, without a thought, but I would sacrifice my claim on you to no one and to nothing. It is all-exorbitant. I make enormous demands. I must have you exclusively for myself."

He teased her,—

"You refuse to marry me."

She was serious.

"Freedom, Julian! Romance! The world before us, to roam at will; fairs to dance at; strange people to consort with, to see the smile in their eyes, and the tolerant "Lovers!" forming on their lips. To tweak the nose of Propriety, to snatch away the chair on which she would sit down! Who in their senses would harness the divine courser to a mail-cart?"

She seemed to him lit by an inner radiance, that shone through her eyes and glowed richly in her smile.

"Vagabond!" he said. "Is life to be one long carnival?"

"And one long honesty. I'll own you before the world—and court its disapproval. I'll release you—no, I'll leave you—when you tire of me. I wouldn't clip love's golden wings. I wouldn't irk you with promises, blackmail you into perjury, wring from you an oath we both should know was made only to be broken. We'll leave that to middle-age. Middle-age—I have been told there is such a thing? Sometimes it is fat, sometimes it is wan, surely it is always dreary! It may be wise and successful and contented. Sometimes, I'm told, it even loves. We are young. Youth!" she said, sinking her voice, "the winged and the divine."

When he talked to her about the Islands, she did not listen, although she dared not check him. He talked, striving to interest her, to fire her enthusiasm. He talked, with his eyes always upon the sea, since some obscure instinct warned him not to keep them bent upon her face; sometimes they were amongst the vines, which in the glow of their September bronze and amber resembled the wine flowing from their fruits, and from here the sea shimmered, crudely and cruelly blue between those flaming leaves, undulating into smooth, nacreous folds; sometimes they were amongst the rocks on the lower levels, on a windier day, when white crests spurted from the waves, and the foam broke with a lacy violence against the island at the edge of the green shallows; and sometimes, after dusk, they climbed to the olive terraces beneath the moon that rose through the trees in a world strangely gray and silver, strangely and contrastingly deprived of colour. He talked, lying on the ground, with his hands pressed close against the soil of Aphros. Its contact gave him the courage he needed. . . . He talked doggedly; in the first week with the fire of inspiration, after that with the perseverance of loyalty. These monologues ended always in the same way. He would bring his glance from the sea to her face, would break off his phrase in the middle, and, coming suddenly to her, would cover her hair, her throat, her mouth, with kisses. Then she would turn gladly and luxuriously towards him, curving in his arms, and presently the grace of her murmured speech would again bewitch him, until upon her lips he forgot the plea of Aphros.

There were times when he struggled to escape her, his physical and mental activity rebelling against the subjection in which she held him. He protested that the affairs of the Islands claimed him; that Herakleion had granted but a month of negotiations; precautions must be taken, and the scheme of government amplified and consolidated. Then the angry look came over her face, and all the bitterness of her resentment broke loose. Having captured him, much of her precocious wisdom seemed to have abandoned her.

"I have waited for you ten years, yet you want to leave me. Do I mean less to you than the Islands? I wish the Islands were at the bottom of the sea instead of on the top of it."

"Be careful, Eve."

"I resent everything which takes you from me," she said recklessly.

Another time she cried, murky with passion—

"Always these councils with Tsigaridis and the rest! always these secret messages passing between you and Kato! Give me that letter."

He refused, shredding Kato's letter and scattering the pieces into the sea.

"What secrets have you with Kato, that you must keep from me?"

"They would have no interest for you," he replied, remembering that she was untrustworthy—that canker in his confidence.

The breeze fanned slightly up the creek where they were lying on the sand under the shadow of a pine, and out in the dazzling sea a porpoise leapt, turning its slow black curve in the water. The heat simmered over the rocks.

"We share our love," he said morosely, "but no other aspect of life. The Islands are nothing to you. An obstacle, not a link." It was a truth that he rarely confronted.

"You are wrong: a background, a setting for you, which I appreciate."

"You appreciate the picturesque. I know. You are an artist in appreciation of the suitable stage-setting. But as for the rest . . ." he made a gesture full of sarcasm and renunciation.

"Give me up, Julian, and all my shortcomings. I have always told you I had but one virtue. I am the first to admit the insufficiency of its claim. Give yourself wholly to your Islands. Let me go." She spoke sadly, as though conscious of her own irremediable difference and perversity.

"Yet you yourself—what were your words?—said you believed in me; you even wrote to me, I remember still, 'conquer, shatter, demolish!' But I must always struggle against you, against your obstructions. What is it you want? Liberty and irresponsibility, to an insatiable degree!"

"Because I love you insatiably."

"You are too unreasonable sometimes!" ("Reason!" she interrupted with scorn, "what has reason got to do with love?") "you are unreasonable to grudge me every moment I spend away from you. Won't you realise that I am responsible for five thousand lives? You must let me go now; only for an hour. I promise to come back to you in an hour."

"Are you tired of me already?"

"Eve . . ."

"When we were in Herakleion, you were always saying you must go to Kato; now you are always going to some council; am I never to have you to myself?"

"I will go only for an hour. I *must* go, Eve, my darling."

"Stay with me, Julian. I'll kiss you. I'll tell you a story." She stretched out her hands. He shook his head, laughing, and ran off in the direction of the village.

When he returned, she refused to speak to him.

But at other times they grew marvellously close, passing hours and days in unbroken union, until the very fact of their two separate personalities became an exasperation. Then, silent as two souls tortured, before a furnace, they struggled for the expression that ever eludes; the complete, the satisfying expression that shall lay bare one soul to another soul, but that, ever failing, mockingly preserves the unwanted boon of essential mystery.

That dumb frenzy outworn, they attained, nevertheless, to a nearer comradeship, the days, perhaps, of their greatest happiness, when with her reckless fancy she charmed his mind; he thought of her then as a vagrant nymph, straying from land to land, from age to age, decking her spirit with any flower she met growing by the way, chastely concerned with the quest of beauty, strangely childlike always, pure as the fiercest, tallest flame. He could not but bow to that audacity, that elemental purity, of spirit. Untainted by worldliness, greed, or malice. . . . The facts of her life became clearer to him, startling in their consistency. He could not associate her with possessions, or a fixed abode, she who was free and elusive as a swallow, to whom the slightest responsibility was an intolerable and inadmissible yoke from beneath which, without commotion but also without compunction, she slipped. On no material point could she be touched—save her own personal luxury, and that seemed to grow with her, as innocent of effort as the colour on a flower; she kindled only in response to music, poetry, love, or laughter, but then with what a kindling! she flamed, she glowed; she ranged over spacious and fabulous realms; her feet never touched earth, they were sandal-shod and carried her in the clean path of breezes, and towards the sun, exalted and ecstatic, breathing as the common air the rarity of the upper spaces. At such times she seemed a creature blown from legend, deriving from no parentage; single, individual, and lawless.

He found that he had come gradually to regard her with a superstitious reverence.

He evolved a theory, constructed around her, dim and nebulous, yet persistent; perforce nebulous, since he was dealing with a matter too fine, too subtle, too unexplored, to lend itself to the gross imperfect imprisonment of words. He never spoke of it, even to her, but staring at her sometimes with a reeling head he felt himself transported, by her medium, beyond the matter-of-fact veils that shroud the limit of human vision. He felt illuminated, on the verge of a new truth; as though by stretching out his hand he might touch something no hand of man had ever touched before, something of unimaginable consistency, neither matter nor the negation of matter; as though he might brush the wings of truth, handle the very substance of a thought. . . .

He felt at these times like a man who passes through a genuine physical experience. Yes, it was as definite as that; he had the glimpse of a possible revelation. He returned from his vision—call it what he would, vision would serve as well as any other word—he returned with that sense of benefit by which alone such an excursion—or was it incursion?—could be justified. He brought back a benefit. He had beheld, as in a distant prospect, a novel balance and proportion of certain values. That alone would have left him enriched for ever.

Practical as he could be, theories and explorations were yet dear to him: he was an inquisitive adventurer of the mind no less than an active adventurer of the world. He sought eagerly for underlying truths. His apparently inactive moods were more accurately his fallow moods. His thought was as an ardent plough, turning and shifting the loam of his mind. Yet he would not allow his fancy to outrun his conviction; if fancy at any moment seemed to lead, he checked it until more lumbering conviction could catch up. They must travel ever abreast, whip and reins alike in his control.

Youth—were the years of youth the intuitive years of perception? Were the most radiant moments the moments in which one stepped farthest from the ordered acceptance of the world? Moments of danger, moments of inspiration, moments of self-sacrifice, moments of perceiving beauty, moments of love, all the drunken moments! Eve moved, he knew, permanently upon that plane. She led an exalted, high-keyed inner life. The normal mood to her was the mood of a sensitive person caught at the highest pitch of sensibility. Was she unsuited to the world and to the necessities of the world because she belonged, not here, but to another sphere apprehended by man only in those rare, keen moments that Julian called the drunken moments? apprehended by poet or artist—the elect, the aristocracy, the true path-finders among the race of man!—in moments when sobriety left them and they passed beyond?

Was she to blame for her cruelty, her selfishness, her disregard for truth? was she, not evil, but only alien? to be forgiven all for the sake of the rarer, more distant flame? Was the standard of cardinal virtues set by the world the true, the ultimate standard? Was it possible that Eve made part of a limited brotherhood? was indeed a citizen of some advanced state of such perfection that this world's measures and ideals were left behind and meaningless? meaningless because unnecessary in such a realm of serenity?

Aphros, then—the liberty of Aphros—and Aphros meant to him far more than merely Aphros—that was surely a lovely and desirable thing, a worthy aim, a high beacon? If Eve cared nothing for the liberty of Aphros, was it because in *her* world (he was by now convinced of its existence) there was no longer any necessity to trouble over such aims, liberty being as natural and unmeditated as the air in the nostrils?

(Not that this would ever turn him from his devotion; at most he could look upon Aphros as a stage upon the journey towards that higher aim—the stage to which he and his like, who were nearly of the elect, yet not of them, might aspire. And if the day should ever come when disillusion drove him down; when, far from becoming a citizen of Eve's far sphere, he should cease to be a citizen even of Aphros and should become a citizen merely of the world, no longer young, no longer blinded by ideals, no longer nearly a poet, but merely a grown, sober man—then he would still keep Aphros as a bright memory of what might have been, of the best he had grasped, the possibility which in the days of youth had not seemed too extravagantly unattainable.)

But in order to keep his hold upon this world of Eve's, which in his inner consciousness he already recognised as the most valuable rift of insight ever vouchsafed to him, it was necessary that he should revolutionise every ancient gospel and reputable creed. The worth of Eve was to him an article of faith. His intimacy with her was a privilege infinitely beyond the ordinary privilege of love. Whatever she might do, whatever crime she might commit, whatever baseness she might perpetrate, her ultimate worth, the core, the kernel, would remain to him unsullied and inviolate. This he knew blindly, seeing it as the mystic sees God; and knew it the more profoundly that he could have defended it with no argument of reason.

What then? the poet, the creator, the woman, the mystic, the man skirting the fringes of death—were they kin with one another and free of some realm unknown, towards which all, consciously or unconsciously, were journeying? Where the extremes of passion (he did not mean only the passion of love), of exaltation, of danger, of courage and vision—where all these extremes met—was it there, the great crossways where the moral ended, and the divine began? Was it for Eve supremely, and to a certain extent for all women and artists—the visionaries, the lovely, the graceful, the irresponsible, the useless!—was it reserved for them to show the beginning of the road?

Youth! youth and illusion! to love Eve and Aphros! when those two slipped from him he would return sobered to the path designated by the sign-posts and milestones of man, hoping no more than to keep as a gleam within him the light glowing in the sky above that unattainable but remembered city.

He returned to earth; Eve was kneading and tormenting a lump of putty, and singing to herself meanwhile; he watched her delicate, able hands, took one of them, and held it up between his eyes and the sun.

"Your fingers are transparent, they're like cornelian against the light," he said.

She left her hand within his grasp, and smiled down at him.

"How you play with me, Julian," she said idly.

"You're such a delicious toy."

"Only a toy?"

He remembered the intricate, untranslatable thoughts he had been thinking about her five minutes earlier, and began to laugh to himself.

"A great deal more than a toy. Once I thought of you only as a child, helpless, irritating, adorable child, always looking for trouble, and turning to me for help when the trouble came."

"And then?"

"Then you made me think of you as a woman," he replied gravely.

"You seemed to hesitate a good deal before deciding to think of me as that."

"Yes, I tried to judge our position by ordinary codes; you must have thought me ridiculous."

"I did, darling." Her mouth twisted drolly as she said it.

"I wonder now how I could have insulted you by applying them to you," he said with real wonderment; everything seemed so clear and obvious to him now.

"Why, how do you think of me now?"

"Oh, God knows!" he replied. "I've called you changeling sometimes, haven't I?" He decided to question her. "Tell me, Eve, how do you explain your difference? you outrage every accepted code, you see, and yet one retains one's belief in you. Is one simply deluded by your charm? or is there a deeper truth? can you explain?" He had spoken in a bantering tone, but he knew that he was trying an experiment of great import to him.

"I don't think I'm different, Julian; I think I feel things strongly, no more."

"Or else you don't feel them at all."

"What do you mean?"

"Well—Paul," he said reluctantly.

"You have never got over that, have you?"

"Exactly!" he exclaimed. "It seems to you extraordinary that I should still remember Paul, or that his death should have made any impression upon me. I ought to hate you for your indifference. Sometimes I have come very near to hating you. But now—perhaps my mind is getting broader—I blame you for nothing because I believe you are simply not capable of understanding. But evidently you can't explain yourself. I love you!" he said, "I love you!"

He knew that her own inability to explain herself—her unselfconsciousness—had done much to strengthen his new theories. The flower does not know why or how it blossoms. . . .

On the day that he told her, with many misgivings, that Kato was coming to Aphros, she uttered no word of anger, but wept despairingly, at first without speaking, then with short, reiterated sentences that wrung his heart for all their unreason—"We were alone. I was happy as never in my life. I had you utterly. We were alone. Alone! Alone!"

"We will tell Kato the truth," he soothed her; "she will leave us alone still."

But it was not in her nature to cling to straws of comfort. For her, the sunshine had been unutterably radiant; and for her it was now proportionately blackened out.

"We were alone," she repeated, shaking her head with unspeakable mournfulness, the tears running between her fingers.

For the first time he spoke to her with a moved, a tender compassion, full of reverence.

"Your joy . . . your sorrow . . . equally over-whelming and tempestuous. How you feel—you tragic child! Yesterday you laughed and made yourself a crown of myrtle."

She refused to accompany him when he went to meet Kato, who, after a devious journey from Athens, was to land at the rear of the island away from the curiosity of Herakleion. She remained in the cool house, sunk in idleness, her pen and pencil alike neglected. She thought only of Julian, absorbingly, concentratedly. Her past life appeared to her, when she thought of it at all, merely as a period in which Julian had not loved her, a period of waiting, of expectancy, of anguish sometimes, of incredible reticence supported only by the certainty which had been her faith and her inspiration . . .

To her surprise, he returned, not only with Kato but with Grbits.

Every word and gesture of the giant demonstrated his enormous pleasure. His oddly Mongolian face wore a perpetual grin of triumphant truancy. His good-humour was not to be withstood. He wrung Eve's hands, inarticulate with delight. Kato, her head covered with a spangled veil—Julian had never seen her in a hat—stood by, looking on, her hands on her hips, as though Grbits were her exhibit. Her little eyes sparkled with mischief.

"He is no longer an officer in the Serbian army," she said at last, "only a free-lance, at Julian's disposal. Is it not magnificent? He has sent in his resignation. His career is ruined. The military representative of Serbia in Herakleion!"

"A free-lance," Grbits repeated, beaming down at Julian. (It annoyed Eve that he should be so much the taller of the two.)

"We sent you no word, not to lessen your surprise," said Kato.

They stood, all four, in the courtyard by the fountain.

"I told you on the day of the elections that when you needed me I should come," Grbits continued, his grin widening.

"Of course, you are a supreme fool, Grbits," said Kato to him.

"Yes," he replied, "thank Heaven for it."

"In Athens the sympathy is all with the Islands," said Kato. She had taken off her veil, and they could see that she wore the gold wheat-ears in her hair. Her arms were, as usual, covered with bangles, nor had she indeed made any concessions to the necessities of travelling, save that on her feet, instead of her habitual square-toed slippers, she wore long, hideous, heelless, elastic-sided boots. Eve reflected that she had grown fatter and more stumpy, but she was, as ever, eager, kindly, enthusiastic, vital; they brought with them a breath of confidence and efficiency, those disproportionately assorted travelling companions; Julian felt a slight shame that he had neglected the Islands for Eve; and Eve stood by, listening to their respective recitals, to Grbits' startling explosions of laughter, and Kato's exuberant joy, tempered with wisdom. They both talked at once, voluble and excited; the wheat-ears trembled in Kato's hair, Grbits' white regular teeth flashed in his broad face, and Julian, a little bewildered, turned from one to the other with his unsmiling gravity.

"I mistrust the forbearance of Herakleion," Kato said, a great weight of meditated action pressing on behind her words; "a month's forbearance! In Athens innumerable rumours were current: of armed ships purchased from the Turks, even of a gun mounted on Mylassa—but that I do not believe. They have given you, you say, a month in which to come to your senses. But they are giving themselves also a month in which to prepare their attack," and she plied him with practical questions that demonstrated her clear familiarity with detail and tactic, while Grbits contributed nothing but the cavernous laugh and ejaculations of his own unquestioning optimism.

Five

The second attack on Aphros was delivered within a week of their arrival.

Eve and Kato, refusing the retreat in the heart of the island, spent the morning together in the Davenant house. In the distance the noise of the fighting alternately increased and waned; now crackling sharply, as it seemed, from all parts of the sea, now dropping into a disquieting silence. At such times Eve looked mutely at the singer. Kato gave her no comfort, but, shaking her head and shrugging her shoulders, expressed only her ignorance. She found that she could speak to Julian sympathetically of Eve, but not to Eve sympathetically of Julian. She had made the attempt, but after the pang of its effort, had renounced it. Their hostility smouldered dully under the shelter of their former friendship. Now, alone in the house, they might indeed have remained for the most time apart in separate rooms, but the common anxiety which linked them drew them together, so that when Kato moved Eve followed her, unwillingly, querulously; and expressions of affection were even forced from them, of which they instantly repented, and by some phrase of veiled cruelty sought to counteract.

No news reached them from outside. Every man was at his post, and Julian had forbidden all movement about the village. By his orders also the heavy shutters had been closed over the windows of the Davenant drawing-room, where Eve and Kato sat, with the door open on to the courtyard for the sake of light, talking spasmodically, and listening to the sounds of the firing. At the first quick rattle Kato had said, "Machine-guns," and Eve had replied, "Yes; the first time—when we were here alone—he told me they had a machine-gun on the police-launch;" then Kato said, after a pause of firing, "This time they have more than one."

Eve raised tormented eyes.

"Anastasia, he said he would be in shelter."

"Would he remain in shelter for long?" Kato replied scornfully.

Eve said, "He has Grbits with him."

Kato, crushing down the personal preoccupation, dwelt ardently on the fate of her country. She must abandon to Eve the thought of Julian, but of the Islands at least she might think possessively, diverting to their dear though inanimate claim all the need of passion and protection humanly denied her. From a woman of always intense patriotism, she had become a fanatic. Starved in one direction, she had doubled her energy in the other, realising, moreover, the power of that bond between herself and Julian. She could have said with thorough truthfulness that her principal cause of resentment against Eve was Eve's indifference toward the Islands—a loftier motive than the more human jealousy. She had noticed Julian's reluctance to mention the Islands in Eve's presence. Alone with herself and Grbits, he had never ceased to pour forth the flood of his scheme, both practical and utopian, so that Kato could not be mistaken as to the direction of his true preoccupations. She had seen the vigour he brought to his governing. She had observed with a delighted grin to Grbits that, despite his Socialistic theories, Julian had in point of fact instituted a complete and very thinly-veiled autocracy in Hagios Zacharie. She had seen him in the village assembly, when in spite of his deferential appeals to the superior experience of the older men, he steered blankly past any piece of advice that ran contrary to the course of his own ideas. She knew that, ahead of him, when he should have freed himself finally of Herakleion (and that he would free himself he did not for a moment doubt), he kept always the dream of his tiny, ideal state. She revered his faith, his energy, and his youth, as the essence in him most worthy of reverence. And she knew that Eve, if she loved these things in him, loved them only in theory, but in practice regarded them with impatient indifference. They stole him away, came between him and her. . . . Kato knew well Eve's own ideals. Courage she exacted. Talents she esteemed. Genius, freedom, and beauty she passionately worshipped as her gods upon earth. But she could tolerate nothing material, nor any occupation that removed her or the other from the blind absorption of love.

Kato sighed. Far otherwise would she have cared for Julian! She caught sight of herself in a mirror, thick, squat, black, with little sparkling eyes; she glanced at Eve, glowing with warmth, sleek and graceful as a little animal, idle and seductive. Outside a crash of firing shook the solid house, and bullets rattled upon the roofs of the village.

It was intolerable to sit unoccupied, working out bitter speculations, while such activity raged around the island. To know the present peril neither of Julian nor of Aphros! To wait indefinitely, probably all day, possibly all night!

"Anastasia, sing."

Kato complied, as much for her own sake as for Eve's. She sang some of her own native songs, then, breaking off, she played, and Eve drew near to her, lost and transfigured by the music; she clasped and unclasped her hands, beautified by her ecstasy, and Kato's harsh thoughts vanished; Eve was, after all, a child, an all too loving and passionate child, and not, as Kato sometimes thought her, a pernicious force of idleness and waste. Wrong-headed, tragically bringing sorrow upon herself in the train of her too intense emotions. . . . Continuing to play, Kato observed her, and felt the light eager fingers upon her arm.

"Ah, Kato, you make me forget. Like some drug of forgetfulness that admits me to caves of treasure. Underground caves heaped with jewels. Caves of the winds; zephyrs that come and go. I'm carried away into oblivion."

"Tell me," Kato said.

Obedient to the lead of the music, Eve wandered into a story—

"Riding on a winged horse, he swept from east to west; he looked down upon the sea, crossed by the wake of ships, splashed here and there with islands, washing on narrow brown stretches of sand, or dashing against the foot of cliffs—you hear the waves breaking?—and he saw how the moon drew the tides, and how ships came to rest for a little while in harbours, but were homeless and restless and free; he passed over the land, swooping low, and he saw the straight streets of cities, and the gleam of fires, the neat fields and guarded frontiers, the wider plains; he saw the gods throned on Ida, wearing the clouds like mantles and like crowns, divinely strong or divinely beautiful; he saw things mean and magnificent; he saw the triumphal procession of a conqueror, with prisoners walking chained to the back of his chariot, and before him white bulls with gilded horns driven to the sacrifice, and children running with garlands of flowers; he saw giants hammering red iron in northern mountains; he saw all the wanderers of the earth; Io the tormented, and all gipsies, vagabonds, and wastrels: all jongleurs, poets, and mountebanks; he saw these wandering, but all the staid and solemn people lived in the cities and counted the neat fields, saying, 'This shall be mine and this shall be yours.' And sometimes, as he passed above a forest, he heard a scurry of startled feet among crisp leaves, and sometimes he heard, which made him sad, the cry of stricken trees beneath the axe."

She broke off, as Kato ceased playing.

"They are still firing," she said.

"Things mean and magnificent," quoted Kato slowly. "Why, then, withhold Julian from the Islands?"

She had spoken inadvertently. Consciousness of the present had jerked her back from remembrance of the past, when Eve had come almost daily to her flat in Herakleion, bathing herself in the music, wrapped up in beauty; when their friendship had hovered on the boundaries of the emotional, in spite of—or perhaps because of?—the thirty years that lay between them.

"I heard the voice of my fantastic Eve, of whom I once thought," she added, fixing her eyes on Eve, "as the purest of beings, utterly removed from the sordid and the ugly."

Eve suddenly flung herself on her knees beside her. "Ah, Kato," she said, "you throw me off my guard when you play to me. I'm not always hard and calculating, and your music melts me. It hurts me to be, as I constantly am, on the defensive. I'm too suspicious by nature to be very happy, Kato. There are always shadows, and . . . and tragedy. Please don't judge me too harshly. Tell me what you mean by sordid and ugly—what is there sordid and ugly in love?"

Kato dared much: she replied in a level voice, "Jealousy. Waste. Exorbitance. Suspicion. I am sometimes afraid of your turning Julian into another of those men who hoped to find their inspiration in a woman, but found only a hindrance."

She nodded sagely at Eve, and the gold wheat-ears trembled in her hair.

Eve darkened at Julian's name; she got up and stood by the door looking into the court. Kato went on, "You are so much of a woman, Eve, that it becomes a responsibility. It is a gift, like genius. And a great gift without a great soul is a curse, because such a gift is too strong to be disregarded. It's a force, a danger. You think I am preaching to you," Eve would never know what the words were costing her—"but I preach only because of my belief in Julian—and in you," she hastened to add, and caught Eve's hand; "don't frown, you child. Look at me; I have no illusions and no sensitiveness on the score of my own appearance; look at me hard, and let me speak to you as a sexless creature."

Eve was touched in spite of her hostility. She was also shocked and distressed. There was to her, so young herself, so insolently vivid in her sex-pride, something wrong and painful in Kato's renunciation of her right. She had a sense of betrayal.

"Hush, Anastasia," she whispered. They were both extremely moved, and the constant volleys of firing played upon their nerves and stripped reserve from them.

"You don't realise," said Kato, who had, upon impulse, sacrificed her pride, and beaten down the feminine weakness she branded as unworthy, "how finely the balance, in love, falters between good and ill. You, Eve, are created for love; any one who saw you, even without speaking to you, across a room, could tell you that." She smiled affectionately; she had, at that moment, risen so far above all personal vanity that she could bring herself to smile affectionately at Eve. "You said, just now, with truth I am sure, that shadows and tragedy were never far away from you; you're too *rare* to be philosophical. I wish there were a word to express the antithesis of a philosopher; if I could call you by it, I should have said all that I could wish to say about you, Eve. I'm so much afraid of sorrow for you and Julian . . ."

"Yes, yes," said Eve, forgetting to be resentful, "I am afraid, too; it overcomes me sometimes; it's a presentiment." She looked really haunted, and Kato was filled with an immense pity for her.

"You mustn't be weak," she said gently. "Presentiment is only a high-sounding word for a weak thought."

"You are so strong and sane, Kato; it is easy for you to be—strong and sane."

They broke off, and listened in silence to an outburst of firing and shouts that rose from the village.

Grbits burst into the room early in the afternoon, his flat sallow face tinged with colour, his clothes torn, and his limbs swinging like the sails of a windmill. In one enormous hand he still brandished a revolver. He was triumphantly out of breath.

"Driven off!" he cried. "They ran up a white flag. Not one succeeded in landing. Not one." He panted between every phrase. "Julian—here in a moment. I ran. Negotiations now, we hope. Sea bobbing with dead."

"Our losses?" said Kato sharply.

"Few. All under cover," Grbits replied. He sat down, swinging his revolver loosely between his knees, and ran his fingers through his oily black hair, so that it separated into straight wisps across his forehead. He was hugely pleased and good-humoured and grinned widely upon Eve and Kato. "Good fighting—though too much at a distance. Julian was grazed on the temple—told me to tell you," he added, with the tardy haste of a child who has forgotten to deliver a message. "We tied up his head, and it will be nothing of a scratch.—Driven off! They have tried and failed. The defence was excellent. They will scarcely try force again. I am sorry I missed the first fight. I could have thrown those little fat soldiers into the sea with one hand, two at a time."

Kato rushed up to Grbits and kissed him; they were like children in their large, clumsy excitement.

Julian came in, his head bandaged; his unconcern deserted him as he saw Kato hanging over the giant's chair. He laughed out loud.

"A miscellaneous fleet!" he cried. "Coastal steamers, fort tugs, old chirkets from the Bosphorous—who was the admiral, I wonder?"

"Panaioannou," cried Grbits, "his uniform military down one side, and naval down the other."

"Their white flag!" said Julian.

"Sterghiou's handkerchief!" said Grbits.

"Coaling steamers, mounting machine-guns," Julian continued.

"Stavridis must have imagined that," said Kato.

"Play us a triumphal march, Anastasia!" said Grbits.

Kato crashed some chords on the piano; they all laughed and sang, but Eve, who had taken no part at all, remained in the window-seat staring at the ground and her lips trembling. She heard Julian's voice calling her, but she obstinately shook her head. He was lost to her between Kato and Grbits. She heard them eagerly talking now, all three, of the negotiations likely to follow. She heard the occasional shout with which Grbits recalled some incident in the fighting, and Julian's response. She felt that her ardent hatred of the Islands rose in proportion to their ardent love. "He cares nothing for me," she kept repeating to herself, "he cares for me as a toy, a pastime, nothing more; he forgets me for Kato and the Islands. The Islands hold his true heart. I am the ornament to his life, not life itself. And he is all my life. He forgets me. . . ." Pride alone conquered her tears.

Later, under cover of a white flag, the ex-Premier Malteios was landed at the port of Aphros, and was conducted—since he insisted that his visit was unofficial—to the Davenant house.

Peace and silence reigned. Grbits and Kato had gone together to look at the wreckage, and Eve, having watched their extraordinary progress down the street until they turned into the market-place, was alone in the drawing-room. Julian slept heavily, his arms flung wide, on his bed upstairs. Zapantiotis, who had expected to find him in the court or in the drawing-room, paused perplexed. He spoke to Eve in a low voice.

"No," she said, "do not wake Mr. Davenant," and, raising her voice, she added, "His Excellency can remain with me."

She was alone in the room with Malteios, as she had desired.

"But why remain thus, as it were, at bay?" he said pleasantly, observing her attitude, shrunk against the wall, her hand pressed to her heart. "You and I were friends once, mademoiselle. Madame?" he substituted.

"Mademoiselle," she replied levelly.

"Ah? Other rumours, perhaps—no matter. Here upon your island, no doubt, different codes obtain. Far be it from me to suggest. . . . An agreeable room," he said, looking round, linking his fingers behind his back, and humming a little tune; "you have a piano, I see; have you played much during your leisure? But, of course, I was forgetting: Madame Kato is your companion here, is she not? and to her skill a piano is a grateful ornament. Ah, I could envy you your evenings, with Kato to make your music. Paris cries for her; but no, she is upon a revolutionary island in the heart of the Aegean! Paris cries the more. Her portrait appears in every paper. Madame Kato, when she emerges, will find her fame carried to its summit. And you, Mademoiselle Eve, likewise something of a heroine."

"I am here in the place of my cousin," Eve said, looking across at the ex-Premier.

He raised his eyebrows, and in a familiar gesture, smoothed away his beard from his rosy lips with the tips of his fingers.

Is that indeed so? A surprising race, you English. Very surprising. You assume or bequeath very lightly the mantle of government, do you not? Am I to understand that you have permanently replaced your cousin in the—ah!—presidency of Hagios Zacharie?"

"My cousin is asleep; there is no reason why you should not speak to me in his absence."

"Asleep? but I must see him, mademoiselle."

"If you will wait until he wakes."

"Hours, possibly!"

"We will send to wake him in an hour's time. Can I not entertain you until then?" she suggested, her natural coquetry returning.

She left the wall against which she had been leaning, and, coming across to Malteios, gave him her fingers with a smile. The ex-Premier had always figured picturesquely in her world.

"Mademoiselle," he said, kissing the fingers she gave him, "you are as delightful as ever, I am assured."

They sat, Malteios impatient and ill at ease, unwilling to forego his urbanity, yet tenacious of his purpose. In the midst of the compliments he perfunctorily proffered, he broke out,—"Children! *Ces gosses. . . . Mais il est fou, voyons, votre cousin.* What is he thinking about? He has created a ridiculous disturbance; well, let that pass; we overlook it, but this persistence. . . . Where is it all to end? Obstinacy feeds and grows fat upon obstinacy; submission grows daily more impossible, more remote. His pride is at stake. A threat, well and good; let him make his threat; he might then have arrived at some compromise. I, possibly, might myself have acted as mediator between him and my friend and rival, Gregori Stavridis. In fact, I am here today in the hope that my effort will not come too late. But after so much fighting! Tempers run high no doubt in the Islands, and I can testify that they run high in Herakleion. Anastasia—probably you know this already—Madame Kato's flat is wrecked. Yes, the mob. We are obliged to keep a cordon of police always before your uncle's house. Neither he nor your father and mother dare to show themselves at the windows. It is a truly terrible state of affairs."

He reverted to the deeper cause of his resentment—

"I could have mediated, in the early days, so well between your cousin and Gregori Stavridis. "Pity, pity, pity!" he said, shaking his head and smiling his benign, regretful smile that today was tinged with a barely concealed bitterness, "a thousand pities, mademoiselle."

He began again, his mind on Herakleion—

"I have seen your father and mother, also your uncle. They are very angry and impotent. Because the people threw stones at their windows and even, I regret to say, fired shots into the house from the *platia,* the windows are all boarded over and they live by artificial light. I have seen them breakfasting by candles. Yes. Your father, your mother, and your uncle, breakfasting together in the drawing-room with lighted candles on the table. I entered the house from the back. Your father said to me apprehensively, "I am told Madame Kato's flat was wrecked last night?" and your mother said, "Outrageous! She is infatuated, either with those Islands or with that boy. She will not care. All her possessions, littering the quays! An outrage." Your uncle said to me, "See the boy, Malteios! Talk to him. We are hopeless." Indeed they appeared hopeless, although not resigned, and sat with their hands hanging by their sides instead of eating their eggs; your mother, even, had lost her determination.

"I tried to reassure them, but a rattle of stones on the boarded windows interrupted me. Your uncle got up and flung away his napkin. 'One cannot breakfast in peace,' he said petulantly, as though that constituted his most serious grievance. He went out of the room, but the door had scarcely closed behind him before it reopened and he came back. He was quite altered, very irritable, and all his courteous gravity gone from him. 'See the inconvenience,' he said to me, jerking his hands, 'all the servants have gone with my son, all damned islanders.' I found nothing to say."

"Kato may return to Herakleion with you?" Eve suggested after a pause during which Malteios recollected himself, and tried to indicate by shrugs and rueful smiles that he considered the bewilderment of the Davenants a deplorable but nevertheless entertaining joke. At the name of Kato, a change came over his face.

"A fanatic, that woman," he replied; "a martyr who will rejoice in her martyrdom. She will never leave Aphros while the cause remains.—A heroic woman," he said, with unexpected reverence.

He looked at Eve, his manner veering again to the insinuating and the crafty; his worse and his better natures were perpetually betraying themselves.

"Would she leave Aphros? no! Would your cousin leave Aphros? no! They have between them the bond of a common cause. I know your cousin. He is young enough to be an idealist. I know Madame Kato. She is old enough to applaud skilfully. Hou!" He spread his hands. "I have said enough."

Eve revealed but little interest, though for the first time during their interview her interest was passionately aroused. Malteios watched her, new schemes germinating in his brain; they played against one another, their hands undeclared, a blind, tentative game. This conversation, which had begun as it were accidentally, fortuitously, turned to a grave significance along a road whose end lay hidden far behind the hills of the future. It led, perhaps, nowhere. It led, perhaps . . .

Eve said lightly, "I am outdistanced by Kato and my cousin; I don't understand politics, or those impersonal friendships."

"Mademoiselle," Malteios replied, choosing his words and infusing into them an air of confidence, "I tell you an open secret, but one to which I would never refer save with a sympathetic listener like yourself, when I tell you that for many years a friendship existed between myself and Madame Kato, political indeed, but not impersonal. Madame Kato," he said, drawing his chair a little nearer and lowering his voice, "is not of the impersonal type."

Eve violently rebelled from his nearness; fastidious, she loathed his goatish smile, his beard, his rosy lips, but she continued to smile to him, a man who held, perhaps, one of Julian's secrets. She was aware of the necessity of obtaining that secret. Of the dishonour towards Julian, sleeping away his fatigue and his hurts in the room above, she was blindly unaware. Love to her was a battle, not a fellowship. She must know! Already her soul, eagerly receptive and bared to the dreaded blow, had adopted the theory of betrayal. In the chaos of her resentments and suspicions, she remembered how Kato had spoken to her in the morning, and without further reflection branded that conversation as a blind.

She even felt a passing admiration for the other woman's superior cleverness. She, Eve, had been completely taken in. . . . So she must contend, not only against the Islands, but against Kato also? Anguish and terror rushed over her. She scarcely knew what she believed or did not believe, only that her mind was one seething and surging tumult of mistrust and all-devouring jealousy. She was on the point of abandoning her temperamentally indirect methods, of stretching out her hands to Malteios, and crying to him for the agonising, the fiercely welcome truth, when he said—

"Impersonal? Do you, mademoiselle, know anything of your sex? An, charming! disturbing, precious, indispensable, even heroic, *tant que vous voudrez,* but impersonal, no! Man, yes, sometimes. Woman, never. Never." He took her hand, patted it, kissed the wrist, and murmured, "Chère enfant, these are not ideas for your pretty head."

She knew from experience that his preoccupation with such theories, if no more sinister motive, would urge him towards a resumption of the subject, and after a pause full of cogitation he continued,—

"Follow my advice, mademoiselle: never give your heart to a man concerned in other affairs. You may love, both of you, but you will strive in opposite directions. Your cousin, for example. . . . And yet," he mused, "you are a woman to charm the leisure of a man of action. The toy of a conqueror." He laughed. "Fortunately, conquerors are rare." But she knew he hovered round the image of Julian. "Believe me, leave such men to such women as Kato; they are more truly kin. You—I discover you—are too exorbitant; love would play too absorbing a role. You would tolerate no rival, neither a person nor a fact. Your eyes smoulder; I am near the truth?"

"One could steal a man from his affairs," she said almost inaudibly.

"The only hope," he replied.

A long silence fell, and his evil benevolence gained on her; on her aroused sensitiveness his unspoken suggestions fell one by one as definitely as the formulated word. He watched her; she trembled, half compelled by his gaze. At length, under the necessity of breaking the silence, she said,

"Kato is not such a woman; she would resent no obstacle."

"Wiser," he added, "she would identify herself with it." He began to banter horribly—

"Ah, child, Eve, child made for love, daily bless your cousinship! Bless its contemptuous security. Smile over the confabulations of Kato and your cousin. Smile to think that he, she, and the Islands are bound in an indissoluble trilogy. If there be jealousy to suffer, rejoice in that it falls, not to your share, but to mine, who am old and sufficiently philosophical. Age and experience harden, you know. Else, I could not see Anastasia Kato pass to another with so negligible a pang. Yet the imagination makes its own trouble. A jealous imagination. . . . Very vivid. Pictures of Anastasia Kato in your cousin's arms—ah, crude, crude, I know, but the crudity of the jealous imagination is unequalled. Not a detail escapes. That is why I say, bless your cousinship and its security." He glanced up and met her tortured eyes. "As I bless my philosophy of the inevitable," he finished softly, caressing her hand which he had retained all the while.

No effort at "Impossible!" escaped her; almost from the first she had blindly adopted his insinuations. She even felt a perverse gratitude towards him, and a certain fellowship. They were allies. Her mind was now set solely upon one object. That self-destruction might be involved did not occur to her, nor would she have been deterred thereby. Like Samson, she had her hands upon the columns. . . .

"Madame Kato lives in this house?" asked Malteios, as one who has been following a train of thought.

She shook her head, and he noticed that her eyes were turned slightly inwards, as with the effort of an immense concentration.

"You have power," he said with admiration.

Bending towards her, he began to speak in a very low, rapid voice; she sat listening to him, by no word betraying her passionate attention, nodding only from time to time, and keeping her hands very still, linked in her lap. Only once she spoke, to ask a question, "He would leave Herakleion?" and Malteios replied, "Inevitably; the question of the Islands would be for ever closed for him"; then she said, producing the words from afar off, "He would be free," and Malteios, working in the dark, following only one of the two processes of her thought, reverted to Kato; his skill could have been greater in playing upon the instrument, but even so it sufficed, so taut was the stringing of the cords. When he had finished speaking, she asked him another question, "He could never trace the thing to me?" and he reassured her with a laugh so natural and contemptuous that she, in her ingenuity, was convinced. All the while she had kept her eyes fastened on his face, on his rosy lips moving amongst his beard, that she might lose no detail of his meaning or his instructions, and at one moment he had thought, "There is something terrible in this child," but immediately he had crushed the qualm, thinking "By this recovery, if indeed it is to be, I am a made man," and thanking the fate that had cast this unforeseen chance across his path. Finally she heard his voice change from its earnest undertone to its customary platitudinous flattery, and turning round she saw that Julian had come into the room, his eyes already bent with brooding scorn upon the emissary.

Six

She was silent that evening, so silent that Grbits, the unobservant, commented to Kato; but after they had dined, all four, by the fountain in the court, she flung aside her preoccupation, laughed and sang, forced Kato to the piano, and danced with reckless inspiration to the accompaniment of Kato's songs. Julian, leaning against a column, watched her bewildering gaiety. She had galvanised Grbits into movement—he who was usually bashful with women especially with Eve, reserving his enthusiasm for Julian—and as she passed and re-passed before Julian in the grasp of the giant she flung at him provocative glances charged with a special meaning he could not interpret; in the turn of her dance he caught her smile and the flash of her eyes, and smiled in response, but his smile was grave, for his mind ran now upon the crisis with Herakleion, and, moreover, he suffered to see Eve so held by Grbits, her turbulent head below the giant's shoulder, and regretted that her gaiety should not be reserved for him alone. Across the court, through the open door of the drawing-room, he could see Kato at the piano, full of delight, her broad little fat hands and wrists racing above the keyboard, her short torso swaying to the rhythm, her rich voice humming, and the gold wheat-ears shaking in her hair. She called to him, and, drawing a chair close to the piano, he sat beside her, but through the door he continued to stare at Eve dancing in the court. Kato said as she played, her perception sharpened by the tormented watch she kept on him,—"Eve celebrates your victory of yesterday," to which he replied, deceived by the kindly sympathy in her eyes, "Eve celebrates her own high spirits and the enjoyment of a new partner; my doings are of the least indifference to her."

Kato played louder; she bent towards him—

"You love her so much, Julian?"

He made an unexpected answer—

"I believe in her."

Kato, a shrewd woman, observed him, thinking, "He does not; he wants to convince himself."

She said aloud, conscientiously wrenching out the truth as she saw it, "She loves you; she is capable of love such as is granted to few; that is the sublime in her."

He seized upon this, hungrily, missing meanwhile the sublime in the honesty of the singer—"Since I am given so much, I should not exact more. The Islands . . . She gives all to me. I ought not to force the Islands upon her."

"Grapes of thistles," Kato said softly.

"You understand," he murmured with gratitude. "But why should she hamper me, Anastasia? are all women so irrational? What am I to believe?"

"We are not so irrational as we appear," Kato said, "because our wildest sophistry has always its roots in the truth of instinct."

Eve was near them, crying out, "A tarantella, Anastasia!"

Julian sprang up; he caught her by the wrist, "Gipsy!"

"Come with the gipsy?" she whispered.

Her scented hair blew near him, and her face was upturned, with its soft, sweet mouth.

"Away from Aphros?" he said, losing his head.

"All over the world!"

He was suddenly swept away by the full force of her wild, irresponsible seduction.

"Anywhere you choose, Eve."

She triumphed, close to him, and wanton. "You'd sacrifice Aphros to me?"

"Anything you asked for," he said desperately.

She laughed, and danced away, stretching out her hands towards him—"Join in the saraband, Julian?"

She was alone in her room. Her emotions and excitement were so intense that they drained her of physical strength, leaving her faint and cold; her eyes closed now and then as under the pressure of pain; she yawned, and her breath came shortly between her lips; she sat by the open window, rose to move about the room, sat again, rose again, passed her hand constantly over her forehead, or pressed it against the base of her throat. The room was in darkness; there was no moon, only the stars hung over the black gulf of the sea. She could see the long, low lights of Herakleion, and the bright red light of the pier. She could hear distant shouting, and an occasional shot. In the room behind her, her bed was disordered. She wore only her Spanish shawl thrown over her long nightgown; her hair hung in its thick plait. Sometimes she formed, in a whisper, the single word, "Julian!"

She thought of Julian. Julian's rough head and angry eyes. Julian when he said, "I shall break you," like a man speaking to a wild young supple tree. (Her laugh of derision, and her rejoicing in her secret fear!) Julian in his lazy ownership of her beauty. Julian when he allowed her to coax him from his moroseness. Julian when she was afraid of him and of the storm she had herself aroused: Julian passionate. . . .

Julian whom she blindly wanted for herself alone.

That desire had risen to its climax. The light of no other consideration filtered through into her closely shuttered heart. She had waited for Julian, schemed for Julian, battled for Julian; this was the final battle. She had not foreseen it. She had tolerated and even welcomed the existence of the Islands until she began to realise that they took part of Julian from her. Then she hated them insanely, implacably; including Kato, whom Julian had called their tutelary deity, in that hatred. Had Julian possessed a dog, she would have hated that too.

The ambitions she had vaguely cherished for him had not survived the test of surrendering a portion of her own inordinate claim.

She had joined battle with the Islands as with a malignant personality. She was fighting them for the possession of Julian as she might have fought a woman she thought more beautiful, more unscrupulous, more appealing than herself, but with very little doubt of ultimate victory. Julian would be hers, at last; more completely hers than he had been even in those ideal, uninterrupted days before Grbits and Kato came, the days when he forgot his obligations, almost his life's dream for her. Love all-eclipsing. . . . She stood at the window, oppressed and tense, but in the soft silken swaying of her loose garments against her limbs she still found a delicately luxurious comfort.

Julian had been called away, called by the violent hammering on the house-door; it had then been after midnight. Two hours had passed since then. No one had come to her, but she had heard the tumult of many voices in the streets, and by leaning far out of the window she could see a great flare burning up from the market-place. She had thought a house might be on fire. She could not look back over her dispositions; they had been completed in a dream, as though under direct dictation. It did not occur to her to be concerned as to their possible miscarriage; she was too ignorant of such matters, too unpractical, to be troubled by any such anxiety. She had carried out Malteios's instructions with intense concentration; there her part had ended. The fuse which she had fired was burning. . . . If Julian would return, to put an end to her impatience!

(Down in the market-place the wooden school-buildings flamed and crackled, redly lighting up the night, and fountains of sparks flew upward against the sky. The lurid market-place was thronged with sullen groups of islanders, under the guard of the soldiers of Herakleion. In the centre, on the cobbles, lay the body of Tsigaridis, on his back, arms flung open, still, in the enormous pool of blood that crept and stained the edges of his spread white fustanella. Many of the islanders were not fully dressed, but had run out half-naked from their houses, only to be captured and disarmed by the troops; the weapons which had been taken from them lay heaped near the body of Tsigaridis, the light of the flames gleaming along the blades of knives and the barrels of rifles, and on the bare bronzed chests of men, and limbs streaked with tricklets of bright red blood. They stood proudly, contemptuous of their wounds, arms folded, some with rough bandages about their heads. Panaioannou, leaning both hands on the hilt of his sword, and grinning sardonically beneath his fierce moustaches, surveyed the place from the steps of the assembly-room.)

Eve in her now silent room realised that all sounds of tumult had died away. A shivering came over her, and, impelled by a suddenly understood necessity, she lit the candles on her dressing-table and, as the room sprang into light, began flinging the clothes out of the drawers into a heap in the middle of the floor. They fluttered softly from her hands, falling together in all their diverse loveliness of colour and fragility of texture. She paused to smile to them, friends and allies. She remembered now, with the fidelity of a child over a well-learnt lesson, the final words of Malteios, "A boat ready for you both tonight, secret and without delay," as earlier in the evening she had remembered his other words, "Midnight, at the creek at the back of the islands . . ."; she had acted upon her lesson mechanically, and in its due sequence, conscientious, trustful.

She stood amongst her clothes, the long red sari which she had worn on the evening of Julian's first triumph drooping from her hand. They foamed about her feet as she stood doubtfully above them, strangely brilliant herself in her Spanish shawl. They lay in a pool of rich delicacy upon the floor. They hung over the backs of chairs, and across the tumbled bed. They pleased her; she thought them pretty. Stooping, she raised them one by one, and allowed them to drop back on to the heap, aware that she must pack them and must also dress herself. But she liked their butterfly colours and gentle rustle, and, remembering that Julian liked them too, smiled to them again. He found her standing there amongst them when after a knock at her door he came slowly into her room.

He remained by the door for a long while looking at her in silence. She had made a sudden, happy movement towards him, but inexplicably had stopped, and with the sari still in her hand gazed back at him, waiting for him to speak. He looked above all, mortally tired. She discovered no anger in his face, not even sorrow; only that mortal weariness. She was touched; she to whom those gentler emotions were usually foreign.

"Julian?" she said, seized with doubt.

"It is all over," he began, quite quietly, and he put his hand against his forehead, which was still bandaged, raising his arm with the same lassitude; "they landed where young Zapantiotis was on guard, and he let them through; they were almost at the village before they were discovered. There was very little fighting. They have allowed me to come here. They are waiting for me downstairs. I am to leave."

"Yes," she said, and looked down at her heap of clothes.

He did not speak again, and gradually she realised the implications of his words.

"Zapantiotis. . . ." she said.

"Yes," he said, raising his eyes again to her face, "yes, you see, Zapantiotis confessed it all to me when he saw me. He was standing amongst a group of prisoners, in the market-place, but when I came by he broke away from the guards and screamed out to me that he had betrayed us. Betrayed us. He said he was tempted, bribed. He said he would cut his own throat. But I told him not to do that."

She began to tremble, wondering how much he knew.

He added, in the saddest voice she had ever heard, "Zapantiotis, an islander, could not be faithful."

Then she was terrified; she did not know what was coming next, what would be the outcome of this quietness. She wanted to come towards him, but she could only remain motionless, holding the sari up to her breast as a means of protection.

"At least," he said, "old Zapantiotis is dead, and will never know about his son. Where can one look for fidelity? Tsigaridis is dead too, and Grbits. I am ashamed of being alive."

She noticed then that he was disarmed.

"Why do you stand over there, Julian?" she said timidly.

"I wonder how much you promised Zapantiotis?" he said in a speculative voice; and next, stating a fact, "You were, of course, acting on Malteios's suggestion."

"You know?" she breathed. She was quite sure now that he was going to kill her.

"Zapantiotis tried to tell me that too—in a strange jumble of confessions. But they dragged him away before he could say more than your bare name. That was enough for me. So I know, Eve."

"Is that all you were going to say?"

He raised his arms and let them fall.

"What is there to say?"

Knowing him very well, she saw that his quietness was dropping from him; she was aware of it perhaps before he was aware of it himself. His eyes were losing their dead apathy, and were travelling round the room; they rested on the heap of clothes, on her own drawing of himself hanging on the wall, on the disordered bed. They flamed suddenly, and he made a step towards her.

"Why? why? why?" he cried out with the utmost anguish and vehemence, but stopped himself, and stood with clenched fists. She shrank away. "All gone—in an hour!" he said, and striding towards her he stood over her, shaken with a tempest of passion. She shrank farther from him, retreating against the wall, but first she stooped and gathered her clothes around her again, pressing her back against the wall and cowering with the clothes as a rampart round her feet. But as yet full realisation was denied her; she knew that he was angry, she thought indeed that he might kill her, but to other thoughts of finality she was, in all innocence, a stranger.

He spoke incoherently, saying, "All gone! All gone!" in accents of blind pain, and once he said, "I thought you loved me," putting his hands to his head as though walls were crumbling. He made no further reproach, save to repeat, "I thought the men were faithful, and that you loved me," and all the while he trembled with the effort of his self-control, and his twitching hands reached out towards her once or twice, but he forced them back. She thought, "How angry he is! but he will forget, and I shall make up to him for what he has lost." So, between them, they remained almost silent, breathing hard, and staring at one another.

"Come, put up your clothes quickly," he said at last, pointing; "they want us off the island, and if we do not go of our own accord they will tie our hands and feet and carry us to the boat. Let us spare ourselves that ludicrous scene. We can marry in Athens tomorrow."

"Marry?" she repeated.

"Naturally. What else did you suppose? That I should leave you? now? Put up your clothes. Shall I help you? Come!"

"But—marry, Julian?"

"Clearly: marry," he replied, in a harsh voice and added, "Let us go. For God's sake, let us go now! I feel stunned, I mustn't begin to think. Let us go." He urged her towards the door.

"But we had nothing to do with marriage," she whispered.

He cried, so loudly and so bitterly that she was startled—

"No, we had to do only with love—love and rebellion! And both have failed me. Now, instead of love, we must have marriage; and instead of rebellion, law. I shall help on authority, instead of opposing it." He broke down and buried his face in his hands.

"You no longer love me," she said slowly, and her eyes narrowed and turned slightly inwards in the way Malteios had noticed. "Then the Islands. . . ."

He pressed both hands against his temples and screamed like one possessed, "But they were all in all in all! It isn't the thing, it's the soul behind the thing. In robbing me of them you've robbed me of more than them—you've robbed me of all the meaning that lay behind them." He retained just sufficient self-possession to realise this. "I knew you were hostile, how could I fail to know it? but I persuaded myself that you were part of Aphros, part of all my beliefs, even something beyond all my beliefs. I loved you, so you and they had to be reconciled. I reconciled you in secret. I gave up mentioning the Islands to you because it stabbed me to see your indifference. It destroyed the illusion I was cherishing. So I built up fresh, separate illusions about you. I have been living on illusions, now I have nothing left but facts. I owe this to you, to you, to you!"

"You no longer love me," she said again. She could think of nothing else. She had not listened to his bitter and broken phrases. "You no longer love me, Julian."

"I was so determined that I would be deceived by no woman, and like every one else I have fallen into the trap. Because you were you, I ceased to be on my guard. Oh, you never pretended to care for Aphros; I grant you that honesty; but I wanted to delude myself and so I was deluded. I told myself marvellous tales of your rarity; I thought you were above even Aphros. I am punished for my weakness in bringing you here. Why hadn't I the strength to remain solitary? I reproach myself; I had not the right to expose my Islands to such a danger. But how could I have known? how could I have known?"

"Clearly, you no longer love me," she said for the third time.

"Zapantiotis sold his soul for money—was it money you promised him?" he went on. "So easily—just for a little money! His soul, and all of us, for money. Money, father's god; he's a wise man, father, to serve the only remunerative god. Was it money you promised Zapantiotis?" he shouted at her, seizing her by the arm, "or was he, perhaps, like Paul, in love with you? Did you perhaps promise him yourself? How am I to know? There may still be depths in you—you woman—that I know nothing about. Did you give yourself to Zapantiotis? Or is he coming tonight for his reward? Did you mean to ship me off to Athens, you and your accomplices, while you waited here in this room—*our* room—for your lover?"

"Julian!" she cried—he had forced her on to her knees—"you are saying monstrous things."

"You drive me to them," he replied; "when I think that while the troops were landing you lay in my arms, here, knowing all the while that you had betrayed me—I could believe anything of you. Monstrous things! Do you know what monstrous things I am thinking? That you shall not belong to Zapantiotis, but to me. Yes, to me. You destroy love, but desire revives, without love; horrible, but sufficient. That's what I am thinking. I dare say I could kiss you still, and forget. Come!"

He was beside himself.

"Your accusations are so outrageous," she said, half-fainting, "your suggestions are obscene, Julian; I would rather you killed me at once."

"Then answer me about Zapantiotis. How am I to know?" he repeated, already slightly ashamed of his outburst, "I'm readjusting my ideas. Tell me the truth; I scarcely care."

"Believe what you choose," she replied, although he still held her, terrified, on the ground at his feet, "I have more pride than you credit me with—too much to answer you."

"It was money," he said after a pause, releasing her. She stood up; reaction overcame her, and she wept.

"Julian, that you should believe that of me! You cut me to the quick—and I gave myself to you with such pride and gladness," she added almost inaudibly.

"Forgive me; I suppose you, also, have your own moral code; I have specu-
lated sufficiently about it, Heaven knows, but that means very little to me now,"
he said, more quietly, and with even a spark of detached interest and curiosity.
But he did not pursue the subject. "What do you want done with your clothes?
We have wasted quite enough time."

"You want me to come with you?"

"You sound incredulous; why?"

"I know you have ceased to love me. You spoke of marrying me. Your love
must have been a poor flimsy thing, to topple over as it has toppled! Mine is
more tenacious, alas. It would not depend on outside happenings."

"How dare you accuse me?" he said, "You destroy and take from me all that
I care for" ("Yes," she interpolated, as much bitterness in her voice as in his
own—but all the time they were talking against one another—"you cared for
everything but me"), "then you brand my love for you as a poor flimsy thing. If
you have killed it, you have done so by taking away the one thing . . ."

"That you cared for more than for me," she completed.

"With which I would have associated you. You yourself made that association
impossible. You hated the things I loved. Now you've killed those things, and
my love for you with them. You've killed everything I cherished and possessed."

"Dead? Irretrievably?" she whispered.

"Dead."

He saw her widened and swimming eyes and added, too much stunned for
personal malice, yet angry because of the pain he was suffering, "You shall never
be jealous of me again. I think I've loved all women, loved you—gone through
the whole of love, and now washed my hands of it; I've tested and plumbed your
vanity, your hideous egotism"—she was crying like a child, unreservedly, her face
hidden against her arm—"your lack of breadth in everything that was not love."

As he spoke, she raised her face and he saw light breaking on her—although it
was not, and never would be, precisely the light he desired. It was illumination and
horror; agonised honor, incredulous dismay. Her eyes were streaming with tears,
but they searched him imploringly, despairingly, as in a new voice she said—

"I've hurt you, Julian . . . how I've hurt you! Hurt you! I would have died for
you. Can't I put it right? oh, tell me! Will you kill me?" and she put her hand
up to her throat, offering it. "Julian, I've hurt you . . . my own, my Julian. What
have I done? What madness made me do it? Oh, what is there now for me to
do? only tell me; I do beseech you only to tell me. Shall I go—to whom?—to
Malteios? I understand nothing; you must tell me. I wanted you so greedily; you
must believe that. Anything, anything you want me to do. . . . It wasn't sufficient, to love you, to want you; I gave you all I had, but it wasn't sufficient. I
loved you wrongly, I suppose; but I loved you, I loved you!"

He had been angry, but now he was seized with a strange pity; pity of her childish bewilderment: the thing that she had perpetrated was a thing she could not understand. She would never fully understand. . . . He looked at her as she stood crying, and remembered her other aspects, in the flood-time of her joy, careless, radiant, irresponsible; they had shared hours of illimitable happiness.

"Eve! Eve!" he cried, and through the wrenching despair of his cry he heard the funeral note, the tear of cleavage like the downfall of a tree.

He took her in his arms and made her sit upon the bed; she continued to weep, and he sat beside her, stroking her hair. He used terms of endearment towards her, such as he had never used in the whole course of their passionate union, "Eve, my little Eve"; and he kept on repeating, "my little Eve," and pressing her head against his shoulder.

They sat together like two children. Presently she looked up, pushing back her hair with a gesture he knew well.

"We both lose the thing we cared most for upon earth, Julian, you lose the Islands, and I lose you."

She stood up, and gazed out of the window towards Herakleion. She stood there for some time without speaking, and a fatal clearness spread over her mind, leaving her quite strong, quite resolute, and coldly armoured against every shaft of hope.

"You want me to marry you," she said at length.

"You must marry me in Athens tomorrow, if possible, and as soon as we are married we can go to England."

"I utterly refuse," she said, turning round towards him.

He stared at her; she looked frail and tired, and with one small white hand held together the edges of her Spanish shawl. She was no longer crying.

"Do you suppose," she went on, "that not content with having ruined the beginning of your life for you—I realise it now, you see—I shall ruin the rest of it as well? You may believe me or not, I speak the truth like a dying person when I tell you I love you to the point of sin; yes, it's a sin to love as I love you. It's blind, it's criminal. It's my curse, the curse of Eve, to love so well that one loves badly. I didn't see. I wanted you too blindly. Even now I scarcely understand how you can have ceased to love me.—No, don't speak. I do understand it—in a way; and yet I don't understand it. I don't understand that an idea can be dearer to one than the person one loves. . . . I don't understand responsibilities; when you've talked about responsibilities I've sometimes felt that I was made of other elements than you . . . But you're a man and I'm a woman; that's the rift. Perhaps it's a rift that can never be bridged. Never mind that. Julian, you must find some more civilised woman than myself; find a woman who will be a friend, not an enemy. Love makes me into an enemy, you see. Find somebody more tolerant, more unselfish.

More maternal. Yes, that's it," she said, illuminated, "more maternal; I'm only a lover, not a mother. You told me once that I was of the sort that sapped and destroyed. I'll admit that, and let you go. You mustn't waste yourself on me. But, oh, Julian," she said, coming close to him, "if I give you up—because in giving you up I utterly break myself—grant me one justice: never doubt that I loved you. Promise me, Julian. I shan't love again. But don't doubt that I loved you; don't argue to yourself, 'She broke my illusions, therefore she never loved me,' let me make amends for what I did, by sending you away now without me."

"I was angry; I was lying; I wanted to hurt you as you had hurt me," he said desperately. "How can I tell what I have been saying to you? I've been dazed, struck. . . . It's untrue that I no longer love you. I love you, in spite, in spite . . . Love can't die in an hour."

"Bless you," she said, putting her hand for a moment on his head, "but you can't deceive me. Oh," she hurried on, "you might deceive yourself; you might persuade yourself that you still loved me and wanted me to go with you; but I know better. I'm not for you. I'm not for your happiness, or for any man's happiness. You've said it yourself: I am different. I let you go because you are strong and useful—oh, yes, useful! so disinterested and strong, all that I am not—too good for me to spoil. You have nothing in common with me. Who has? I think I haven't any kindred. I love you! I love you better than myself!"

He stood up; he stammered in his terror and earnestness, but she only shook her head.

"No, Julian."

"You're too strong," he cried, "you little weak thing; stronger than I."

She smiled; he was unaware of the very small reserve of her strength.

"Stronger than you," she repeated; "yes."

Again he implored her to go with him; he even threatened her, but she continued to shake her head and to say in a faint and tortured voice, "Go now, Julian; go, my darling; go now, Julian."

"With you, or not at all." He was at last seriously afraid that she meant what she said.

"Without me."

"Eve, we were so happy. Remember! Only come; we shall be as happy again."

"You mustn't tempt me; it's cruel," she said, shivering. "I'm human."

"But I love you!" he said. He seized her hands, and tried to drag her towards the door.

"No," she answered, putting him gently away from her. "Don't tempt me, Julian, don't; let me make amends in my own way."

Her gentleness and dignity were such that he now felt reproved, and, dimly, that the wrong done was by him towards her, not by her towards him.

"You are too strong—magnificent, and heartbreaking," he said in despair.

As strong as a rock," she replied, looking straight at him and thinking that at any moment she must fall. But still she forced her lips to a smile of finality.

"Think better of it," he was beginning, when they heard a stir of commotion in the court below.

"They are coming for you!" she cried out in sudden panic. "Go; I can't face any one just now . . ."

He opened the door on to the landing.

"Kato!" he said, falling back. Eve heard the note of fresh anguish in his voice.

Kato came in; even in that hour of horror they saw that she had merely dragged a quilt round her shoulders, and that her hair was down her back. In this guise her appearance was indescribably grotesque.

"Defeated, defeated," she said in lost tones to Julian. She did not see that they had both involuntarily recoiled before her; she was beyond such considerations.

"Anastasia," he said, taking her by the arm and shaking her slightly to recall her from her bemusement, "here is something more urgent—thank God, you will be my ally—Eve must leave Aphros with me; tell her so, tell her so; she refuses." He shook her more violently with the emphasis of his words.

"If he wants you. . . ." Kato said, looking at Eve, who had retreated into the shadows and stood there, half fainting, supporting herself against the back of a chair. "If he wants you. . . ." she repeated, in a stupid voice, but her mind was far away.

"You don't understand, Anastasia," Eve answered; "it was I that betrayed him." Again she thought she must fall.

"She is lying!" cried Julian.

"No," said Eve. She and Kato stared at one another, so preposterously different, yet with currents of truth rushing between them.

"You!" Kato said at last, awaking.

"I am sending him away," said Eve, speaking as before to the other woman.

"You!" said Kato again. She turned wildly to Julian. "Why didn't you trust yourself to me, Julian, my beloved?" she cried; "I wouldn't have treated you so, Julian; why didn't you trust yourself to me?" She pointed at Eve, silent and brilliant in her coloured shawl; then, her glance falling upon her own person, so sordid, so unkempt, she gave a dreadful cry and looked around as though seeking for escape. The other two both turned their heads away; to look at Kato in that moment was more than they could bear.

Presently they heard her speaking again; her self-abandonment had been brief; she had mastered herself, and was making it a point of honour to speak with calmness.

"Julian, the officers have orders that you must leave the island before dawn; if you do not go to them, they will fetch you here. They are waiting below in the courtyard now. Eve"—her face altered—"Eve is right: if she has indeed done as she says, she cannot go with you. She is right; she is more right, probably, than she has ever been in her life before or ever will be again. Come, now; I will go with you."

"Stay with Eve, if I go," he said.

"Impossible!" replied Kato, instantly hardening, and casting upon Eve a look of hatred and scorn.

"How cruel you are, Anastasia!" said Julian, making a movement of pity towards Eve.

"Take him away, Anastasia," Eve murmured, shrinking from him.

"See, she understands me better than you do, and understands herself better too," said Kato, in a tone of cruel triumph; "if you do not come, Julian, I shall send up the officers." As she spoke she went out of the room, her quilt trailing, and her heel-less slippers clacking on the boards.

"Eve, for the last time . . ."

A cry was wrenched from her, "Go! if you pity me!"

"I shall come back."

"Oh, no, no!" she replied, "you'll never come back. One doesn't live through such things twice." She shook her head like a tortured animal that seeks to escape from pain. He gave an exclamation of despair, and, after one wild gesture towards her, which she weakly repudiated, he followed Kato. Eve heard their steps upon the stairs, then crossing the courtyard, and the tramp of soldiers; the house-door crashed massively. She stooped very slowly and mechanically, and began to pick up the gay and fragile tissue of her clothes.

Seven

She laid them all in orderly fashion across the bed, smoothing out the folds with a care that was strongly opposed to her usual impatience. Then she stood for some time drawing the thin silk of the sari through her fingers and listening for sounds in the house; there were none. The silence impressed her with the fact that she was alone.

"Gone!" she thought, but she made no movement.

Her eyes narrowed and her mouth became contracted with pain.

"Julian," she murmured, and, finding some slippers, she thrust her bare feet into them with sudden haste and threw the corner of her shawl over her shoulder.

She moved now with feverish speed; any one seeing her face would have exclaimed that she was not in conscious possession of her will, but would have shrunk before the force of her determination. She opened the door upon the dark staircase and went rapidly down; the courtyard was lit by a torch the soldiers had left stuck and flaring in a bracket. She had some trouble with the door, tearing her hands and breaking her nails upon the great latch, but she felt nothing, dragged it open, and found herself in the street. At the end of the street she could see the glare from the burning buildings of the market-place, and could hear the shout of military orders.

She knew she must take the opposite road; Malteios had told her that. "Go by the mule-path over the hill; it will lead you straight to the creek where the boat will be waiting, he had said. "The boat for Julian and me," she kept muttering to herself as she speeded up the path stumbling over the shallow steps and bruising her feet upon the cobbles. It was very dark. Once or twice as she put out her hand to save herself from falling she encountered only a prickly bush of aloe or gorse, and the pain stung her, causing a momentary relief.

"I mustn't hurry too much," she said to herself, "I mustn't arrive at the creek before they have pushed off the boat. I mustn't call out . . ."

She tried to compare her pace with that of Julian, Kato, and the officers, and ended by sitting down for a few minutes at the highest point of the path, where it had climbed over the shoulder of the island, and was about to curve down upon the other side. From this small height, under the magnificent vault studded with stars, she could hear the sigh of the sea and feel the slight breeze ruffling her hair. "Without Julian, without Julian—no, never," she said to herself, and that one thought revolved in her brain. "I'm alone," she thought, "I've always been alone. . . . I'm an outcast, I don't belong here. . . ." She did not really know what she meant by this, but she repeated it with a blind conviction, and a terrible loneliness overcame her. "Oh, stars!' she said aloud, putting up her hands to them, and again she did not know what she meant, either by the words or the gesture. Then she realised that it was dark, and standing up she thought, "I'm frightened," but there was no reply to the appeal for Julian that followed immediately upon the thought. She clasped her shawl round her, and tried to stare through the night; then she thought "People on the edge of death have no need to be frightened," but for all that she continued to look fearfully about her, to listen for sounds, and to wish that Julian would come to take care of her.

She went down the opposite side of the hill less rapidly than she had come up. She knew she must not overtake Julian and his escort. She did not really know why she had chosen to follow them, when any other part of the coast would have been equally suitable for what she had determined to do. But she kept thinking, as though it brought some consolation, "He passed along this path five-ten-minutes ago; he is there somewhere, not far in front of me." And she remembered how he had begged her to go with him. " . . . But I couldn't have gone!" she cried, half in apology to the dazzling happiness she had renounced, "I was a curse to him—to everything I touch. I could never have controlled my jealousy, my exorbitance. . . . He asked me to go, to be with him always," she thought, sobbing and hurrying on; and she sobbed his name, like a child, "Julian! Julian! Julian!"

Presently the path ceased to lead downhill and became flat, running along the top of the rocky cliff about twenty feet above the sea. She moved more cautiously, knowing that it would bring her to the little creek where the boat was to be waiting; as she moved she blundered constantly against boulders, for the path was winding and in the starlight very difficult to follow. She was still fighting with herself, "No, I could not go with him; I am not fit. . . . I don't belong here . . ." that reiterated cry. "But without him—no, no, no! This is quite simple. Will he think me bad? I hope not; I shall have done what I could . . . Her complexity had entirely deserted her, and she thought in broad, childish lines. "Poor Eve," she thought suddenly, viewing herself as a separate person, "she was very young" (in her eyes youth amounted to a moral virtue), "Julian, Julian, be a little sorry for her—I was cursed, I was surely cursed," she added, and at that moment she found herself just above the creek.

The path descended to it in rough steps, and with a beating heart she crept down, helping herself by her hands, until she stood upon the sand, hidden in the shadow of a boulder. The shadows were very black and hunched, like the shadows of great beasts. She listened, the softness of her limbs pressed against the harshness of the rocks. She heard faint voices, and, creeping forward, still keeping in the shadows, she made out the shape of a rowing-boat filled with men about twenty yards from the shore.

"Kato has gone with him" was her first idea, and at that all her jealousy flamed again—the jealousy that, at the bottom of her heart, she knew was groundless, but could not keep in check. Anger revived her—"Am I to waste myself on him?" she thought, but immediately she remembered the blank that that one word "Never!" could conjure up, and her purpose became fixed again. "Not life without him," she thought firmly and unchangeably, and moved forward until her feet were covered by the thin waves lapping the sandy edge of the creek. She had thrown off her shoes, standing barefoot on the soft wet sand.

Here she paused to allow the boat to draw farther away. She knew that she would cry out, however strong her will, and she must guard against all chance of rescue. She waited at the edge of the creek, shivering and drawing her silk garments about her, and forcing herself to endure the cold horror of the water washing round her ankles. How immense was the night, how immense the sea!—The oars in the boat dipped regularly; by now it was almost undistinguishable in the darkness.

"What must I do?" she thought wildly, knowing the moment had come. "I must run out as far as I can. . . . She sent an unuttered cry of "Julian!" after the

278 / VITA SACKVILLE-WEST

boat, and plunged forward; the coldness of the water stopped her as it reached her waist, and the long silk folds became entangled around her limbs, but she recovered herself and fought her way forward. Instinctively she kept her hands pressed against her mouth and nostrils, and her staring eyes tried to fathom this cruelly deliberate death. Then the shelving coast failed her beneath her feet; she had lost the shallows and was taken by the swell and rhythm of the deep. A thought flashed through her brain, "This is where the water ceases to be green and becomes blue"; then in her terror she lost all self-control and tried to scream; it was incredible that Julian, who was so near at hand, should not hear and come to save her; she felt herself tiny and helpless in that great surge of water; even as she tried to scream she was carried forward and under, in spite of her wild terrified battle against the sea, beneath the profound serenity of the night that witnessed and received her expiation.

SEDUCERS IN ECUADOR (1924)

Included complete in this volume is the brief and brilliant Seducers in Ecuador. *Among all Vita Sackville-West's writings, this very short novel, or novella, stands out as the most complex and the most highly stylized, the most interesting and the most modernist of Vita Sackville-West's works. Unsurprisingly, it is also the one of Vita's productions that most appealed to Virginia Woolf, to whom it is dedicated. "I wish I had written it," said she. With its plot dependent upon the varying colors of spectacles chosen by the hero, each of which determines a way of not just seeing but acting upon what he sees, it exudes an air of high modernist experiment. The shifting perspective calls forth the very "curious world so recently his own."*

Blue glasses were all the rage at the time that this work was written. Duncan Grant had seen a listing of Cézanne's painting of six apples, simply called "Pommes," at the Degas sale, and suggested to John Maynard Keynes that to acquire this painting would be a good way to repay some of Britain's debt to France. With Sir Charles Holmes, Director of the National Gallery, they set off for Paris. Sir Charles—eager to acquire the painting anonymously—wore blue glasses throughout the sale, and Keynes acquired the painting. But when he arrived at Charleston, in the evening of March 28, 1918, he had too much baggage and so left the painting in the hedge just outside.[1] A few days later, at Gordon Square, Vanessa Bell brought out the painting for Virginia Woolf, Keynes, classical scholar J. T. Sheppard, and Roger Fry. What she brought was, as Virginia Woolf writes:

. . . a small parcel about the size of a large slab of chocolate. On one side are painted 6 apples by Cézanne. Roger very nearly lost his senses. I've never seen such a sight of intoxication. He was like a bee on a sunflower. Imagine snow falling outside, a wind like there is in the Tube, an atmosphere of yellow grains of dust, and us all gloating upon these apples.[2]

The color of glasses, of course, determines the twists, turns, and changeability in Seducers in Ecuador, and in this way, the novella is quite unlike the straightforward and successful views promoted in the Edwardians *and* All Passion Spent, *the best known of Vita's works. For present-day readers, more given to the brief and the complex, it has a completely different appeal. Vita was clearly fascinated by this kind of alteration of perspective. One of her gardening pieces included here, "Full-bosomed trollop of a rose," begins with a gentleman "wearing amber-colored spectacles." He urges the narrator to try on his glasses: "look at your roses; look also at your brown-tiled roofs; look at the clouds in the sky." Everything is intensified, deepened, and made far more interesting.*

"Look, he said. . . ." This could well be Vita's message to the reader.

SEDUCERS IN ECUADOR

It was in Egypt that Arthur Lomax contracted the habit which, after a pleasantly varied career, brought him finally to the scaffold.

In Egypt most tourists wear blue spectacles. Arthur Lomax followed this prudent if unbecoming fashion. In the company of three people he scarcely knew, but into whose intimacy he had been forced by the exigencies of yachting, straddling his long legs across a donkey, attired in a suit of white ducks, a solar topee on his head, his blue spectacles on his nose, he contemplated the Sphinx. But Lomax was less interested in the Sphinx than in the phenomenon produced by the wearing of those coloured glasses. In fact, he had already dismissed the Sphinx as a most overrated object, which, deprived of the snobbishness of legend to help it out, would have little chance of luring the traveller over fifteen hundred miles of land and sea to Egypt. But, as so often happens, although disappointed in one quarter he had been richly and unexpectedly rewarded in another. The world was changed for him, and, had he but known it, the whole of his future altered, by those two circles of blue glass. Unfortunately one does not recognise the turning-point of one's future until one's future has become one's past.

Whether he pushed the glasses up on to his forehead, and looked out from underneath them, or slid them down to the tip of his nose, and looked out above them, he confronted unaided the too realistic glare of the Egyptian sun. When, however, he readjusted them to the place where they were intended to be worn, he immediately re-entered the curious world so recently become his own.

It was more than curious; it was magical. A thick green light shrouded every-thing, the sort of light that might be the forerunner of some undreamed-of storm, or hang between a dying sun and a dead world. He wondered at the poverty of the common imagination, which degraded blue glasses into a prosaic, even a comic, thing. He resolved, however, not to initiate a soul into his dis-covery. To those blessed with perception, let perception remain sacred, but let the obtuse dwell for ever in their darkness.

But for Bellamy, Lomax would not have been in Egypt at all. Bellamy owned the yacht. A tall, cadaverous man, with a dark skin, white hair, and pale blue eyes, he belonged to Lomax's club. They had never taken any notice of one an-other beyond a nod. Then one evening Bellamy, sitting next to Lomax at din-ner, mentioned that he was sailing next day for Egypt. He was greatly put out because his third guest, a man, had failed him. "Family ties," he grumbled; and then, to Lomax, "somehow you don't look as though you had any." "I haven't," said Lomax. "Lucky man," grumbled Bellamy. "No," said Lomax, "not so much lucky as wise. A man isn't born with wife and children, and if he acquires them he has only himself to blame." This appeared to amuse Bellamy, especially com-ing from Lomax, who was habitually taciturn, and he said, "That being so, you'd better come along to Egypt tomorrow." "Thanks," said Lomax, "I will."

This trip would serve to pass the time. A yachting trip was a pleasant, civilised thing to undertake, and Lomax appreciated pleasant, civilised things. He had very little use for the conspicuous or the arresting. Such inclinations as he had towards the finer gestures—and it is not to be denied that such inclinations were latent in him—had been judiciously repressed, until Lomax could congratulate himself on having achieved the comfortable ideal of all true Englishmen. From this trip, then, he anticipated nothing but six or seven agreeable weeks of sight-seeing in company as civilised as his own. It is, however, the purpose of this story to demonstrate the danger of becoming involved in the lives of others without having previously tested the harmlessness of those others, and the danger above all of contracting in middle-age a new habit liable to release those lions of folly which prowl about our depths, and which it is the duty of every citizen to keep securely caged.

Of course one cannot blame Lomax. He knew nothing of Bellamy, and for Miss Whitaker his original feeling was one of purely chivalrous compassion. Be-sides, it must be remembered that under the new influence of his spectacles he was living in a condition of ecstasy—a breathless condition, in which he was hurried along by his instincts, and precipitated into compromising himself be-fore he had had time to remove his spectacles and consult his reason. Indeed, with a rapidity that he was never well able to understand, he found himself in such a position that he no longer dared to remove his spectacles at all; he could not face a return to the daylight mood; realism was no longer for him. And the spectacles, having once made him their slave, served him well. They altered the world in the most extraordinary way. The general light was green instead of yellow, the sky and the desert both turned green, reds became purple, greens were almost black. It produced an effect of stillness, everything seemed muffled. The noises of the world lost their significance. Everything became at once intensified and remote. Lomax found it decidedly more interesting than the sights of Egypt. The sights of Egypt were a fact, having a material reality, but here was a phenomenon that presented life under a new aspect. Lomax knew well enough that to present life under a new aspect is the beginning and probably also the end of genius; it is therefore no wonder that his discovery produced in him so profound and sensational an excitement. His companions thought him silent; they thought him even a little dull. But they were by that time accustomed to his silence; they no longer regarded him as a possible stimulant; they regarded him merely as a fixture—uncommunicative, but emanating an agreeable if undefined sense of security. Although they could not expect to be amused by him, in each one of them dwelt an unphrased conviction that Lomax was a man to be depended upon in the event of trouble. The extent to which he could be depended upon they had yet to learn.

It is now time to be a little more explicit on the question of the companions of Lomax.

Perhaps Miss Whitaker deserves precedence, since it was she, after all, who married Lomax.

And perhaps Bellamy should come next, since it was he, after all, for whose murder Lomax was hanged.

And perhaps Artivale should come third, since it was to him, after all, that Lomax bequeathed his, that is to say Bellamy's, fortune.

The practised reader will have observed by now that the element of surprise is not to be looked for in this story.

"Lord Carnarvon would be alive today if he had not interfered with the Tomb," said Miss Whitaker to Lomax.

Lomax, lying in a deck-chair in the verandah of their hotel, expressed dissent.

"I *know* it," said Miss Whitaker with extreme simplicity.

"Now how do you know it?" said Lomax, bored.

But Miss Whitaker never condescended to the direct explanation. She preferred to suggest reserves of information too recondite to be imparted. She had, too, that peculiarly irritating habit of a constant and oblique reference to absent friends, which makes present company feel excluded, insignificant, unadventurous and contemptible. *"You and I* would never agree on those questions," she replied on this occasion.

Lomax asked her once where she lived in London. She looked at him mistrustfully, like a little brown animal that fears to be enticed into a trap, and replied that she was to be found at a variety of addresses. "Not that *you'd* find me there," she added, with a laugh. Lomax knew that she did not mean to be rude, but only interesting. He was not interested; not interested enough even to ask Bellamy. Bellamy, now, interested him a great deal, though he would always have waited for Bellamy to take the first step towards a closer intimacy. Bellamy, however, showed no disposition to take it. He was civil and hospitable to his guests, but as aloof as a peak. Lomax knew him to be very rich and very delicate, and that was about the sum of his knowledge. Bellamy's reticence made his confidences, when they did finally come, all the more surprising.

Artivale, the fourth member of the party, was on the contrary as expansive as he well could be. He was a dark, slim, poor, untidy young scientist, consumed by a burning zest for life and his profession. His youth, his zeal, and his ability were his outstanding characteristics. Bellamy in his discreet way would smile at his exuberance, but everybody liked Artivale except Miss Whitaker, who said he was a bounder. Miss Whitaker admired only one type of man, and dismissed as perverts or bounders all those who did not belong to it; which was unfortunate for Lomax, Bellamy, and Artivale, none of whom conformed. Her friends, she let it be understood, were men of a very different stamp. Artivale did not appear to suffer under her disapprobation, and his manner towards her remained as candid and as engaging as towards everybody else, no less sure of his welcome than a puppy or a child. With him alone Lomax might have shared the delight of the coloured spectacles, had he felt any desire so to share. Artivale had skirted the subject; he had settled his spectacles, peered about him, and laughed. "By Jove, what a queer world! Every value altered." He dashed off to other trains of thought—he couldn't stay long poised on any one thing—giving Lomax just a second in which to appreciate the exactness of his observation.

Artivale was like that—swift and exact; and always uninsistent.

Lomax went to the chemist in Cairo, and bought all the coloured spectacles he could find. He had already his blue pair, bought in London; in Cairo he bought an amber pair, and a green, and a black. He amused himself by wearing them turn and turn about; but soon it ceased to be an amusement and became an obsession—a vice. Bellamy with his reserve, and Heaven knows what tragedy at the back of it; a finished life, Bellamy's, one felt, without knowing why. Miss Whitaker with her elaborate mystery; an empty life, one felt, at the back of it; empty as a sail inflated by wind—and how the sails bellied white, across the blue Mediterranean! Artivale with his energy; a bursting life, one felt, thank God, beside the other two. Lomax with his spectacles. All self-sufficient, and thereby severed from one another. Lomax thought himself the least apart, because, through his glasses, he surveyed.

He was wearing the black ones when he came on Miss Whitaker, sobbing in the verandah.

Miss Whitaker had not taken much notice of him on the journey. She had not, in fact, taken much notice of anybody, but had spent her time writing letters, which were afterwards left about in subtle places, addressed to Ecuador. Arrived in Egypt, she had emerged from her epistolary seclusion. Perhaps it had not aroused the comment she hoped for. She had then taken up Lomax, and dealt out to him the fragments of her soul. She would not give him her address in London, but she would give him snippets of her spiritual experience. Allusive they were, rather than explicit; chucked at him, with a sort of contempt, as though he were not worthy to receive them, but as though an inner pressure compelled their expectoration. Lomax, drunk behind his wall of coloured glass, played up to the impression he was expected to glean. He knew already—and his glasses deepened the knowledge—that life was a business that had to be got through; nor did he see any reason, in his disheartened way, why Bellamy's queer yachting party shouldn't enrich his ennui as far as possible.

He was, then, wearing his black spectacles when he came on Miss Whitaker sobbing in the verandah.

The black ones were, at the moment, his favourites. You know the lull that comes over the world at the hour of solar eclipse? How the birds themselves cease to sing, and go to roost? How the very leaves on the trees become still and metallic? How the heaven turns to copper? How the stars come out, terrible in the daytime, with the clock at midday instead of at midnight? How all is hushed before the superstition of impending disaster? So, at will, was it with Lomax. But Miss Whitaker, for once, was a natural woman.

"Oh," she said, looking up at last, "do for goodness' sake take off those horrid spectacles."

Lomax realised then the gulf between himself, dwelling in his strange world, and the rest of mankind in a wholesome day. But he knew that if he took them off, Miss Whitaker would immediately become intolerable.

"The glare hurts my eyes," he said. So do we lie. Miss Whitaker little knew what she gained. Looking at Lomax, she saw a man made absurd. Looking at Miss Whitaker, Lomax saw a woman in distress. All womanhood in distress; all womanhood pressed by catastrophe. His common sense was divinely in abeyance; and he kept it there. What else, indeed, was worth while?

To Miss Whitaker, too, was communicated a certain imminence. Her own stories were marvellously coming true. Indeed, to her, they were always true; what else was worth while? But that the truth of fact should corroborate the truth of imagination! Her heart beat. She kept her eyes averted from Lomax; it was her only chance. He kept his eyes bent upon her; it was his. At all costs she must not see the glasses, and at all costs he must see through them, and through them alone. He gazed. The chair she sat in was a smoky cloud; her fragility was duskily tinged. Her tears were Ethiopian jewels; black pearls; grief in mourning. Yet Lomax had been, once, an ordinary man, getting through life; not more cynical than most. An ordinary man, with nothing in the world to keep him busy. Perhaps that had been his trouble. Anyway, that was, now extravagantly remedied.

It took a long time to get a confession out of Miss Whitaker. She could write Ecuador on an envelope, and without comment allow it to be observed, but she could not bring herself to utter so precise a geographical statement. There were moments when it seemed to Lomax, even behind the black glasses, perfectly ridiculous that he should suggest marriage to Miss Whitaker. He did not even know her; but then, certainly, the idea of marriage with a woman one did not know had always appeared to him a degree less grotesque than the reverse. The only woman in his life being inaccessible, one reason for marriage with anybody else was as good as another. And what better reason than that one had found a lonely woman in tears, and had looked on her through coloured glasses?

Miss Whitaker knew only that she must keep her head. She had not thought that the loose strands cast by her about Lomax could have hardened so suddenly into a knot. She had never known them so harden before. But what an extraordinary man! Having spent her life in the hopes of coming across somebody who would play up, she was astonished now that she had found him. He was too good to be believed in. Very rapidly—for he was pressing her—she must make up her mind. The situation could not be allowed to fritter out into the commonplace. It did not occur to her that the truth was as likely to increase his attention as any fiction. She was not alone in this; for who stands back to perceive the pattern made by their own lives? They plaster on every sort of colour, which in due time flakes off and discovers the design beneath. Miss Whitaker only plastered her colour a little thicker than most. She was finding, however, that Lomax had got hold of her paint-brush and was putting in every kind of chiaroscuro while she, helplessly, looked on. Now it was the grey of disillusion, now the high light of faith. The picture shaped itself under her eyes. She tried to direct him, but he had bolted with her. "Ten days ago," she tried to say, "you didn't know me." And, to make matters more disconcerting, Lomax himself was evidently in some great distress. He seemed to be impelled by some inner fire to pronounce the words he was pronouncing; to be abandoning all egoism under the exaltation of self-sacrifice. The absurd creature believed in his mission. And Miss Whitaker was not slow to kindle at his flame. They were both caught up, now, in their own drama. Intent, he urged details from her, and with now a sigh escaping her, and now a little flare of pride, she hinted confirmation. It was really admirable, the background which between them they contrived to build up;

personalities emerged, three-dimensional; Ecuador fell into its place with a click. Even the expedition to Egypt fitted in—Miss Whitaker had accepted Bellamy's invitation in order to escape the vigilance of a brother. He had a hot temper, this brother—Robert; any affront to his sister, and he would be flying off to Ecuador. Robert was immensely wealthy; he owned an oil-field in Persia; he would spare no expense in searching Ecuador from end to end. He had already been known to scour Russia to avenge a woman. By this time Lomax was himself ready to scour Ecuador. Miss Whitaker wavered; she relished the idea of a Lomax with smoking nostrils ransacking Central America, but on second thoughts she dissuaded him; she didn't want, she said, to send him to his death. Lomax had an idea that the man—still anonymous—would not prove so formidable. Miss Whitaker constructed him as very formidable indeed; one of the world's bad lots, but in every sense of the word irresistible. Lomax scorned the adjective; he had no use, he said, for bad lots so callous as to lay the sole burden of consequences upon the woman. He used a strong word. Miss Whitaker blinked. The men she admired did not use such words in the presence of women. Still, under the circumstances, she made no comment; she overlooked the irregularity. She merely put up a chiding finger, not a word of blame was to be uttered in her hearing.

"By the way," said Lomax, as they finally parted to dress for dinner, "perhaps you wouldn't mind telling me your Christian name?"

The hotel facade was a concrete wall pierced with windows; the rooms were square compartments enclosing single individuals. Sometimes they enclosed couples, linked together by convention or by lust. In either case the persons concerned were really quite separate, whether they wanted to be or whether they didn't. They had no choice in the matter. Boots and shoes stood outside the doors, in a row down the passage. The riding-boots of soldiers, tanned and spurred. High-heeled, strapped shoes of women. Sometimes two pairs stood side by side, right and proper, masculine and feminine; and this made the single pairs look forlorn. Surely, if they could have walked without feet in them, they would have edged together? The little Anglo-Egyptian wife of the colonel, carefully creaming her nose before powdering it, wished that that Mr. Bellamy, who looked so distinguished, would ask them down to his yacht at Alexandria.

The colonel, in his shirt sleeves, wished only that his stud would go into his collar. Artivale, bending over a dead chameleon, slit up its belly neatly with his nail scissors. The little Swiss waiter in his cupboard of a bedroom saw the sweat from his forehead drip upon the floor as he pared away the corn upon his toe. He sat, unconsciously, in the attitude of the Tireur d'Epines. But Lomax and Miss Whitaker, on reaching their bedrooms, paused appalled at their own madness as the blessing of solitude enclosed them with the shutting of the door.

It is not really difficult to get a marriage licence. Besides, once one has committed oneself to a thing, pride forbids that one should draw back. Nevertheless, Lomax was married in his spectacles—the blue ones. Without them, he could not have gone through the ceremony. They walked home, when it was over, via the bazaars. They had to flatten themselves against the wall to let a string of camels go by. The din and shouting of the bazaar rose round them; Achmed Ali, with cheap carpets over his arm, displayed to Miss Whitaker his excellent teeth and his bad Assiout shawls; some one smashed a bottle of scent and its perfume rose up under their feet, like incense before a sacrifice. Still they made no reference to what had just taken place. It was in their covenant that no reference should be made, neither between one another, nor to any one else. Time enough for that, thought Lomax, an indeterminate number of months hence. That was Miss Whitaker's business. When she needed him, she had only to send him a message. In the meantime, Bellamy met them on the steps of the hotel, more genial than usual, for he had been talking to the colonel's wife and she had amused him—a transient amusement, but better than nothing to that sad man.

"Been sight-seeing?" he inquired; and then, as Miss Whitaker passed into the hotel, "It's really noble of you, my dear Lomax," he said, "to have taken Miss Whitaker off like that for a whole morning."

Marion Vane's husband died that afternoon. She had sat by his bedside trying loyally not to think that now she would be free to marry Lomax. She did not know where Lomax was, for they had long since settled that it was better for them not to communicate. He would see the death in the papers, of course, and perhaps he would write her a formal letter of condolence, but she knew she could trust him not to come near her until she sent for him. This was April; in October she would send. Then she was startled by a faint throaty sound, and saw that the fingers which had been picking the blankets were once convulsed, and then lay still.

The *Nereid* set sail from Alexandria two days later. Bellamy did not seem able to make up his mind where he wanted to go. Sicily was talked of, the Dalmatian coast, the Piraeus, and Constantinople. The others were quite passive under his vacillations. Now they were afloat, and had re-entered that self-contained little world which is in every ship at sea; temporary, but with so convincing an illusion of permanence; a world weighing so many tons, confined within a measure of so many paces, limited to a population of so many souls, a world at the same time restricted and limitless, here closely bound by the tiny compass of the ship, and there subject to no frontiers but those of the watery globe itself. In a ship at sea our land life slips away, and our existence fills with the new conditions. Moreover in a sailing ship the governing laws are few and simple; a mere question of elements. Bellamy was sailor enough—eccentric enough, said some—to despise auxiliary steam. Appreciative of caprice, in the wind he found a spirit capricious enough to satisfy his taste. In a calm he was patient, and in a storm amused, and for the rest he comported himself in this matter, as in all others (according to his set and general principle), as though he had the whole leisure of life before him.

No shore was visible, for Bellamy liked to keep the shore out of sight. It increased, he explained, not only the sense of space but also the sense of time. So they lounged along, having the coasts of Barbary somewhere over the horizon, and being pleasantly independent of century; indeed, the hours of their meals were of greater import to them than the interval elapsed since the birth of Christ. This, Bellamy said, was the wholesome attitude. Bellamy, in his courteous, sophisticated, and ironical way, was ever so slightly a tyrant. He did not dictate to them, but he suggested, not only where they should go, but also what they should think. It was very subtly done. There was not enough, not nearly enough, for them to resent; there was only enough to make them, sometimes, for a skimming moment, uneasy. What if Bellamy, when they wanted to go home, wouldn't go home? What if, from being a host, he should slide into being a jailer?

But in the meantime it was pleasant enough to cruise in the *Nereid*, lying in deck-chairs, while Bellamy, with his hand on the helm and the great blade of the mainsail above him, watched from under the peak of his cap, not them, but the sea.

Very blue it was too, and the *Nereid*, when she was not running before a fair wind on an even keel, lay over to the water, so low that now and then she shipped a gobbet of sea, only a thin little runnel that escaped at once through the open scuppers of the lee runner, in a hurry to get back to its element. Bellamy was bored by a fair wind; he hated the monotony of a day with the sheet out and the beautiful scooped shape of the spinnaker, and the crew asleep for'ard, since there was no handling of gear to keep them on the run. What he liked was a day with plenty of tacking, and then he would turn the mate or the captain off and take the wheel himself, and cry "Lee-o!" to the crew. And what pleased him even better was to catch the eye of the mate and give the order with only a nod of the head, so that his unwarned guests slithered across the deck as the ship went about, when he would laugh and apologise with perfect urbanity; but they noticed that next time he had the chance he did precisely the same thing again. "Bellamy likes teasing us," said Lomax, with a good deal of meaning in his tone. Bellamy did, even by so slight an irritation. And once he brought off a Dutchman's gybe, which nearly shot Lomax, who was lying asleep under the mizzen-boom, into the sea.

One sleeps a great part of the time on a yacht. Artivale fished, and dissected the fish he caught, so that a section of the deck was strewn with little ribs and spines. Lomax surveyed these through his spectacles. Artivale had long slim fingers, and he took up and set down the little bones, fitting them together, with the dexterity of a lace-maker among her bobbins. Tailor-wise he sat, his hair lifted by the wind, and sometimes he looked up with a full smile into the disapproving face of Miss Whitaker. "Play spillikins, Miss Whitaker?" he asked, jumbling his fish bones all together into a heap.

Very blue and white it all was. Soft, immense white clouds floated, and the sails were white, and Artivale's tiny graveyard, but the scrubbed deck, which in Southampton Water had looked white, here appeared pale yellow by contrast. The sails threw blue shadows. The crew ran noiselessly on bare feet. "When shall we get there?" Lomax wondered, but since he did not know where "there" was, and since all the blueness and whiteness were to him overlaid as with the angry cloud of an impending storm, he was content to hammock himself passively in the amplitude of enveloping time, He was, indeed, in no hurry, for his land-life, now withdrawn, had been merely a thing to be got through; he had an idle curiosity to see what was going to happen in these changed aeons that stretched before him; nor did he know that Marion Vane's husband was dead. So he lay in his deck-chair, speculating about Bellamy, watching Artivale, aware of the parallel proximity of Miss Whitaker—who was his wife—in her deck-chair, and occasionally, by way of refreshment, turning his eyes behind their owlish spectacles over the expanse of his lurid sea and sky.

What of it, anyway? There were quite a number of other communities in the world beside this little community, microscopic on the Mediterranean. Lomax saw the blue as it was not, the others saw or thought they saw the blue as it was, but unless and until our means of communication become more subtle than they at present are, we cannot even be sure that our eyes see colours alike. How, then, should we know one another? Lomax lived alone with his secret, Bellamy with his; and as for Miss Whitaker, if Truth be indeed accustomed to dwell at the bottom of a well, at the bottom of Miss Whitaker's heart she must surely have found a dwelling suited to her taste. Artivale, being a scientist intent upon a clue, probably knew more of the secrets of life than the seamen who begot their offspring in the rude old fashion, but it is to be doubted whether even Artivale knew much that was worth knowing. He claimed to have produced a tadpole by ectogenetic birth, but, having produced it, he was quite unable to tell that tadpole whither it was going when it inconsiderately died, and, moreover, as he himself observed, there were tadpoles enough in the world already.

Volcanic islands began, pitting the sea; white towns and golden temples clung to a violet coast. Bellamy suggested to them that they did not want to land, a suggestion in which they acquiesced. They shared a strange disinclination to cross Bellamy. They were sailing now within a stone's throw of a wild, precipitous coast, their nights and their days boundaried by magnificent sunsets and splendid dawns. But for those, time did not exist. Geography did not exist either; Bellamy referred to Illyria, and they were content to leave it at that. It fitted in with the unreality of their voyage. There are paintings of ships setting sail into a haze of sunlight, ships full-rigged, broad-beamed, with tracery of rope, pushing off for the unknown, voyages to Cythera, misty and romantic; Lomax wore the amber spectacles, and saw a golden ship evanescent in golden air. Morning and evening flamed upon the sea; each day was a lagoon of blue. Islets and rocks stained the shield of water; mountains swept down and trod the sea; cities of Illyria rose upon the breast of the coastline; rose; drew near; and faded past. Venice and Byzantium in spire and cupola clashed the arms of peace for ever on the scene of their exploits. But towns were rare; they passed not more than one in every four-and-twenty hours. For the rest, they were alone with that piratical seaboard descending barbarously to the sea; never a hut, never a road, never a goat to hint at life, but caves and creeks running between the headlands, and sullen mountains like a barrier between the water and the inland tracts. The little ship sailed lonely beneath the peaks. Day after day she sailed, idly coasting Illyria, and Bellamy waited for the storm. "Treacherous waters," he had observed on entering them. Indeed it seemed incongruous that the sea should be so calm and the shore so wild. Day after day unbroken, with that angry coast always on their right hand and the placid sea on their left; day after day of leisure, with a wall of disaster banking higher and higher against them.

Those paintings of ships show the ship setting sail in fair weather; they never follow her into the turbulence of her adventure. Friends speed her with waving handkerchiefs, and turn away, and know nothing of her till a letter comes saying that she has arrived at her place of port. And, for the matter of that, the lives of friends touch here and there in the same fashion, and the gap over the interval is never bridged, knowledge being but a splintered mirror which shall never gather to a smooth and even surface.

The *Nereid* then, with her living freight, saw the serenity of Illyria broken up into a night of anger, but the wives of the crew, lighting their lamps in brick cottages at Brightlingsea, knew nothing of it, and the wife of the captain writing to her aunt said, "Joe has a nice job with a gentleman name of Bellamy on a yorl in the Mediterranean," and Marion Vane with an edging of white lawn to her mourning at neck and cuffs was vague to her trustee at dinner regarding the disposal of her country house, for she believed that this time next year she would be married to Lomax. The *Nereid* was not broad-beamed; she was slim as a hound, and it was not with a plebeian solidity but with an aristocratic mettle that she took the storm. Her canvas rapidly furled, she rode with bare masts crazily sawing the sky. Black ragged night enveloped her; the coast, although invisible, contributed to the tempest, throwing its boulders against the waves as the waves hurled themselves against its boulders. The little boat, a thing of naught, was battered at that meeting-place of enemies. Rain and spray drove together across the deck, as momently the storm increased and the wind tore howling through the naked spars. The men were black figures clinging to stays for support, going down with the ship when she swooped from the crest down into the trough, rising again with her, thankful to find the deck still there beneath their feet, lashed by the rain, blinded by the darkness, unable to see, able only to feel, whether with their hands that, wet and frozen, clung to rail and stanchion, or with their bodies that sank and rose, enduring the tremendous buffeting of the tossing ship, and the shock of water that, as it broke over the deck, knocked the breath from their lungs and all but swept them from their refuge into the hopeless broiling of the sea.

Lomax was in the deck-house. There, he was dry, and could prop himself to resist the rearing and plunging; and could almost enjoy, moreover, the drench of water flung against the little hutch, invisible, but mighty and audible, streaming away after sweeping the ship from end to end. A funny lot they would be to drown, he reflected; and he remembered their departure from Southampton, all a little shy and constrained, with Miss Whitaker sprightly but on the defensive. How long ago that was, he failed to calculate. They had drifted down to Calshot, anchoring there on a washed April evening, between a liquid sky and oily lagoon-like reaches, gulls and sea-planes skimming sea and heaven, in the immense primrose peace of sunset. And they had known nothing of one another, and Miss Whitaker had written letters after dinner in the saloon. Well, well! thought Lomax.

There came a fumbling at the deck-house door, a sudden blast of wind, a shower of spray, and Bellamy, in glistening oilskins, scrambled into the shelter, slamming the door behind him. A pool began to gather immediately round him on the floor. Lomax thought that he looked strangely triumphant, as though this were his hour. "Glad to have got us all into this mess," he thought meanly. It aggravated him that he should never yet have found the key to Bellamy.

"I want to talk to you," cried Bellamy, rocking on his feet as he stood.

He wanted to talk. External danger, then, gave him internal courage.

"Come into my cabin," he cried to Lomax over his shoulder as he began to make his way down the companion.

But Lomax, really, knew nothing of all this. The storm, really, had not entered his consciousness at all; Bellamy, and Bellamy alone, had occupied it all the while. All that he knew, really, was that he found himself in Bellamy's cabin.

In Bellamy's cabin, everything loose had been stowed away, so that it was bare of personal possessions; the narrow bunk, the swinging lamp, the closed cupboards alone remained untouched in the cabin that had sheltered the privacy of Bellamy's midnight hours. Lomax, as he lurched in through the door and was violently thrown against the bunk, reflected that he had never before set foot in the owner's quarters. They were small, low, and seamanlike; no luxury of chintz softened the plain wooden fittings; Lomax forgot the delicate yacht, and saw himself only in the presence of a sailor aboard his vessel, for Bellamy in his sou'wester and streaming oilskins, straddling in sea-boots beneath the lamp, had more the aspect of a captain newly descended from the bridge than of the millionaire owner of a pleasure yawl. He kept his feet, too, in spite of the violent motion, while Lomax, clinging to the side of the bunk, could barely save himself from being flung again across the cabin. But Bellamy stood there full of triumph, fully alive for the first time since Lomax had known him; his courteous languor dropped from him, he looked like a happy man. "This weather suits you," Lomax shouted above the din.

The yacht strained and creaked; now she lifted high on a wave, now fell sickeningly down into the trough. Water dashed against the closed port-hole and streamed past as the ship rose again to take the wave. Cast about in all directions, now dipping with her bows, now rolling heavily from furrow to furrow, she floundered with no direction and with no purpose other than to keep afloat; govern herself she could not, but maintain her hold on life she would. Lomax, who in the cabin down below could see nothing of the action of the sea, felt only the ship shaken in an angry hand, and heard the crash of tumult as the seas struck down upon the deck. "Will she live through it?" he screamed.

"If she isn't driven ashore," cried Bellamy with perfect indifference. "Come nearer, we can't make ourselves heard in this infernal noise."

It did not occur to him to move nearer to Lomax; perhaps he took pride in standing in the middle of the cabin, under the lamp now madly swaying in its gimbals, with the water still dripping from his oilskins into a pool on the floor. Lomax staggered towards him, clinging on to the edge of the bunk. It crossed his mind that this was a strange occasion to choose for conversation, but his standard of strangeness being now somewhat high he did not pause for long to consider that.

"I want to have a talk with you," said Bellamy again.

An enormous shock of water struck the ship overhead, and for a moment she quivered through all her timbers—a moment of stillness almost, while she ceased to roll, and nothing but that shudder ran through her. "Stood that well," said Bellamy, listening. Then she plunged; plunged as though never to rise any more, falling down as though a trap in the waters had opened to receive her; but she came up, lifted as rapidly as she had fallen, with a tremendous list over on to her side; righted herself, and took again to her rolling. The mate appeared in the doorway.

"Dinghy's gone, sir."

The man poured with water; in his black oilskins, his black sou'wester, he was a part of the black, wet night made tangible. Bellamy turned to Lomax. "So we're isolated. Not that a boat could have lived in a sea like this."

"What are you really thinking?" cried Lomax. "Not of the dinghy, or the sea, but something you've had in your mind all these weeks. And why tell it to me? You don't know me," but he remembered that he did not know Miss Whitaker, yet he had married her.

"Know you! Know you!" said Bellamy impatiently. "What's knowing, at best? I want you to do me a favour. I want a promise from you. I know you enough to know you won't refuse it."

"Why do you wear those glasses here?" cried Bellamy, staring at his guest.

Lomax, contriving to seat himself on the edge of the bunk, and holding on to the rod, shouted back, "If I took them off I might refuse any promise."

"I like you," said Bellamy. "I want you to come to me any day I should send for you—in England."

"So we are going back to England, are we?" said Lomax. He remembered their speculations about Bellamy. And so accustomed had he grown to the close limitation of the yacht and their four selves inhabiting it, that the prospect of disintegration was not only unconvincing, but positively distasteful. "We had," he said, "an idea that you wouldn't allow us to go back," but he wondered as he said it why men should take pleasure in bringing pain upon one another.

"Was I so sinister a figure?" said Bellamy. He took off his helmet, shining from the wet, and the lamp over his head gleamed upon his thick white hair and carved the shadows of weariness on his face, shadows that moved and shifted with the swinging of the lamp. "I was inconsiderate, doubtless—exasperating—wouldn't make plans—I owe you all an apology. I am an egoist, you see, Lomax. I was thinking of myself. There were certain things I wanted to allow myself the luxury of forgetting."

It was intolerable that Bellamy should heap this blame upon himself.

"You teased us," muttered Lomax in shamed justification.

"Yes, I teased you," said Bellamy. "I apologise again, I disturbed your comfort. But knowing myself to be a dying man, I indulged myself in that mischief. I had moods, I confess, when the sight of your comfort and your security irritated me even into the desire to drown you all. It's bad thinking, of a very elementary sort, and the foundation of most cynicism. I accept your rebuke."

"Damn you," said Lomax, twisting his hands.

"Nevertheless," Bellamy continued, "I shan't scruple to ask of you the favour I was going to ask. I am a coward, Lomax. I am afraid of pain. I am afraid of disease—of long, slow, disgusting disease—you understand me? And I have long been looking for some one who, when the moment came, would put me out of it."

"You can count on me," said Lomax. At the same time he could not help hoping that the moment had not come there and then. Procastination and a carefully chosen pair of spectacles would make him a very giant of decision.

Lomax went up on deck; he wanted a storm outside his head as well as a storm within it. The rain had ceased, and the tall spars swayed across a cloudy sky, rent between the clouds to show the moon. The sea was very rough and beautiful beneath the moon. It was good to see the storm at last, to see as well as to feel. Stars appeared, among the rack of the clouds, and vaguely astronomical phrases came into Lomax's mind: Nebulae, Inter-planetary space, Asteroids, Eighty thousand miles a second; he supposed that there were men to whom trillions were a workable reality, just as there were men who could diagnose Bellamy's disease and give him his sentence of death for the sum of two guineas. Two guineas was a contemptible sum to Bellamy, who was so rich a man. To Artivale, what did two guineas mean? A new retort? A supply of chemical? And to Lomax himself—a new pair of glasses? Tossed on Illyrian billows, he saw a lunar rainbow standing suddenly upon the waves, amazingly coloured in the night of black and silver. Life jumbled madly in his brain. There was Marion, too, lost to him from the moment he had stepped out of that system in which existence was simply a thing to be got through as inconspicuously as possible; and leaning against the deck-house for support he came nearer to tears than he had ever been in his life.

Of course it was to be expected that the death of so wealthy a man as Bellamy should create a certain sensation. There were headlines in the papers, and Arthur Lomax, who had dined with him that evening and had been the last person to see him alive, spent tiresome days evading reports. Veronal it was; no question or doubt about that; the tumbler containing the dregs of poison and the dregs of whisky and soda was found quite frankly standing on the table beside him. Lomax's evidence at the inquest threw no light on the suicide; no, Mr. Bellamy had not appeared depressed; yes, Mr. Bellamy had mixed a whisky and soda and drunk it off in his, Lomax's, presence. He had not seen Mr. Bellamy add anything to the contents of the tumbler. He was unable to say whether Mr. Bellamy had mixed a second whisky and soda after he, Lomax, had left the house. What time had he left? Late; about one in the morning. They had sat up talking. No, he had not known Mr. Bellamy very long, but they had been for a yachting cruise together, lasting some weeks. He would not say that they had become intimate. He knew nothing of Mr. Bellamy's private affairs. He had been very much shocked to read of the death next morning in the papers. Thank you, Mr. Lomax, that will do.

Bellamy was buried, and Lomax, Artivale, and Miss Whitaker attended the funeral, drawn together again into their little group of four—if you counted Bellamy, invisible, but terribly present, in his coffin. To be buried in the rain is dreary, but to be buried on a morning of gay sunshine is more ironical. Fortunately for Lomax, he was able to obscure the sunshine by the use of his black glasses; and heaven knows he needed them. He was either indifferent or oblivious to the remarkable appearance he offered, in a top-hat, a black coat, and black spectacles. "Weak eyes," noted the reporters. In fact he cared nothing for externals now, especially with the memory of his last meeting with Bellamy strong upon him. On seeing Miss Whitaker he roused himself a little, just enough to look at her with a wondering curiosity; he had forgotten her existence lately, except for the dim but constant knowledge that something stood blocked between him and Marion Vane, a something that wore neither name nor features, and whose materialisation he recognised, briefly puzzled by her importance, as Miss Whitaker. Important yet not important, for, in the muffled world which was his refuge, nothing mattered; events happened, but his mind registered nothing. Marion Vane herself was but a figure coming to him with outstretched hands, a figure so long desired, wearing that very gesture seemingly so impossible; and, in that gesture finally made, so instantly repudiated. His whole relationship with Marion Vane seemed now condensed into that moment of repudiation. "I am the resurrection and the life," saith the Lord, but the clods thumped down with very convincing finality into Bellamy's grave. Miss Whitaker stood near him, in black, very fragile; yes, she too had her pathos. Whether she had or had not trapped him with a lie . . . well, the lie, and the necessity for the lie, were of a deeper pathos than any truth she might have chosen to exploit. It is less pathetic to have a seducer in Ecuador than to have no seducer anywhere. But she might, thought Lomax, at least have acted up to her own invention. She might, knowing that she was going to meet him at the funeral, at least have thrust a cushion up under her skirt. A coarse man, Lomax. But perhaps she would have thought that irreverent at a funeral. There was no telling what queer superstitions people had; half the time, they did not know themselves, until a test found them out. Perhaps Miss Whitaker had boggled at that. Give her the benefit of the doubt; oh, surely better to credit her with a scruple than with lack of imagination! "I am become the first-fruits of them that sleep"—what did it all mean, anyway? Bellamy and the storm; why should the storm have given Bellamy courage? brought, so to speak, his hitherto only speculative courage to a head? Where was the relationship? What bearing had the extrinsic world upon the intrinsic? Why should the contemplation of life through coloured glasses make that life the easier to ruin? Why should reality recede? What *was* reality? Marion with her hands outstretched; so sure of him. Better to have helped Bellamy; better to have helped Miss Whitaker. Even though Miss Whitaker's need of help was, perhaps, fictitious? Yes, even so. The loss was hers, not his. Her falsity could not impair his quixotism; that was a wild, irrational thing, separate, untouched, independent. It flamed out of his life—for all the unreality of Miss Whitaker, that actual Miss Whitaker who subscribed to the census paper, paid rates and taxes, and had an existence in the eyes of the law— it flamed as a few things flamed: his two meetings with Bellamy, his repudiation of Marion Vane. There were just a few gashes of life, bitten in; that was all one could hope for. Was it worth living seventy, eighty years, to accumulate half-a-dozen scars? Half-a-dozen ineradicable pictures, scattered over the monotony of seventy, eighty pages. He had known, when he married Miss Whitaker, that he repudiated Marion Vane; to repudiate her when she came with outstretched hands was but the projection of the half-hour in the Cairo registry office. But it was that that he remembered. And her hurt incredulous eyes; as it was Bellamy's cry that he remembered; always the tangible thing—such was the weakness of the human, fleshly system. Now Bellamy would rot and be eaten, "Earth to earth, dust to dust"; his sickly body corrupting within the senseless coffin; and by that Lomax would be haunted, rather than by his spiritual tragedy; the tangible again, in the worms crawling in and out of a brain its master had preferred to still into eternal nescience. How long did it take for the buried flesh to become a skeleton? So long, and no less, would Lomax be haunted by the rotting corpse of Bellamy, as he would not have been haunted by the man dragging out a living death. Illogical, all of it; based neither upon truth nor upon reason, but always upon instinct, which reason dismissed as fallacious. Lomax opened his eyes, which he had closed; saw the world darkened, though he knew the sun still shone; and regretted nothing.

He had never before seen Miss Whitaker's house. It was small, and extremely conventional. He sat drinking her tea, and telling himself over and over again that she was his wife. There were letters on her writing-table, and he caught himself looking for the foreign stamp; but he could see nothing but bills. He suspected her correspondence of containing nothing more intimate. Yet here she was, a woman secretly married; that, at any rate, was true, whatever else might be false. He wondered whether she hinted it to her acquaintances, and whether they disbelieved her.

"Why did you laugh?" said Miss Whitaker.

They resumed their conversation. It was feverishly impersonal, yet they both thought it must end by crashing into the shrine of intimacy. But as though their lives depended upon it they juggled with superficiality. Lomax devoted only half his attention to their talk, which indeed was of a nature so contemptibly futile as to deserve no more; the rest of his attention wandered about the room, inquiring into the sudden vividness of Miss Whitaker's possessions: her initials on a paper-cutter, E. A. W.; the photograph of a woman, unknown to him, on the mantel-piece; a little stone Buddha; a seal in the pen-tray. Lomax saw them all through his darkened veil. This was her present—this small, conventional room; here she opened her morning paper, smoked her after-breakfast cigarette; here she re-turned in the evening, removed her hat, sat down to a book, poked the fire. But her past stretched away behind her, a blank to Lomax. No doubt she had done sums, worn a pig-tail, cried, and had a mother. So far, conjectures were safe. But her emotional interludes? All locked up? or hadn't there been any? What, to her, was the half-hour in the Cairo registry office? Did it bulk, to her, as Bellamy and Marion Vane bulked to him? One could never feel the shape of another person's mind; never justly apprehend its population. And he was not at all anxious to plumb the possibly abysmal pathos of Miss Whitaker; he didn't want those friends of hers, those strong manly men, to evaporate beneath the crudity of his search. He didn't want to be faced with the true desolation of the little room.

The rumours about Bellamy's death became common property only a few weeks later. They apparently had their origin in Bellamy's will, by which the fortune went to Lomax, turning him from a poor man into a rich one, to his embar-rassed astonishment. He wondered vaguely whether the rumours had been set afoot by Miss Whitaker, but came to the conclusion that fact or what she be-lieved to be fact had less allurement for her than frank fiction. Ergo, he said, her seducer in Ecuador interests her more than her secret husband in London. And he reasoned well.

Bellamy's body was exhumed. No one understood why, since the administra-tion of veronal had never been disputed. It was exhumed secretly, at night, by the light of a lantern, and carried into an empty cottage next to the graveyard. The papers next day gave these details. Lomax read them with a nauseous hor-ror. Bellamy, who had abjured life so that his tormented body might be at peace! And now, surrounded by constables, officers of the Law, on a rainy night, lit by the gleams of a hurricane lantern, what remained of his flesh had been smuggled into a derelict cottage and investigated by the scalpel of the anatomist. Truly the grave was neither fine nor private.

Then the newspaper accounts ceased; Bellamy was reburied; and the world went on as usual.

A friendship flared up—surely the queerest in London—between Lomax and Miss Whitaker. They met quite often. They dined together; they went to theatres. One afternoon they chartered a taxi and did a London round: they went to Sir John Soane's Museum, to Mme. Tussaud's, and the Zoo. Side by side, they looked at Mme. Tussaud's own modelling of Marie Antoinette's severed head fresh from the basket; they listened to somebody's cook beside them, reading from her catalogue: "Mary Antonette, gelatined in 1792; Lewis sixteen—why, he was gelatined too"; they held their noses in the Small Cats' House, appreciated the Coati, who can turn his long snout up or down, to left or right, without moving his head, and contemplated at length the Magnificent Bird of Paradise, who hopped incessantly, and the Frogmouth, who, of all creation, has in the supremest degree the quality of immobility and identification with his bough. Lomax found Miss Whitaker quite companionable on these occasions. If she told him how often she had observed the Magnificent Bird and the Frogmouth in their native haunts, he liked her none the less for that; a piquancy was added to her otherwise drab little personality, for he was convinced that she had never stirred out of England save in Bellamy's yacht. And certainly there had been neither Magnificent Bird nor Frogmouth in Illyria.

How romantic were the journeys of Miss Whitaker! How picturesque her travelling companions!

It must not be thought, however, that she incessantly talked about herself, for the very reverse was true; the allusions which she let fall were few, but although few they were always most startling.

Her company was usually, if not immediately, available. That was a great advantage to Lomax, who soon found that he could depend upon her almost at a moment's notice. Sometimes, indeed, a little obstacle came back to him over the telephone: "Lunch today? oh dear, I am so sorry I can't; I promised Roger that I would lunch with him," or else, "I promised Carmen that I would motor down to Kew." Lomax would express his regret. And Miss Whitaker, "But wait a moment, if you will ring off now I will try to get through to him (or her), and see if I can't put it off." And twenty minutes later Lomax's telephone bell would ring, and Miss Whitaker would tell him how angry Roger (or Carmen) had been, declaring that she was really too insufferable, and that he (or she) would have nothing more to do with her.

Miss Whitaker, indeed, was part of the fantasy of Lomax's life. He took a great interest in Roger and Carmen, and was never tired of their doings or their tempers. He sometimes arrived at Miss Whitaker's house to find a used tea-cup on the tray, which was pointed out to him as evidence of their recent departure. He sympathised over a bruise inflicted by the jealousy of Roger. On the whole, he preferred Carmen, for he liked women to have pretty hands, and Carmen's were small, southern, and dimpled; in fact, he came very near to being in love with Carmen. He beheld them, of course, as he now beheld Miss Whitaker, as he beheld everything, through the miraculous veil of his spectacles; crudity was tempered, criticism in abeyance; only compassion remained, and a vast indifference. All sense of reality had finally left him on the day that he repudiated Marion Vane; he scarcely suffered now, and even the nightmare which was beginning to hem him in held no personal significance; he was withdrawn. He heard the rumours about Bellamy's death, as though they concerned another man. He was quite sure that he regretted nothing he had done.

He was staring at the card he held in his hand: MR. ROBERT WHITAKER.

So Robert existed. Robert who had scoured Russia to avenge a woman. He was disappointed in Miss Whitaker. Since Robert existed, what need had she to mention him? An imaginary brother might tickle the fancy; a real brother was merely commonplace. With a sigh he gave orders for the admission of Robert. He awaited him, reflecting that the mortification of discovering that which one believed true to be untrue is as nothing compared to the mortification of discovering that which one believed untrue to be true. All art, said Lomax, is a lie; but that lie contains more truth than the truth. But here was Robert.

He was large and angry; lamentably like his sister's presentment of him. Lomax began to believe both in his Persian oil-field and in his exaggerated sense of honour. And when he heard Robert's business, he could no longer cherish any doubts as to Miss Whitaker's veracity. Here was Robert, large as life, and unmistakably out for revenge.

Lomax sat smiling, examining his finger-nails, and assenting to everything. Yes, he had been secretly married to Robert's sister in Cairo. Yes, it was quite possible, if Robert liked to believe it, that he was a bigamist. A seducer of young women. At that Lomax frankly laughed. Robert did not at all like the note in his laughter, mocking? satirical? He did not like it at all. Did Mr. Lomax at least realise that he would have Miss Whitaker's family to reckon with? He, Robert, had heard things lately about Mr. Lomax which he would not specify at present, but which would be investigated, with possibly very unpleasant results for Mr. Lomax. They were things which were making Miss Whitaker's family most uneasy. He did not pretend to know what Lomax's little game had been, but he had come today to warn him that he had better lie low and be up to no tricks. Lomax was greatly amused to find himself regarded as an adventurer. He put on a bland manner towards Robert which naturally strengthened Robert's conviction. And his last remark persuaded Robert that he was not only dangerous, but eccentric.

"By the way," he said, stopping Robert at the door; "would you mind telling me whether you have ever been in Russia? And did you catch your man?"

Robert stared angrily, and said, "Yes, to both questions."

"Ah, pity, pity!" said Lomax regretfully, shaking his head. There was another illusion gone.

He was almost tempted to wonder whether he ought not to believe again, as he had believed originally, in the seducer in Ecuador.

When he next saw Miss Whitaker he made no allusion to Robert's visit; neither did she, though she must have known of it. She had received an anonymous letter threatening abduction, and was full of that; she showed it to Lomax, who considered it with suitable gravity. He found Miss Whitaker's adventures most precious to him in his state of life and of mind. He clung on to them, for he knew that his own danger was becoming urgent. He had heard the phrase, "living on a volcano," but until now it had had as little meaning as it has for the rest of us. But now he knew well enough the expectation of being blown, at any moment, sky-high.

With these thoughts in his head, Lomax decided that he must see Artivale before it was too late. Before it was too late. Before, that is to say, he had been deprived of the liberty of action; that was the first step, that deprivation, to be followed by the second step: deprived of speech, gesture, thought—deprived of life itself. Before he was reduced, first to a prisoner, and then to a limp body lifted from under the gallows by the hands of men.

He must see Artivale.

Artivale lived in Paris. Lomax travelled to Paris, surprised, almost, to find his passport unchallenged and himself unchecked as he climbed into a train or crossed the gangway of a boat. Again and again surprise returned to him, whether he ordered a cup of tea in his Pullman or sat in his corner of the French compartment looking at La Vie Parisienne like any ordinary man. He was going to Paris. He had bought his ticket, and the clerk in the booking-office had handed it to him without comment. That meant freedom—being a free man. The privileges of freedom. He looked at his fellow-travellers and wondered whether they knew how free they were. How free to come and go, and how quickly their freedom might be snatched from them. He wondered what they would say if they knew that a condemned man travelled with them. Time was the important thing; whether he had time enough to do what he had to do before the hand fell upon him. "But," thought Lomax, laughing to himself, "they are all condemned, only they forget about it; they know it, but they forget." And as he looked at them through his spectacles—the black ones—moving as though they had eternity before them in a world dim, unreal, and subdued, they seemed to him in their preoccupation and their forgetfulness extremely pitiful.

Under the great girders of the Gare du Nord they scurried, tiny figures galvanised suddenly into shouting and haste. But it was not the recollection of their ultimate condemnation that made them hurry; it was the returning urgency of their own affairs after the passivity of the journey. After all, the train is going as fast as it can, and the most impatient traveller can do no more than allow himself to be carried. But on arrival it is different. Porters may be speeded up by abuse, other travellers may be shoved out of the way, one may capture the first taxi in the rank rather than the last. All these things are of great importance. Perversely, Lomax, as soon as he had descended from the train, began to dawdle. The station, that great cavern full of shadows, swallowing up the gleaming tracks, stopping the monstrous trains as with a wall of finality; those tiny figures so senselessly hurrying; those loads of humanity discharged out of trains from unknown origins towards unknown destinations; all this appeared to him as the work of some crazy etcher, building up a system of lit or darkened masses, here a column curving into relief, there a cavernous exit yawning to engulf, here groins and iron arches soaring to a very heaven of night, there metallic perspectives diminishing towards a promise of day; and everywhere the tiny figures streaming beneath the architectural nightmare, microscopic bodies of men with faces undistinguishable, flying as for their lives along passage—ways between eddies of smoke in a fantastic temple of din and murk and machinery. Moreover, he was wearing, it must be remembered, the black glasses. That which was sombre enough to other eyes, to him was sinister as the pit. He knew the mood which the black glasses induced; yet he had deliberately come away with no other pair in his pocket. The fear which troubled him most was the thought that in his imprisonment his glasses might be taken from him—he had dim recollections, survivals from a life in which the possibility of imprisonment played no part, that condemned criminals must be deprived of all instruments of suicide. And the black glasses, of them all, best suited his natural humour. Therefore he had indulged himself, on perhaps his last opportunity, by bringing no alternative pair. Since he had lost everything in life, he would riot in the luxury of beholding life through an extravagance of darkness.

A dragon pursued him, clanging a bell; mechanically he moved aside, and the electric luggage-trucks passed him, writhing into the customs-house at the end of the station. Artivale lived in the Quartier Latin; it was necessary to get there before the hand fell on his shoulder. Paris taxi-drivers were mad, surely, and their taxis on the verge of disintegration; chasing enormous trams, charged by demoniac lorries, hooting incessantly and incessantly hooted at, Lomax in his wheeled scrap-iron rattled across a Paris darkened into the menace of an imminent cataclysm. A heaven of lead hung over the ghastly streets. All condemned, thought Lomax, as he racketed through the procession of life that was so gaily unconscious of the night in which it moved.

He arrived at Artivale's house.

Artivale himself opened the door.

"Good God!" he said on seeing Lomax, "what . . . But come in.—You're ill," he continued, when he had got Lomax inside the door.

"No," said Lomax, oblivious of the startling appearance he presented, with haggard cheeks behind the absurd spectacles; "only, I had to see you—in a hurry."

"In a hurry?" said Artivale, accustomed to think of Lomax as a man without engagements, occupations, or urgency.

"You see," said Lomax, "I murdered Bellamy and I may be arrested at any moment."

"Of course that does explain your hurry," said Artivale, "but would you mind coming down to the kitchen, where I want to keep my eye on some larvae? We can talk there. My servants don't understand English."

Lomax followed him downstairs to the basement, where in a vaulted kitchen enormous blue butterflies circled in the air and a stout negress stoked the oven. The room was dark and excessively hot. "We're in the tropics," said Lomax, looking at the butterflies.

Artivale apologised for the atmosphere. "I have to keep it hot for the sake of the larvae," he explained, "and I had to import the black women because no French servant would stand the heat. These are the larvae," and he showed Lomax various colourless smudges lying on the tables and the dresser. "Now tell me about Bellamy."

The negress beamed upon them benevolently, showing her teeth. A negro girl came from an inner room, carrying a pile of plates. A butterfly of extraordinary brilliancy quivered for a moment on the kitchen clock, and swept away, up into the shadows of the roof, fanning Lomax with its wings in passing.

"The murder was nothing," said Lomax; "he asked me to do it. He was ill, you see—mortally—and he was afraid of pain. That's all very simple. He left me his fortune, though."

"Yes," said Artivale, "I read his will in the paper."

"I am leaving that to you," said Lomax.

"To me—but, my dear fellow, you're not going to die."

"Oh yes," said Lomax, "I shall be hung, of course. Besides, we are all condemned, you know."

"Ultimately, yes," replied Artivale, "but not imminently."

"That's why people forget about it," said Lomax, gazing at him very intently.

Artivale began to wonder whether Lomax suffered from delusions.

"Could you take off those spectacles?" he asked.

"No," said Lomax. "I should go mad if I did. You have no idea how beautiful your butterflies are, seen through them—the blue through a veil of black.

But to go back to the fortune. I ought, perhaps, to leave it to Miss Whitaker, but she has enough of her own already."

"Why to Miss Whitaker?" asked Artivale.

"I married her in Cairo," replied Lomax; "I forgot to tell you that. It is so difficult to remember all these things."

"Are you telling me that you and Miss Whitaker were married all that time on the yacht?"

"Exactly. She was going to have a child, you know—by another man."

"I see," said Artivale.

"But of course all these things that I am telling you are private."

"Oh, quite," said Artivale. "Miss Whitaker was going to have a child, so you married her, Bellamy had a mortal illness, so you murdered him. Private and confidential. I quite understand."

"I hope you will have no scruples about accepting the fortune," said Lomax anxiously. "I am leaving it to you, really, as I should leave it to a scientific institute—because I believe you will use it to the good of humanity. But if you make any difficulties I shall alter my will and leave it to the Royal Society."

"Tell me, Lomax," said Artivale, "do you care a fig for humanity?"

"There is nothing else to care about," said Lomax.

"Of course I accept your offer—though not for myself," said Artivale.

"That's all right then," said Lomax, and he rose to go.

"Stay a moment," said Artivale. "Naturally, you got Bellamy to sign a paper stating that you were about to murder him at his own request?"

"No," said Lomax; "it did cross my mind, but it seemed indelicate, somehow—egotistic, you know, at a moment like that, to mention such a thing—and as he didn't suggest it I thought I wouldn't bother him. After all, he was paying me a great compliment—a very great compliment."

"Oh, undoubtedly!" said Artivale, "but I think, if you will forgive my saying so, that your delicacy outran your prudence. Any evidence that I can give . . ."

"But you have only my word, and that isn't evidence," replied Lomax, smiling.

At that moment a bell pealed through the house upstairs.

"That will be for me," said Lomax; "how lucky that I had time to say what I wanted to say."

"Oh, you are lucky, aren't you?" cried Artivale wildly; "a lucky, lucky dog. Your luck's inconceivable. Lomax—look Lomax—you must get out of this house. The back door.

The bell rang again.

"It's only a question of sooner or later," said Lomax gently; "for everybody, you know; not only for me. If they let me keep the spectacles I don't mind. With them, I don't see things as they are. Or perhaps I do. It doesn't make much difference which. If you won't go up and open that door, I shall go and open it myself."

They took Lomax away in a cab. He was not allowed to keep his spectacles. Artivale came downstairs again to the kitchen, and watched a peacock butterfly of humming-bird proportions crawl free of its cocoon and spread its wings in flight.

It was only during the course of his trial that Lomax discovered how pitiable a weapon was truth. A law-court is a place of many contradictions; pitch-pine walls and rows of benches give it the appearance of a school treat, white wigs and scarlet and phraseology erect it into a seeming monument to all civilisation, but of the helplessness of the victim there is at least no doubt at all. His bewilderment is the one certain factor. Lomax in the days when he might meet fact with fantasy had been a contented man; now, when he tried to meet with fact the fantastical world which so suddenly and so utterly swamped him, was a man confounded, a man floundering for a foothold. He had lost his spectacles. He had lost his attitude towards life. He had lost Miss Whitaker, or at any rate had exchanged her for a Miss Whitaker new and formidable, a Miss Whitaker who, astonishingly and catastrophically, spoke a portion of the truth. If earth had turned to heaven and heaven to earth a greater chaos could not have resulted in his mind.

The public see me in the dock; they do not see me in my cell. Let me look at the walls; they are white, not clouded into a nameless colour, as once they would have been. Uncompromisingly white. How ugly, how bare! But I must remember: this is a prison cell. I have no means of turning it into anything else. I am a prisoner on trial for my life. That's fact. A plain man, suffering the consequences for the actions of a creature enchanted, now disappeared. The white walls are fact. Geometry is a fact—or so they say—but didn't some one suggest that in another planetary system the laws of geometry might be reversed? This cell is geometrical; square floor, square ceiling, square walls, square window intersected by bars. Geometrical shadows, Euclidean angles. White light. Did I, or did I not, do this, that, and the other? I did, but . . . No buts. Facts are facts. Yes or no. Geometrical questions require geometrical answers. If A be equal to B, then C . . . But either I am mad, or they are mad, or the King's English no longer means what it used to mean.

In the dock again. Amazing statements, in substance true, in essence madly false. He must neither interrupt nor attempt to justify. All these events, which dance round him pointing crooked fingers, disfiguring their aspects into such caricatures, all these events came about so naturally, so inevitably. He knows that, as a lesson learnt, though the enchantment is gone from him. If he might speak, even, what should he relate of that experience? If he might speak! But when he speaks he damns himself. His counsel speaks for him, well-primed, so far as his client's idea of honour has been allowed to prime him; but Lomax knows all the time that his life is of no real consequence to his counsel, except in so far as success provides advertisement; he knows that after the trial is over, one way or the other, his counsel will meet the opposing counsel in the lobby and stop to joke with him, "Got the better of you that time," or, "Well, you were too much for me."

Meanwhile his counsel has been eloquent, in an academic way. Lomax has nothing to complain of. The opening speech for the defence. A simple defence: murder at the victim's request; a man threatened by a mortal disease. An act of friendship; an exaggerated act of friendship, it may be said; but shall it be called the less noble for that? But Lomax sees it coldly; he judges dispassionately, as though the story were not his own. Here stands this man; the jury will hear him tell how, out of compassion for a man he barely knew, he exposed himself to the utmost risk; even the precautions of common prudence were neglected by him in the urgency and delicacy of the circumstances. Another man would have refused this friendly office; or, accepting it, would have ensured his personal safety by a written assurance; or, thirdly, would have hurried from the house before the death had taken place. Not so the prisoner. Prisoner had remained for two hours with the dead body of his friend in the room, dealing with his private papers according to instructions previously received. (Here the prisoner was observed to show some signs of emotion.) Again, the prisoner might have pleaded not guilty; but, regretting his inaccuracies at the time of the inquest, had refused to do so. He was determined to tell the whole truth and to throw himself upon the mercy of the jury.

Lomax realised fully the impossible task his obstinacy had imposed upon his unfortunate counsel.

He realised too, however, that the difficulties improved the game, from the point of view of his counsel. How great would his triumph be, supposing . . . ! And, after all, it was nothing but a game.

"A hopeless fellow," said counsel to his wife that night, over his port. "I never had to deal with such a case—never. Of course, if I can get him off, I'm made," and he fell to ruminating, and his wife who was in love with him, knew better than to interrupt.

How strange a colour were faces in the mass! A face examined separately and in detail was pink, porous, distinctive with mouth and eyebrows, but taken collectively they were of a uniform buff, and wore but one expression, of imbecile curiosity. Upturned, vacuous curiosity. Lomax had a prolonged opportunity for looking down upon such a mass. Here and there he picked out a face he knew— Artivale, Robert Whitaker, the captain of the *Nereid*,—and wondered vaguely what strands had drawn them all together at that place. Only by an effort of concentration could he connect them with himself. The voice went on, telling the truth on his behalf. The jury leaned forward to stare at him. The judge, with a long face and dewlaps like a bloodhound, up under his canopy, drew pictures on his blotting-paper. Outside in the streets, sensational posters flowered against the railings with the noonday editions. The Coati in the Zoo waggled his snout; at Mme. Tussaud's the waxen murderers stood accumulating dust in the original dock of the Old Bailey; the *Nereid,* stripped of her wings, swayed a forlorn hulk in the mud at Brightlingsea.

The prosecution was thick with argument. It bore down upon Lomax like a fog through which he could not find his way. He heard his piteous motives scouted; he heard the exquisite ridicule: he saw a smile of derision flicker across the jury. And he sympathised. He quite saw that he could not expect to be believed. If only Bellamy had not left him that fortune, he might have stood a chance. But he would not be so ungenerous as to criticise Bellamy.

That was the first day of the prosecution. Lomax at night in his cell was almost happy: he was glad to endure this for Bellamy's sake. He had loved Bellamy. He was glad to know at last how much he had loved Bellamy. And his privilege had been to spare Bellamy years of intolerable life. He never stopped to argue that Bellamy might just as well have performed the function for himself; for Bellamy was a coward—had said so once and for all, and Lomax had accepted it. Lomax did not sleep much that night, but a sort of exultation kept him going: he had saved Bellamy, Artivale would have the money, and it was still just possible that to Miss Whitaker he had rendered a service. Not much of a service, certainly, to provide her with a convicted murderer upon whom to father her child; but, between himself and his own conscience, he knew that his intentions had been honourable. His brain was perfectly clear that night. He knew that he must hold on to those three things, and he would go compensated to the scaffold.

On the second day two of his three things were taken from him.

The first was the harder to bear. Post-mortem had revealed no mortal disease in the exhumed body. Lomax, lack-lustre in the dock stirred to brief interest: so Bellamy, too, had been of the same company? But what Bellamy had really believed would now never be known.

The second concerned Miss Whitaker. Before she was called, the court was cleared, counsel submitting that the evidence about to be produced was of too delicate and private a character for publication. Ah, thought Lomax, here is a delicacy they can understand! He sat quiet while feet shuffled out of the court, herded away by a bailiff. Then when the doors were closed he heard the now familiar voice: Evelyn Amy Whitaker.

She was in the witness-box. She was very much frightened but she had been subpoenaed, and Robert had terrorised her. She would not look at Lomax. Was she resident at 40 College Buildings, Kensington? She was. She had known the prisoner since April of the present year. She had met him on Mr. Bellamy's yacht. They had sailed from Southampton to Alexandria and from thence had travelled by train to Cairo. In Cairo she had married the prisoner.

Here Lomax's counsel protested that the evidence was irrelevant.

Counsel for the Crown maintained that the evidence was necessary to throw light upon the prisoner's character, and the objection was overruled.

Examination continued: the marriage took place entirely at the prisoner's suggestion. He had appeared very strange, and insisted upon wearing coloured spectacles even when not in the sun—but here another protest was raised, and allowed by his lordship. Prisoner had always been very much interested in Mr. Bellamy, and occasionally said he could not understand him; also asked witness and Mr. Artivale their opinion. She had never heard Mr. Bellamy make any reference to his health. She had known Mr. Bellamy and the prisoner to be closeted for long talks in Mr. Bellamy's cabin.

Cross-examined by counsel for the defence: was it not a fact that she had led the prisoner to believe that she was with child by a man then living abroad? and that prisoner's suggestion of marriage was prompted by considerations of chivalry? Certainly not.

Dr. Edward Williams, of Harley Street, gynaecologist, examined: he had attended the witness, and could state upon oath that she was not in the condition described. The lady was, in fact, he might add, a virgin.

Lomax listened to this phantasmagoria of truth and untruth. He could have thanked the doctor for the outstanding and indubitable accuracy of his statement. It shone out like a light in darkness.

His lordship, much irritated: "I cannot have this."

As your lordship pleases.

But the jury looked paternally at Miss Whitaker, thinking that she had had a lucky escape.

And again Lomax sympathised with the scepticism of the jury. Again he saw that he could not expect to be believed. "People don't do such things"; men were not quixotic to that extent. Of course they could not believe. Why, he himself, in his pre-spectacle days, would not have believed. He scarcely believed now. The spectacles were really responsible; but it would only make matters worse to tell the jury about the spectacles. There was no place for such things in a tribunal; and, since all life was a tribunal, there should be no place for such things in life. The evidence for the defence was already sufficiently weak. Lomax had never known the name of the doctor who had given Bellamy his death-sentence, and advertisement had failed to produce him. Artivale, an impassioned witness, had had his story immediately pulled to pieces. Lomax himself was examined. But it all sounded very thin. And now that he was deprived of his spectacles—was become again that ordinary man, that Arthur Lomax getting through existence, with only the information of that fantastic interlude, as though it concerned another man, the information rather than the memory, since it existed now for him in words and not in sensation—now that he was returned to his pre-spectacle days, he could survey his story with cold hard sense and see that it could bear no relation to a world of fact. It was a mistake, he had always known that it was a mistake, to mix one's manners. And for having permitted himself that luxury, he was about to be hanged. It was perhaps an excessive penalty, but Lomax was not one to complain.

Miss Whitaker came to visit him in prison. She was his wife, however shamefully he had treated her, and had no difficulty in obtaining the necessary permission from compassionate authority. Lomax was pleased to see her. She reminded him of Illyria and the Coati—though, of course, Illyria and the Coati were things he knew of only by hearsay. But Miss Whitaker herself was a little embarrassed; was almost sorry she had come. Like Lomax, she found reality confusing. "I am afraid you have ruined your life," she said, looking round Lomax's neat cell.

"Not at all," said Lomax politely, "so long as I haven't ruined yours. I am only sorry my counsel should have mentioned that about the child. He got it out of me in an unguarded moment. I am glad to have this opportunity of apologising."

"Yes, poor little thing," said Miss Whitaker. "But as my name hasn't appeared, no harm was done. I was sorry, too, that I had to give evidence against you. Robert insisted—I always warned you that Robert was very revengeful."

"Quite," said Lomax.

"I ought to tell you," said Miss Whitaker, looking down at her shoes, "that *he* is coming home. He has been among the Indians for the last six months, and it has broken his health. He lands at Southampton—where we sailed from, do you remember?—just before Christmas."

"I am sorry," said Lomax, "that I shan't have the pleasure of meeting him."

"No," said Miss Whitaker, and then, seeming to lose her head a little, she again said, "No; of course you won't. Perhaps I ought to be going?"

Anyway, Artivale would have the money. Lomax hugged that to his breast. Science would have the money; and science was a fact, surely, incapable of caricature; absolute, as mathematics were absolute. He had had enough of living in a world where truth was falsehood and falsehood truth. He was about to abandon that world, and his only legacy to it should be to an incorruptible province;

let him hold that comfort, where all other comforts had turned to so ingenious a mockery.

Shortly after Lomax had been hanged, Bellamy's nearest relations, two maiden ladies who lived at Hampstead and interested themselves in the conversion of the heathen, entered a plea that Bellamy's will had been composed under the undue influence of Arthur Lomax. The case was easily proved, and it was understood that the bulk of the fortune would be placed by the next-of-kin as conscience money at the disposal of His Majesty's Treasury.

FROM *ALL PASSION SPENT* (1931)

This book, probably Vita's best-known production apart from her garden columns, essays, and radio broadcasts, was written in May of 1930, just when Vita had made an offer for the purchase of Sissinghurst Castle. Sissinghurst had to be renovated, and so there was again the question, as often there was, of Vita having to make money for the family. The novel was begun just when she had finished correcting the proofs of The Edwardians, *which was set against the background of a large house and was an instant bestseller by early June of 1930. During this period she also wrote the poem "Sissinghurst," which she dedicated to Virginia Woolf, enraging B. M., who would have liked it dedicated to herself.*

Of all Vita's books, All Passion Spent *has remained in print the longest, and was even made into a television show. Its dedication to Vita's sons:*

> For Benedict and Nigel
> Who are young
> This story of people who are old.

In All Passion Spent, *Lady Slane, the gentle aged widow who had given up her own ambition to be a painter in order to be a proper wife to her husband, has an admirable spaciousness of mind. She will encourage the ambition of young Deborah, her great-granddaughter, who is herself determined to be a musician, remembering how her own potential career as a painter was stifled. Lady Slane's stiff children, who want to arrange her life and that of the younger generation, have a far more constricted point of view than hers. The point is firmly made about women, old and young, following their own bent and having their own careers. Lady Slane, now eighty-eight, who has devoted herself to her husband and his career, has made the decision to take no interest in her children, who are prim, proper, and boring, and has moved to the country, away from the* society she despises, accompanied only by her French maid, Genoux. Nearby, she has for company three elderly gentleman friends: her landlord and adviser, Mr. Bucktrout; a carpenter, Mr. Gosheron, who will give his finest piece of wood for her coffin; and an eccentric millionaire friend, FitzGeorge, whom she had loved many years before and whose fortune she has refused.

Lady Slane's encouragement of her granddaughter is based on her own loss of "what she herself wanted to be . . . the girl was talking as she herself would have talked. . . . If she wanted approval, she should have it. 'Of course you are right, my dear,' she said quietly." Vita's passionate belief that women should be as free as men to develop and assert their own passions impels her encouragement of others.

This novel had such immediate success that Virginia Woolf wrote to Vita of her exhaustion wrapping it up to send to those who have ordered it. She exclaims how her fingers are red from doing up the parcels: "Oh Lord what it is to publish a best seller— when shall I be able to hold a pen again? . . . Yes, I'll come to Sissinghurst. But when will you come here—all covered with gold as you are? You must sign my 6 thousandth copy . . . What fun it all is to be sure—selling 6,000."[3]

The pages reprinted here are the final ones. Many readers consider this novel Vita's finest, and certainly it is her most influential. The freedom for the young women here suggested, advised, demanded, and, ultimately, taken is couched in terms available and moving. Considering Vita's problematic relation with her mother, whose harsh judgement of her was, on all counts, the opposite of Lady Slane's encouragement of the younger generation of women, it is all the more remarkable that she should have written such a convincing novel on the topics of age and women's self-determination.

ALL PASSION SPENT

Common sense rarely laid its fingers on Lady Slane, these days. It did occur to her to wonder, however, what the young people had thought of her renunciation of FitzGeorge's fortune. They had been indignant probably; they had cursed their great-grandmother soundly for defrauding them of a benefit which would eventually have been theirs. They would certainly have given her no credit for romantic motives. Perhaps she owed them an explanation, though not an apology? But how could she get into touch with them, now especially? Pride caught her wrist even as she stretched her pen out towards the ink. She had, after all, behaved towards them in what to any reasonable person must seem a most unnatural way; first she had refused to see them, and then she had eliminated from their future the possibility of great and easy wealth. She must appear to them as the incarnation of egoism and inconsideration. Lady Slane was distressed, yet she knew that she had acted according to her convictions. Had not

FitzGeorge himself once taken her to task for sinning against the light? And suddenly, in a moment of illumination, she understood why FitzGeorge had tempted her with this fortune: he had tempted her only in order that she should find the strength to reject it. He had offered her not so much a fortune as a chance to be true to herself. Lady Slane bent down and stroked the cat, whom as a rule she did not much like. "John," she said, "John—how fortunate that I did what he wanted, before I realised what he wanted."

After that she was happy, though her qualms about her young descendants continued to worry her. By a curious twist, her qualms of conscience about them increased now that she had satisfactorily explained her own action to herself, as though she blamed herself for some extravagant gesture of self-indulgence. Perhaps she had come too hastily to her decision? Perhaps she had treated the children unfairly? Perhaps one should not demand sacrifices of others, consequent upon one's own ideas? She had consulted her own ideas entirely, with the added spice of pleasure, she must admit, in annoying Carrie, Herbert, Charles, and William. It had seemed wrong to her that private people should own such possessions, such exaggerated wealth; therefore she had hastened to dispose of both, the treasures to the public and the money to the suffering poor; the logic was simple though trenchant. Stated in these terms, she could not believe in her own wrong-doing; but, on the other hand, should she not have considered her great-grandchildren? It was a subtle problem to decide alone; and Mr. Bucktrout, to whom she confided it, gave her no help, for not only was he entirely in sympathy with her first instinct but, moreover, in view of the approaching end of the world, he could not see that it mattered very much one way or the other. "My dear lady," he said, "when your Cellinis, your Poussins, your grandchildren, and your great-grandchildren are all mingled in planetary dust your problem of conscience will cease to be of much importance." That was true rather than helpful. Astronomical truths, enlarging though they may be to the imagination, contain little assistance for immediate problems. She continued to gaze at him in distress, a distress which at that very moment had been augmented by a sudden thought of what Henry, raising his eyebrows, would have said.

"Miss Deborah Holland," said Genoux, throwing open the door. She threw it open in such a way as to suggest that she was retrospectively aping the manner of the grand major-domo at the Paris Embassy.

Lady Slane rose in a fluster, with the usual soft rustle of her silks and laces; her knitting slipped to the floor; she stooped ineffectually to retrieve it; her mind swept wildly round, seeking to reconcile this improbable encounter between her great-granddaughter, Mr. Bucktrout, and herself. The circumstances were too complicated for her to govern successfully in a moment's thought. She had never been good at dealing with a situation that demanded nimbleness of wit; and, considering the conversations she had had with Mr. Bucktrout about her great-grandchildren, of whom Herbert's granddaughter thus suddenly presented herself as a specimen, the situation demanded a very nimble wit indeed. "My *dear* Deborah," said Lady Slane, scurrying affectionately, dropping her knitting, trying to retrieve it, abandoning the attempt midway, and finally managing to kiss Deborah on the cheek.

She was the more confused, for Deborah was the first young person to enter the house at Hampstead since Lady Slane had removed herself from Elm Park Gardens. The house at Hampstead had opened its doors to no one but Mr. Fitz-George, Mr. Bucktrout, and Mr. Gosheron—and, of course, on occasion, to Lady Slane's own children, who, although they might be unwelcome, were at any rate advanced in years. Deborah came in the person of youth knocking at the doors. She was pretty, under her fur cap; pretty and elegant; the very girl Lady Slane would have expected from her photographs in the society papers. In the year since Lady Slane had seen her, she had changed from a schoolgirl into a young lady. Of her activities in the fashionable world since she became a young lady, Lady Slane had had ample evidence. This observation reminded Lady Slane of her press-cutting album, which was lying on the table under the lamp; releasing Deborah's hand, she hurriedly removed the album to a dark place, as though it were a dirtied cup of tea. She put the blotter over it. A narrow escape; narrow and unforeseen; but now she felt safe. She came back and introduced Deborah formally to Mr. Bucktrout.

Mr. Bucktrout had the tact to take his leave almost immediately. Lady Slane, knowing him, had feared that he might plunge instantly into topics of the deepest import, with references to her own recent and eccentric conduct, thereby embarrassing both the girl and herself. Mr. Bucktrout, however, behaved most unexpectedly as a man of the world. He made a few remarks about the beginning of spring—about the reappearance of flowers on barrows in the London streets—about the longevity of anemones in water, especially if you cut their stems—about the bunches of snowdrops that came up from the country, and how soon they would be succeeded by bunches of primroses—about Covent Garden. But about cosmic catastrophes or the right judgment of Deborah Holland's great-grandmother he said nothing. Only once did he verge on an indiscretion, when he leant forward, putting his finger against his nose, and said, "Miss Deborah, you bear a certain resemblance to Lady Slane whom I have the honour to call my friend." Fortunately, he did not follow up the remark, but after the correct interval merely rose and took his leave. Lady Slane was grateful to him, yet it was with dismay that she saw him go, leaving her face to face with a young woman bearing what had once been her own name.

She expected an evasive and meaningless conversation as a start, dreading the chance phrase that would fire it into realities, growing swiftly like Jack's beanstalk into a tangle of reproaches; she expected anything in the world but that Deborah should sit at her knee and thank her with directness and simplicity for what she had done. Lady Slane made no answer at all, except to lay her hand on the girl's head pressed against her knee. She was too much moved to answer; she preferred to let the young voice go on, imagining that she herself was the speaker, reviving her adolescent years and deluding herself with the fancy that she had at last found a confidant to whom she could betray her thoughts. She was old, she was tired, she lost herself willingly in the sweet illusion. Was it an echo that she heard? or had some miracle wiped out the years? were the years being played over again, with a difference? She allowed her fingers to ruffle Deborah's hair, and, finding it short instead of ringleted, supposed vaguely that she had put her own early plans for escape into execution. Had she then really run away from home? had she, indeed, chosen her own career instead of Henry's? Was she now sitting on the floor beside a trusted friend, pouring out her reasons, her aspirations, and her convictions, with a firmness and a certainty lit as by a flame from within? Fortunate Deborah! she thought, to be so firm, so trustful, and by one person at least so well understood; but to which Deborah she alluded, she scarcely knew.

She had told herself after FitzGeorge's death that no strange and lovely thing would ever enter her life again, a foolish prophecy. This unexpected confusion of her own life with that of her great-granddaughter was as strange and as lovely. FitzGeorge's death had aged her; at her time of life people aged suddenly and alarmingly; her mind was, perhaps, no longer very clear; but at least it was clear enough for her to recognise its weakness, and to say, "Go on, my darling; you might be myself speaking." Deborah, in her young egoism, failed to pick up the significance of that remark, which Lady Slane, indeed, had inadvertently let slip. She had no intention of revealing herself to her great-granddaughter; her hand upon the latch of the door of death, she had no intention of troubling the young with a recital of her own past problems; enough for her, now to submerge herself into a listener, a pair of ears, though she might still keep her secrets running in and out of her mind according to her fancy—for it must be remembered that Lady Slane had always relished the privacy of her enjoyments. This enjoyment was especially private now, though not very sharp; it was hazy rather than sharp, her perceptions intensified and yet blurred, so that she could feel intensely without being able or obliged to reason. In the deepening twilight of her life, in the maturity of her years, she returned to the fluctuations of adolescence; she became once more the reed wavering in the river, the skiff reaching out towards the sea, yet blown back again and again into the safe waters of the estuary. Youth!

youth! she thought; and she, so near to death, imagined that all the perils again awaited her, but this time she would face them more bravely, she would allow no concessions, she would be firm and certain. This child, this Deborah, this self, this other self, this projection of herself, was firm and certain. Her engagement, she said, was a mistake; she had drifted into it to please her grandfather; (Mother doesn't count, she said, nor does Granny—poor Mabel!); her grandfather had ambitions for her, she said; he liked the idea of her being, some day, a duchess; but what was that, she said, compared with what she herself wanted to be, a musician?

When she said "a musician," Lady Slane received a little shock, so confidently had she expected Deborah to say "a painter." But it came to much the same thing, and her disappointment was quickly healed. The girl was talking as she herself would have talked. She had no prejudice against marriage with someone who measured his values against the same rod as herself. Understanding was impossible between people who did not agree as to the yard and the inch. To her grandfather and her late fiance, wealth and so great a title measured a yard—two yards—a hundred yards—a mile. To her, they measured an inch—half an inch. Music, on the other hand, and all that it implied, could be measured by no terrestrial scale. Therefore she was grateful to her great-grandmother for reducing her value in the worldly market. "You see," she said amused, "for a week I was supposed to be an heiress, and when it was found that I wasn't an heiress at all it became much easier for me to break off my engagement."

"When did you break it off?" asked Lady Slane, thinking of her newspaper cuttings which had not mentioned the fact.

"The day before yesterday."

Genoux came in with the evening post, glad of a pretext to take another look at Deborah. Lady Slane slipped the green packet under her knitting. "I didn't know," she said, "that you had broken it off."

And such a relief it was, said Deborah, wriggling her shoulders. She would have no more to do, she said, with that crazy world. "Is it crazy, great-grandmother," she asked, "or am I? Or am I merely one of the people who can't fit in? Am I just one of the people who think a different set of things important? Anyhow, why should I accept other people's ideas? My own are just as likely to be right—right for me. I know one or two people who agree with me, but they are always people who don't seem to get on with grandfather or great-aunt Carrie. And another thing"—she paused.

"Go on," said Lady Slane, moved to the heart by this stumbling and perplexed analysis.

"Well," said Deborah, "there seems to be a kind of solidarity between grandfather and great-aunt Carrie and the people that grandfather and great-aunt

Carrie approve of. As though cement had been poured over the whole lot. But the people *I* like always seem to be scattered, lonely people—only they recognise each other as soon as they come together. They seem to be aware of something more important than the things grandfather and great-aunt Carrie think important. I don't yet know exactly what that something is. If it were religion—if I wanted to become a nun instead of a musician—I think that even grandfather would understand dimly what I was talking about. But it isn't religion; and yet it seems to have something of the nature of religion. A chord of music, for instance, gives me more satisfaction than a prayer."

"Go on," said Lady Slane.

"Then," said Deborah, "among the people I like, I find something hard and concentrated in the middle of them, harsh, almost cruel. A sort of stone of honesty. As though they were determined at all costs to be true to the things that they think matter. Of course," said Deborah dutifully, remembering the comments of her grandfather and her great-aunt Carrie, "I know that they are, so to speak, very useless members of society." She said it with a childish gravity.

"They have their uses," said Lady Slane; "they act as a leaven."

"I never know how to pronounce that word," said Deborah; "whether to rhyme with even or seven. I suppose you are right about them, great-grandmother. But the leaven takes a long time to work, and even then it only works among people who are more or less of the same mind."

"Yes," said Lady Slane, "but more people are really of the same mind than you would believe. They take a great deal of trouble to conceal it, and only a crisis calls it out. For instance, if you were to die,"—but what she really meant was, If I were to die—"I daresay you would find that your grandfather had understood you (me) better than you (I) think."

"That's mere sentimentality," said Deborah firmly; "naturally, death startles everybody, even grandfather and great-aunt Carrie—it reminds them of the things they prefer to ignore. My point about the people I like is not that they dwell morbidly on death, but that they keep continually a sense of what, to them, matters in life. Death, after all, is an incident. Life is an incident too. The thing I mean lies outside both. And it doesn't seem compatible with the sort of life grandfather and great-aunt Carrie think I ought to lead. Am I wrong, or are they?"

Lady Slane perceived one last opportunity for annoying Herbert and Carrie. Let them call her a wicked old woman! she knew that she was no such thing. The child was an artist and must have her way. There were other people in plenty to carry on the work of the world, to earn and enjoy its rewards, to suffer its malice and return its wounds in kind; the small and rare fraternity to which Deborah belonged, indifferent to gilded lures, should be free to go obscurely but ardently about its business. In the long run, with the strange bedlam always in process of sorting itself out, as the present-day became history, the poets and the prophets counted for more than the conquerors. Christ himself was of their company.

She could form no estimate of Deborah's talents; that was beside the point. Achievement was good, but the spirit was better. To reckon by achievements was to make a concession to the prevailing system of the world; it was a departure from the austere, disinterested, exacting standards that Lady Slane and her kindred recognised. Yet what she said was not at all in accordance with her thoughts; she said, "Oh dear, if I hadn't given away that fortune I could have made you independent."

Deborah laughed. She wanted advice, she said, not money. Lady Slane knew very well that she did not really want advice either; she wanted only to be strengthened and supported in her resolution. Very well, if she wanted approval, she should have it. "Of course you are right, my dear," she said quietly.

They talked for a while longer, but Deborah, feeling herself folded into peace and sympathy, noticed that her great-grandmother's mind wandered a little into some maze of confusion to which Deborah held no guiding thread. It was natural at Lady Slane's age. At moments she appeared to be talking about herself, then recalled her wits, and with pathetic clumsiness tried to cover up the slip, rousing herself to speak eagerly of the girl's future, not of some event which had gone wrong in the distant past. Deborah was too profoundly lulled and happy to wonder much what that event could be. This hour of union with the old woman soothed her like music, like chords lightly touched in the evening, with the shadows closing and the moths bruising beyond an open window. She leaned against the old woman's knee as a support, a prop, drowned, enfolded, in warmth, dimness, and soft harmonious sounds. The hurly-burly receded; the clangour was stilled; her grandfather and her great-aunt Carrie lost their angular importance and shrivelled to little gesticulating puppets with parchment faces and silly wavering hands; other values rose up like great archangels in the room, and towered and spread their wings. Inexplicable associations floated into Deborah's mind; she remembered how once she had seen a young woman in a white dress leading a white borzoi across the darkness of a southern port. This physical and mental contact with her great-grandmother—so far removed in years, so closely attuned in spirit—stripped off the coverings from the small treasure of short experience that she had jealously stored away. She caught herself wondering whether she could afterwards recapture the incantation of this hour sufficiently to render it into terms of music. Her desire to render an experience in terms of music transcended even her interest in her great-grandmother as a human being; a form of egoism which she knew her great-grandmother would neither resent nor misunderstand. The impulse which had led her to her great-grandmother was a right impulse. The sense of enveloping music proved that. On some remote piano the chords were struck, and they were chords which had no meaning, no existence, in the world inhabited by her grandfather and her great-aunt Carrie; but in her great-grandmother's world they had their value and their significance. But she must not tire her great-grandmother, thought Deborah, suddenly realising that the old voice had ceased its maunderings and that the spell of an hour was broken. Her great-grandmother was asleep. Her chin had fallen forward on to the laces at her breast. Her lovely hands were limp in their repose. As Deborah rose silently, and silently let herself out into the street, being careful not to slam the door behind her, the chords of her imagination died away.

Genoux, bringing in the tray an hour later, announcing *"Miladi est servie,"* altered her formula to a sudden, *"Mon Dieu, mais qu'est-ce que c'est ça—Miladi est morte."*

"It was to be expected," said Carrie, mopping her eyes as she had not mopped them over the death of her father; "it was to be expected, Mr. Bucktrout. Yet it comes as a shock. My poor mother was such a very exceptional woman, as you know—though I'm sure I don't see how you should have known it, for she was, of course, only your tenant. A correspondent in *The Times* described her this morning as a rare spirit. Just what I always said myself: a rare spirit." Carrie had forgotten the many other things she had said. "A little difficult to manage sometimes," she added, stung by a sudden thought of FitzGeorge's fortune; "unpractical to a degree, but practical things are not the only things that count, are they, Mr. Bucktrout?" *The Times* had said that too. "My poor mother had a beautiful nature. I don't say that I should always have acted myself as she sometimes acted. Her motives were sometimes a little difficult to follow. Quixotic, you know, and—shall we say?—injudicious. Besides, she could be very stubborn. There were times when she wouldn't be guided, which was unfortunate, considering how unpractical she was. We should all be in a very different position now had she been willing to listen to us. However, it's no good crying over spilt milk, is it?" said Carrie, giving Mr. Bucktrout what was meant to be a brave smile.

Mr. Bucktrout made no answer. He disliked Carrie. He wondered how anyone so hard and so hypocritical could be the daughter of someone so sensitive and so honest as his old friend. He was determined to reveal to Carrie by no word or look how deeply he felt the loss of Lady Slane.

"There is a man downstairs who can take the measurements for the coffin, should you wish," he said.

Carrie stared. So they had been right about this Mr. Bucktrout: a heartless old man, lacking the decency to find one suitable phrase about poor mother; Carrie herself had been generous enough to repeat those words about the rare spirit; really, on the whole, she considered her little oration over her mother to be a very generous tribute, when one remembered the tricks her mother had played on them all. She had felt extremely righteous as she pronounced it, and according to her code Mr. Bucktrout ought to have said something graceful in reply. No doubt he had expected to pull some plums out of the pudding himself, and had been embittered by his failure. The thought of the old shark's discomfiture was Carrie's great consolation. Mr. Bucktrout was just the sort of man who tried to hook an unsuspecting old lady. And now, full of revengefulness, he fell back on bringing a man to make the coffin.

"My brother, Lord Slane, will be here shortly to make all the necessary arrangements," she replied haughtily.

Mr. Gosheron, however, was already at the door. He came in tilting his bowler hat, but whether he tilted it towards the silent presence of Lady Slane in her bed, or towards Carrie standing at the foot, was questionable. Mr. Gosheron in his capacity as an undertaker was well accustomed to death; still, his feeling for Lady Slane had always been much warmer than for a mere client. He had already tried to give some private expression to his emotion by determining to sacrifice his most treasured piece of wood as the lid for her coffin.

"Her ladyship makes a lovely corpse," he said to Mr. Bucktrout.

They both ignored Carrie.

"Lovely in life, lovely in death, is what I always say," said Mr. Gosheron. "It's astonishing, the beauty that death brings out. My old grandfather told me that, who was in the same line of business, and for fifty years I've watched to see if his words were true. 'Beauty in life,' he used to say, 'may come from good dressing and what-not, but for beauty in death you have to fall back on character.' Now look at her ladyship, Mr. Bucktrout. Is it true, or isn't it? To tell you the truth," he added confidentially, "if I want to size a person up, I look at them and picture them dead. That always gives it away, especially as they don't know you're doing it. The first time I ever set eyes on her ladyship, I said, yes, she'll do; and now that I see her as I pictured her then I still say it. She wasn't never but half in this world, anyhow."

"No, she wasn't," said Mr. Bucktrout, who, now that Mr. Gosheron had arrived, was willing to talk about Lady Slane, "and she never came to terms with it either. She had the best that it could give her—all the things she didn't want. She considered the lilies of the field, Mr. Gosheron."

"She did, Mr. Bucktrout; many a phrase out of the Bible have I applied to her ladyship. But people will stand things in the Bible that they won't stand in common life. They don't seem to see the sense of it when they meet it in their own homes, although they'll put on a reverent face when they hear it read out from a lectern."

Oh goodness, thought Carrie, will these two old men never stop talking across mother like a Greek chorus? She had arrived at Hampstead in a determined frame of mind: she would be generous, she would be forgiving—and some genuine emotion had come to her aid—but now her self-possession cracked and her ill-temper and grievances came boiling up. This agent and this undertaker, who talked so securely and so sagaciously, what could they know of her mother?

"Perhaps," she snapped, "you had better leave my mother's funeral oration to be pronounced by one of her own family."

Mr. Bucktrout and Mr. Gosheron both turned gravely towards her. She saw them suddenly as detached figures; figures of fun certainly, yet also figures of justice. Their eyes stripped away the protection of her decent hypocrisy. She felt that they judged her; that Mr. Gosheron, according to his use and principle, was imagining her as a corpse; was narrowing his eyes to help the effort of his imagination; was laying her out upon a bed, examining her without the defences she could no longer control. That phrase about the rare spirit shrivelled to a cinder. Mr. Bucktrout and Mr. Gosheron were in league with her mother, and no phrases could cover up the truth from such an alliance.

"In the presence of death," she said to Mr. Gosheron, taking refuge in a last convention, "you might at least take off your hat."

PART IX

POEMS

Vita's poetry is very much of her time and place. This is definitely the least modern side of her writing, and yet we can scarcely fail to be aware of the richness of her natural perception, the high color of her love for places and persons.

Travel Poems

Vita's love of travel was, of course, paramount. Her poems, whether from Turkey, from Persia, or from Provence, all depict her ability to observe what was new, specific to the geography, and in the long run most unforgettable. Her 1913 poem about Constantinople was written when Harold was posted there as third secretary in the British Embassy, and they were living in their first married quarters, on a hill overlooking the Bosphorus. It was part of Eight Poems, *published privately in 1915. After returning from Persia, which had inspired her superb travel book* Passenger to Teheran, *that land was always in her memory. It provided the model for her famous White Garden at Sissinghurst. From Isfahan, she had brought back the blue beads celebrated in one poem, and of which she had given a string, after a night together, to the adoring Christopher St. John (Christabel Marshall, who called herself St. John out of fervor for Catholicism and St. John the Baptist). Vita's affairs were, like her travels, nothing if not exotic.*

Her travel poems, of which a selection is included here, are in general associated with an object, like that bowl of blue beads, or a person to whom the poem is dedicated explicitly (for example, to Hilda Matheson) or implicitly (Evelyn Irons). Of all places she liked touring, France, where she traveled widely, held her interest longest; her 1928 trip with Virginia Woolf, from which her diary is published in this volume, is the most well-known of those voyages. In 1929, she traveled in the Val d'Isère in the Savoie with Hilda Matheson, director of talks for the BBC, thus the dedication to her of the poem about the storm in the mountains. In 1931, she traveled in Provence with her new love, Evelyn Irons, the thirty-year-old Scot who was editor of the women's page for the Daily Mail.

The landscape and feeling of Provence are particularly sensed in the poems set in the high then-deserted town of Les Baux above St. Rémy, memorializing both their love and that high ruin of rock, which she designated in one of these poems the "Temple of Love." Vita's intense love of Provence was reawakened when she was 63 and on a driving trip with Harold. She describes in a letter to Alvilde Lees-Milne (also a friend of Violet Trefusis, thus providing the triangular love tension Vita so cherished) the scenery through the Gorges of the Tarn and the high and beautiful Provençal scenery between Sisteron and Digne. For Vita, nothing is lost, everything intensified by the accumulating affairs, and she retains her gift of friendship along with her more ephemeral and more passionate involvements. Each emotion is clarified by its setting. This letter dates from October 13, 1955, and was written from Aix, recalling that trip: "Oh goodness what a beautiful country it is, from Brantôme to Aix we have had nothing but one beauty after the other. The Dordogne was flaming red and gold, the Gorges du Tarn more tremendous than I had imagined, never having been there before, and of course Provence is always like itself. Have you ever been to Roussillon? A blood-red village, the colours of Coulonges-la-Rouge, with a canyon of cliffs to match?"

And Vita's enthusiasm was always awakened every time by travel, to which the poems included here bear witness, just as her poems The Land *and* The Garden *speak, at far greater length, of her love of Sussex. Even the poem about Charleston, South Carolina, written on her last stop with Harold and just after their visit to the Grand Canyon, during her lecture trip to the United States in 1933, recalls England, which she greatly missed. Always and everywhere, she is fully aware of place.*

"THE MUEZZIN" (CONSTANTINOPLE, 1913)

Above the city at his feet,
Above the dome, above the sea,
He rises unconfined and free
To break upon the noonday heat.

He turns around the parapet,
Black-robed against the marble tower;
His singing gains or loses power
In pacing round the minaret.

A brother to the singing birds
He never knew restraining walls,
But freely rises, freely falls
The rhythm of the sacred words.

I would that it to me were given
To climb each day the muezzin's stair
And in the warm and silent air
To sing my heart out into heaven.

"A BOWL OF BLUE BEADS" (1928)

I bought these beads in Isfahan;
I bought a handful for a kran,
—That's sixpence—at the motley stall
Against the Meidan's northern wall,
At evening when the plane-tree's cool
Shadow blessed the dirty pool,

And the great arch of the bazaar
Gaped like a cave crepuscular.
Blue beads to keep the evil eye
Away as horse and mule go by
Through narrow streets between the brown
High walls of mud that make the town,
And gain the melon-fields that lie
Where the desert meets the sky.

Now, in a bowl, in exile, they
Speak Persia to an English day;
Blue as the skies that once in March
Were framed for me beneath the arch
Of a ruined caravanserai.
And oh, how glad, how glad am I
That Persia is no lovely lie
For me, but sharp reality.

—February 1928

"PERSIA" (1928)

The passes are blocked by snow.
No word comes through, no message, and no letter.
Only the eagles plane above the snow,
And wolves come down upon the villages.
The barrier of mountains is the end,
The edge of the world to us in wintry Persia.
We are self-contained, shut off.
Only the telegraph ticks out its flimsy sheets,
Bringing the distant news of deaths of princes.
Day after day the cold and marvellous sun
Rides in the cold, the pale, the marvellous heaven,
Cutting the blue and icy folds of shadow
Aslant the foothills where the snow begins.
So would I have it, pure in isolation,
With scarcely a rumour of the varied world
Leaping the mountain-barrier in disturbance.

Are there not hearts that find their high fulfilment
Alone, with ice between them and their friends?

"NOSTALGIA" (1932)

That day must come, when I shall leave my friends,
My loves, my garden, and the bush of balm
That grows beside my door, for the world's ends:

A Persian valley where I might find calm.

And this is no romance, the place is no
Vague lovely Persia of a poet's tale,
But a very valley where some cornfields grow
And peasants beat the harvest with a flail.

I saw it, as I saw the pigeon-towers
Streaked white with dung, and goat-kids born in blood;
And saw the early almond spray its flowers
Through breaches in the wall of sun-burnt mud.

Brutality and beauty shared the sun;
Necessity of crops the river-bed;
And I without such sunlight am undone,
Without such rivers wilt unharvested.

"PALMYRA" (1927)

This is the street of a hundred golden columns,
But the pavement is of sand;
Sand of the desert, a white, a wind-blown
Forgotten strand.

These are the columns that were raised by Arabs,
Arabs who had heard of Rome;
But the wild bees hang in the arches to build
Their honey-comb.

Sand of the desert has blown and silted
Half a column high;
Now no longer the proud Odenathus
Goes riding by.

Only a caravan of laden camels
Slouching with noiseless pad,
Goes stringing out at dawn on the desert
Towards Baghdad.

"STORM IN THE MOUNTAINS" (SAVOY, 1929)

For Hilda Matheson

The rags of storm are on the hills;

The gathering dusk is shot with light;
One peak is dark, another bright,
And every vein of valley fills,
With wind as on a message sent:
The thunder bruises through the clouds,
And spears of lightning tear the shrouds
Behind the mountains' tattered tent,
But distant still the muted storm
Waiting, like anger, for the spark,
Delays in masses bright and dark,
And drapes with threat the ranges' form,
Yet will not break.
Those slatted beams stand upright from the mountains' flanks
As laddered for celestial ranks
In tall and misty golden gleams.
Enormous stage, with curtains hung
Of mournful purple in the deeps,
And midnight blue upon the steeps
From ropes of slanting sunlight slung,
And solitude that empty holds
The scarp, the crag, the valleys' cleft,
As though no son of man were left
To stride between the curtains' folds!

The butterflies that fanned the stone
With azure or with speckled wing
Are fled before the shadowing;
A few last fugitives are blown
About the upland meadow's slope
In wild and windy path too frail
To choose a way before the gale,
But still held up on gusty hope,
Unlike the lowly, rooted flowers
That tethered to their fate remain,
Among the grass a painted stain
In sunny or in savage hours,
Such hours as they, familiar, knew
Since first upon a shaping world
The veils of such a storm were furled,
And peaks rose up, and gentians grew.

"MIDDLETON PLACE, SOUTH CAROLINA" (1933)

Stand I indeed in England? Do I dream?
Those broken steps, those grassy terraces,

Those water-meadows and that ample stream,
Those woods that take the curve of distances,
Those still reflections mirrored in the faint
And milky waters under milky skies
     That Constable might paint,
Do they indeed but cheat my heart, my eyes,
With their strange likeness to the thing they seem?

Tricked at each turn by nature's difference
Englishmen came, and cut their English shapes
Out of the virgin forest and the dense
Tangle of branches loaded with wild grapes;
Pointing their axis to the river's bend,
Sleepy as Thames.
Content as one who finds
     An unexpected friend
In alien lands where blood more closely binds,
Rejoiced they at the forced coincidence.
  . . .
Look closer; never in an English glade
Flashed scarlet wings, nor grew the northern larch
In onyx pools as here the cypress staid;
Nor flamed the azalea in an English March
Down paths of fallen petals, aisle on aisle;
Nor climbed the tall liana to the sun,
     Nor squatted near a pile
Of oranges, their morning labour done,
That group of negroes idle in the shade.

Nor from the branches hung the parasite
Of greybeard moss bewitching ancient trees,
Blowing aslant through ilex-woods at night
In pointed cobwebs streaming on the breeze;
Singular veils of spectral nameless plot,
The unrelated symbol of a spell
     Once potent, now forgot;
Some lost mythology of woods where dwell
The shorn and lockless spirits shunning light.

Pensive within its evening of decay
The garden slopes towards the river reaches;
Deepens the sunset of the southern day
In sombre ilexes and coral peaches.
No England! but a look, an echoing tone
Such as may cross the voice of distant kin,
     Caught briefly, swiftly flown,

Different in resemblance, held within
A heart still mindful of the English way.
—Charleston, South Carolina, April 1933

OTHER POEMS

Although her upbringing in privilege and her decidedly chilly attitude toward those of different classes might seem to disqualify Vita Sackville-West for the idealized role of female intellectual, her extraordinary production and passion in relation to creativity and literary life go far to combat that.

Vita spent much of her life writing and lecturing for the radio and literary audience on society and on gardening, on England, its literature and its history, and on her travels. From her early diary entry about the first fee she earned for writing a poem to her essays on other poets, her deep concern with things of the mind is clear. Her small book on Alexander Marvell contains a wonderful passage on the word (and color) "green," reflecting, as in her other writing, her care for the meaningful literary detail. Her unpublished lecture "Some Tendencies of Modern English Poetry," given October 17, 1926, and her unpublished story "The Poetry Reading," reveal, perhaps as much as her own poetry, her concern with that particular genre, her favorite.

Vita spent much of her time at Sissinghurst in her writing tower, coming down for meals, and that, not always. Even on her travels she was constantly writing poems. She wanted above all, says her son Nigel, to be known as a poet. Her poetry can only be evaluated as part of its time and place. This is definitely the part of her work that seems the least "modernist." But her poems, including "The Land" and "The Garden," depend on the whole and very English tradition of writing about the land and the seasons: James Thompson's The Seasons forms the background for her epic poems of working the land, and of loving it. Also, her love of gardening informs her writing of these epic works, and if they seem to us at the present moment somewhat sentimental, we can scarcely fail to be aware of the richness of her natural perception, the high color of her love.

If we can lay aside our preconceived notions of what twentieth-century poetry is meant to be, even in the early part of the century, we can enter the stateliness and interior order of these verses, provided we take the time. It is a privilege to do so.

"WINTER AFTERNOON"

Summer may boast her sweets, but sterner days
Strip country bare and gild the nervous trees
With an ancient light that summer never knew,

Low and experienced sun, aslant, askew,
Old man of seasons bent on crooked knees.

(See, on the moat's embankment, like a frieze,
The slow procession leads the punctual hour
Across the primrose of the evening's flower:
Two heifers treading the appointed ways,
Followed by man with stick
And waddling cygnet and a dozen ducks
Strung out in ludicrous yet due design,
In grave march, never quick,
All homing in their usual evening line.)

Here is no colour, here but gold and ash.
Cold, cold the night will be; the dusk is chilled
Already with the winter's coiling lash;
Earth to the moon will blanch.
Yet, rare musician sumptuously skilled,
The sunlight with a sinking finger plucks.
Last notes from each bare branch.
Goldsmith of fields already brownly tilled
Gilder of ridges left behind the plough,
Layer of gold-leaf where no leaf remains,
The sunlight in an aged actor's bow
Takes rich and low farewell of summer's strains.

Ah, with what beauty did he touch the trees,
Ah, with what beauty did he touch the fields.
So delicate, so rich, so altering a touch
It held the heart confuted in a clutch;
An altering touch that magnified the heart
And set it from the cannon apart.
Such moments come and shatter prudent shields
Our poor reminders of mortalities.

(See, up the track come waggons strongly drawn,
Passing the window with their outer life;
Trusses of fodder, timber newly sawn
Loads for a sturdy team.
The ruts are frosted, and the horses steam with foot-fall effort up
    the lane;
The carter's boy alongside leaves the rein,
And pares a hazel switch with sharpened knife.
How calm, how strong, how permanent, how sane,
The venerable necessary theme!)

Is this the world's last day so placid seen
Earth and her beasts and men and women's range?
So, for a million years, has life worked on
Varied from continent to continent

From Asia to a patch of little Kent,
A ploughshare carving through the centuries.
Is this the world's last day, that may exchange
Traditions for catastrophes?
All effort, patient or heroic, gone?
The little knowledge perilously won
Since men desire, enquire, and still aspire,
Scrapped on a planet's paltry pyre
To perish half-way done?

Reprieve and ruin, ruin and reprieve.
Still the dread sentence rumbles like a far
Delaying storm above the herded sheep,
So long delaying that the soul takes leave
In reassurance still to disbelieve,
And still to live, and still to sow and reap.
Still rises once again the evening star
In ordered juncture as we, singly blest,
Turn our brave planet to a further rest
And let our hamlets fold themselves in sleep.

"The Intellectual to His Puppy"

Golden lad, what art thou eating?
Feathered slipper, silken sock?
Filthy muck I call manure?
Drop it, drop it, pretty sweeting.
That's a trick I can't endure.

Little one, what art thou doing?
Puddles on my Persian rug?
O poetry
Out with you, you dirty varmint,
Make them on the garden dug.

That's the place for all your messes,
But you must not bury bones
Where our precious plants are planted,
Nor between our paving stones.

"THE PUPPY TO HIS NEW OWNER"

Naughty, naughty, always naughty.
How can puppies hope to please?
All you folk are far too haughty,
Far too tidy, far too smart.
What I want's a loving heart.
Oh this place is far too cold!
And the place where I was wanted,
Where I came from—that was home.
Not this place where it is always
"Brandy, no! hey nonny, NO!"

"IN MEMORIAM: VIRGINIA WOOLF"

[with Vita's changes after publication in *The Observer,* April 1941]

Many words crowd, and all and each unmeaning.
The simplest words in sorrow are the best.

So let us say, she loved the water-meadows,
The Downs; her friends; her books; her memories;
The room which was her own.
London by twilight; shops and Mrs. Brown;

Donne's church; the Strand; the buses, and the large
Smell of humanity that passed her by.

I remember she told me once that she, a child,
Trapped evening moths with honey round a tree-trunk,
And with a lantern watched their antic flight.
So she, a poet, caught her special prey
With words of honey and lamp of wit.

Frugal, austere, fine, proud,
Rich in her contradictions, rich in love,
So did she capture all her moth-like self:
Her fluttered spirit, delicate and soft,
Bumping against the lamp of life, too hard, too glassy,

Yet kept a sting beneath the brushing wing,
Her blame astringent and her praise supreme.

How small, how petty seemed the little men
Measured against her scornful quality.

Some say, she lived in an unreal world,
Cloud-cuckoo-land. Maybe. She now has gone
Into the prouder world of immortality.

POEMS OF HOUSE, LAND, AND SEASONS

Vita's love of her homes and her land often finds its expression in her poetry. The
Land *and* The Garden, *as well as "Sissinghurst" and "Winter Afternoon," speak*
abundantly of that feeling.

On Sissinghurst

Vita's intense and enduring attachment to Sissinghurst appears frequently in the many
forms of her writing. In a letter to Alvilde Lees-Milne of December 11, 1954, she ex-
claims: "I can't tell you how much it touches me that you should have this apprecia-
tion of my odd inconvenient Sissinghurst. You seem to understand it; and it takes a
great deal of understanding. I wish you had seen it in the full moonlight two nights
ago. It was a dream of unreality." Everything about Sissinghurst was of great appeal to
Vita, even the times when the garden was barren of flowers, and all of it typified her
beloved Kent. In another letter to Alvilde Lees-Milne of September 2, 1955, she exclaims
how "The whole of Sissinghurst reeks of hops, which I find an agreeably Kentish smell."

Vita began this long poem in 1930, immediately after acquiring Sissinghurst. It is
dedicated to Virginia Woolf, whose Hogarth Press published it in 1931.

"SISSINGHURST"

A tired swimmer in the waves of time
I throw my hands up: let the surface close:
Sink down through centuries to another clime,
And buried find the castle and the rose.
Buried in time and sleep,
So drowsy, overgrown,
That here the moss is green upon the stone,
And lichen stains the keep.
I've sunk into an image, water-drowned,
Where stirs no wind and penetrates no sound,
Illusive, fragile to a touch, remote,
Foundered within the well of years as deep
As in the waters of a stagnant moat.
Yet in and out of these decaying halls
I move, and not a ripple, not a quiver,
Shakes the reflection though the waters shiver—

My tread is to the same illusion bound.
Here, tall and damask as a summer flower,
Rise the brick gable and the spring tower;
Invading Nature crawls
With ivied fingers over rosy walls,
Searching the crevices,
Clasping the mullion, riveting the crack,
Binding the fabric crumbling to attack,
And questing feelers of the wandering fronds
Grope for interstices,
Holding this myth together under-seas,
Anachronistic vagabonds!
And here, by birthright far from present fashion,
As no disturber of the mirrored trance
I move, and to the world above the waters
Wave my incognisance.
For here, where days and years have lost their number,
I let a plummet down in lieu of date,
And lose myself within a slumber
Submerged, elate.
This husbandry, this castle, and this I
Moving within the deeps,
Shall be content within our timeless spell,
Assembled fragments of an age gone by,
While still the sower sows, the reaper reaps,
Beneath the snowy mountains of the sky,
And meadows dimple to the village bell.
So plods the stallion up my evening lane
And fills me with a mindless deep repose,
Wherein I find in chain
The castle, and the pasture, and the rose.

Beauty, and use, and beauty once again
Link up my scattered heart, and shape a scheme
Commensurate with a frustrated dream.

The autumn bonfire smokes across the woods
And reddens in the water of the moat;
As red within the water burns the scythe,
And the moon dwindled to her gibbous tithe
Follows the sunken sun afloat.
Green is the eastern sky and red the west;
The hop-kilns huddle under pallid hoods;
The waggon stupid stands with upright shaft,
As daily life accepts the night's arrest.
Night like a deeper sea engulfs the land,
The castle, and the meadows, and the farm;

Only the baying watch-dog looks for harm,
And shakes his chain towards the lunar brand.

In the high room where tall the shadows tilt

For now the apple ripens, now the hop,
And now the clover, now the barley-crop;
Spokes bound upon a wheel forever turning,
Wherewith I turn, no present manner learning;
Cry neither "Speed your processes!" nor "Stop!"
I am content to leave the world awry
(Busy with politic perplexity,)
If still the cart-horse at the fall of day
Clumps up the lane to stable and to hay,
And tired men go home from the immense
Labour and life's expense
That force the harsh recalcitrant waste to yield
Corn and not nettles in the harvest-field;
As candle-flames blow crooked in the draught,
The reddened sunset on the panes was spilt,
But now as black as any nomad's tent
The night-time and the night of time have blent
Their darkness, and the waters doubly sleep.
Over my head the years and centuries sweep,
The years of childhood flown,
The centuries unknown;
I dream; I do not weep.

—1930

FROM *THE GARDEN* (1946)

Presented here is a large portion of the last part of The Garden, *entitled "Autumn," which won the Heinemann prize for poetry. Although Vita began* The Garden *in 1926 as a companion to the prizewinning* The Land, *she set it aside and didn't resume writing it until 1939. She worked on the poem intermittently over the war years; it was published in 1946 by Michael Joseph in London.* The Land *and* The Garden *were republished together in 1989 by Webb and Bower in London.*

AUTUMN

Autumn in felted slipper shuffles on,
Muted yet fiery—Autumn's character.
Brown as a monk yet flaring as a whore,

And in the distance blue as Raphael's robe
Tender around the Virgin.
    Blue the smoke
Drifting across brown woods; but in the garden
Maples are garish, and surprising leaves
Make sudden fires with sudden crests of flame
Where the sun hits them; in the deep-cut leaf
Of peony, like a mediaeval axe
Of rusty iron; fervour of azalea
Whose dying days repeat her June of flower;
In Sargent's cherry, upright as a torch
Till ravelled sideways by the wind to stream
Disorderly, and strew the mint of sparks
In coins of pointed metal, cooling down;
And that true child of Fall, whose morbid fruit
Ripens, with walnuts, only in November,

The Medlar lying brown across the thatch;
Rough elbows of rough branches, russet fruit
So blet it's worth no more than sleepy pear,
But in its motley pink and yellow leaf
A harlequin that some may overlook
Nor ever think to break and set within
A vase of bronze against a wall of oak,
With Red-hot Poker, Autumn's final torch.
The medlar and the quince's globe of gold.
How rich and fat those yellow fruits do hang!
They were light blossom once, a light-foot girl,
All cream and muslin once, now turned to age
Mellow with fine experience. The sun
Burnt in one season what the years must need
For a girl's ripening. He was the lover
In dilatory half-awakened Spring;
He was the husband of the fruitful Summer,
Father of pregnancy that brings those fruits
Ready to drop at the first touch of hand
Carefully lifting at the parting stalk,
Or at the first wild breath of wind, so soft
You think it harmless, till it blows the vanes
Crooked this way and that, a treacherous wind
Bringing the apples down before their date.

All's brown and red: the robin and the clods,
And umber half-light of the potting-shed,
The terra-cotta of the pots, the brown
Sacking with its peculiar autumn smell,

Musty in corners, where the cobweb panes
Filter the sun, to bronze the patient heaps
Of leaf-mould, loam, and tan of wholesome peat;
And sieves that orderly against the wall
Dangle from nail, with all the panoply
(Brightened by oily rag) of shining tools,
The gardener's armour, pewter as a lake,
And good brown wood in handles and in shafts;
Plump onion and thin bassen raffia
Slung from the rafters where the ladders prop.

And in the gloom, with his slow gesture, moves
The leathern demiurge of this domain,
Like an old minor god in corduroy
Setting and picking up the things he needs,
Deliberate as though all Time were his.
Honour the gardener! that patient man
Who from his schooldays follows up his calling,
Starting so modestly, a little boy
Red-nosed, red-fingered, doing what he's told,
Not knowing what he does or why he does it,
Having no concept of the larger plan.
But gradually (if the love be there,
Irrational as any passion, strong),
Enlarging vision slowly turns the key
And swings the door wide open on the long
Vistas of true significance. No more
Is toil a vacant drudgery, when purport
Attends each small and conscientious task
—As the stone-mason setting yard by yard
Each stone in place, exalting not his gaze
To measure growth of structure or assess
That slow accomplishment, but in the end
Tops the last finial and, stepping back
To wipe the grit for the last time from eyes,
Sees that he built a temple—so the true
Born gardener toils with love that is not toil
In detailed time of minutes, hours, and days,
Months, years, a life of doing each thing well;
The Life-line in his hand not rubbed away
As you might think, by constant scrape and rasp,
But deepened rather, as the line of Fate,
By earth imbedded in his wrinkled palm;
A golden ring worn thin upon his finger,
A signet ring, no ring of human marriage,
On that brown hand, dry as a crust of bread,

A ring that in its circle belts him close
To earthly seasons, and in its slow thinning
Wears out its life with his.
That hand, that broke with tenderness and strength
Clumps of the primrose and the primula,
Watched by a loving woman who desired
Such tenderness and strength to hold her close,
And take her passionate giving, as he held
His broken plants and set them in the ground,
New children; but he had no thought of her.
She only stood and watched his capable hand
Brown with the earth and golden with the ring,
And knew her part was small in his lone heart.
[Centered Ellipses, as shown here] . . .
As the poor orphan that the Fates maltreat
Toughens uncoddled in the frost, the sleet,
Expecting nothing else from world unkind
Where he who lives not, dies;
But at the first soft touch awakes to throw
Blossoms of thankfulness in wild surprise
Such different aspect of the world to find,
And in the kiss of sun forgets the snow.
So Autumn's not the end, not the last rung
Of any ladder in the yearly climb,
When that is deathly old which once was young,
Since time's no ladder but a constant wheel
Like an old paddled mill that dips and churns
The mill-race, and upon the summit turns
Unceasingly to heel
Over, and scoop fresh water out of time.

Autumn's a preparation for renewal,
Yet not entirely shorn
Of tardy beauty, last and saddest jewel
Bedizening where it may not adorn.
Few of the autumn blooms are deeply dear,
Lacking the spirit volatile and chaste
That blows across the ground when pied appear
The midget sweets of Spring, and in their haste
The vaporous trees break blossom pale and clear,
—Carpet and canopy, together born.
    . . .
Pack the dark fibre in the potter's bowl;
Set bulbs of hyacinth and daffodil,
Jonquil and crocus (bulbs both sound and whole),
Narcissus and the blue Siberian squill.

Set close, but not so tight
That flow'ring heads collide as months fulfil
Their purpose, and in generous sheaf expand
Obedient to th' arrangement of your hand.
Yours is the forethought, yours the sage control.

Keep the too eager bulbs from ardent light;
Store in a gloomy cupboard, not too chill;
Give grateful moisture to the roots unseen,
And wait until the nose of bleached shoot
Pushes its inches up, in evidence
That many worms of root
Writhe whitely down to fill
The darkness of the compost, tangled, dense.
Then may you set your bowls on window sill
And smile to see the pallor turn to green.
Fat, pregnant, solid horns, that overnight
Swell into buds, and overnight again
Explode in colour, morning's sudden stain,
In long succession, nicely planned between
Epiphany and Easter, if so be
Easter falls early and the window-pane
Still shows the fine the crisp anatomy
Of fern-like frosted frond,
And nothing in the waiting soil beyond.

But in October, later, shall you stand
With paper sack of bulbs and plunge your hand
And careless fling your bulbs both large and small
To roll, to topple, settling sparse or thick,
Over the grass, and plant them where they fall
(Legitimate device, a sanctioned trick).
Thus in a drift as though by Nature planned
Snowdrops shall blow in spreading tide,
Little white horses breaking on the strand
At edge of orchard; and the orange-eyed
Narcissus of the poets in a wide
Lyrical river flowing as you pass
Meandering along the path of grass.
. . .
Now the dark yew, that sombre secret soul,
Bears fruit, more coral than our ugly blood;
Bright wax within the green, a tallow stud
Most exquisite in substance and in form,
Strewn by the birds and by the soft wild storm
In sprinkled carpet underneath the bays

Of taxine carpentry, these autumn days.

The breeze that autumn night was hot and south.
I met a frog that carried in his mouth
One of those berries, on unknown intent.
So brisk, so earnest, in his ranine hurry,
I stood aside to let him take his bent.
He had his right to's life as I to mine;
I had my right to my descriptive line,
He had his right to his more precious berry.
I stopped, he hopped, I watched him where he went.
He had no fear of me and could not doubt
What love I had for him, that blebbed and queer
Visitant from the woodland mere
Who, gaudy with his berry sticking out,
Met me beneath the cavern of the porch
As we were meant to meet,
—Miniature monster circled at my feet
Within the coin of my miraculous torch.

He lowly, and the architectural porch so tall,
But he, in *his* way, also a miracle.
. . .
Low sinks the sun, and long the shadows fall.
The sun-clock, faithful measurer of time,
Fixed to man's dwelling on his flimsy wall
Or tabled flat on curving pedestal
Amongst his dying flowers, tells the last
Hours of the year as to a funeral,
With silent music, solemn and sublime.
Now is the sunlight ebbing, faint and fast
In intermittent gleams that seldom cut
Throughout the day the quadrant of our fate
With the slow stroke that says TOO SOON . . . TOO LATE . . .
The stroke that turns our present to our past.
BEWARE, THE OPEN GATE WILL SOON BE SHUT.

November sun that latens with our age,
Filching the zest from our young pilgrimage,
Writing old wisdom on our virgin page.
Not the hot ardour of the Summer's height,
Not the sharp-minted coinage of the Spring
When all was but a delicate delight
And all took wing and all the bells did ring;
Not the spare Winter, clothed in black and white,
Forcing us into fancy's eremite,

But gliding Time that slid us into gold
Richer and deeper as we grew more old
And saw some meaning in this dying day;
Travellers of the year, who faintly say
How could such beauty walk the common way?

. . .

POEMS OF PROVENCE

The Provence poems of 1931 are love poems to Evelyn Irons, the editor of the women's page of the Daily Mail. *Vita had been interviewed by Irons and then invited her to Sissinghurst; they fell in love. Sometime after Evelyn's March 6 visit, Vita wrote what she called a "diary poem," a spontaneous poem not intended for publication. In contrast to the formal lyricism of her other poems, it reads in part:*

> *This is pain.*
> *I recognize it.*
> *I feared I had forgotten how to feel it.*
> *I feared, that I was so lapped in happiness and security,*
> *That I had forgotten the sting of pain, of sensation;*
> *But here is the familiar turmoil, the stinging.*
> *I welcome it; I fear it; I welcome my own fear of it.*
> *I am glad to find that I can still be afraid of my own sensations.*
> *I am glad to find that I can still be swept by a sensation I cannot logi-*
> *   cally explain to others;*
> *That I am still capable of an irrational passion,*
> *I who had grown so ordered, rational,*
> *I have established my contact with irrational humanity. . . .*

    In the fall of 1931, Vita went with Evelyn to Provence, a trip that she led Harold to believe she was taking alone. They walked from Tarascon to Les Baux, and then visited Arles and Nîmes. Later, Vita wrote "Egypt, Egypt, Egypt" over her diary entries about the episode and changed the "we" to "I," in case Harold should see the diary. All Passion Spent, *about which Vita was less enthusiastic than the public, appeared at the time of her deepest involvement with Evelyn Irons, who lends her name to the heroine of* Family History, *the next of Vita's novels.*

    After Vita's involvement with Violet Trefusis, clearly the most important of her lesbian affairs, that with Evelyn Irons seems to many the most interesting. Evelyn and Vita had worked out their complex relationship as being deliciously many-sided, each of them sharing two genders. Evelyn lived with Olive Rinder, who became understandably jealous, fell ill, and gave up her job. (Vita would support her in later years.) In exasperation, Evelyn wrote Vita, "Damn my married life, as well as yours."[1] Predictably,

since it had happened so many times that Vita was at the center of a triangular affair,
Olive in her turn fell in love with Vita, causing yet another of what Harold and Vita
called Vita's "muddles" or "scrapes." [2]

"The Quarryman (*Les Baux*)"

Surly, the generations sent him out,
Climbing a path as stony as his life,
Through valleys aromatic in the drought
With thyme and lavender among the boulders;
The fierce sun dried his shirt upon his shoulders,
And in his pocket warmed the clasped knife.

But in the quarries underneath the hill
The shadow bent its knee across the portal;
The sun died instantly in sudden chill,
And in the catacombs of tunnelled stone
The candid chips lay strewn as fleshless bone,
And candid shelves awaited urns immortal.

He dumped his saw, his mattock, and his pick;
He dumped his bundle on a handy ledge;
And then by his prepared arithmetic
Spat on his palms and fell to work begun
On similar mornings when the thwarted sun
Into the shadowed pylon drove its wedge.
He laboured, never raising eye from line;
One block completed cost him twenty days;
He gave his life to an unseen design,
Sculptor of mountains while he thought to carve
A living, that his children should not starve,
And with the sunset clattered down his ways.

He laboured at his subterranean craft,
Not seeing that the while, square temple rose,
Roofed over by a mountain, apse and shaft,
Deep-driven, pillared into ivory halls,
Luminous galleries and virgin walls,
Unfinished altars, white as drifted snows.

Through the soft limestone hissed the rhythmic saw;
The stone was hard without, but soft within,
As he, whose hard exterior hid the flaw
Of softness prey to ignorance and doubt;

How grey, how beaten by the years without,
How white, how tender when the tests begin!

New shapes, new planes, undreamed by architect;
An accidental beauty, born of need;
Beauty of angles, vertical, erect,
And monolithic as a sea-cut cave
Where the withdrawal of the millionth wave
Leaves the smooth surface when the tides recede.

To what new god he left it dedicate,
This straight new temple lit by crooked day,
The smokeless altars, and the height elate,
The slabs for sacrifice, the mounting stairs,
The naves and transepts risen unawares,
The sunlight and the shadow, who shall say?

                                                           1931

"The Temple Of Love (*Les Baux*)"

To put a circle round the courts of Love,
I need but slip a ring upon your finger,
And swear—brown earth beneath, blue skies above,
In vineyards where the latened clusters linger—
That I will love you till this you, this I,
Give our dear flesh to worm or else to ash,
Rotting in earth or smoking to the sky,
When Death, at last, brings down his scarlet slash.

Such easy uses whispered in your ear
Reach you as lovers' threadbare vows perhaps,
And yet, perennial as the vintage here,
They hold their truth beyond such brief collapse,
Lifting me to the realms where constant are
The dark companion and uncertain star.

                                                           —1931

"Dawn (*Les Baux*)"

What archer shot that arrow through my panes?
A huntress moon that flees the hunter day,
Or hunter day that masculine arraigns
His right above his Cynthia's soft affray?
An arrow in my heart; I am transfixed;

A bow in heaven snapped; the arrow sticks;
My window widens; Phoebus in pursuit
Chases a Cynthia wan and dissolute.

—1931

PART X

ANIMAL REFLECTIONS

One of Vita's more engaging traits was her keen fondness for animals—and, in partic-
ular, for dogs of all breeds. She had many dogs over the years, often several at the same
time. When she would go to see Virginia Woolf, the latter would write her to "come and
be sure to bring Sally," one of Vita's dogs. Pictures abound of Vita and her dogs, of Vita
and Leonard Woolf and the dogs of the two households, or of Vita and her sons and
dogs. In one of Virginia Woolf's famous descriptions of Vita, she sees her striding across
her fields, accompanied by her many noble-featured dogs.

From *Faces* (1961)

Vita's reflections on various dogs, included in the rare volume Faces, are full of humor, affection, and history, both of dog lore and Vita's personal experiences. Her unmistakably negative reaction to the sullen and unappealing Saluki that was given to her by Gertrude Bell in Persia (an event that she recounts at length in the pages of her Passenger to Teheran) is not allowed to influence her reaction here on these ultra-thin, ultra-chic, ultra-sensitive dogs.

Vita is at her most endearing when describing one of her cocker spaniels who gave birth at the same time as one of her cats and borrowed a few kittens to nurse along with the rest of the cocker litter; the Cocker was amused, the cat not a whit. Vita's sense of humor and play is given its full rein in these descriptions. These one-page pieces are among her most delightful productions.

Faces

The Saluki or Gazelle-Hound

The Saluki is an Arab; in fact, *saluk* in Arabic means hound, and it is further suggested, with some plausibility, that the breed originated in the town or district of Saluk. Possibly the oldest breed in the world, their portrait appears in mural paintings in Egyptian tombs, notably in the tomb of Rechmara 1400 B.C. This and the fact that they were also known in Persia and China, despite the reluctance of the Arabs to part with their dogs, implies that they were greatly valued for their swiftness and endurance in hunting and formed an acceptable present to the princes of those distant lands. "Oh my Huntsman," writes a Persian poet in 800 A.D., "bring me my dogs brought by the Kings of Saluk," and remarked further that a Saluki ran so fast that his feet and his head seemed joined in his collar, which is scarcely surprising when we reflect that they were used in the pursuit of gazelle, antelope, and hare. If the cheetah is the swiftest animal on earth, the Saluki must run it very close.

They enjoyed also the honour of being modelled by Benvenuto Cellini for Cosimo de Medici.

These most romantic of dogs were practically unknown in England before the end of the nineteenth century. A Mr. Allen, in the 1880s, had exhibited one Jierma, whose unusual grace aroused much excitement and caused her to be mistakenly described as a Persian greyhound. But it was not until after 1895, when the Hon. Florence Amherst was presented with two puppies bred by sheikhs of a Bedouin tribe, that the breed became established here and caught the popular imagination to such an extent that some exhibitors added an Eastern glamour to the proceedings by appearing in full native dress.

Salukis resemble their native desert in colouring, as any traveller familiar with the desert under varying lights will agree. They may be a plain pale tan, or grizzled, or golden, or cream, or even white as some of the sand-dunes. The lovely creature in the photograph displays the silky ears, and undoubtedly possesses also "feathers" of the same texture down the back of the legs and on the curly tail. There are also smooth-coated Salukis with no feathers, to my mind less attractive.

I once had a Saluki, presented to me in Baghdad straight out of the desert by Miss Gertrude Bell, without exception the dullest dog I ever owned. Salukis are reputed to be very gentle and faithful; this one, Zurcha, meaning the yellow one, was gentle enough because she was completely spiritless, and as for fidelity she was faithful only to the best arm-chair. I took her up from Baghdad into Persia, where nothing would induce her to come out for a walk—perhaps because I omitted to provide a gazelle. In the end I followed the historical tradition and gave her to a Persian prince, who subsequently lost her somewhere in Moscow. I was unlucky, of course, in the only Saluki I ever owned, and these remarks must not be taken as an aspersion upon an incomparably elegant and ancient race.

The Cocker Spaniel

It is not surprising that this silky little creature should be so popular, for it combines sporting instincts in the field with domestic affection in the house, and as a puppy is irresistible. It would seem also that, the sporting instincts denied their scope, it can accommodate itself with the utmost resignation to an uneventful existence. No dog ever led a duller or more sedentary life than Miss Elizabeth Barrett's Flush, whose ears so closely resembled his mistress's curls.

And yet the very name *cocker* was specially applied to a spaniel small enough to penetrate the thick undergrowth where woodcock crouched concealed, and in the reign of Queen Elizabeth I was used to drive game and birds into nets. They are active little dogs, with nothing namby-pamby about them, in spite of a loving nature amounting to sentimentality. Their colour, according to taste, may be red, golden, tan, blue roan, black, or black and white, so there is plenty of variety to choose from.

It is thought that the spaniel originated in Spain, and in the beginning of their recorded history, which goes back to 1387, they were all generically known as spaniels. It was not until 1790 that they began to be divided into separate varieties. After that we get so many types that the amateur may be forgiven for a failure to disentangle them. There is the English Springer, the Clumber, the Sussex, the Welsh Springer, the Irish Water and the Field Spaniel, which is really a larger version of the Cocker. The main difference seems to lie in the size and weight; the Field may weigh anything from 35 lb. to 50 lb., the little Cocker should not exceed 28.

The solemn face in the illustration gives no idea of the cheerful disposition of one that is nicknamed the Merry Cocker. I believe also that they have a sense of humour; some dogs have. I once owned a golden cocker bitch and a cream Persian cat; the spaniel had puppies and the cat kittens at the same time, puppies and kittens being of exactly the same colour. The spaniel used to steal the kittens and deposit them amongst her own offspring, suckling them all indiscriminately, and I would swear that the little dog grinned up at me whenever I went to sort them out. I should add that the cat in her turn stole the puppies, but I was never able to discern the slightest trace of amusement on her face.

The Great Dane

Unlike the Dalmatian, the Great Dane may well come from the country which gives him his name, though he has also been claimed by Germany. This hugely alarming dog, like many large men, usually has the kindliest disposition; I feel sure he enjoyed carrying a lamp in his mouth ahead of benighted travellers, by his mere presence assuring them of their safety, as he was taught to do in the eighteenth century. He could also be sent back five or six miles to retrieve a forgotten parcel. These were among the services he was pleased to render.

It seems scarcely necessary to say that he should be wisely handled from puppyhood, for an undisciplined or irritable Great Dane is a terrifying thought. Even an amiable one, anxious to please, provides some elements of peril. Too exuberant a display of affection will easily land you on the floor, and there is also the tail to be considered. It is long, and as hard as a piece of wood, and unlike a piece of wood it wags. Now this tail may get damaged if the dog is confined in too small a kennel, and so generally is this danger recognised that dog-shops supply a special tail-protector. In my admittedly limited experience of the breed, I have noticed that danger *from* the tail is as much to be taken into account as danger *to* the tail. One happy swoop across a low table, and off go all the tea-cups.

Dear Brutus! the only Great Dane I ever intimately knew. How remorseful he was whenever his enormous clumsiness had led him into transgression. He seemed to say he knew he had done wrong, but how could he help it? His owner, the poet Dorothy Wellesley, forgave him all his trespasses:

> My great marbled hound [she wrote]
> Leaps at them [the rooks] as they fly.

The one in the illustration is a harlequin, which means that he may have a wall-eye and a pink nose. This truly noble dog, this great marbled hound, ought to be seen in his entirety. He stands 30 inches tall, and weighs at the minimum 120 lb., or nearly ten stone. He has been with us for some two hundred years, possibly three hundred, when dogs were used for pulling carts, even as they are used today in Belgium and Holland. So muscular a dog as the Dane, almost the size of a Shetland pony, would have been well-adapted to cart-harness. Why not use him today, to pull the mowing machine?

Considering his size, it is rather surprising to find that he registers over 500 a year in the Kennel Club list.

The Mongrel

Alas, we can honour him with no history, no pedigree. He must speak for himself, with those great wistful eyes, as appealing as a lost child. Fortunately for him he is well able to do so. I have owned, or been owned by, several mongrels in my time, and never have I known dogs more capable of falling on their feet. Some of them have been pi-dogs[1]; one made her way into my house in Constantinople, and, too savage to be ejected, gave birth to a litter of puppies on the drawing-room sofa; another dreadful little object collected me in the bazaars of Teheran, followed me home, and took complete possession. The faces of the Persian servants when I made them give him a bath, badly needed, were worth seeing.

Then there was Micky, who had a dash of Irish terrier in him. I think Micky must be the only dog who has openly walked ashore off a battle-ship on to English soil without being intercepted and clapped into quarantine. I had left him behind in Turkey, when, unable to return myself owing to the outbreak of war, the Ambassador who detested dogs but to whom I remain eternally grateful brought him home to me on a string. Micky it was, too, who, falling through a skylight when he ought by all the rules to have been killed, contrived to land on a bed—though that was perhaps due to good luck rather than to good management.

The worst of mongrels is that they are apt to be so very plain. Micky himself was no beauty. Good breeding tells. One has noticed the extreme ungainliness of dogs lying about the streets of foreign villages, and has been thankful that the proportion of these mistakes is not so high in Britain. But for sheer urchin wit and resourcefulness the mongrel can be hard to beat, only unfortunately when tempted to acquire an irresistible puppy one is seldom aware of its lineage, immediate or remote, and thus cannot estimate what characteristics it is likely to develop in later life. Will it have a bit of the sheep-dog in it, and proudly but inconveniently bring one a flock of sheep belonging to somebody else? Will it have a bit of terrier, and have to be dragged backwards by the tail out of a rabbit-hole? Or will it be merely a small scavenger, preferring unspeakable filth to the nice bowl we painstakingly provide? One must take one's chance, and in most cases one's life is no longer likely to be one's own.

The Collie

There are, roughly speaking, five types of collie: the rough and the smooth, which are large; the Welsh and the Border, which are small; and the Shetland or Sheltie, which is smallest of all. The smooth-coated collie has never been so popular as the rough; some shepherds may have found short coats more convenient in wet weather, but the rough is incomparably the more beautiful animal, with its silky coat, the frill, the gentle expression, the graceful build, the intelligence in those watchful eyes.

> His honest, sonsie, bawsent face
> Aye got him friends in ilka place.

There is also the bearded collie, whose portrait is facing. . . .

All collies are extremely sensitive, which may account for their reputation for a treacherous temper. If offended or frightened, they retaliate. The reverse of the medal is their excessive devotion. Who has not shed a tear for Owd Bob in fiction, or over the recent real-life story of the dog who stayed for three months by the dead body of his shepherd, lost on the snow-bound moors?

Ideally the collie should be a working dog; he should follow his natural profession. Thwarted of this, his hereditary instinct is still predominant, sometimes in amusing ways. My own Border collie, because as a puppy he was never employed in herding sheep, still tries to herd the clumps of daffodils in the orchard, running round them in circles and snapping with exasperation when he cannot get them to move. More regrettably, he also tries to herd people into groups, and is not above giving a nip to the human ankle as he would nip at the fetlock of a recalcitrant sheep. When one thinks of the almost incredible sagacity displayed at the sheep-dog trials, it seems wasteful to turn such marvellous material into a mere pet.

These little cattle-herders, apart from their peculiar aptitude for driving sheep through hurdles where sheep don't want to go, have many pretty and endearing ways. I have never known any other dog who would sit hanging his head, in expectation of a scolding. Puzzling and idiosyncratic companions, I have come to the conclusion that they are a bit fey. It must be due to the Celtic strain in them.

How much one wishes, sometimes, that one's dog could explain what is going on inside his head; and that he could tell one how often in spite of all one's love, one misunderstands him.

PART XI

SUMMARY OF WORKS NOT EXCERPTED

The following are very brief comments on some of the works not excerpted or quoted at any length in the pages of this volume. They are intended only as guides to works that may or may not be available in libraries or in print.

Aphra Behn: The Incomparable Astrea. New York: Russell & Russell, 1927.
Vita describes in this book her chosen involvement with her heroines, pretending to complain, and perhaps in part doing so, about "the tedious hours she has compelled me to spend over her volumes." The book begins by instantly showing us "Aphra Behn, that good-humoured lady, 'dressed in the loose robe de chambre,' but with what fire in her eye!" Behn's novel *Oroonoko,* about the pleasantness of love, was written—as Vita points out—when she had grown into a self as comfortable and "loose" as her costume, into "the loose-living, kindly, successful Astrea of Restoration London," but later than her heyday, when she frequented coffee-houses with Dryden and Otway.[1]

This kind of courage is precisely what appealed to Vita, and her heroines are all of the courageous sort. "Gay, tragic, generous, smutty, rich of nature and big of heart, propping her elbows on the tavern table, cracking her jokes, penning those midnight letters to her sad lover by the light of a tallow dip—this is the Aphra of whom one cannot take leave without respect."[2] Three months in her company, says Vita, she gladly spent.

Her irony and rapidity as a biographer, writer, and critic are in full evidence in this early book. She is amused by the way in which Aphra describes Surinam, where she went as a child, but about which she writes as a grownup: "For the moment, though, let it pass." She is not taken in: about Aphra's writing in her novel *Oroonoko,* she pulls what might be a Jane Austen trick: "You see, of course, what is coming."[3] Indeed we do, but less so in Vita's writings. She is always somewhere else, writing in some other genre: thus her appeal for many of us.

The Edwardians. New York: Doubleday Doran & Co., 1930.

A statement precedes this volume as an author's note, the contrary of the usual disclaimer about the reality of the depictions in relation to the writer's imagination: "No character in this book is wholly fictitious." Beginning on this self-conscious note, the novelist treats herself as a presumably nongeneric "he." "Among the many problems which beset the novelist, not the least weighty is the choice of the moment at which to begin his novel."[4] This hugely successful novel presents a picture of some of the novelist's own problems. Among them, the protagonist's attachment to a great house modeled after Knole, a duchess modeled after Vita's mother, siblings Sebastian and Viola modeled after Vita herself; Sebastian's struggles with life and love, torn between adventure, sin, and conformity to his wealthy upper class expectations and traditions. Most interesting are the descriptions of the house parties and of Sylvia, one of the central female characters, the older woman with whom Sebastian has his first love affair.

On April 19, 1930, *The Edwardians* was presented as a play at the Richmond Theatre, to great acclaim.

Family History. London: Hogarth Press, New York: Doubleday, Doran, 1932.

Written directly after the success of *The Edwardians* and *All Passion Spent,* this novel revolves around the affair of a charming young politician in the Labour party, Miles Vane-Merrick—and an older overly possessive woman, Evelyn Jarrold.

Since Vita's mother took very badly to Vita's having dedicated her poem "Sissinghurst" to Virginia Woolf and not to her, Vita dedicated this book to that fearsome being. (Something of her character can be surmised from her diary, pages of which are printed in this volume.)

Evelyn falls in love with Miles, and their tryst with each other and their different natures as well as the destructive nature of possessive love occupy all the superbly visual central themes. The highly discreet and drawn-out 30-page deathbed conclusion has Miles holding Evelyn's hand as she is dying. Over this conclusion Harold, says Victoria Glendinning, Vita's biographer, wept profusely in the train between Staplehurst and London. As she is about to take the morphine that will help her on her way, Miles stays by her side, as she murmurs: "Don't go. So he stayed for an indefinite period. He was simply merged with her in the dark room, with no physical contact between them except her hand lying in his."[5] This sentimentally satisfactory ending strikes a different note from the extended ecstatic passage of Evelyn's passion. This is Vita at the height of her descriptive powers relating to the emotions. The fact that the hero's home and the setting of much of the novel is a castle resembling her own castle, Sissinghurst, greatly contributes to the interest of the novel.

The fact that her spelling reform of the pronoun "thatt" runs riot through this book is itself odd: she tried it nowhere but here. The point had been to distinguish between "that" as a conjunction and "that" as a pronoun: so "thatt" was the idea that she had entertained.

The Dark Island. New York: Doubleday, Doran, 1936.
Originally called "the dark island," in lower case letters, this very peculiar and brooding novel, dedicated to Gwen St. Aubyn, Harold's younger sister and Vita's lover at the time she wrote it—is, according to Virginia Woolf, too closely associated with the personal for Vita to have the necessary distance to make it a good piece of writing. Woolf cared for it less than for Vita's other writings—and the present editor is in total agreement with her. The location, the island of Storn, is associated with St. Michael's Mount (off the Cornish shore), which Gwen's husband, Francis (Sam) St. Aubyn, the third Baron St. Levan, was to inherit.

Storn, situated off the coast at Port Breton, has a piney wood, a Gull Rock, a castle with a terrace, a cave, a sandy beach, and a village. There is a "map" to show us where the Dark Island is. The willed specificity of these details is meant to make it feel more "real," a qualification arising often in the text. Gwen is pictured as the heroine Shirin (a prefatory note tells the reader to pronounce it Sheereen, just in case we would be speaking it aloud). For Vita's stand-in here, Sir Venn, is a would-be dweller in the mythical, given to flashes of "anger and impatience" and wedded above all to his past—a past he has shared with Shirin—on his hereditary island of Storn. Language is no concern of his, and when Shirin argues with him about words, it only irritates him: "'Are there,' she asks, 'certain words you like, so that they thrust into you whenever you hear them spoken?'

"'There you are,' he said, 'talking real again.' And he thought what a mixture she was, of candour and pretence; of passion and control."[6]

All that interests Venn is the island, dark because inescapably part of him. This Shirin knows, and when the doctor has suggested tearing Venn from his beloved wet and dark island, she thinks: "Venn would never leave Storn. . . . Venn whom she knew as a skilled and audacious sailor, a venturous swimmer, a daring rider! Yet he clung to her now, sobbing, hysterical, all self-respect gone; he would not, could not, die, he said; he would not leave Storn; . . . she must not force him away from Storn. . . ."[7] This attachment to place on the part of the hero/heroine (since it is always Vita, as Venn here and as Julian in *Challenge*) is inescapably part of the dark romanticism, verging on the Gothic, that makes up Vita's writing temperament in her most passionate mode.

Saint Joan of Arc: Born January 6, 1412, Burned as a Heretic, May 30, 1431, Canonized as a Saint, May 6, 1920. New York: Doubleday, Doran, 1938.

Vita had a certain attraction to the idea of religion, finding it a part of tradition, inherently valuable, even if she herself was "pagan." As Nigel Nicolson observed to this author, it was not the ritual side of religion she liked, but the mystical side. Personally believing in "some mysterious central originating force"[8] she concentrated some of her writing energies on the legends of saints, as in her forceful portrayal of the two Teresas in *The Eagle and the Dove,* and in this biography, *Saint Joan of Arc.*

The front cover of this historical biography reads: "an authentic and unprejudiced account of one of the most dramatic and moving stories in the world's history—the thrilling career of the heroic peasant girl who rode triumphantly through brilliant victory to tragic martyrdom." Vita wrote the biography believing that otherwise quite educated persons retain only the impression of Jeanne d'Arc as a peasant girl hearing voices, seeing visions, besieging Orleans, and being burned to death at Rouen; perhaps one remembers the detail of an English soldier making two pieces of wood into a cross he hands her amid the flames. She lays out the history of the moment, the conditions in France and the war raging there for over seventy years as the English claimed sovereignty over it.

Vita's love of details and her assurance in presenting them is authoritative: she does not follow the march towards Reims but interrupts her narrative in Troyes in Burgundy to describe the Franciscan friar called Brother Richard and his role in Troyes' transfer of allegiance to the dauphin. Then she proceeds to the coronation and shows us how Jeanne is the subject of all attention. "But a single figure drew all eyes, the cause, as they said, after God, of this coronation and of all that assembly. Jeanne d'Arc, who kept her place standing beside the King, in armour, her standard in her hand. '*Il avait été à la peine,*' she said, when they asked why her standard had figured at the *sacre, 'c'était bien raison qu'il fut à l'honneur.'*" ("It had been present at the suffering, it is only right it should be present at the honour.")[9]

Joan emerges in her true colors here, or so it feels.

Grand Canyon. London: Michael Joseph, New York: Doubleday, Doran, 1942.

This novel was inspired by the visit Vita and Harold made to the Grand Canyon in 1933 during their lecture tour of the United States. It was the next to last place they visited, before Charleston, South Carolina (to which one of the poems included here, "Middleton Place," is dedicated). Vita declared herself "increased" by that visit,[10] and the setting here, down Bright Angel Trail, exhibits her enthusiasm for the place. The novel was refused by Leonard Woolf—in part for its defeatism, since the Nazis win out in it—in 1941 but published by Doubleday, Doran in New York in 1942.

It is a science-fiction fantasy, Vita's only effort in this genre, imagining what it would be like to live at the bottom of the Grand Canyon if the Nazis, once they had defeated Britain, had conquered America, and New York had tumbled into ruin. In the novel, Germany has persuaded America to make peace—and it has not proved to be a lasting one. The tragedy of Europe is "over and finished. Do not lament over the dead and the conquered," says the protagonist of the book.[11]

The hotel in which two English people, Mrs. Helen Temple and Mr. Lester Dale, have been staying is destroyed by bombs, and they lead the other guests to the bottom of the canyon, for an idyllic existence in Phantom Ranch. Describing the descent down the Bright Angel Trail, which she was awed by, Vita writes: "A long crocodile of marchers switched on their tiny flames, making little circles of light round their feet. They wound down steadily, making towards the bottom of the canyon. . . . It became warmer with every step taken downwards; they passed from a moderate temperature into a semi-tropical."[12] Once arrived in their haven, the survivors (or as the reader later deduces from the story, their spirits) develop as they can in what they have: Their souls are not dead, and they are unsentimental. For beyond life experience is another experience, to be figured only in the imagination. With that, Vita was richly endowed.

The Easter Party. New York: Doubleday, 1953.
This novel, whose beginning Vita had thought very bad, and then less so, shows Vita's indulgence of her own sense of melodrama at its highest peak. "Perhaps one is never able to judge oneself."[13] Such judgement creates only a cloudy experience, she says, hoping the reader will see what is implicit in the author's statement. One might well put under the category of "cloudy experience" *The Dark Island,* and other novels, like the excruciating attempt at sci-fi called *Grand Canyon.*

Whereas the preposterous, glittering, and concise *Seducers in Ecuador* is enlightened by irony, the same is not true of *The Easter Party.* One has only to glance at the terrible plot line through Walter Mortibois's brother, Gilbert, who pretends to put Walter's adored dog Svend to death to teach him a lesson about love. (Vita's own dog Svend was no less adored.) Walter is indeed a chilly figure: When his beautiful house Anstey is burning, he seems exalted. The description of the fire, transparently surnamed Mortibois (dead wood), is as efficacious as terrible in its repetitions: "Anstey was burning and in no mean measure . . . Anstey burnt. It was frightful, and magnificent, to watch the burning. The burning hulk of Anstey poured out its flames. All splendour had departed. . . . There had been a magnificence in ruin; now there was nothing but a dying stench of wet and charred remains."[14] This is not one of the highest peaks of Vita's writing—nevertheless it forms part of her way of seeing things—frequently melodramatic to the point of Gothic stylization.

Daughter of France: The Life of Anne Marie Louise d'Orléans 1627–1693. London: Michael Joseph, 1959.

Vita's relation to history was intense, one might say almost intimate. She had an extraordinary sense of tradition that the haunting loss of Knole exemplifies, but also of French and English history. If she wrote on her grandmother Pepita Duran, she wrote also on La Grande Mademoiselle (Anne Marie Lousie d'Orleans), the two St. Theresas, Joan of Arc, and also a groundbreaking and feminist work on Aphra Behn. She was justly celebrated for her celebration of great figures in history and literature, such as Chatterton, Voltaire, Jean-Baptiste Poquelin, Richelieu, Alcibiades, Alice Meynell, Gottfried Kunstler, Lady Anne Clifford, Walter de la Mare, George Eliot. Vita's sense of English history—"England is always very much the same"—reinforces her notions of heredity: "the instinctive arrogance of the aristocrat," wrote Harold. Her books such as *Family History, The Edwardians,* and *The Heir* reflect her study and her passion. The details she researches and retains put lesser biographers and historians to shame. They are not only historical, they are linguistic: for instance, take her very learned discussion, in the 1947 edition of *Knole and the Sackvilles,* of *Thieves' Cant* (the slang of the vagabond classes, made famous by the medieval French poet Françoise Villon).

Among her historical and biographical works, the one perhaps of most interest to contemporary readers is the heftily titled *Daughter of France: The Life of Anne Marie Louise d'Orléans 1627–1693:* a biography of the duchess of Montpensier who was known as La Grande Mademoiselle. Like her literary research, her historical research into figures as well as houses was all-consuming. As a life-story teller, Vita was highly skilled—her biographies are often more readable than her novels. But she thought this one very bad; her reasoning is clear, and her modesty reassures all of us who write: "Oh Hadji," she writes to Harold on February 26, 1958, "My book is so bad. . . . I read a lot, but I haven't been able to synthesise or compress it as I hoped. It is just a mess. I had a clear picture when I started, but now it has all got muddled up with detail and the outline has got lost."[15]

What is lasting about this book is idiosyncractic and personal. She firmly believes in personal intervention in such writings, the main reason for present-day readers to tackle such a biography. This topic was originally suggested by Raymond Mortimer, who had asked Vita years before, one day in a French vineyard: "Why don't you write the life of the Big Miss?"[16] And so she did. In the middle of the book, which she called an "interlude," she recapitulates the events in reverse order. Since, as she points out, it was never intended to be a scholarly biography, she hopes her "sins as a historian," such as this antilinear one (as we might put it), can be forgiven.[17]

Even in her childhood, the Grande Mademoiselle had a "searching little brain," and was always shrewd, motivating in part Vita's delight in following her adventures. Vita was fluent in French, and here she has translated the words of Mademoiselle and her contemporaries as idiomatically as possible. At a few points, she simply leaves the French; Lauzun insults the king's mistress, Mme de Montespan, when she declares she has tried to arrange the King's consent to his marriage with Mademoiselle de Montpensier but that he has refused. "You lie, *bougresse de putain,*" he cries, saying his spies have told him the contrary. A delicate footnote to this expression that combines the delights of buggerdom and prostitution reads simply: "This, which most French authors would hesitate to print in full, is not an amiable term to apply to a woman."[18]

In the last two chapters about the Grande Mademoiselle's love of the courtier Lauzun and her terrible downfall, Vita's personality makes itself felt: this "fragile theory of her own" is heightened by the death of Mademoiselle at 66, as Vita points out: " the biographer's age writing this book." Here again, the reader feels the force of her personality. Conscious always of heritage, Vita studied it from close up, as she did history and literature. This is the major appeal of her more serious works.

No Signposts in the Sea. London: Michael Joseph, New York: Doubleday, 1961. Vita's last novel, about a cruise, was inspired by one of the six she took with Harold: their 1959 cruise to Port Said, Singapore, and Manila, on the *Cambodge.* (His own book *Journey to Java* was also based on this trip.) It is dedicated to Edie Lamont, a painter friend who lived nearby, of whom Vita was very fond at that point in her life. Edie was on their last cruise with them, and Vita assured Harold that "if either you or I got ill, she would be a rock of help and comfort." Indeed, Edie was the one in whom Vita confided about her cancer, and before dying, asked her to keep Glen, her golden retriever.

The novel centers on Edmund Carr, a journalist on shipboard, who is keeping a diary given to him by his fellow passenger, Laura, and records in it his secret love for her. He intends to throw it into the sea, but he dies before he is able to, yet not until after he has recounted their discussions of their conceptions of love. He wants to believe that he is nearer to her than he would be if she were his, "in the common sense of the word." Their discussion leaves him joyous, but it is in fact the end of his life. The book concludes with his last diary passage:

> I cannot think, I dare not think . . . Folly, folly, folly! She got up and went, leaving me alone with the lighted ship in the night.
> How shall I meet her tomorrow?

Shall I

Edmund Carr was found dead in his cabin the morning after this conversation had taken place. He had fallen forward on to his table, his diary open at the page where he had recorded these last broken-off words . . . Carr had also included a note to the effect that he wished to be buried at sea. These instructions were duly carried out in the Pacific Ocean.

A canister of lighted fuel is thrown in after him to mark the spot, and they watch it burning "as the ship proceeded on her way, until the flame died down and nothing more was seen."[19] Nothing more was seen. . . . The way the ending of this last volume closes off so perfectly in darkness makes it the kind of conclusion to a life befitting Vita's great style. The ending is absolute and gives, were it needed, absolution.

NOTES

Introduction

1. Nigel Nicolson, *Portrait of a Marriage.* London: Futura, 1974, p. 27.
2. Ibid., p. 38.
3. Ibid., p. 105.
4. Ibid., p. 106.
5. Ibid., p. 150.
6. October 25, 1918.
7. See the description of Julian in *Challenge.*
8. Diary entry, Paris, February 14, 1920.
9. Nigel Nicolson and Joanne Traumann, eds., *Letters of Virginia Woolf.* New York and London: Harcourt Brace Jovanovich, 1979, vol 5: 8 November, 1932.
10. Ibid., vol. 3, p. 302.
11. Nicolson, *Portrait,* p. 202.
12. Anne Olivier Bell, ed., assisted by Andrew McNeillie. *The Diaries of Virginia Woolf.* London and New York: Harcourt Brace, Jovanovich, vol. 5, p. 111.
13. Ibid., vol. l June 27, 1940, p. 305.
14. Nicolson, *Letters of Virginia Woolf,* vol.6, March 4, 1941, p. 476.
15. Nigel Nicolson, ed., *Vita and Harold: the Letters of Vita Sackville-West and Harold Nicolson.* New York: Putnam's, 1992, p. 410.
16. Sarah Ruth Watson, *V. Sackville-West.* New York: Twayne, 1972, p. 22.
17. Michael Stevens, *Vita Sackville-West: A Critical Biography.* New York: Scribner's, 1974, p. 14.
18. Nicolson, *Vita and Harold,* p. 42.
19. Nicolson, *Portrait,* p. 175.
20. Nicolson, *Vita and Harold,* p. 336.
21. Victoria Glendinning, *Vita: A Biography of Vita Sackville-West.* London: Weidenfeld and Nicolson, 1983, p. 142.
22. Ibid., p. 143.
23. Ibid., loc. cit.
24. *All Passion Spent,* p. 167.
25. Glendinning, p. 341.
26. Ibid., p. 241.
27. Stevens, p. 14.
28. Glendinning, p. 375.

Part I

1. Nicolson, *Portrait,* p. 26.
2. Ibid., p. 18.

Part III

1. Nicolson, *Vita and Harold,* p. 179.

Part IV

1. Nicolson, in Sackville-West's *Passenger to Teheran,* p. 20.
2. Sackville-West, *Passenger to Teheran,* p. 81
3. Nicolson in Sackville-West's *Passenger to Teheran* (1990), p. 22.
4. Sackville-West in Nicolson and Trautman's *Letters of Virginia Woolf,* vol. III, p. 533.

Part VI

1. Vita Sackville-West, *Knole and the Sackvilles* (London: William Heinemann, 1922), p. 36. Hereafter all subsequent references to this work will be abbreviated as *KS.*
2. Vita Sackville-West, *English Country Houses* (London: Prion, 1941), pp. 40–43, 46.
3. Victoria Glendinning, *Vita: The Life of V. Sackville-West* (London: Weidenfeld and Nicholson; New York: Knopf, 1983), p. 389.
4. From 1947 edition (London: Lindsay Drummond).
5. *Country Notes* (London: Michael Joseph, 1939; New York: Harper, 1940), p. 14. Hereafter all subsequent references to this work will be abbreviated as *CN.*
6. *CN,* p. 113.

Part VII

1. The short story "The Other Two" can be found in *Descent of Man and other Stories* (New York: Scribner's, 1904).
2. "The Poet" was included in *Thirty Clocks Strike the Hour,* published by Doubleday, Doran in 1932, in London and New York.
3. See also Victoria Glendinning, *Vita: The Life of V. Sackville-West* (London: Weidenfeld and Nicolson; New York: Knopf, 1983).

Part VIII

1. Quentin Bell, "A Cézanne in the Hedge," in Hugh Lee, ed., *A Cézanne in the Hedge and other Memories of Charleston and Bloomsbury* (London: Collins and Brown, 1992), pp. 136–139.
2. Nigel Nicolson and Joanne Trautmann, eds. *Letters of Virginia Woolf* (Harcourt Brace Jovanovich, 6 vols., 1975–1980), vol. 2, p. 230.
3. Nigel Nicolson and Joanne Trautman, ed. *Letters of Virginia Woolf* (New York and London: Harcourt Brace, 1979), vol. 5, pp. 110, 100.

Part IX

1. Victoria Glendinning, *Vita: The Life of Vita Sackville-West* (London: Wiederfeld and Nicolson; New York: Knopf, 1983), p. 242.
2. See John Richardson, *Sacred Monsters, Sacred Masters.* (New York: Random House, 2001), on "Vita's Muddles," pp. 112–122.

Part X

1. In a letter to Jacques Raverat, December 26, 1924 (Nigel Nicolson and Joanne Trautman, ed. *Letters of Virginia Woolf* (New York and London: Harcourt Brace, 1979), vol. 5, p 150.

Part XI

1. Vita Sackville-West, *Aphra Behn: the Incomparable Astrea* (New York: Russell & Russell, 1927), pp. 85–86.
2. Ibid., p. 86.
3. Ibid., pp. 16, 18.
4. Vita Sackville-West, *The Edwardians* (New York: Doubleday Doran & Co., 1930), p. 1.
5. Vita Sackville-West, *Family History* (London: Hogarth Press, New York: Doubleday, Doran, 1932), p. 315.
6. Vita Sackville-West, *The Dark Island* (New York: Doubleday, Doran, 1936), pp. 101–102.
7. Ibid., p. 260.
8. Vita Sackville-West, *Saint Joan of Arc: Born January 6, 1412, Burned as a Heretic, May 30, 1431, Canonized as a Saint, May 6, 1920* (New York: Doubleday, Doran, 1938), p. 344.
9. Ibid., p. 223
10. Victoria Glendinning, *Vita: The Life Of Vita Sackville-West* (New York: Knopf, London: Wiedenfeld and Nicolson, 1983), p. 260.
11. Vita Sackville-West, *Grand Canyon* (London: Michael Joseph, New York: Doubleday, Doran, 1942), p. 177.
12. Ibid., p. 171.
13. Vita Sackville-West, *The Easter Party* (New York: Doubleday, 1953), p. 398.
14. Ibid., 228–229.
15. Nigel Nicholson, ed., *Vita and Harold: THe Letters of Vita Sackville-West and Harold Nicholson* (New York: Putman, 1992), p. 424.
16. Vita Sackville-West, *Daughter of France: The Life of Anne Marie Louise d'Orléans 1627–1693* (London: Michael Joseph, 1959), p. 5.
17. Ibid., p. 220.
18. Ibid., p. 299.
19. Vita Sackville-West, *No Signposts in the Sea* (London: Michael Joseph, New York: Doubleday, 1961), p. 156.

BIBLIOGRAPHY

Cross, Robert and Ann Ravescroft-Hulme, eds., *Vita Sackville-West: A Bibliography.* Winchester: St. Paul's Bibliographies; New Castle, Delaware: Oak Knoll Press, 1999.

DeSalvo, Louise and Mitchell A. Leaska, eds. Introduction by Mitchell A. Leaska. *The Letters of Vita Sackville-West to Virginia Woolf.* London: Virago Press, 1992.

Glendinning, Victoria. *Vita: The Life of V. Sackville-West.* London: Weidenfeld and Nicolson; New York: Knopf, 1983.

Lee, Hugh, ed. *A Cézanne in the Hedge and Other Memories of Charleston and Bloomsbury.* London: Collins and Brown, 1992.

Nicolson, Nigel and Joanne Trautmann, eds. *Letters of Virginia Woolf.* Harcourt Brace Jovanovich. 6 vols. 1975–1980.

———. *Portrait of a Marriage.* London: Weidenfeld & Nicolson; New York: Atheneum, 1973.

———, ed. *Vita and Harold: The Letters of Vita Sackville-West and Harold Nicolson.* New York: G. P. Putnam's Sons, 1992.

Raitt, Suzanne, *Vita and Virginia: the Work and Friendship of V. Sackville-West and Virginia Woolf.* Oxford: Clarendon Press, 1993.

Richardson, John, *Sacred Monsters, Sacred Masters.* New York: Random House, 2001.

Souhami, Diana. *Mrs. Keppel and Her Daughter.* New York: St. Martin's Press, Griffin: 1996.

Stevens, Michael, ed. *V. Sackville-West: A Critical Biography.* New York: Scribner's, 1974.

Watson, Sara Ruth. *V. Sackville-West.* New York: Twayne, 1972.

WORKS BY VITA SACKVILLE-WEST

The following is a list of Vita Sackville-West's works that are discussed or mentioned in this volume.

All Passion Spent. London: Hogarth Press; New York Doubleday, Doran, 1931.

Andrew Marvell. London: Faber & Faber, 1929.

Aphra Behn. London: Gerald Howe, 1927; New York: Viking Press, 1928.

Challenge. New York: George H. Doran, 1924.

Collected Poems, vol. 1. London: Hogarth Press. 1933.

Country Notes. London: Michael Joseph, 1939; New York: Harper, 1940.

The Dark Island. London: Hogarth Press; New York: Doubleday, Doran, 1934.

Daughter of France. London: Michael Joseph; New York: Doubleday, 1949.

The Eagle and The Dove. London: Michael Joseph, 1943; New York: Doubleday, Doran, 1944.

The Easter Party. London: Michael Joseph; New York: Doubleday, 1953.

The Edwardians. London: Hogarth Press. New York: Doubleday, Doran, 1930.

"The Engagement," *Tatler,* October 22, 1930, pp. 44–45, 102, 104.

English Country Houses. London: Collins, 1941.

Faces: Profiles of Dogs (with photographs by Laelia Goehr). Harvill Press, London; New York: Doubleday, 1962.

Family History. London: Hogarth Press; New York: Doubleday, Doran, 1932.

The Garden. London: Michael Joseph, 1946.

Grand Canyon. London: Michael Joseph; New York: Doubleday, Doran, 1942.

In Your Garden. London: Michael Joseph, 1951.

A Joy of Gardening: A Selection for Americans, ed. Hermine Popper. New York: Harper, 1958.

Knole and the Sackvilles. London: William Heinemann, 1922.

No Signposts in the Sea. London: Michael Joseph; New York: Doubleday, 1961.

Passenger to Teheran. London: Hogarth Press, 1926; second edition, Cockbird Press, Heathfield, 1990.

Pepita. London: Hogarth Press; New York: Doubleday, 1937.

Poems of East and West. London: Bodley Head, 1917.

Saint Joan of Arc. London: Cobden, Sanderson; New York: Doubleday, Doran, 1936.

Seducers in Ecuador. London: Hogarth Press, 1924; New York: Doran, 1925; Penguin Books, 1989.

Some Tendencies of Modern English Poetry, Essays by Divers Hands (1917), Royal Society of Literature, London.

Thirty Clocks Strike the Hour. New York: Doubleday, Doran, 1932.

Twelve Days. London: Hogarth press, 1928.

INDEX